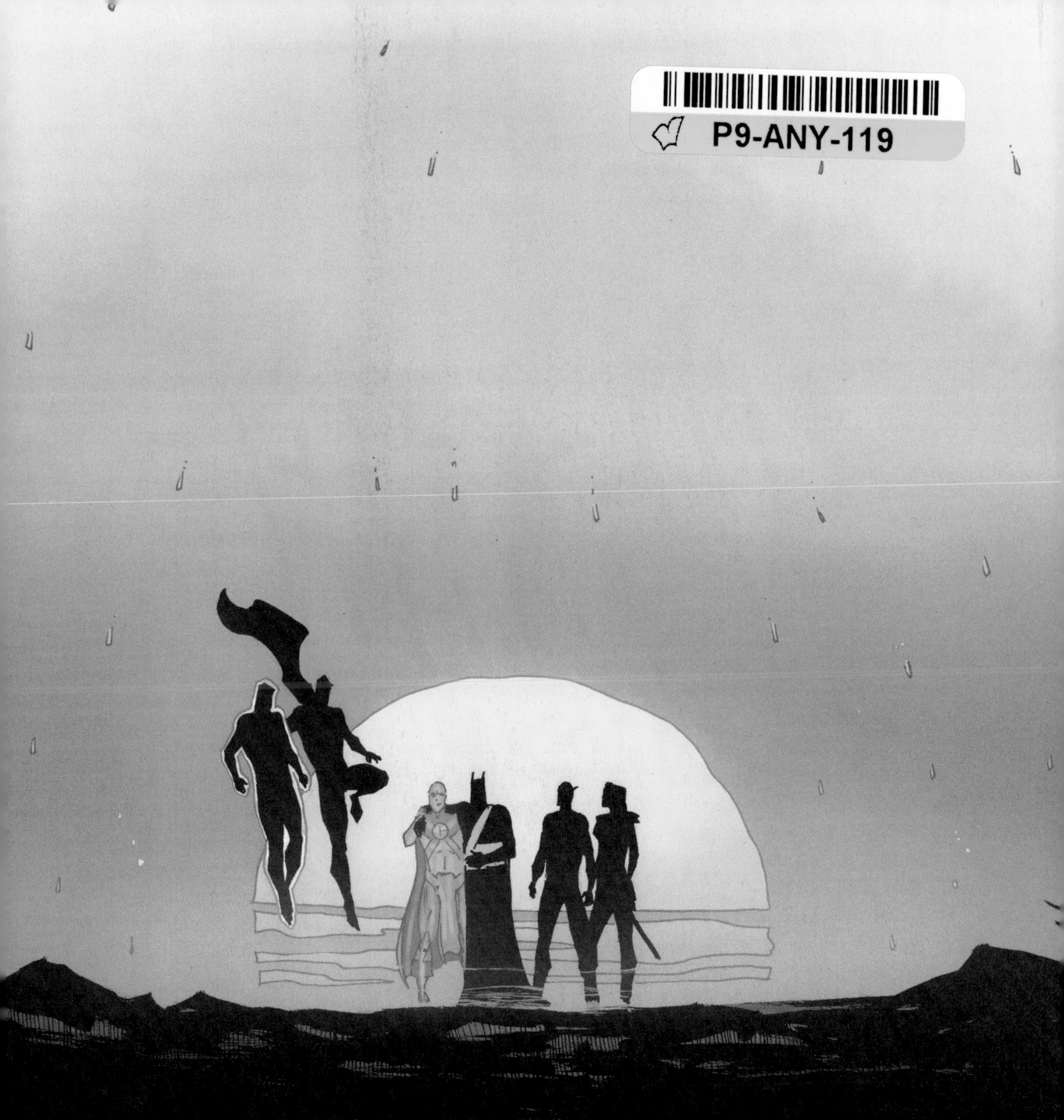

JUSTICE LEAGUE
LAST RIDE

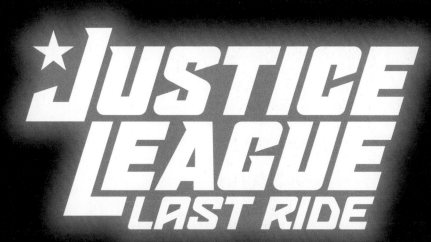

CHIP ZDARSKY
writer

MIGUEL MENDONÇA
artist

ENRICA EREN ANGIOLINI
colorist

ANDWORLD DESIGN
letterer

DARICK ROBERTSON and DIEGO RODRIGUEZ
collection cover artists

Superman created by JERRY SIEGEL and JOE SHUSTER
Supergirl based on the characters created by JERRY SIEGEL and JOE SHUSTER
By special arrangement with the Jerry Siegel Family

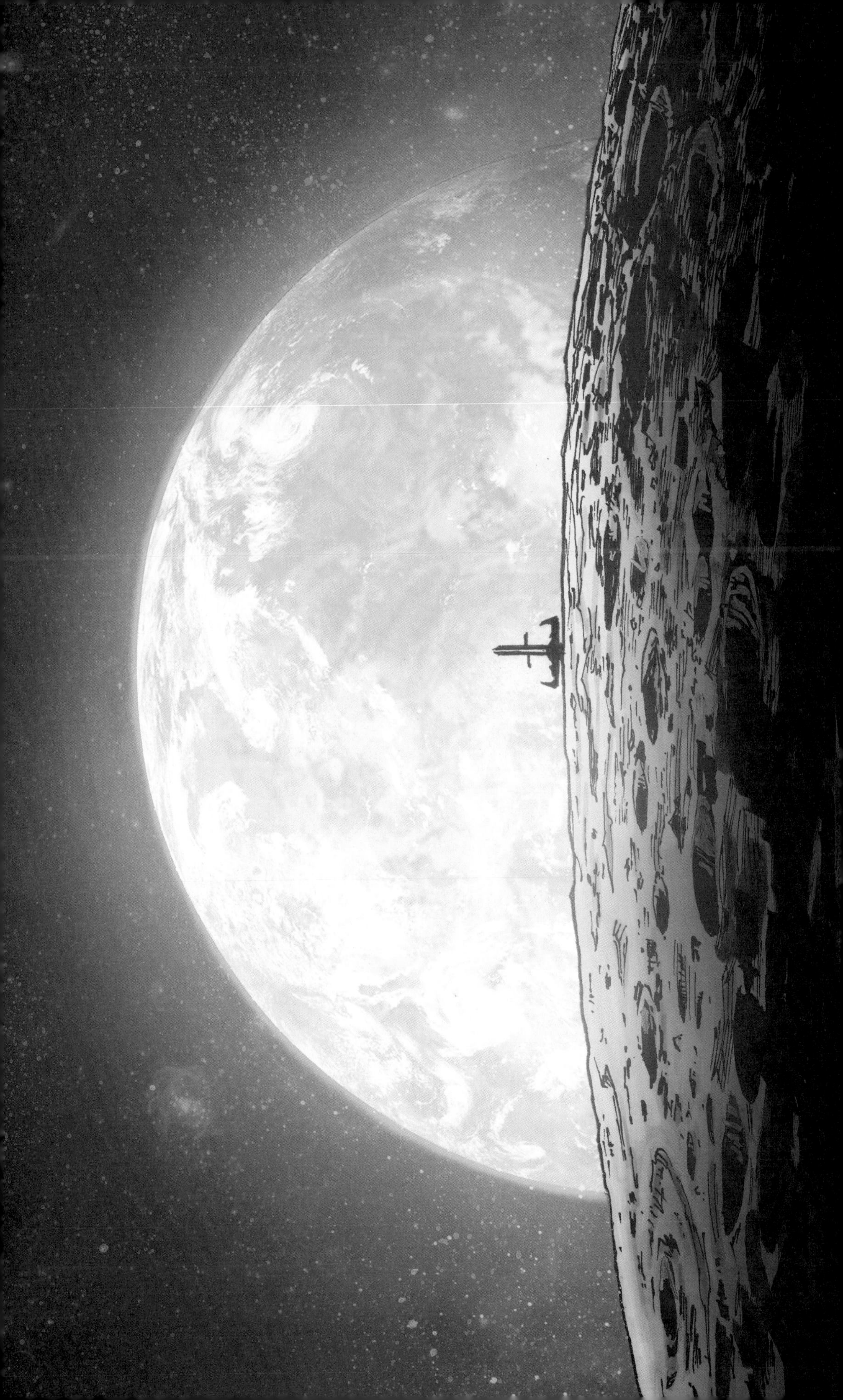

KATIE KUBERT, MICHAEL McCALISTER
Editors – Original Series & Collected Edition

STEVE COOK
Design Director – Books

DAMIAN RYLAND
Publication Design

ERIN VANOVER
Publication Production

MARIE JAVINS
Editor-in-Chief, DC Comics

ANNE DePIES
Senior VP – General Manager

JIM LEE
Publisher & Chief Creative Officer

DON FALLETTI
VP – Manufacturing Operations & Workflow Management

LAWRENCE GANEM
VP – Talent Services

ALISON GILL
Senior VP – Manufacturing & Operations

JEFFREY KAUFMAN
VP – Editorial Strategy & Programming

NICK J. NAPOLITANO
VP – Manufacturing Administration & Design

NANCY SPEARS
VP – Revenue

JUSTICE LEAGUE: LAST RIDE

DC Comics, 2900 West Alameda Ave., Burbank, CA 91505
Printed by Solisco Printers, Scott, QC, Canada. 5/6/22. First Printing. ISBN: 978-1-77951-439-4.

Library of Congress Cataloging-in-Publication Data is available.

PEFC Certified
This product is from sustainably managed forests and controlled sources
PEFC/26-31-02
www.pefc.org

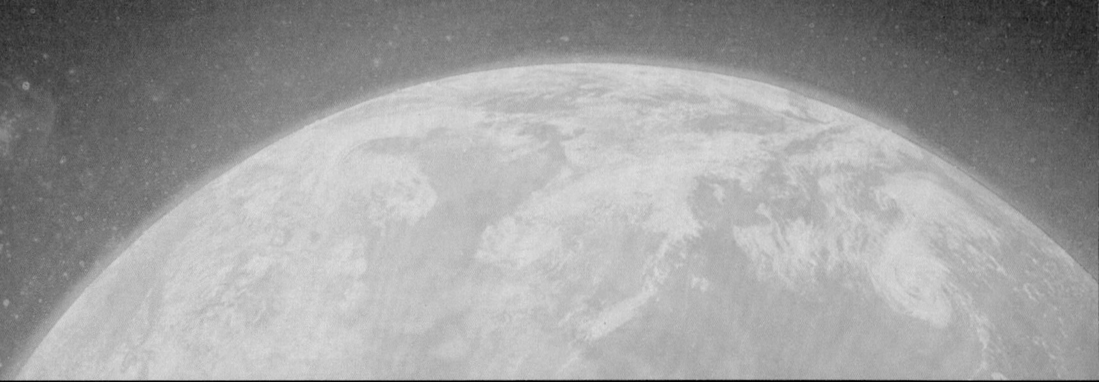

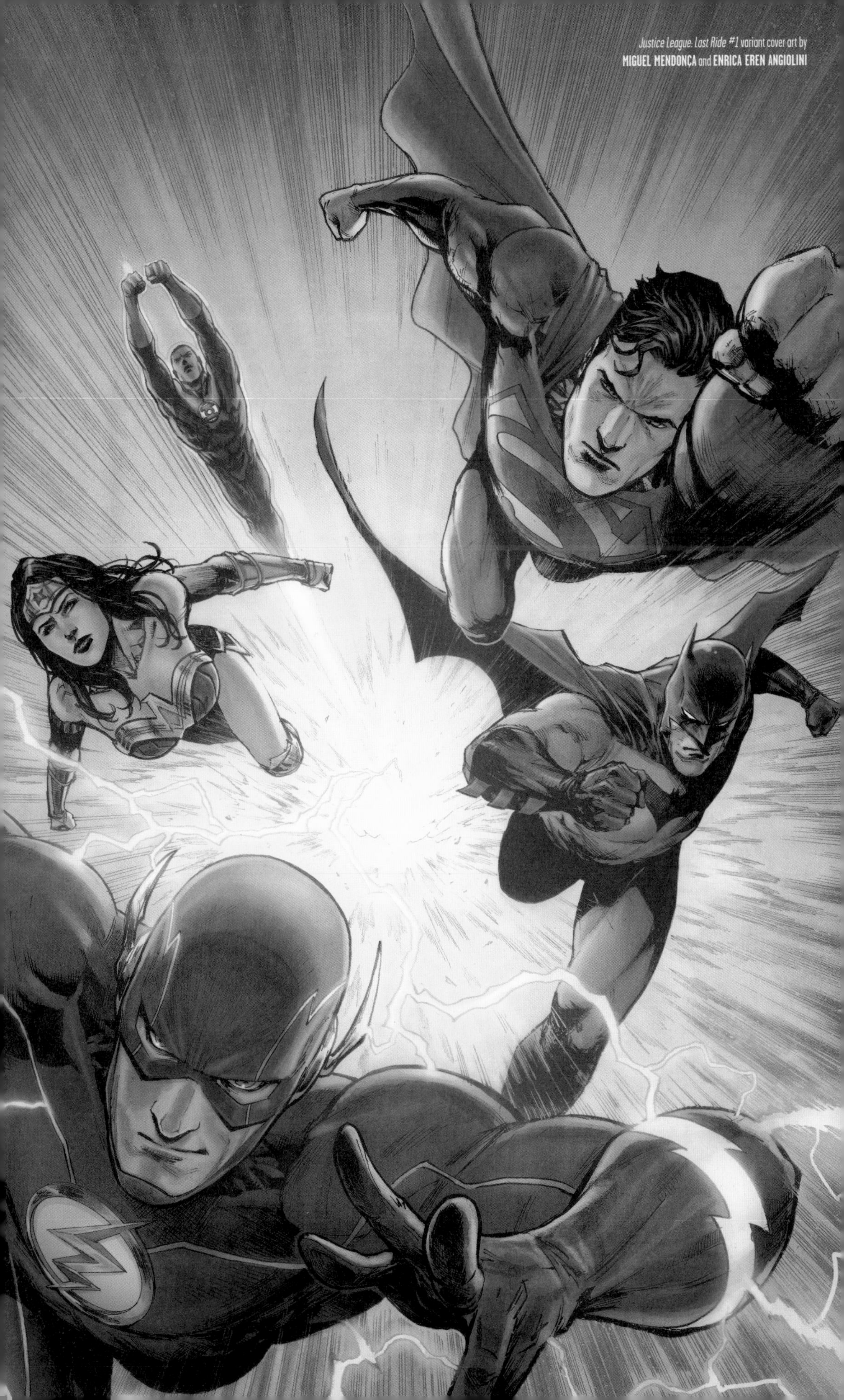

Justice League: Last Ride #1 variant cover art by
MIGUEL MENDONÇA and **ENRICA EREN ANGIOLINI**

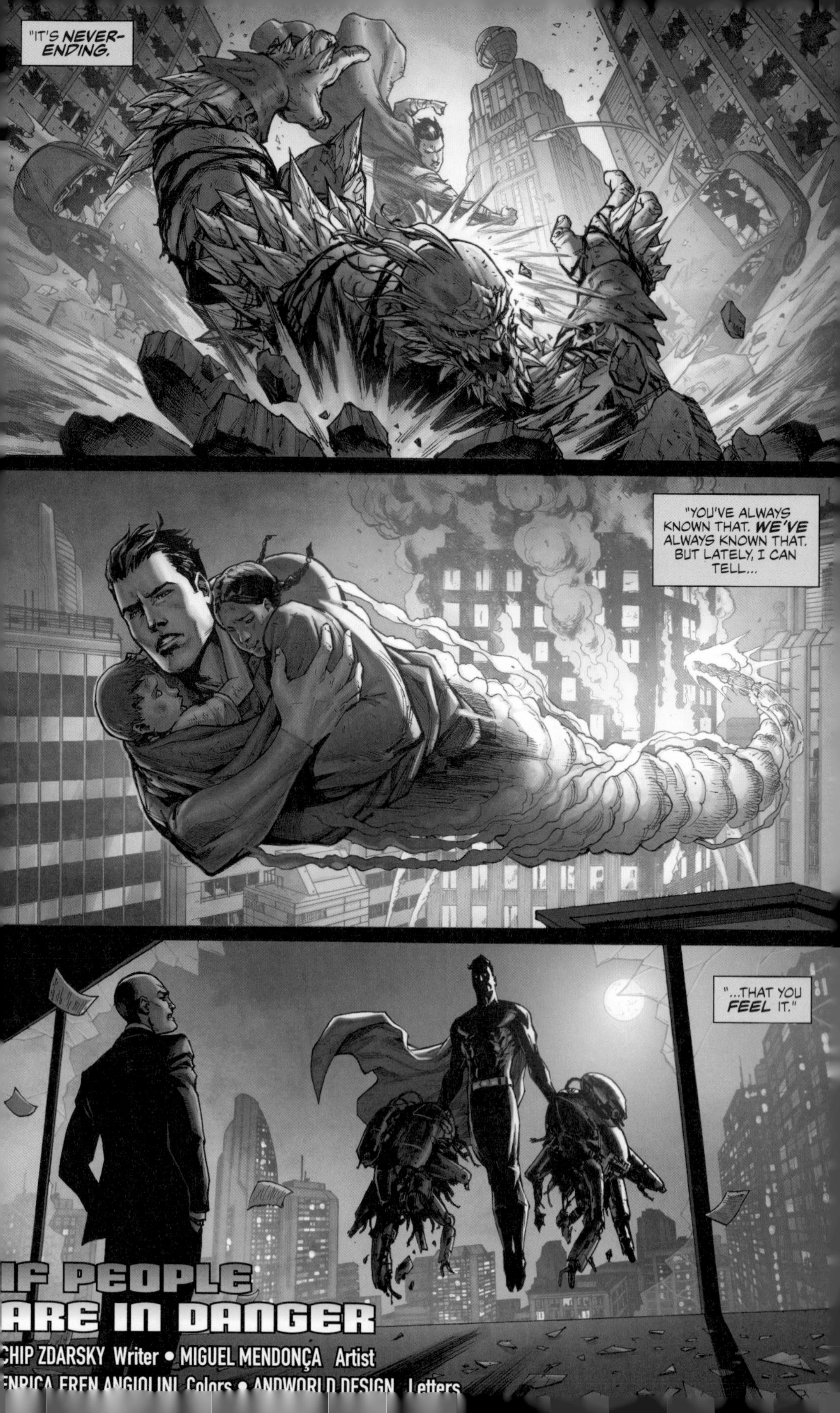
"IT'S NEVER-ENDING.
"YOU'VE ALWAYS KNOWN THAT. WE'VE ALWAYS KNOWN THAT. BUT LATELY, I CAN TELL...
"...THAT YOU FEEL IT."
IF PEOPLE ARE IN DANGER
CHIP ZDARSKY Writer • MIGUEL MENDONÇA Artist
ENRICA EREN ANGIOLINI Colors • ANDWORLD DESIGN Letters

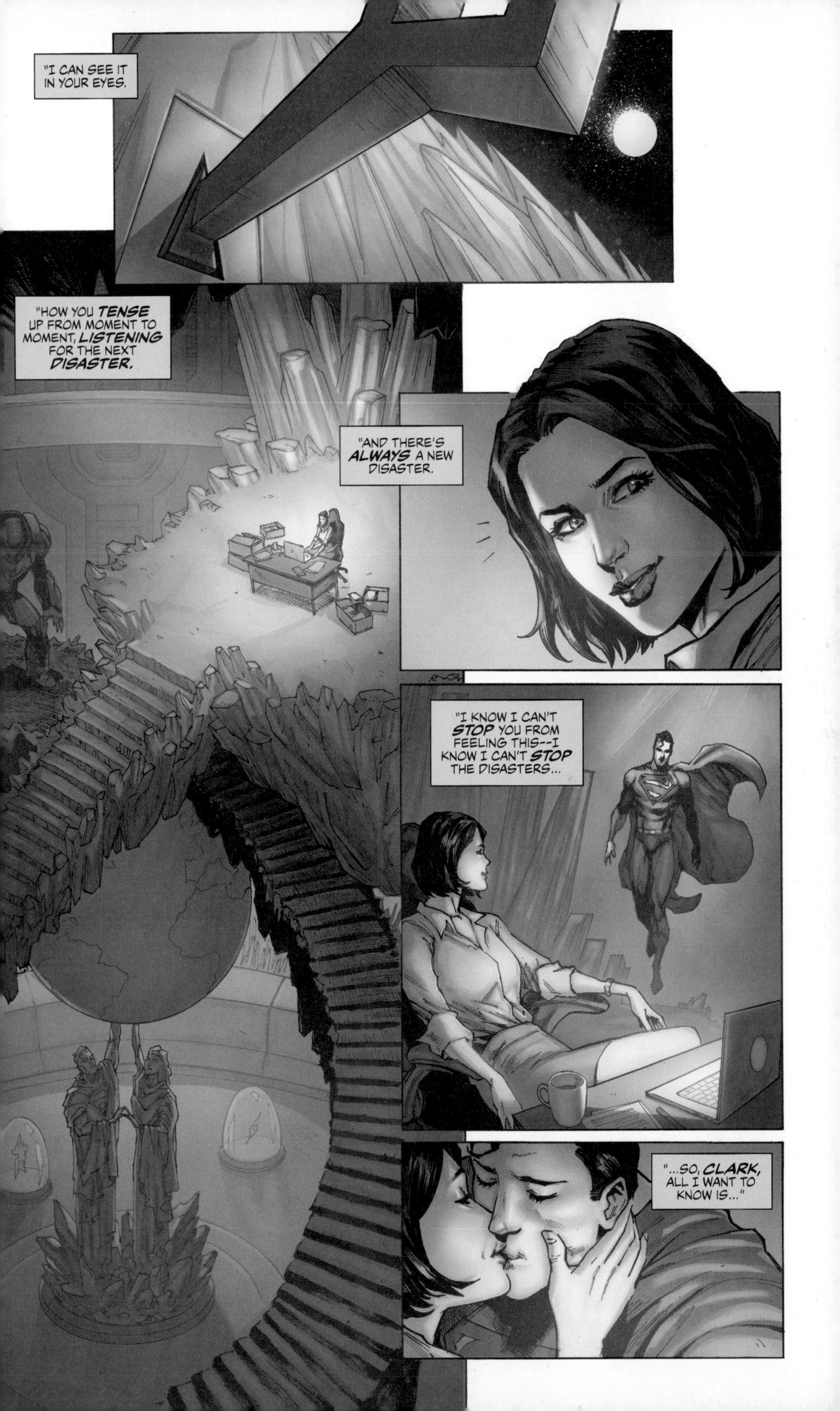
"I CAN SEE IT IN YOUR EYES.
"HOW YOU TENSE UP FROM MOMENT TO MOMENT, LISTENING FOR THE NEXT DISASTER.
"AND THERE'S ALWAYS A NEW DISASTER.
"I KNOW I CAN'T STOP YOU FROM FEELING THIS--I KNOW I CAN'T STOP THE DISASTERS...
"...SO, CLARK, ALL I WANT TO KNOW IS..."

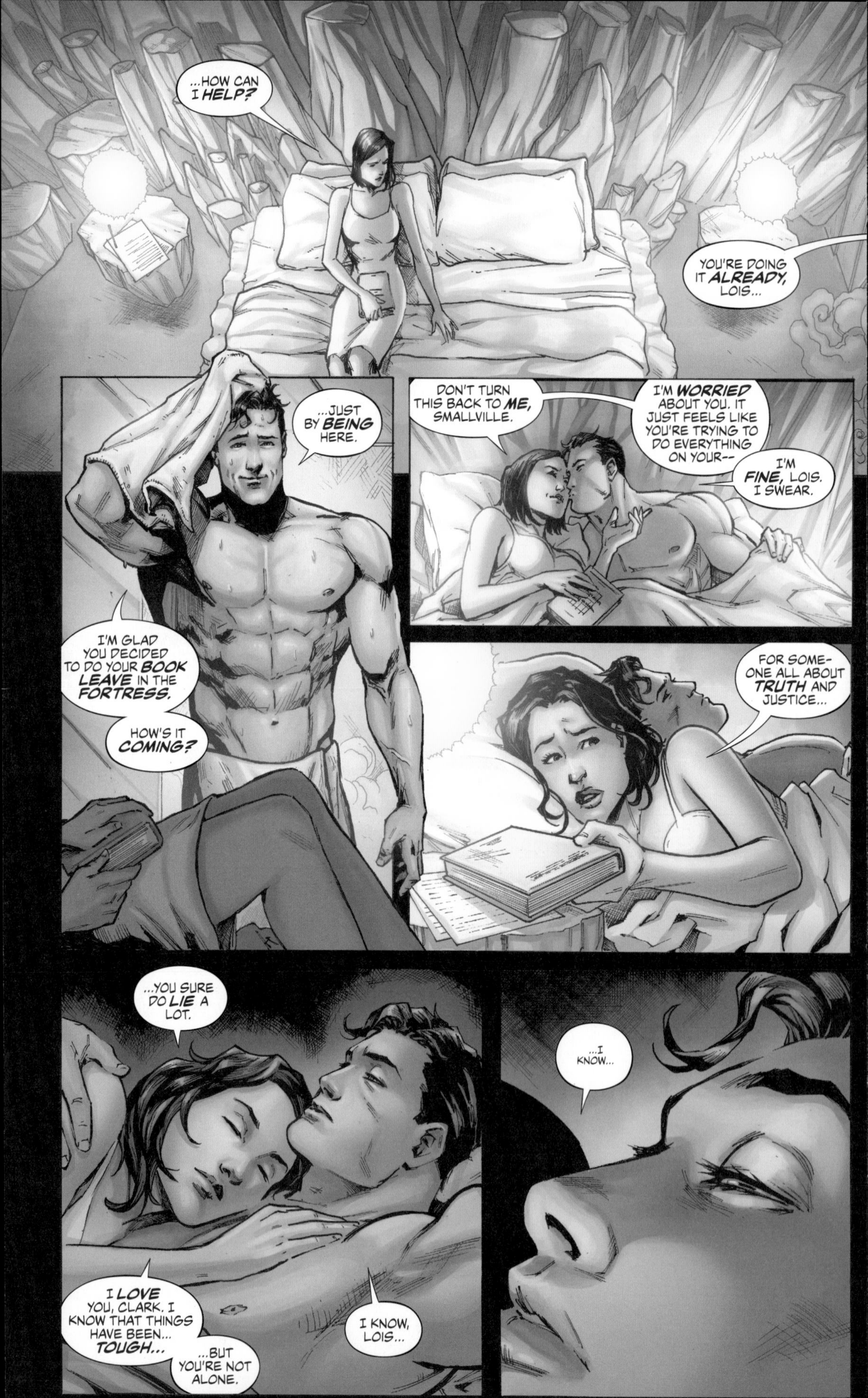
...HOW CAN I HELP?
YOU'RE DOING IT ALREADY, LOIS...
...JUST BY BEING HERE.
I'M GLAD YOU DECIDED TO DO YOUR BOOK LEAVE IN THE FORTRESS.
HOW'S IT COMING?
DON'T TURN THIS BACK TO ME, SMALLVILLE.
I'M WORRIED ABOUT YOU. IT JUST FEELS LIKE YOU'RE TRYING TO DO EVERYTHING ON YOUR--
I'M FINE, LOIS. I SWEAR.
FOR SOME-ONE ALL ABOUT TRUTH AND JUSTICE...
...YOU SURE DO LIE A LOT.
I LOVE YOU, CLARK. I KNOW THAT THINGS HAVE BEEN... TOUGH...
...BUT YOU'RE NOT ALONE.
I KNOW, LOIS...
...I KNOW...

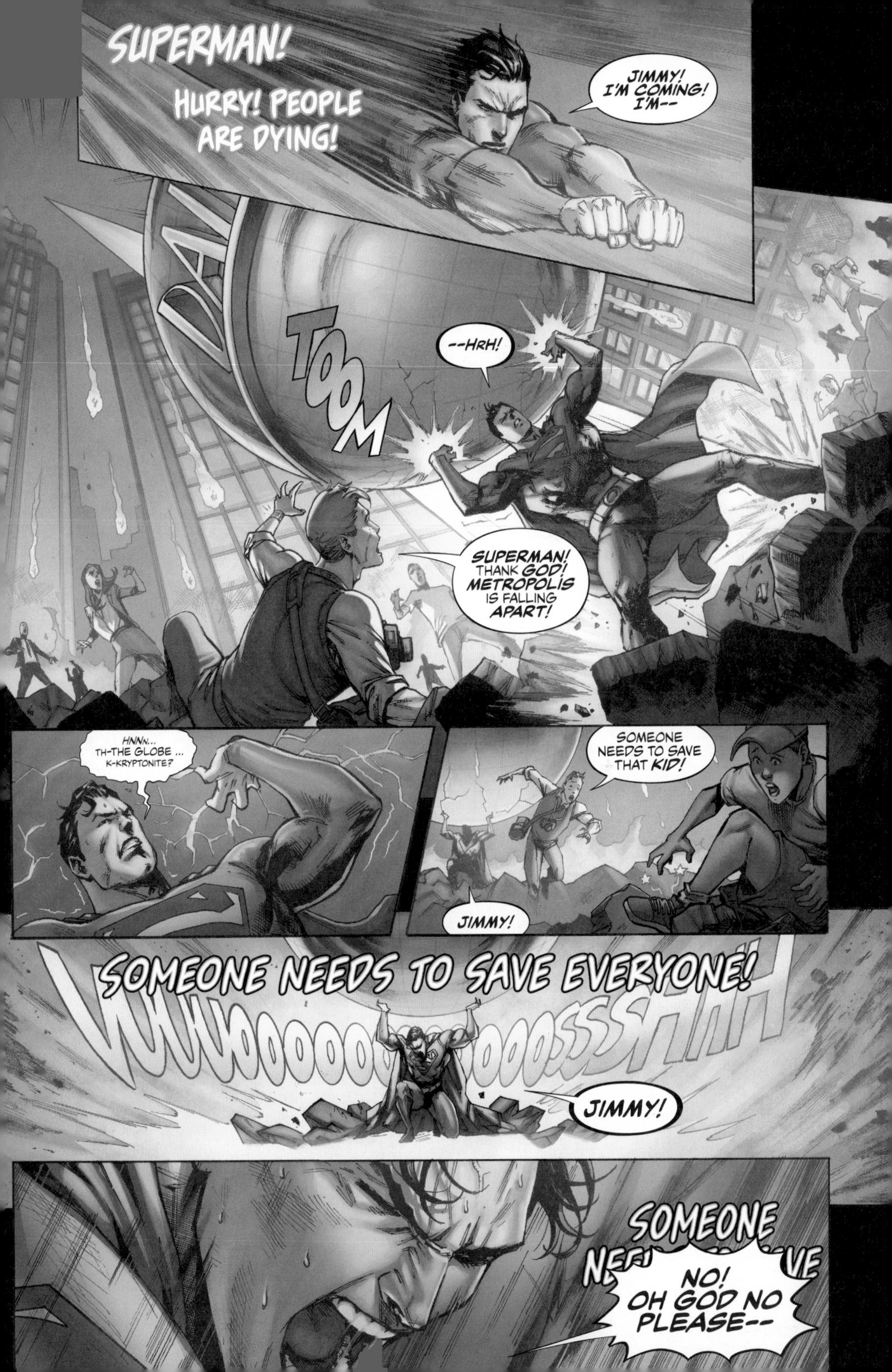
SUPERMAN!
HURRY! PEOPLE ARE DYING!
JIMMY! I'M COMING! I'M--
TOOM
--HRH!
SUPERMAN! THANK GOD! METROPOLIS IS FALLING APART!
HNNN... TH-THE GLOBE ... K-KRYPTONITE?
SOMEONE NEEDS TO SAVE THAT KID!
JIMMY!
SOMEONE NEEDS TO SAVE EVERYONE!
VUUUOOOOOOOOOOOSSSHHH
JIMMY!
SOMEONE
NO! OH GOD NO PLEASE--

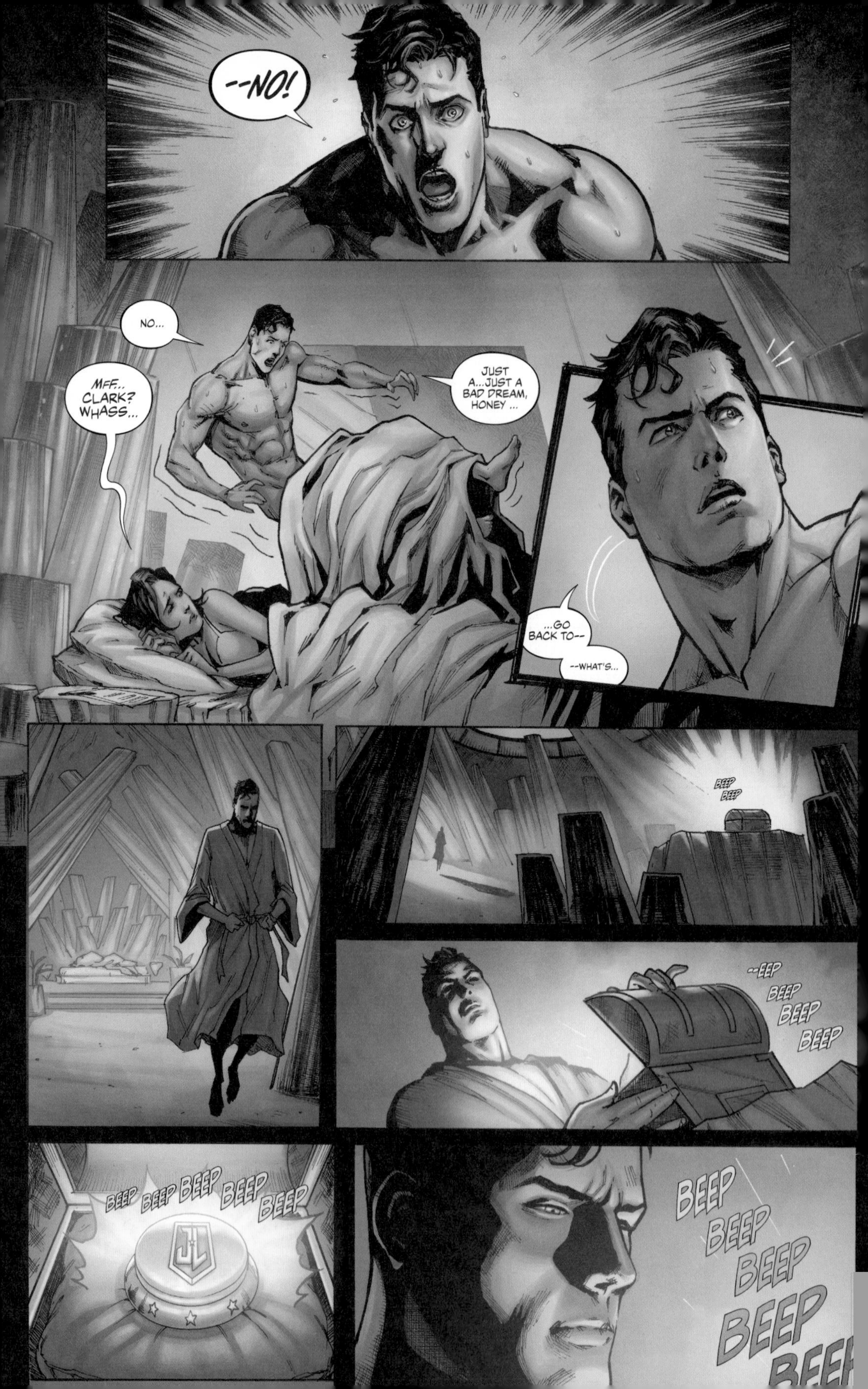
--NO!
NO...
MFF.. CLARK? WHASS...
JUST A...JUST A BAD DREAM, HONEY ...
...GO BACK TO--
--WHAT'S...
BEEP BEEP
--EEP
BEEP
BEEP
BEEP
BEEP BEEP BEEP BEEP BEEP
BEEP
BEEP
BEEP
BEEP

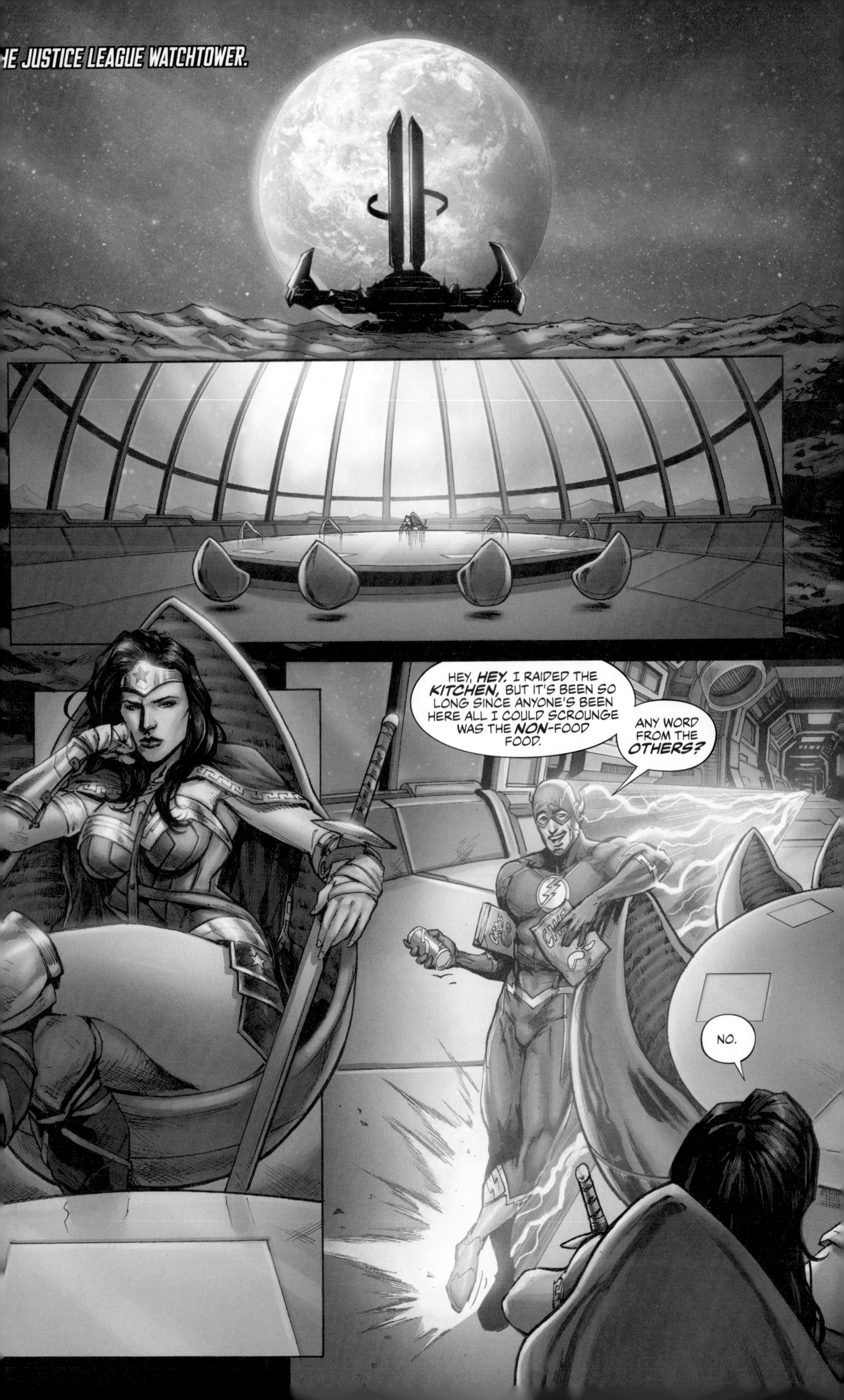
HE JUSTICE LEAGUE WATCHTOWER.
HEY, HEY. I RAIDED THE KITCHEN, BUT IT'S BEEN SO LONG SINCE ANYONE'S BEEN HERE ALL I COULD SCROUNGE WAS THE NON-FOOD FOOD.
ANY WORD FROM THE OTHERS?
NO.

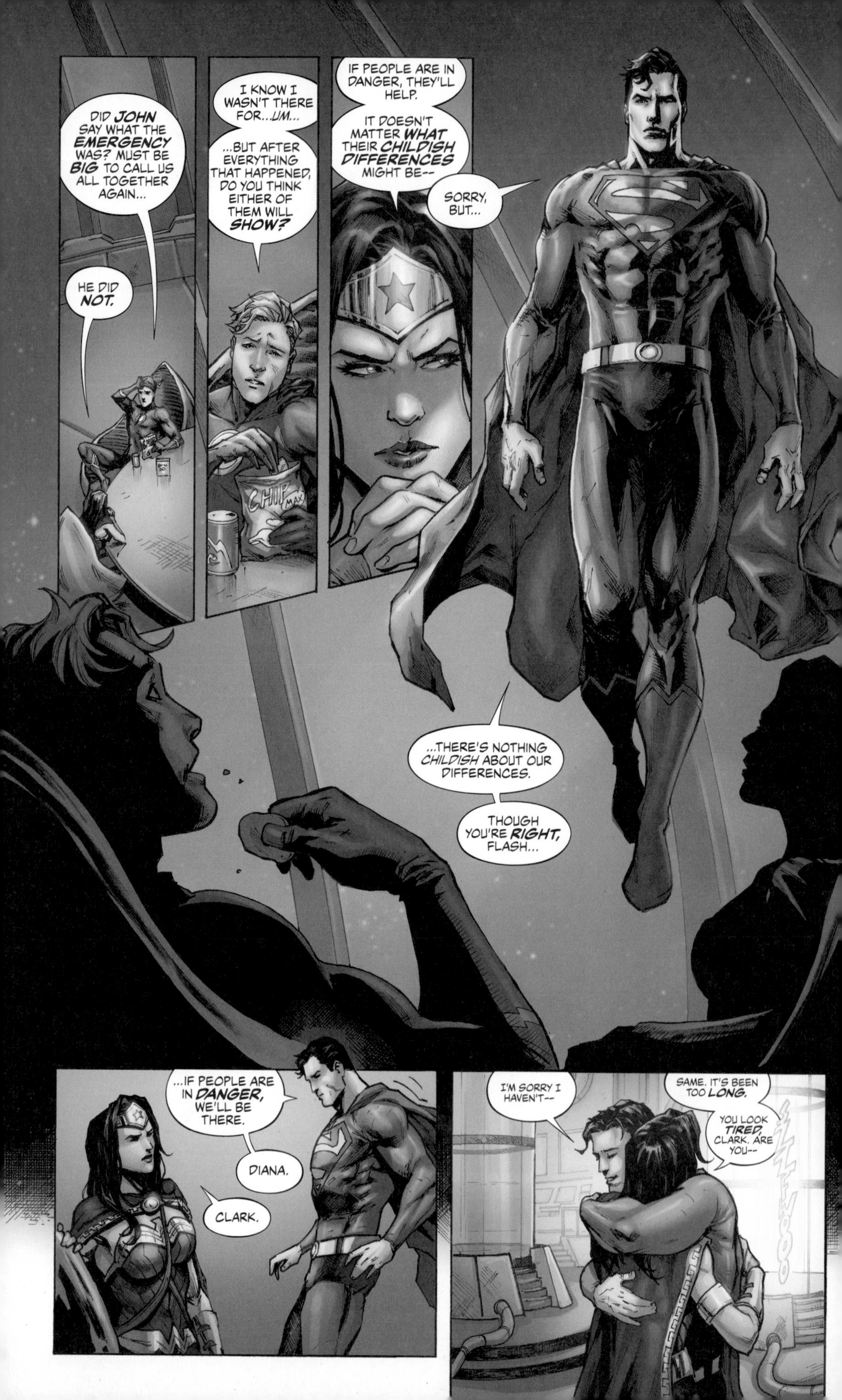

DID JOHN SAY WHAT THE EMERGENCY WAS? MUST BE BIG TO CALL US ALL TOGETHER AGAIN...
HE DID NOT.
I KNOW I WASN'T THERE FOR...UM...
...BUT AFTER EVERYTHING THAT HAPPENED, DO YOU THINK EITHER OF THEM WILL SHOW?
IF PEOPLE ARE IN DANGER, THEY'LL HELP.
IT DOESN'T MATTER WHAT THEIR CHILDISH DIFFERENCES MIGHT BE--
SORRY, BUT...
...THERE'S NOTHING CHILDISH ABOUT OUR DIFFERENCES.
THOUGH YOU'RE RIGHT, FLASH...
...IF PEOPLE ARE IN DANGER, WE'LL BE THERE.
DIANA.
CLARK.
I'M SORRY I HAVEN'T--
SAME. IT'S BEEN TOO LONG.
YOU LOOK TIRED, CLARK. ARE YOU--

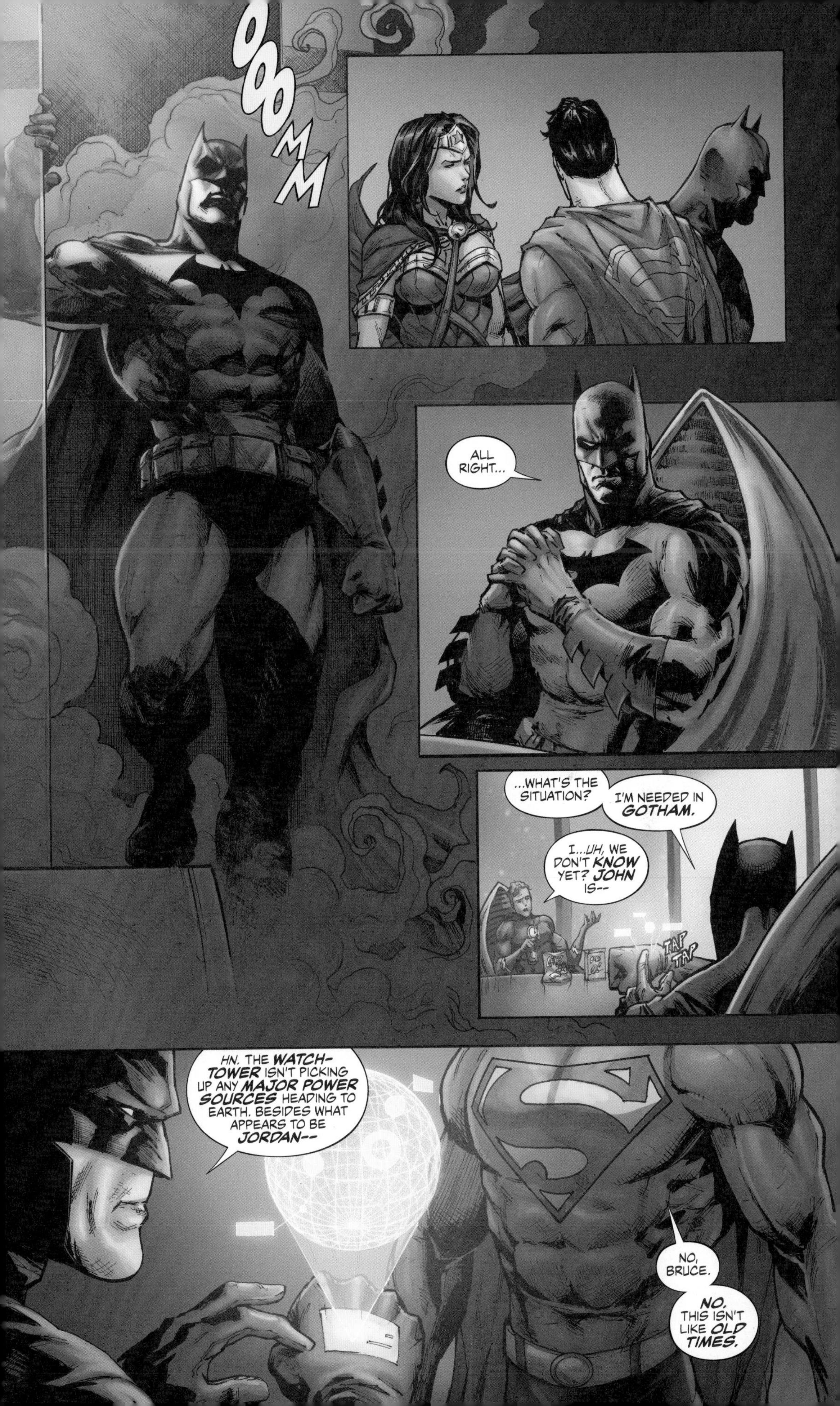
OOOOMMM
ALL RIGHT...
...WHAT'S THE SITUATION?
I'M NEEDED IN GOTHAM.
I...UH, WE DON'T KNOW YET? JOHN IS--
TAP TAP
HN. THE WATCH-TOWER ISN'T PICKING UP ANY MAJOR POWER SOURCES HEADING TO EARTH. BESIDES WHAT APPEARS TO BE JORDAN--
NO, BRUCE.
NO. THIS ISN'T LIKE OLD TIMES.

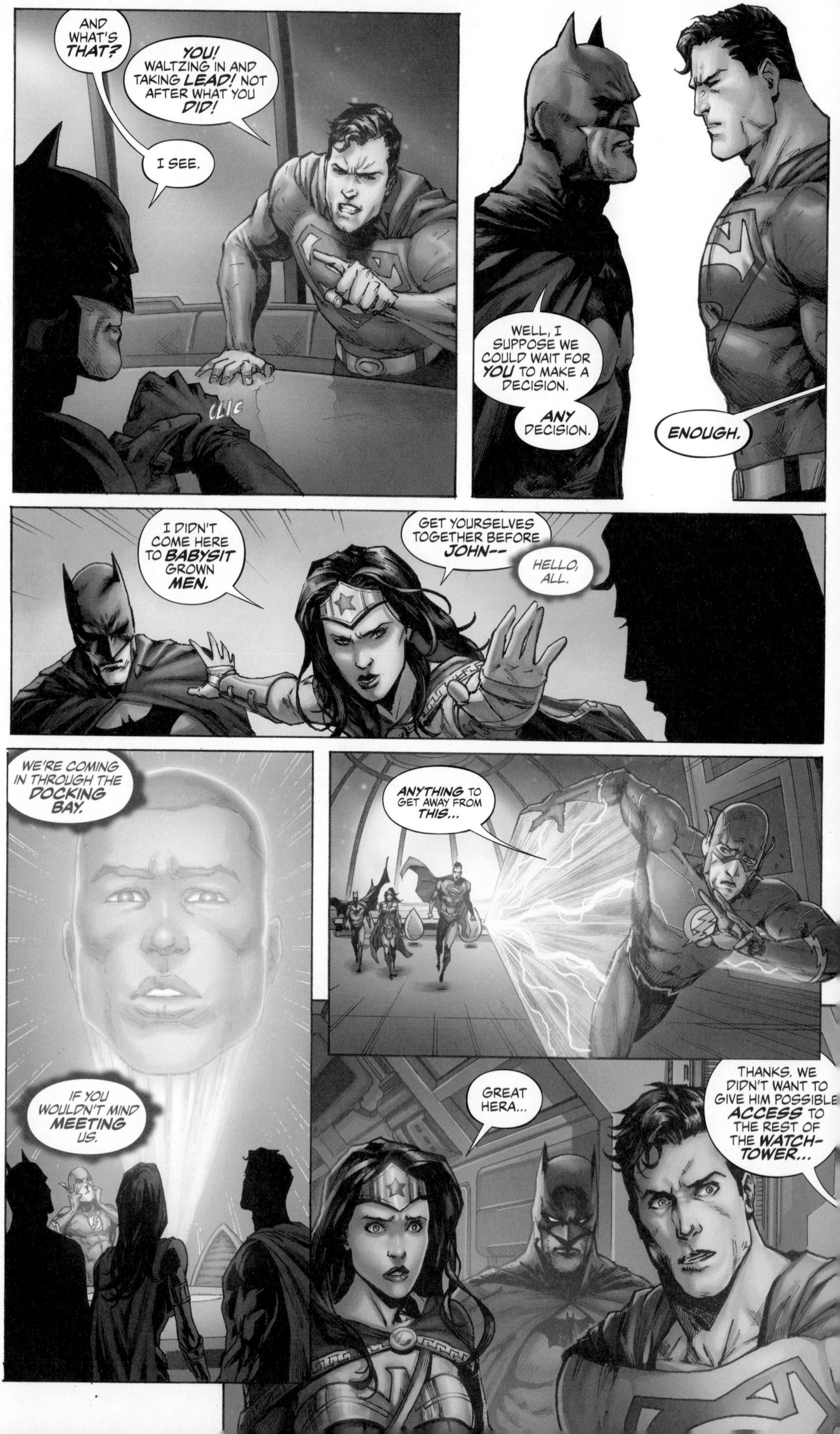

AND WHAT'S THAT?
YOU! WALTZING IN AND TAKING LEAD! NOT AFTER WHAT YOU DID!
I SEE.
CLIC
WELL, I SUPPOSE WE COULD WAIT FOR YOU TO MAKE A DECISION.
ANY DECISION.
ENOUGH.
I DIDN'T COME HERE TO BABYSIT GROWN MEN.
GET YOURSELVES TOGETHER BEFORE JOHN--
HELLO, ALL.
WE'RE COMING IN THROUGH THE DOCKING BAY.
IF YOU WOULDN'T MIND MEETING US.
ANYTHING TO GET AWAY FROM THIS...
GREAT HERA...
THANKS. WE DIDN'T WANT TO GIVE HIM POSSIBLE ACCESS TO THE REST OF THE WATCH-TOWER...

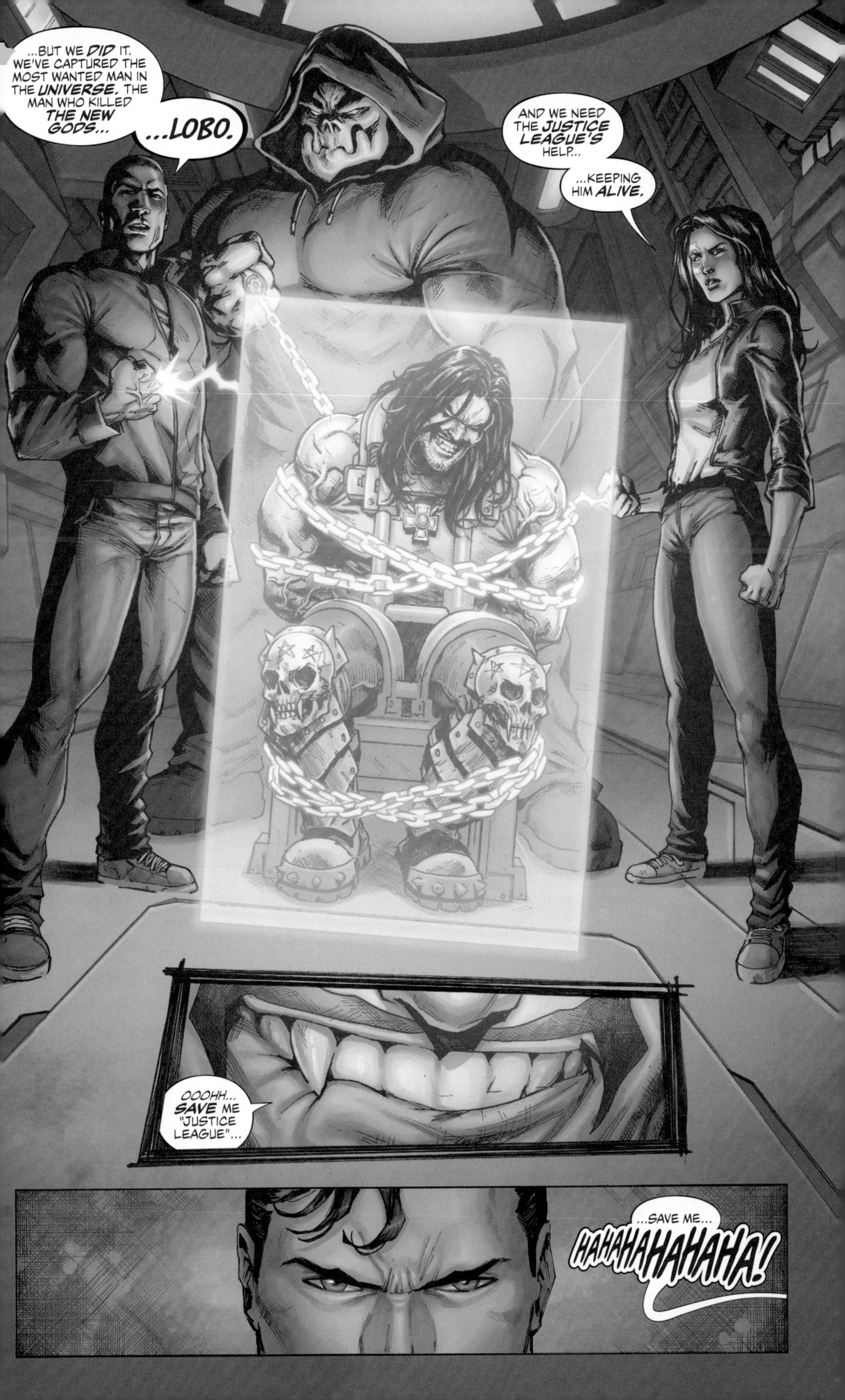
...BUT WE DID IT. WE'VE CAPTURED THE MOST WANTED MAN IN THE UNIVERSE. THE MAN WHO KILLED THE NEW GODS...
...LOBO.
AND WE NEED THE JUSTICE LEAGUE'S HELP...
...KEEPING HIM ALIVE.
OOOHH... SAVE ME "JUSTICE LEAGUE"...
...SAVE ME...
HAHAHAHAHAHAHA!

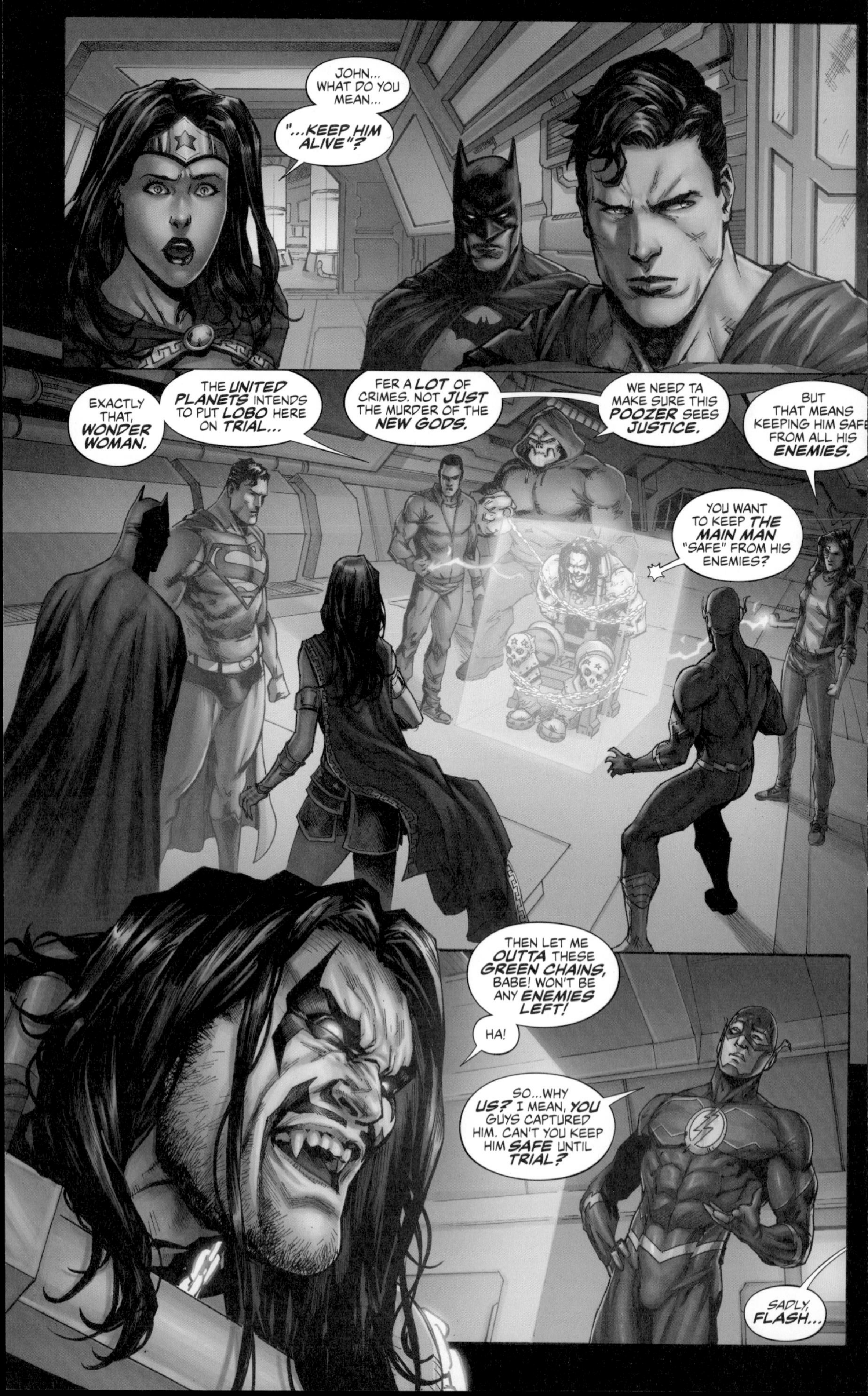
JOHN... WHAT DO YOU MEAN...
"...KEEP HIM ALIVE"?
EXACTLY THAT, WONDER WOMAN.
THE UNITED PLANETS INTENDS TO PUT LOBO HERE ON TRIAL...
FER A LOT OF CRIMES. NOT JUST THE MURDER OF THE NEW GODS.
WE NEED TA MAKE SURE THIS POOZER SEES JUSTICE.
BUT THAT MEANS KEEPING HIM SAFE FROM ALL HIS ENEMIES.
YOU WANT TO KEEP THE MAIN MAN "SAFE" FROM HIS ENEMIES?
THEN LET ME OUTTA THESE GREEN CHAINS, BABE! WON'T BE ANY ENEMIES LEFT!
HA!
SO...WHY US? I MEAN, YOU GUYS CAPTURED HIM. CAN'T YOU KEEP HIM SAFE UNTIL TRIAL?
SADLY, FLASH...

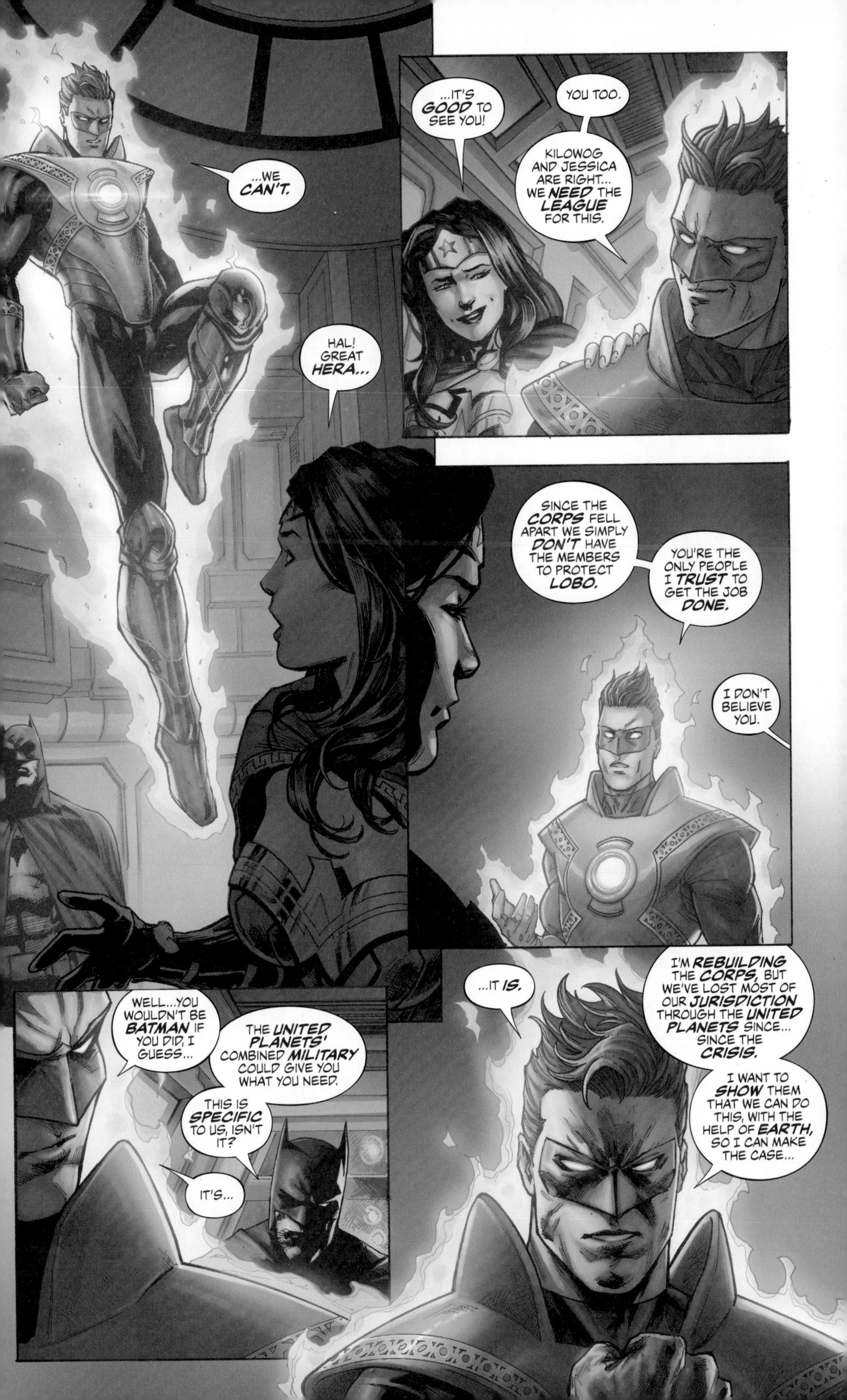
...WE CAN'T.
HAL! GREAT HERA...
...IT'S GOOD TO SEE YOU!
YOU TOO.
KILOWOG AND JESSICA ARE RIGHT... WE NEED THE LEAGUE FOR THIS.
SINCE THE CORPS FELL APART WE SIMPLY DON'T HAVE THE MEMBERS TO PROTECT LOBO.
YOU'RE THE ONLY PEOPLE I TRUST TO GET THE JOB DONE.
I DON'T BELIEVE YOU.
WELL...YOU WOULDN'T BE BATMAN IF YOU DID, I GUESS...
THE UNITED PLANETS' COMBINED MILITARY COULD GIVE YOU WHAT YOU NEED.
THIS IS SPECIFIC TO US, ISN'T IT?
IT'S...
...IT IS.
I'M REBUILDING THE CORPS, BUT WE'VE LOST MOST OF OUR JURISDICTION THROUGH THE UNITED PLANETS SINCE... SINCE THE CRISIS.
I WANT TO SHOW THEM THAT WE CAN DO THIS, WITH THE HELP OF EARTH, SO I CAN MAKE THE CASE...

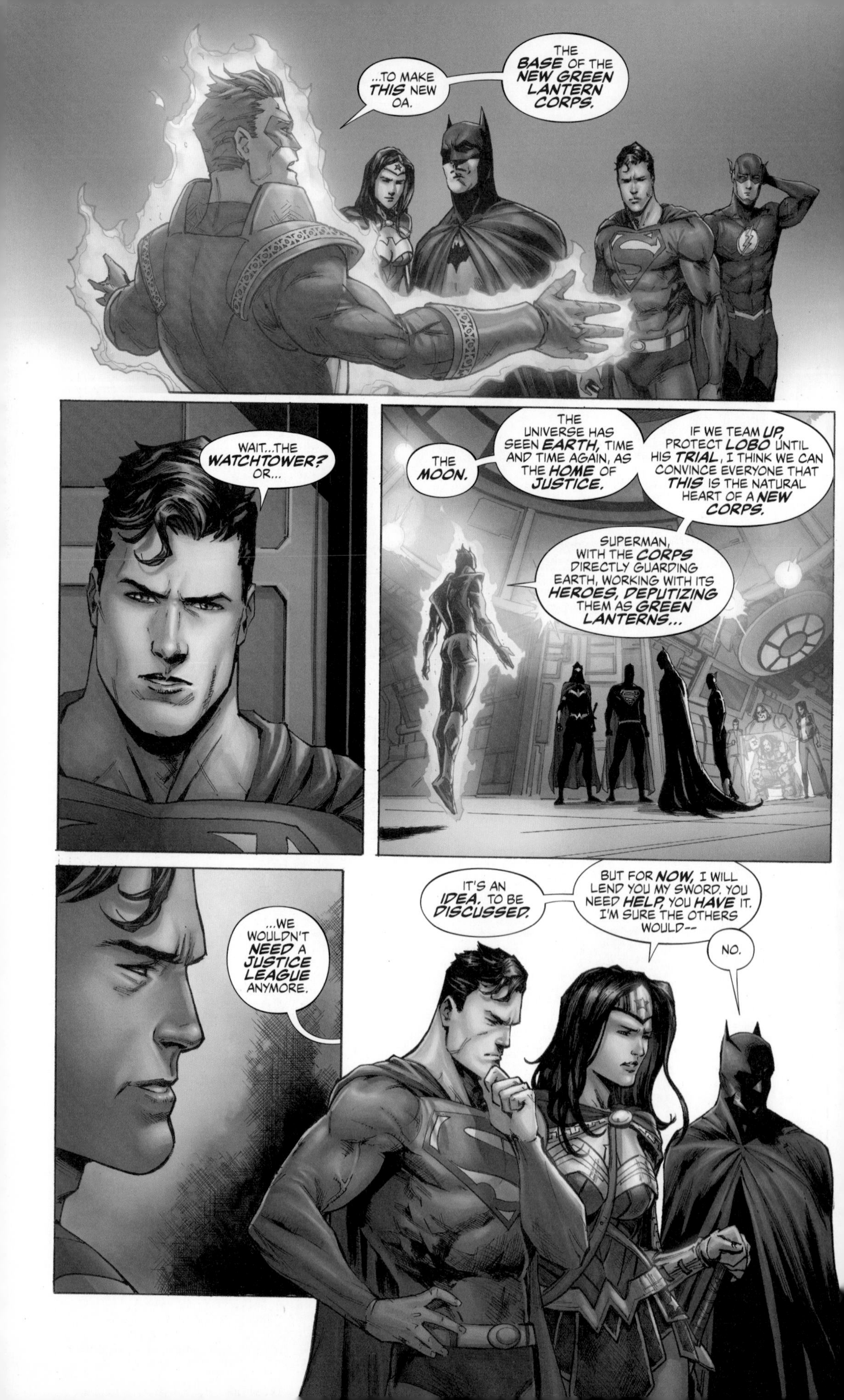
...TO MAKE THIS NEW OA.
THE BASE OF THE NEW GREEN LANTERN CORPS.
WAIT...THE WATCHTOWER? OR...
THE MOON.
THE UNIVERSE HAS SEEN EARTH, TIME AND TIME AGAIN, AS THE HOME OF JUSTICE.
IF WE TEAM UP, PROTECT LOBO UNTIL HIS TRIAL, I THINK WE CAN CONVINCE EVERYONE THAT THIS IS THE NATURAL HEART OF A NEW CORPS.
SUPERMAN, WITH THE CORPS DIRECTLY GUARDING EARTH, WORKING WITH ITS HEROES, DEPUTIZING THEM AS GREEN LANTERNS...
...WE WOULDN'T NEED A JUSTICE LEAGUE ANYMORE.
IT'S AN IDEA. TO BE DISCUSSED.
BUT FOR NOW, I WILL LEND YOU MY SWORD. YOU NEED HELP, YOU HAVE IT. I'M SURE THE OTHERS WOULD--
NO.

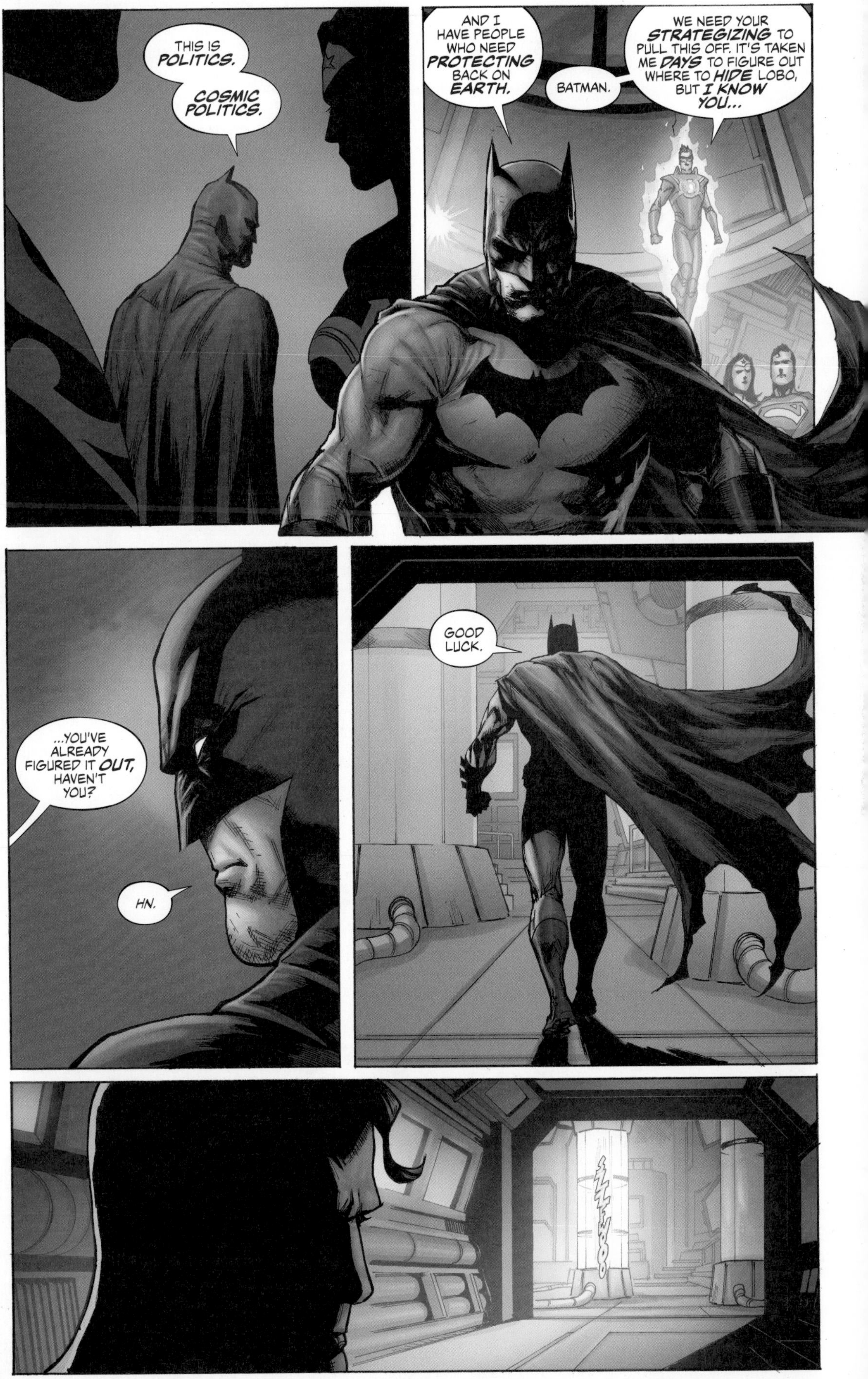

THIS IS POLITICS.
COSMIC POLITICS.
AND I HAVE PEOPLE WHO NEED PROTECTING BACK ON EARTH.
BATMAN.
WE NEED YOUR STRATEGIZING TO PULL THIS OFF. IT'S TAKEN ME DAYS TO FIGURE OUT WHERE TO HIDE LOBO, BUT I KNOW YOU...
...YOU'VE ALREADY FIGURED IT OUT, HAVEN'T YOU?
HN.
GOOD LUCK.

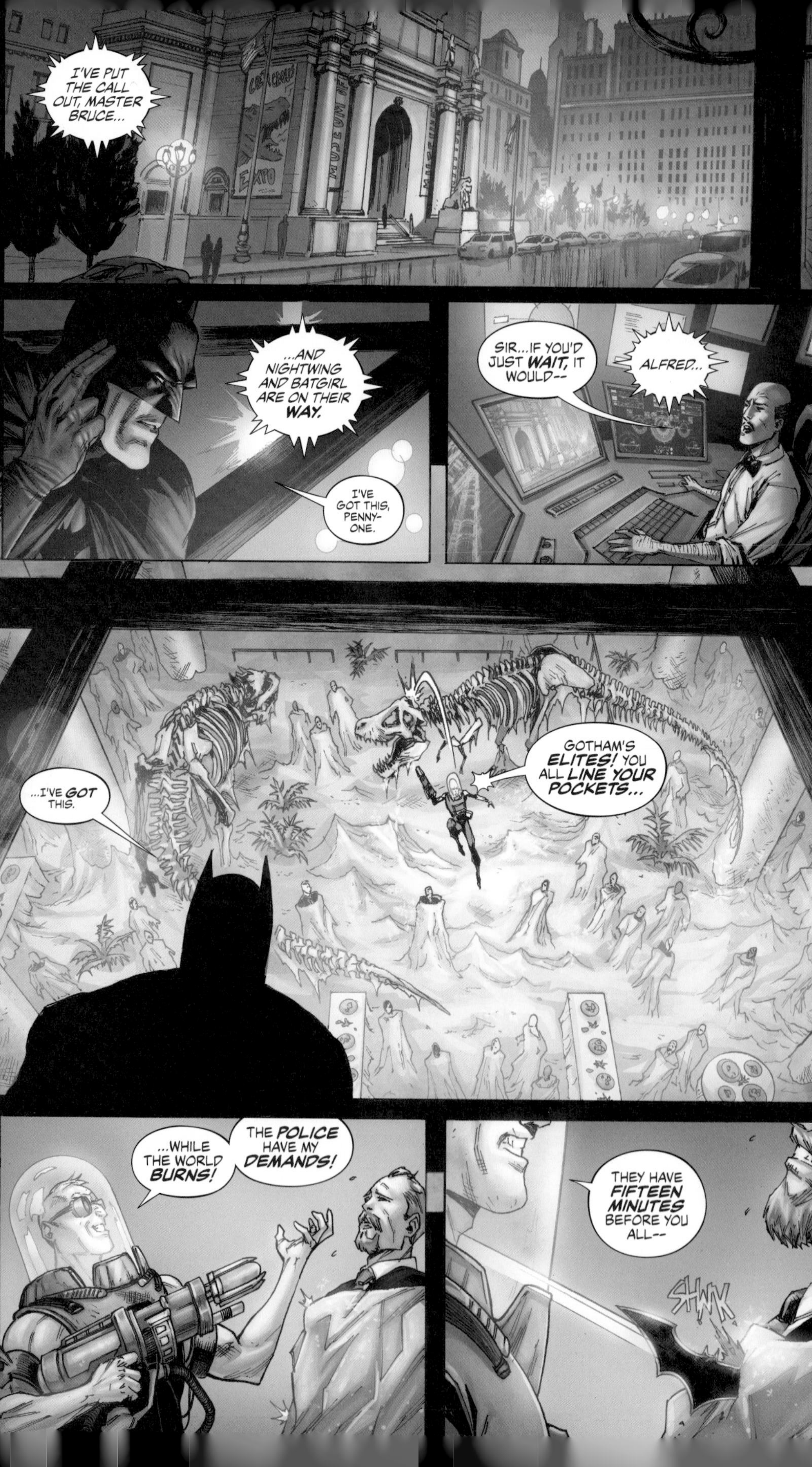

I'VE PUT THE CALL OUT, MASTER BRUCE...
...AND NIGHTWING AND BATGIRL ARE ON THEIR WAY.
I'VE GOT THIS, PENNY-ONE.
SIR...IF YOU'D JUST WAIT, IT WOULD--
ALFRED...
...I'VE GOT THIS.
GOTHAM'S ELITES! YOU ALL LINE YOUR POCKETS...
...WHILE THE WORLD BURNS!
THE POLICE HAVE MY DEMANDS!
THEY HAVE FIFTEEN MINUTES BEFORE YOU ALL--
SHWK

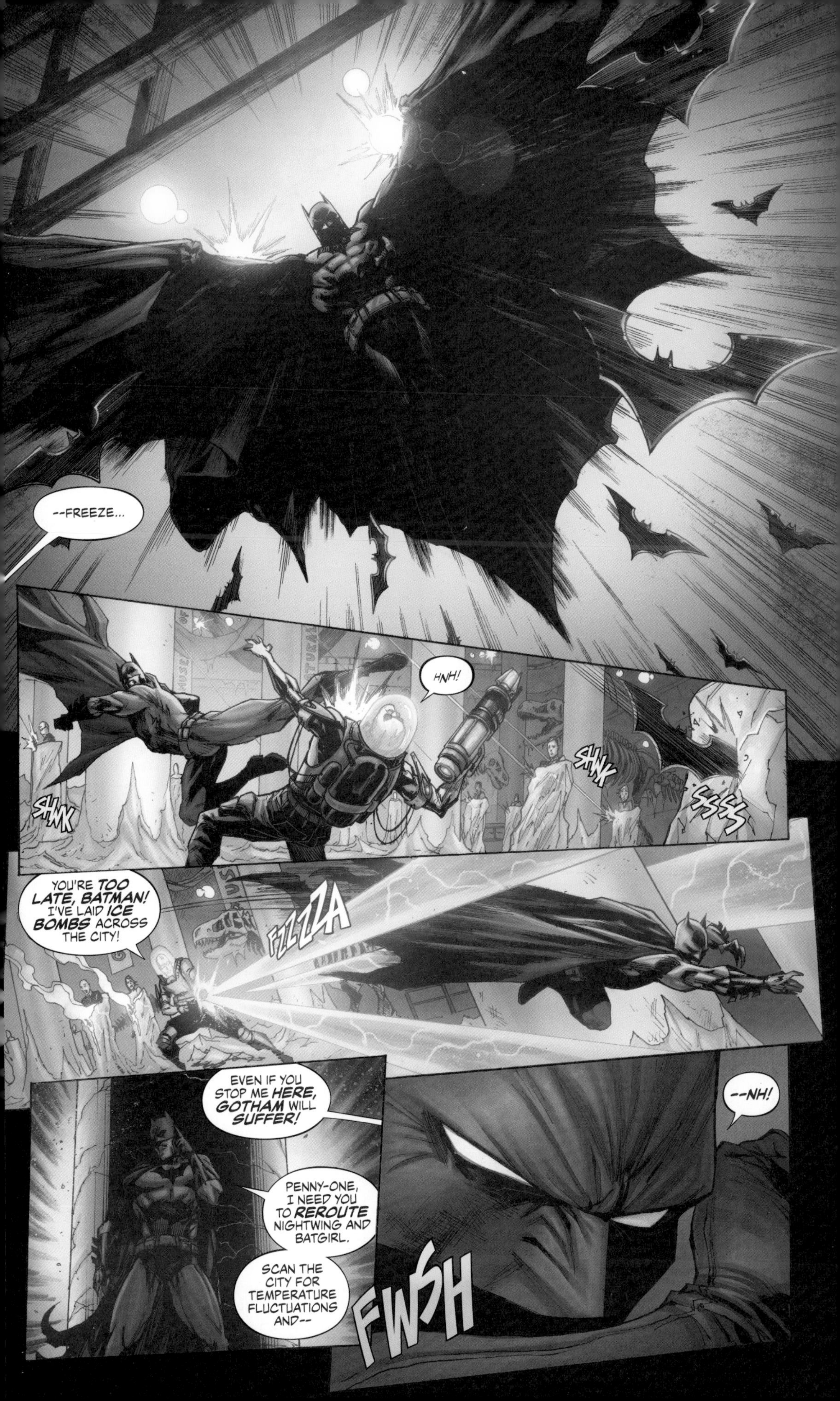
--FREEZE...
HNH!
SHNK
SHNK
SSSS
YOU'RE **TOO LATE, BATMAN!** I'VE LAID **ICE BOMBS** ACROSS THE CITY!
FZZZZA
EVEN IF YOU STOP ME **HERE, GOTHAM** WILL **SUFFER!**
PENNY-ONE, I NEED YOU TO **REROUTE** NIGHTWING AND BATGIRL.
SCAN THE CITY FOR TEMPERATURE FLUCTUATIONS AND--
--NH!
FWSH

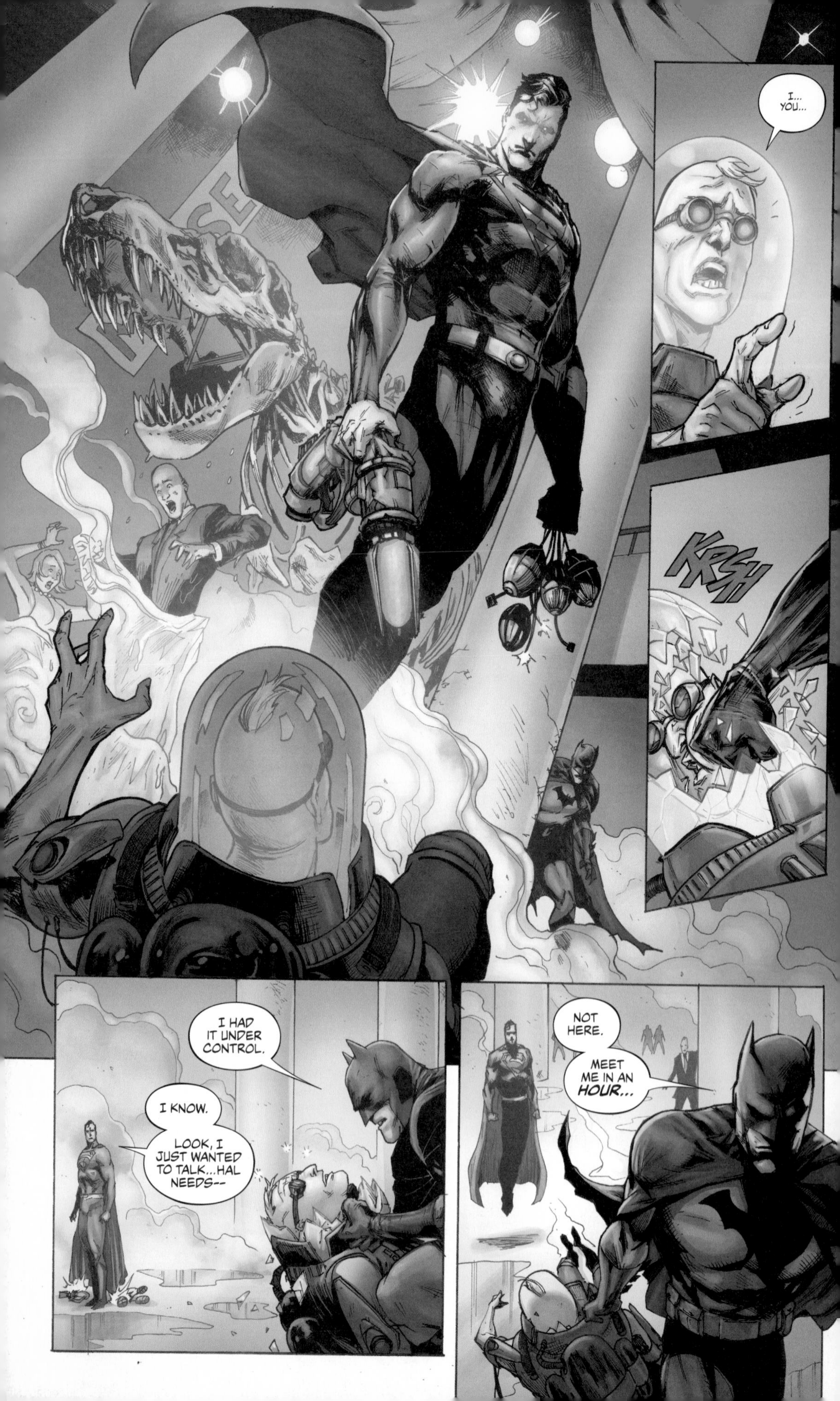

I... YOU...
KRSH
I HAD IT UNDER CONTROL.
I KNOW.
LOOK, I JUST WANTED TO TALK...HAL NEEDS--
NOT HERE.
MEET ME IN AN HOUR...

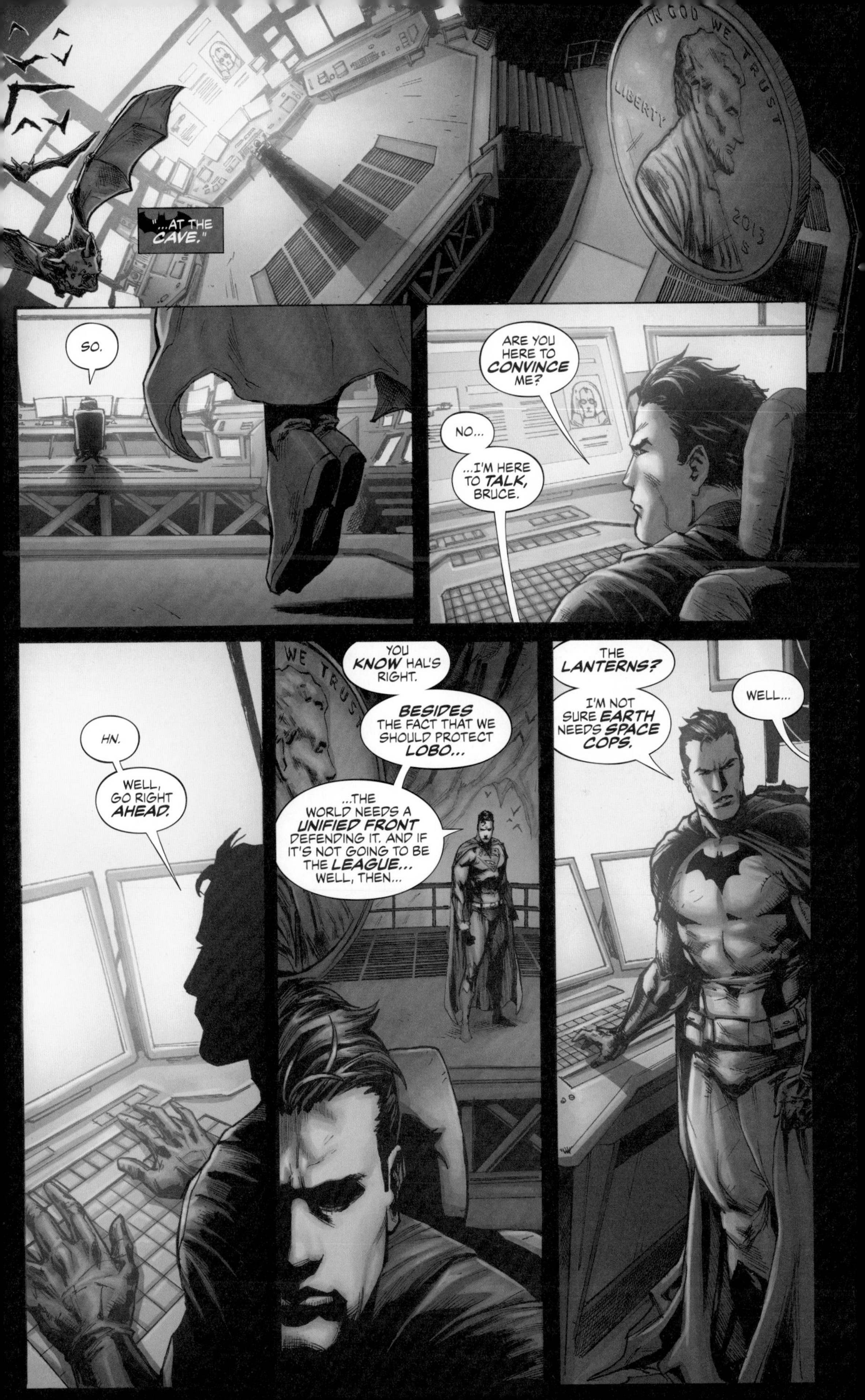
"...AT THE CAVE."
IN GOD WE TRUST
LIBERTY
2013
SO.
ARE YOU HERE TO CONVINCE ME?
NO...
...I'M HERE TO TALK, BRUCE.
HN.
WELL, GO RIGHT AHEAD.
YOU KNOW HAL'S RIGHT.
BESIDES THE FACT THAT WE SHOULD PROTECT LOBO...
...THE WORLD NEEDS A UNIFIED FRONT DEFENDING IT. AND IF IT'S NOT GOING TO BE THE LEAGUE... WELL, THEN...
THE LANTERNS?
I'M NOT SURE EARTH NEEDS SPACE COPS.
WELL...

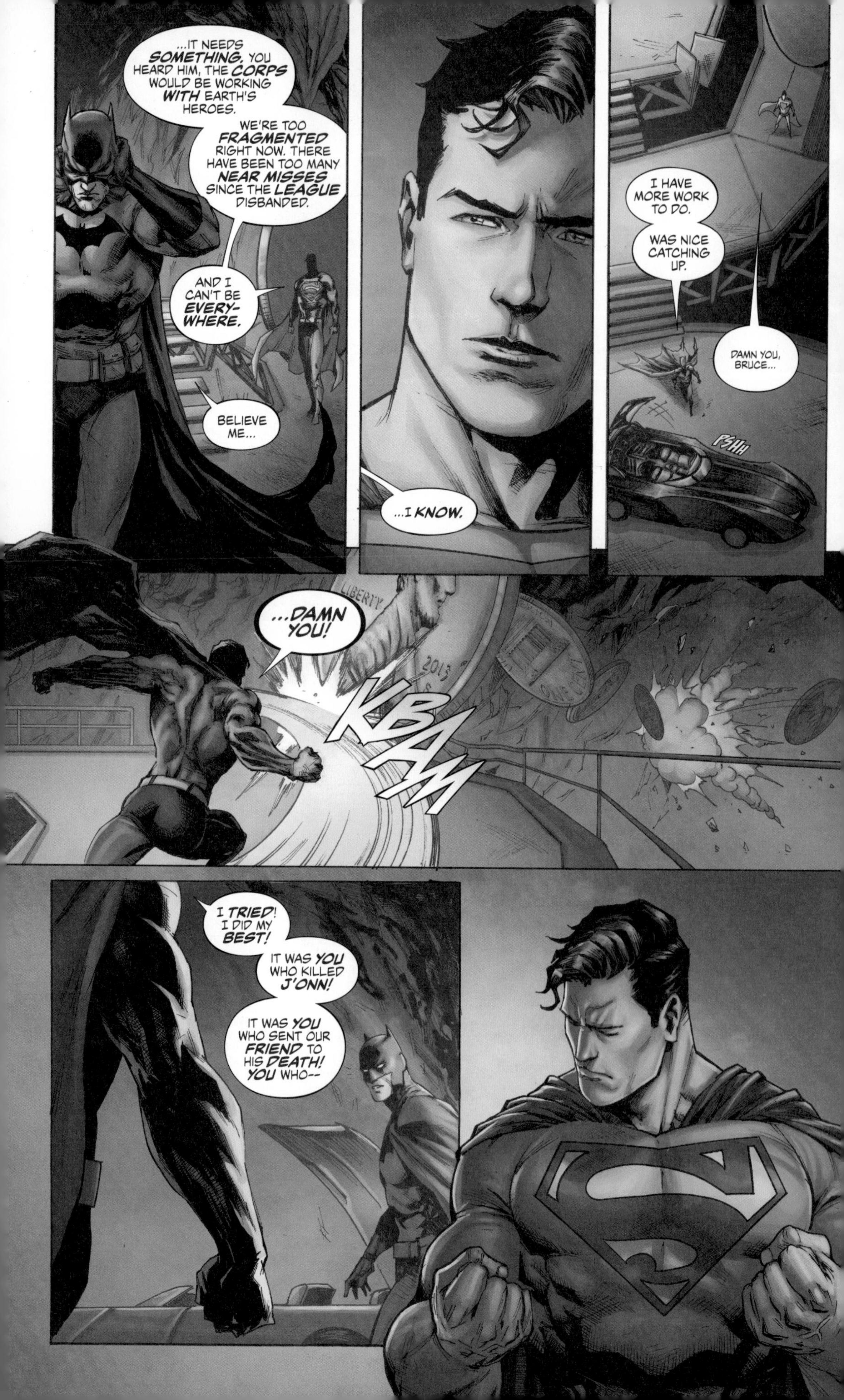
...IT NEEDS SOMETHING. YOU HEARD HIM, THE CORPS WOULD BE WORKING WITH EARTH'S HEROES.
WE'RE TOO FRAGMENTED RIGHT NOW. THERE HAVE BEEN TOO MANY NEAR MISSES SINCE THE LEAGUE DISBANDED.
AND I CAN'T BE EVERY-WHERE.
BELIEVE ME...
...I KNOW.
I HAVE MORE WORK TO DO.
WAS NICE CATCHING UP.
DAMN YOU, BRUCE...
PSHH
...DAMN YOU!
KBAM
I TRIED! I DID MY BEST!
IT WAS YOU WHO KILLED J'ONN!
IT WAS YOU WHO SENT OUR FRIEND TO HIS DEATH! YOU WHO--

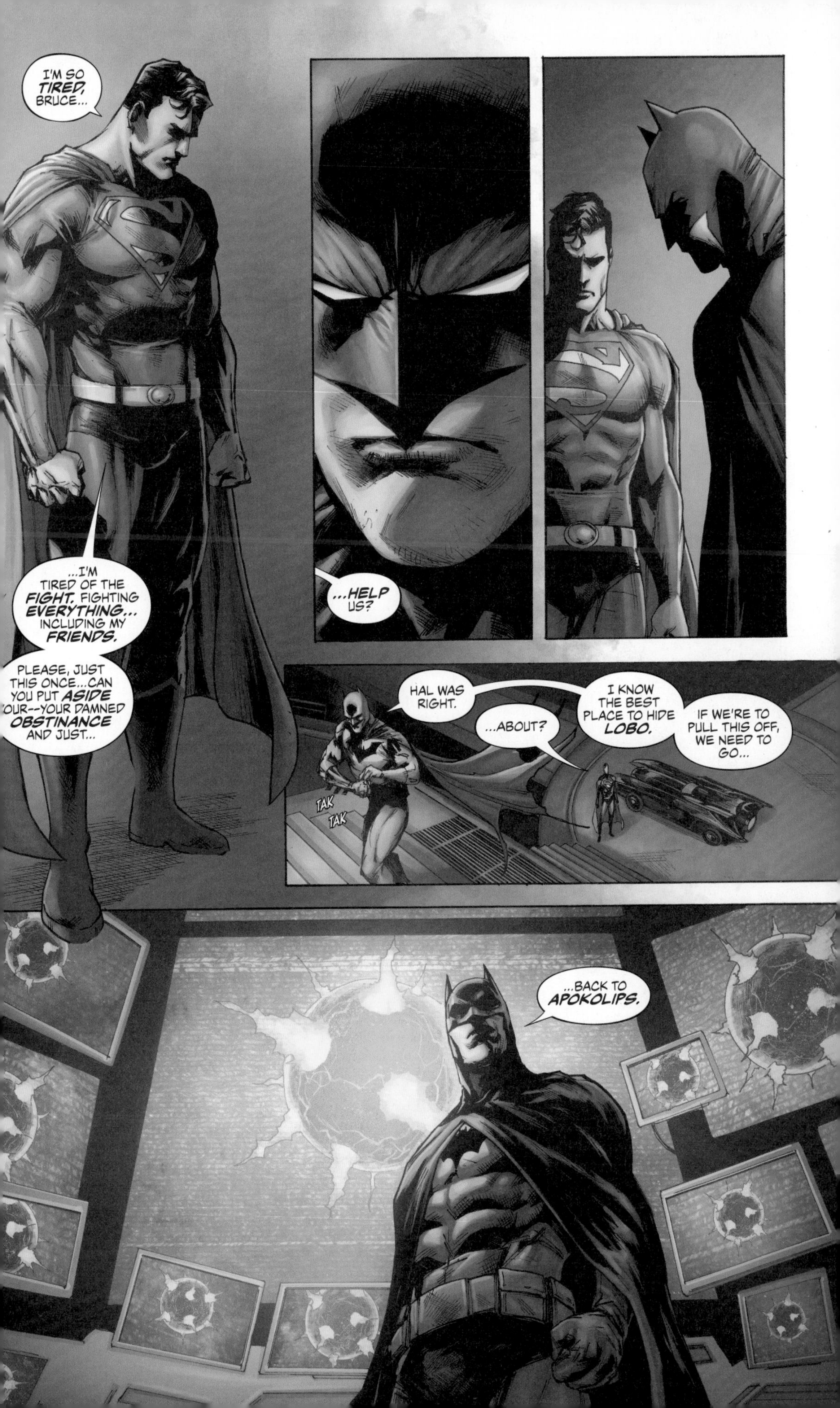
I'M SO TIRED, BRUCE...
...I'M TIRED OF THE FIGHT. FIGHTING EVERYTHING... INCLUDING MY FRIENDS.
PLEASE, JUST THIS ONCE...CAN YOU PUT ASIDE OUR--YOUR DAMNED OBSTINANCE AND JUST...
...HELP US?
HAL WAS RIGHT.
...ABOUT?
I KNOW THE BEST PLACE TO HIDE LOBO.
IF WE'RE TO PULL THIS OFF, WE NEED TO GO...
TAK
TAK
...BACK TO APOKOLIPS.

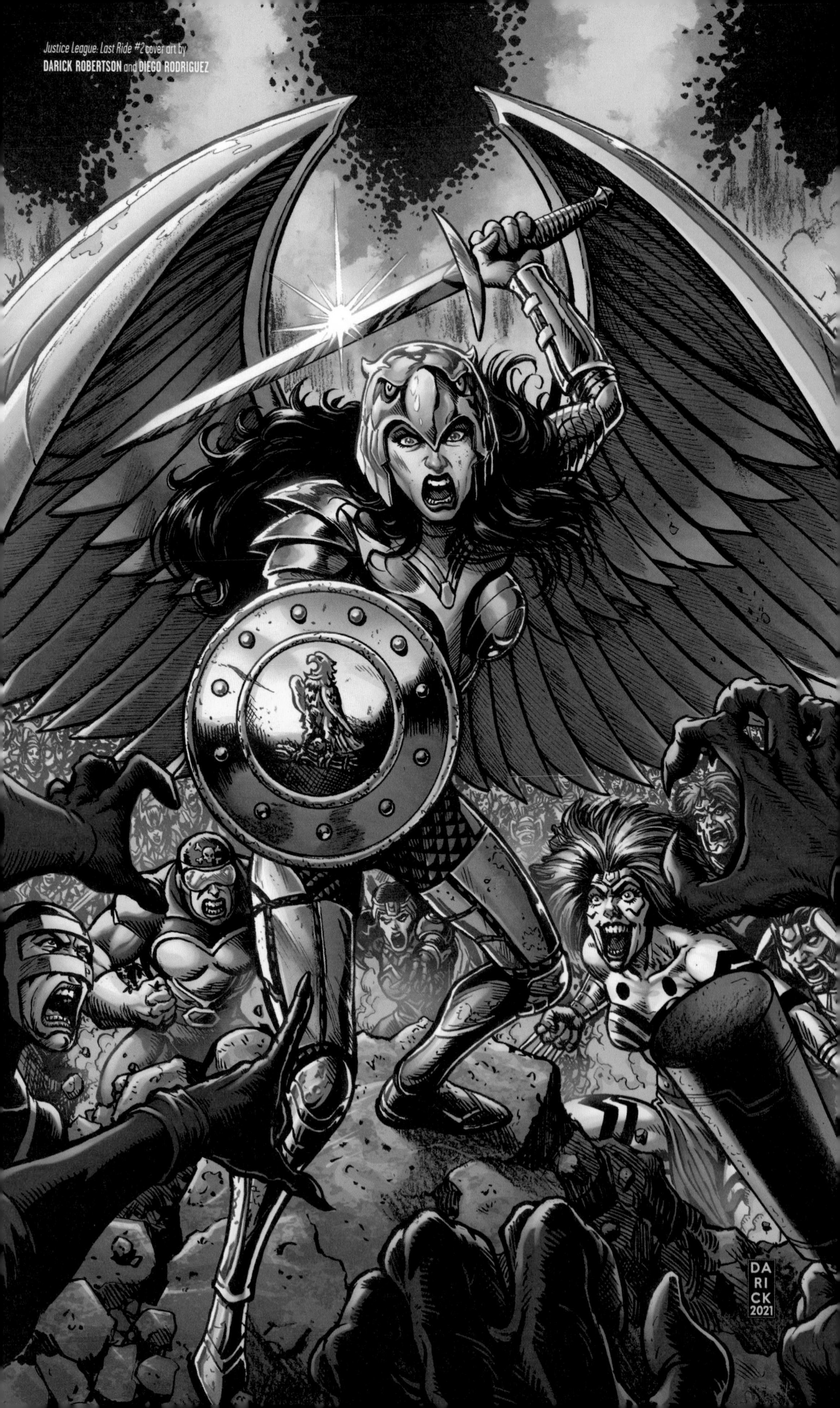
DA
RI
CK
2021

Justice League: Last Ride #2 cover art by
DARICK ROBERTSON and **DIEGO RODRIGUEZ**

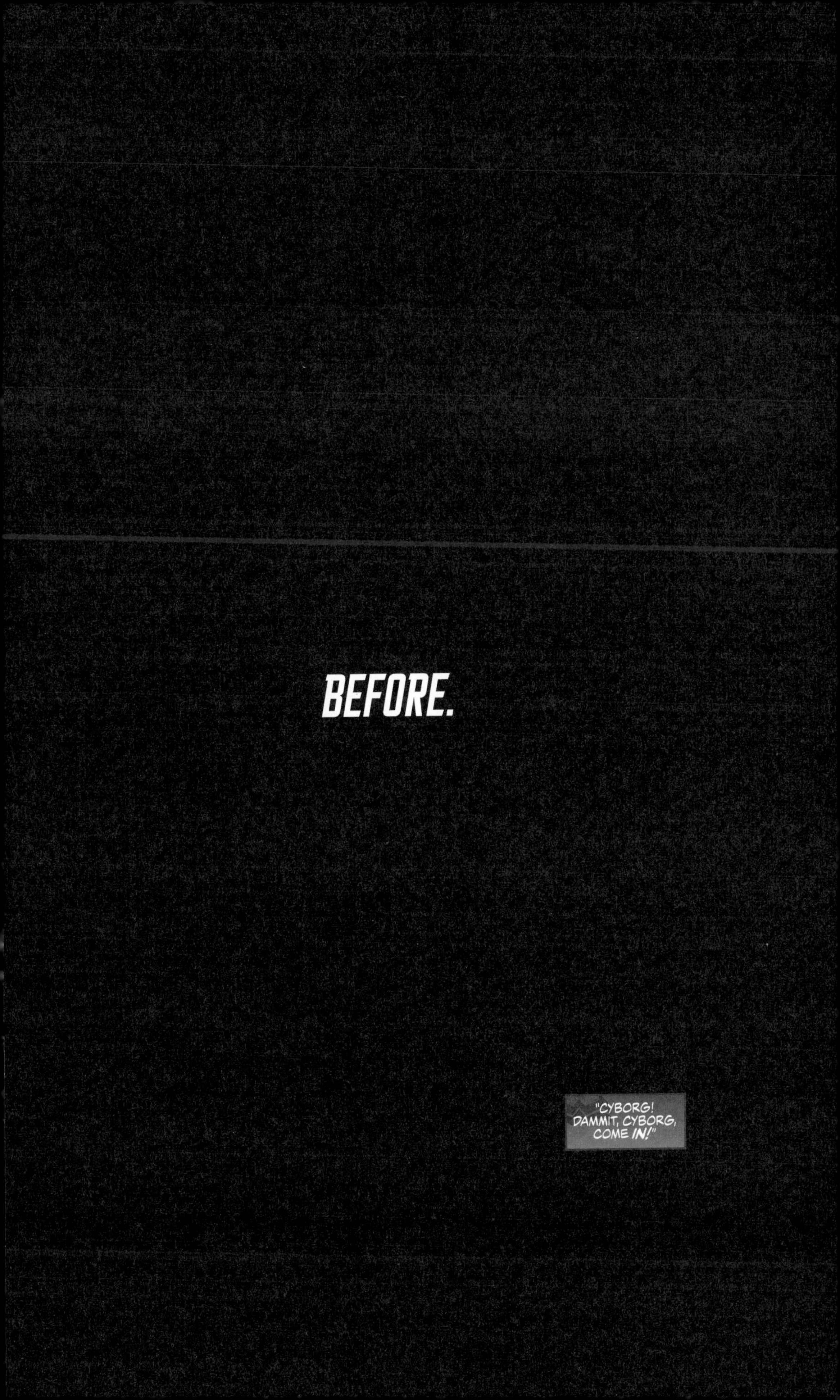
BEFORE.
"CYBORG! DAMMIT, CYBORG, COME IN!"

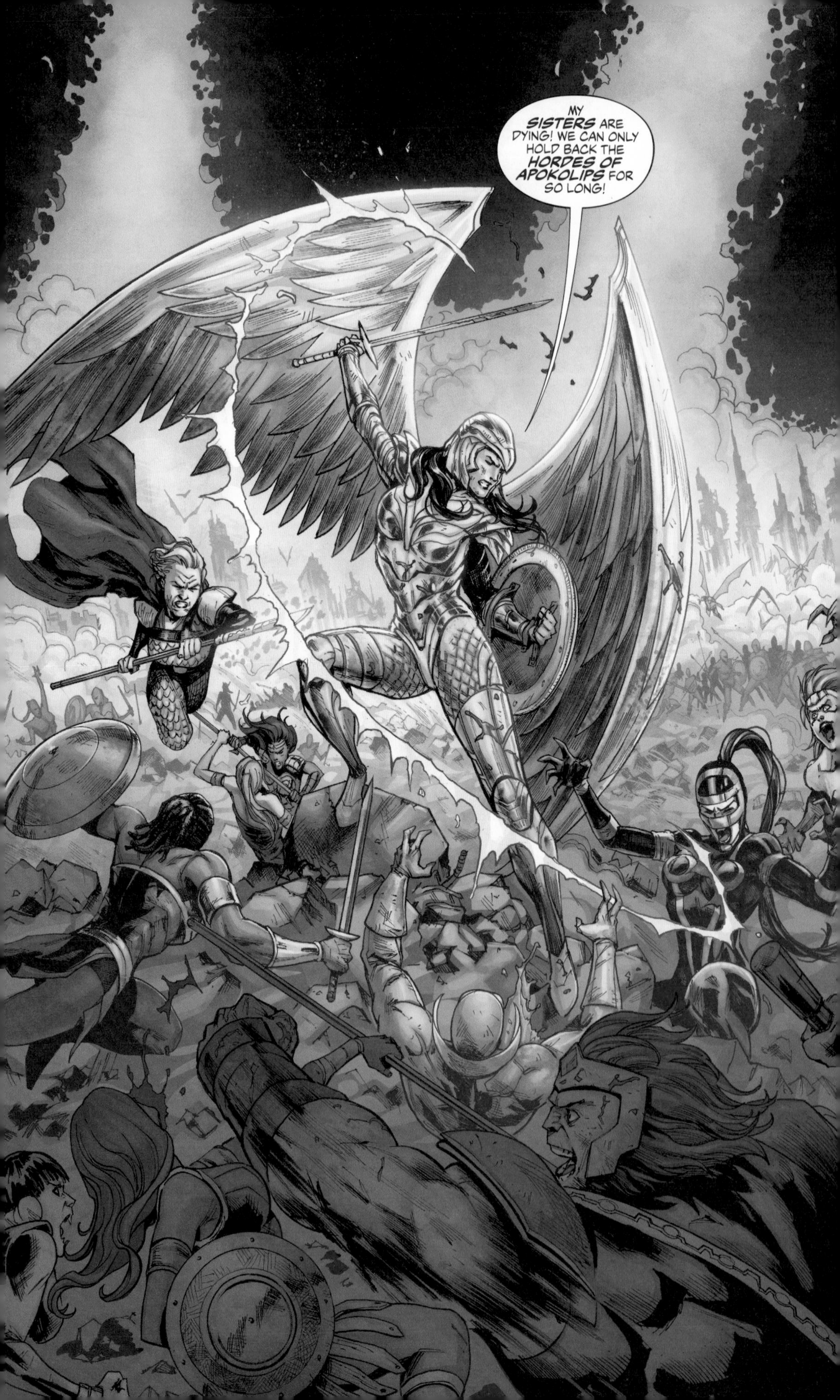
MY SISTERS ARE DYING! WE CAN ONLY HOLD BACK THE HORDES OF APOKOLIPS FOR SO LONG!

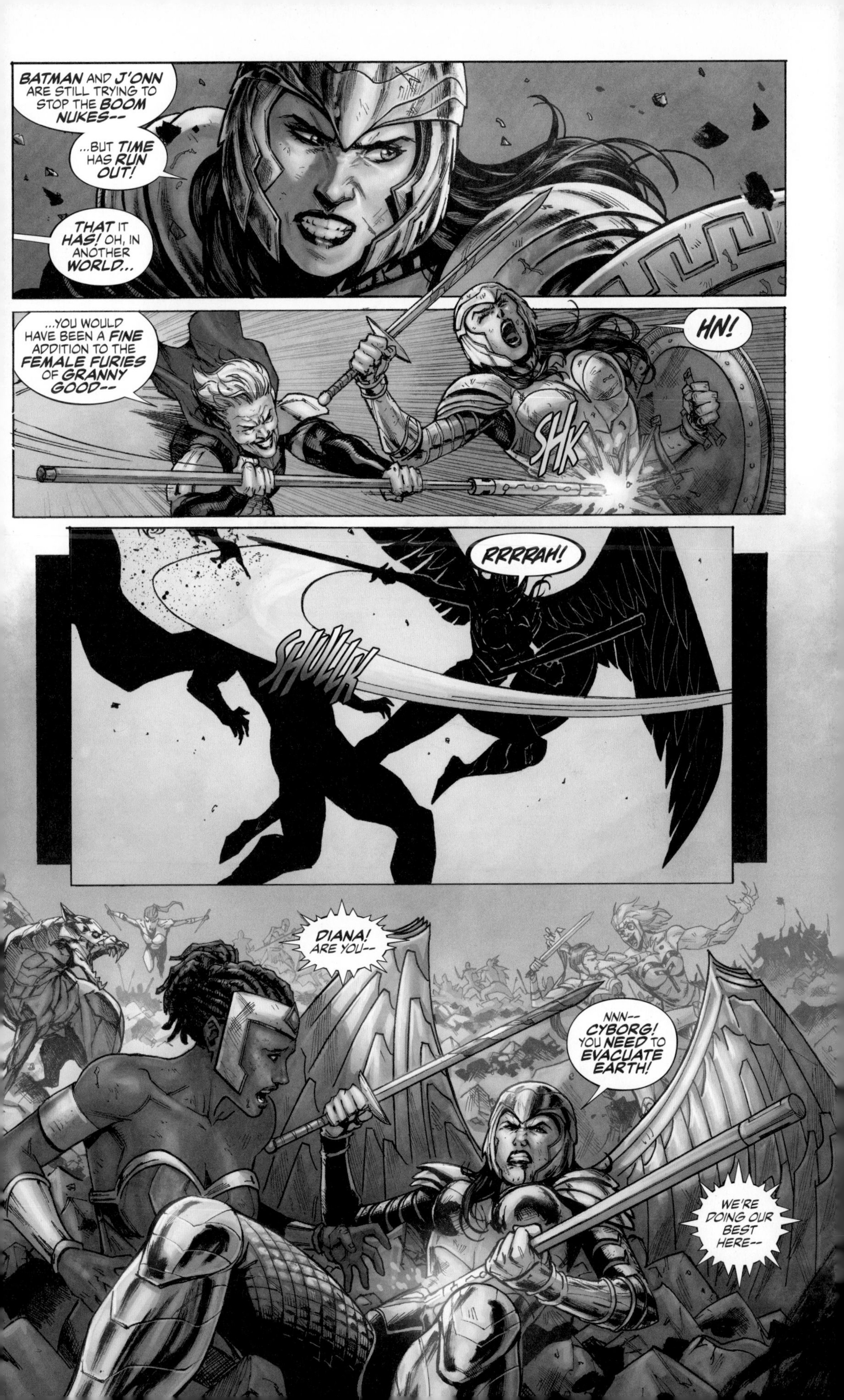

BATMAN AND J'ONN ARE STILL TRYING TO STOP THE BOOM NUKES--
...BUT TIME HAS RUN OUT!
THAT IT HAS! OH, IN ANOTHER WORLD...
...YOU WOULD HAVE BEEN A FINE ADDITION TO THE FEMALE FURIES OF GRANNY GOOD--
HN!
SHK
RRRRAH!
SHUUK
DIANA! ARE YOU--
NNN-- CYBORG! YOU NEED TO EVACUATE EARTH!
WE'RE DOING OUR BEST HERE--

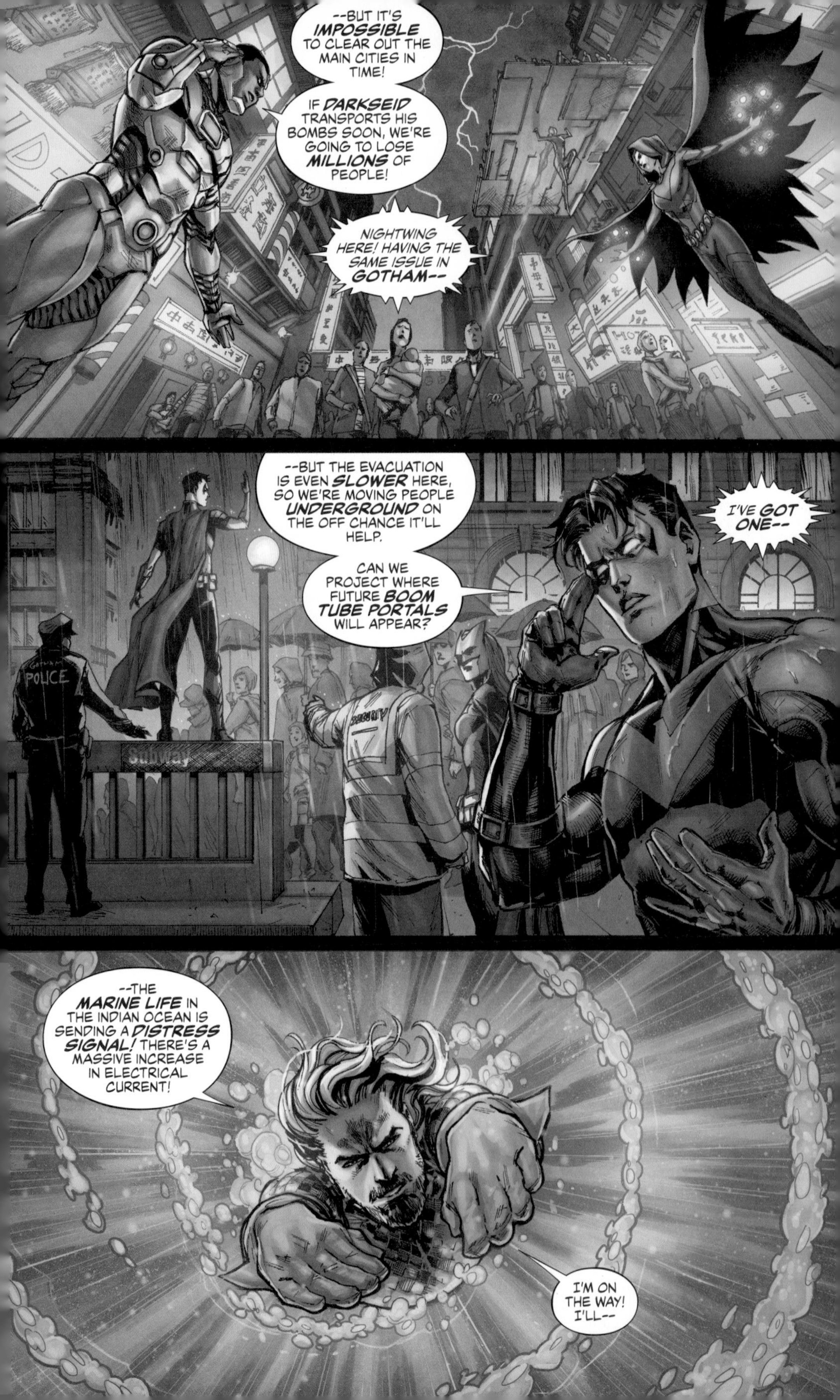
--BUT IT'S IMPOSSIBLE TO CLEAR OUT THE MAIN CITIES IN TIME!
IF DARKSEID TRANSPORTS HIS BOMBS SOON, WE'RE GOING TO LOSE MILLIONS OF PEOPLE!
NIGHTWING HERE! HAVING THE SAME ISSUE IN GOTHAM--
--BUT THE EVACUATION IS EVEN SLOWER HERE, SO WE'RE MOVING PEOPLE UNDERGROUND ON THE OFF CHANCE IT'LL HELP.
CAN WE PROJECT WHERE FUTURE BOOM TUBE PORTALS WILL APPEAR?
I'VE GOT ONE--
POLICE
Subway
--THE MARINE LIFE IN THE INDIAN OCEAN IS SENDING A DISTRESS SIGNAL! THERE'S A MASSIVE INCREASE IN ELECTRICAL CURRENT!
I'M ON THE WAY! I'LL--

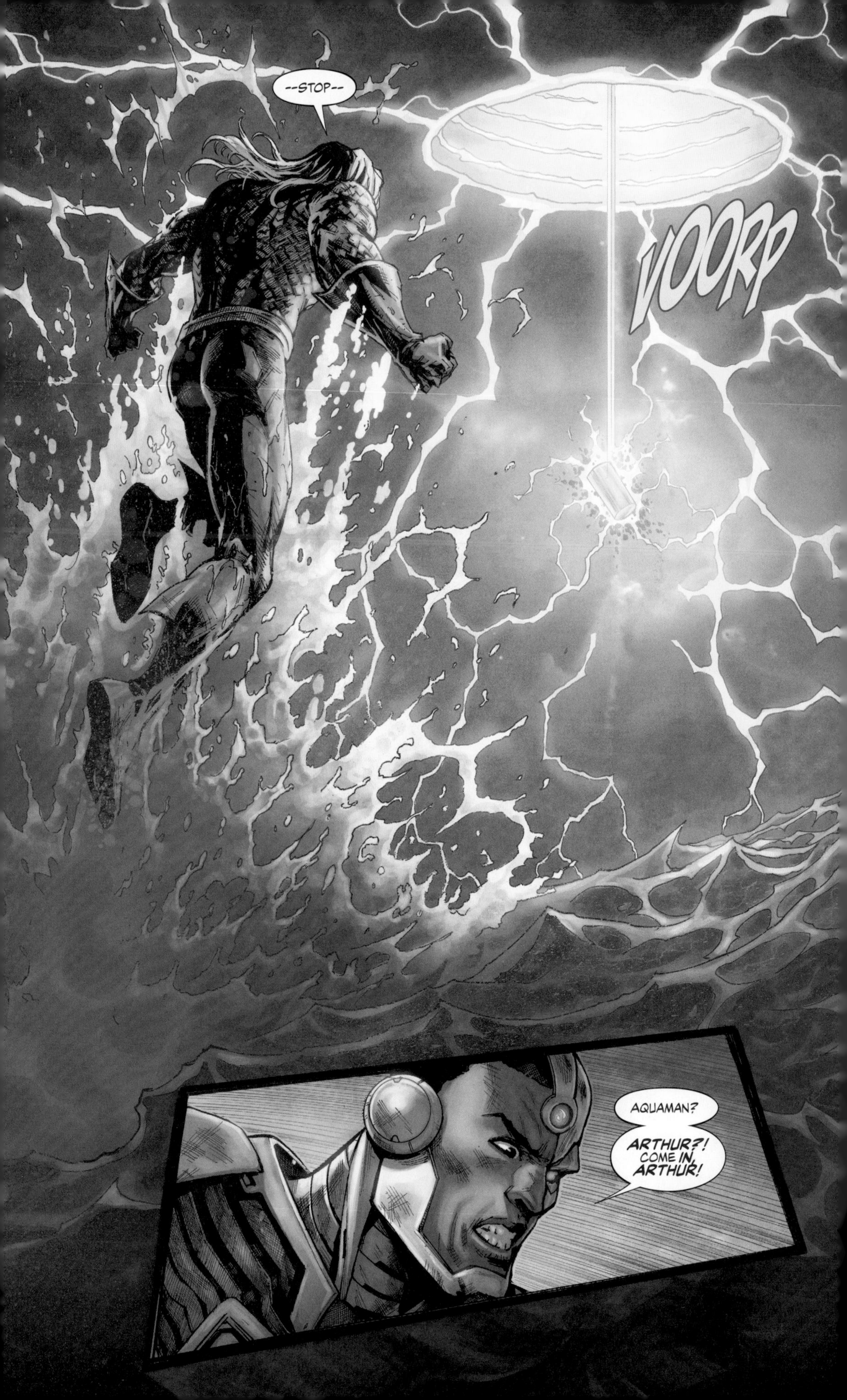
--STOP--
VOORP
AQUAMAN?
ARTHUR?! COME IN, ARTHUR!

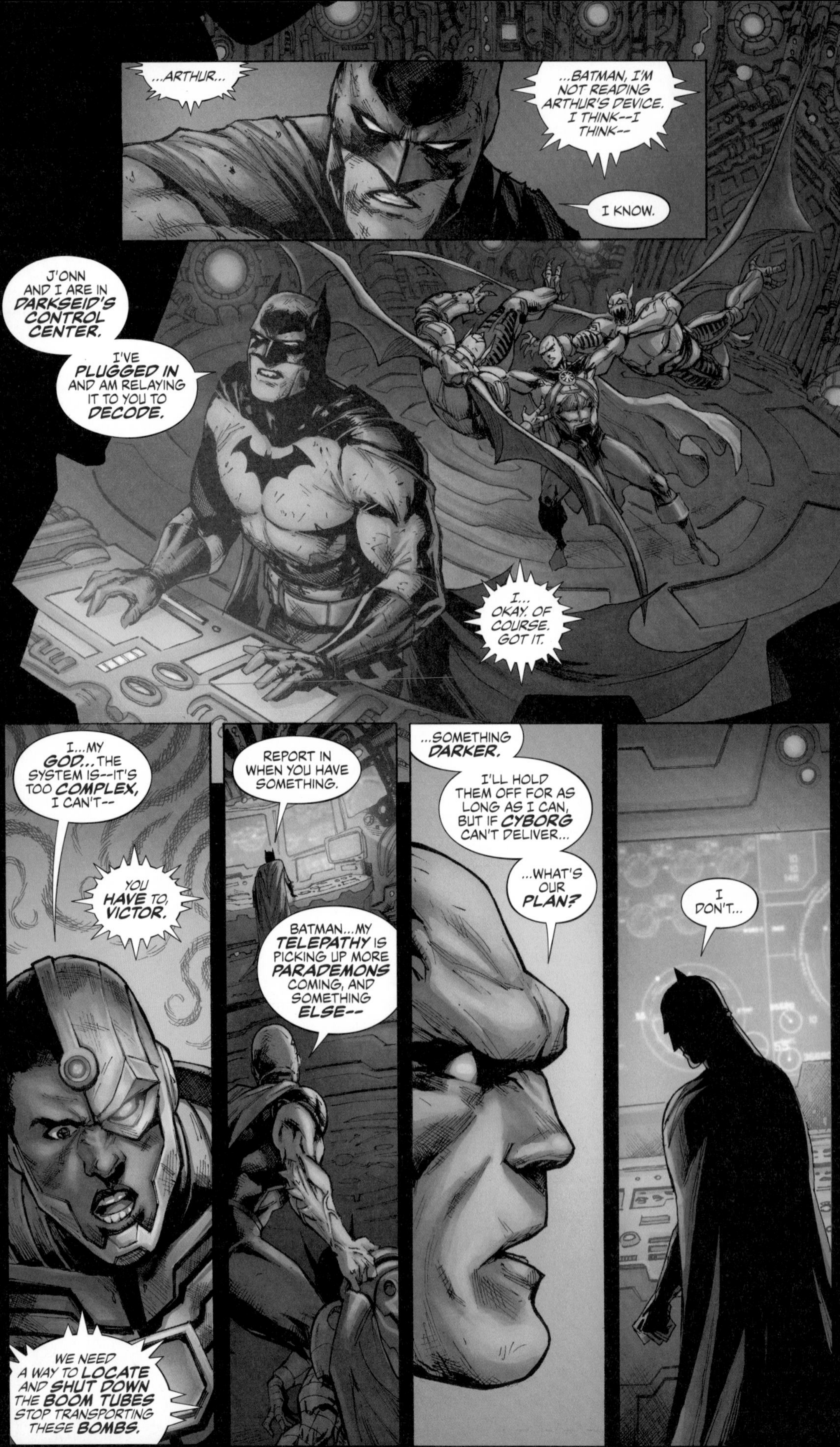
...ARTHUR...
...BATMAN, I'M NOT READING ARTHUR'S DEVICE. I THINK--I THINK--
I KNOW.
J'ONN AND I ARE IN DARKSEID'S CONTROL CENTER.
I'VE PLUGGED IN AND AM RELAYING IT TO YOU TO DECODE.
I... OKAY. OF COURSE. GOT IT.
I...MY GOD...THE SYSTEM IS--IT'S TOO COMPLEX, I CAN'T--
YOU HAVE TO, VICTOR.
WE NEED A WAY TO LOCATE AND SHUT DOWN THE BOOM TUBES STOP TRANSPORTING THESE BOMBS.
REPORT IN WHEN YOU HAVE SOMETHING.
BATMAN...MY TELEPATHY IS PICKING UP MORE PARADEMONS COMING, AND SOMETHING ELSE--
...SOMETHING DARKER.
I'LL HOLD THEM OFF FOR AS LONG AS I CAN, BUT IF CYBORG CAN'T DELIVER...
...WHAT'S OUR PLAN?
I DON'T...

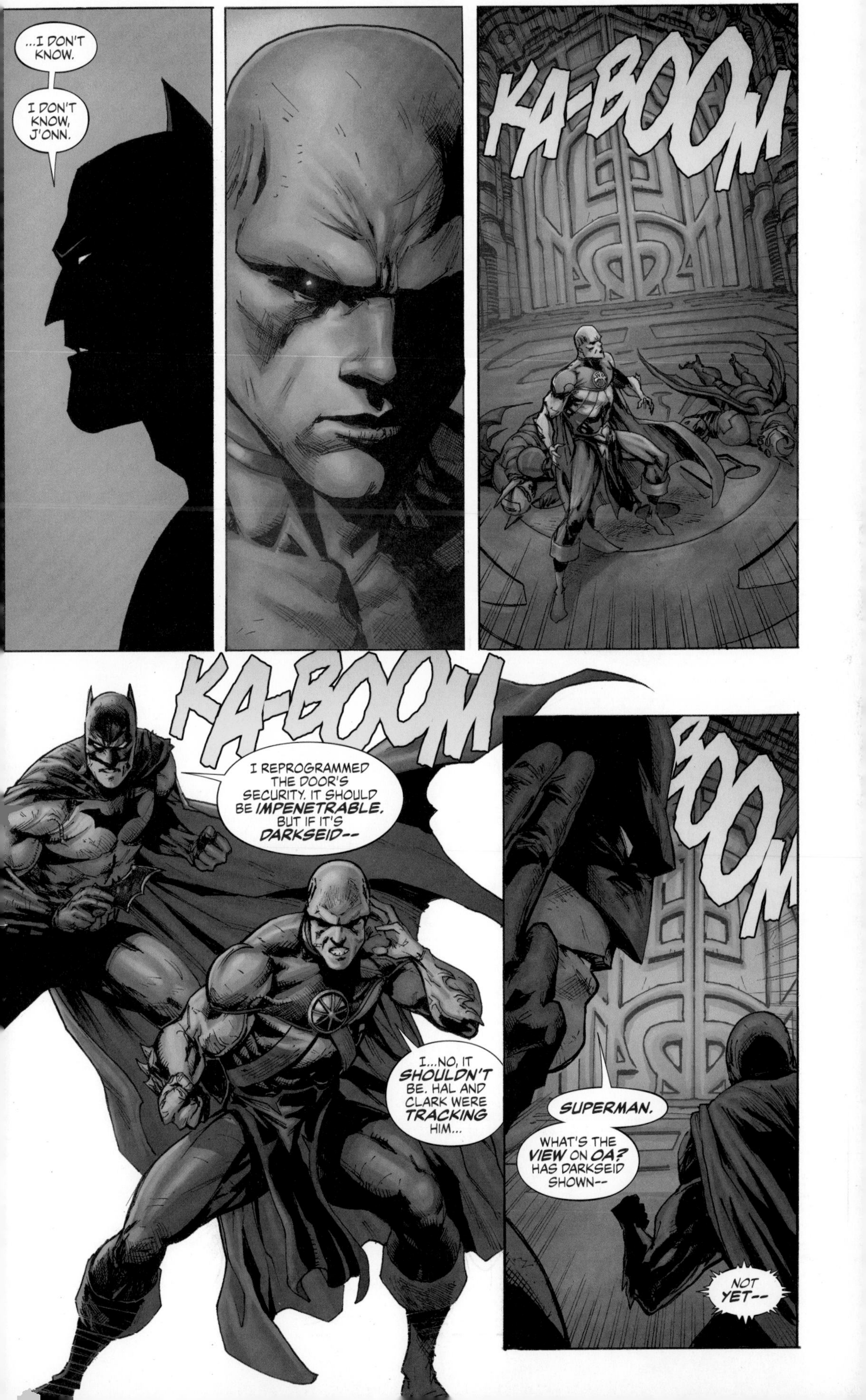
...I DON'T KNOW.
I DON'T KNOW, J'ONN.
KA-BOOM
KA-BOOM
I REPROGRAMMED THE DOOR'S SECURITY. IT SHOULD BE IMPENETRABLE. BUT IF IT'S DARKSEID--
I...NO, IT SHOULDN'T BE. HAL AND CLARK WERE TRACKING HIM...
BOOM
SUPERMAN.
WHAT'S THE VIEW ON OA? HAS DARKSEID SHOWN--
NOT YET--

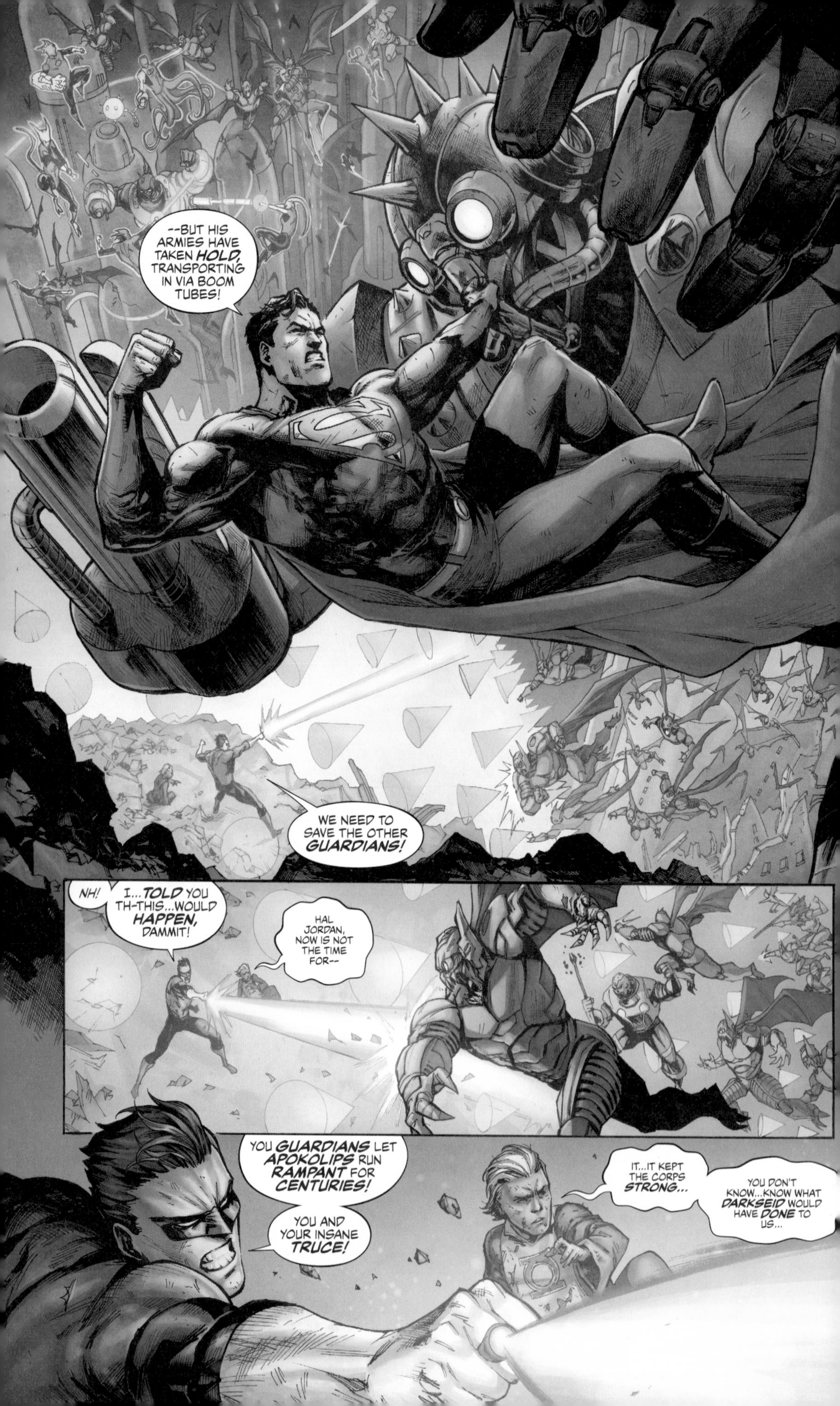
--BUT HIS ARMIES HAVE TAKEN HOLD, TRANSPORTING IN VIA BOOM TUBES!
WE NEED TO SAVE THE OTHER GUARDIANS!
NH!
I...TOLD YOU TH-THIS...WOULD HAPPEN, DAMMIT!
HAL JORDAN, NOW IS NOT THE TIME FOR--
YOU GUARDIANS LET APOKOLIPS RUN RAMPANT FOR CENTURIES!
YOU AND YOUR INSANE TRUCE!
IT...IT KEPT THE CORPS STRONG...
YOU DON'T KNOW...KNOW WHAT DARKSEID WOULD HAVE DONE TO US...

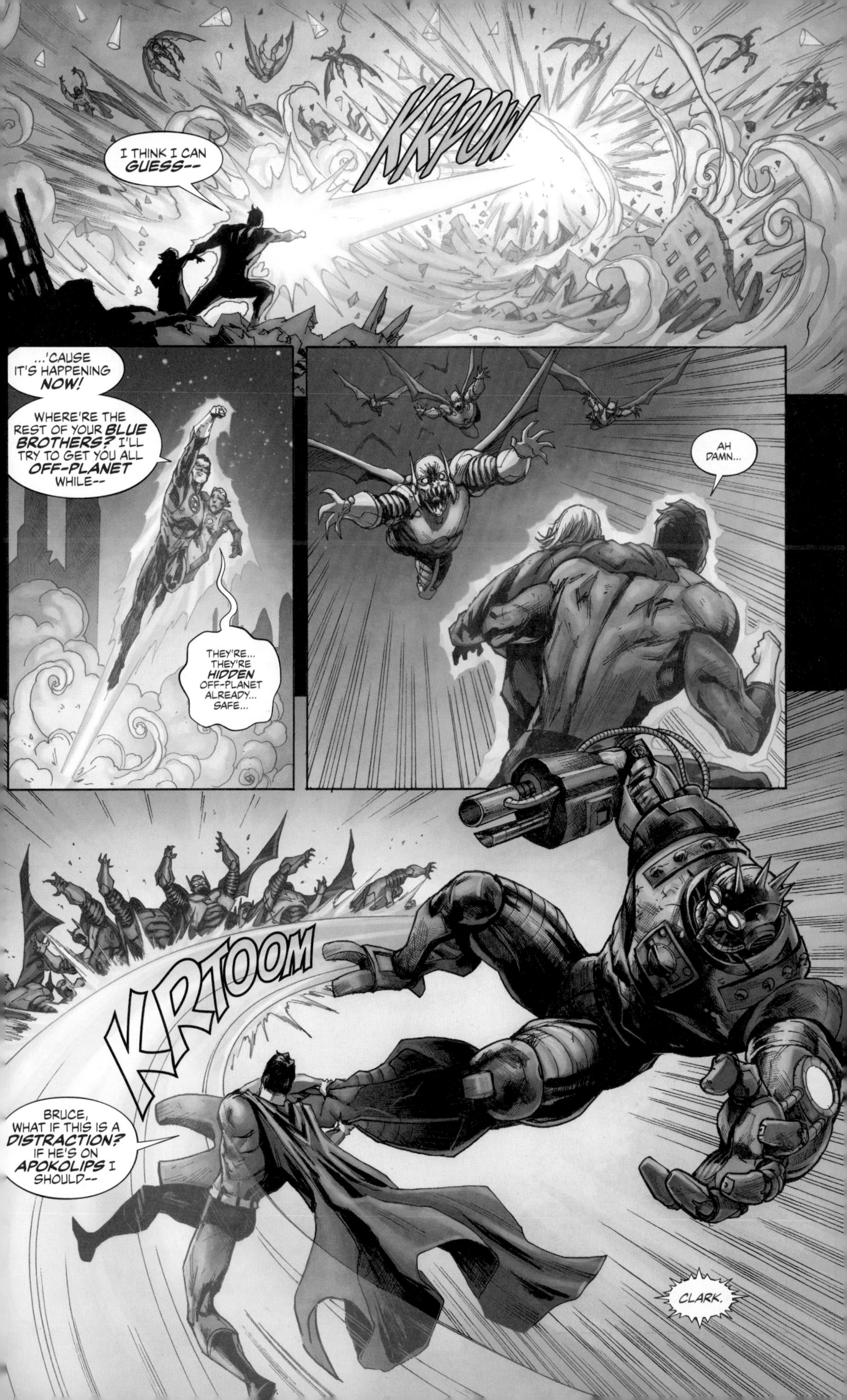
KRPOW
I THINK I CAN GUESS--
...'CAUSE IT'S HAPPENING NOW!
WHERE'RE THE REST OF YOUR BLUE BROTHERS? I'LL TRY TO GET YOU ALL OFF-PLANET WHILE--
THEY'RE... THEY'RE HIDDEN OFF-PLANET ALREADY... SAFE...
AH DAMN...
KRTOOM
BRUCE, WHAT IF THIS IS A DISTRACTION? IF HE'S ON APOKOLIPS I SHOULD--
CLARK.

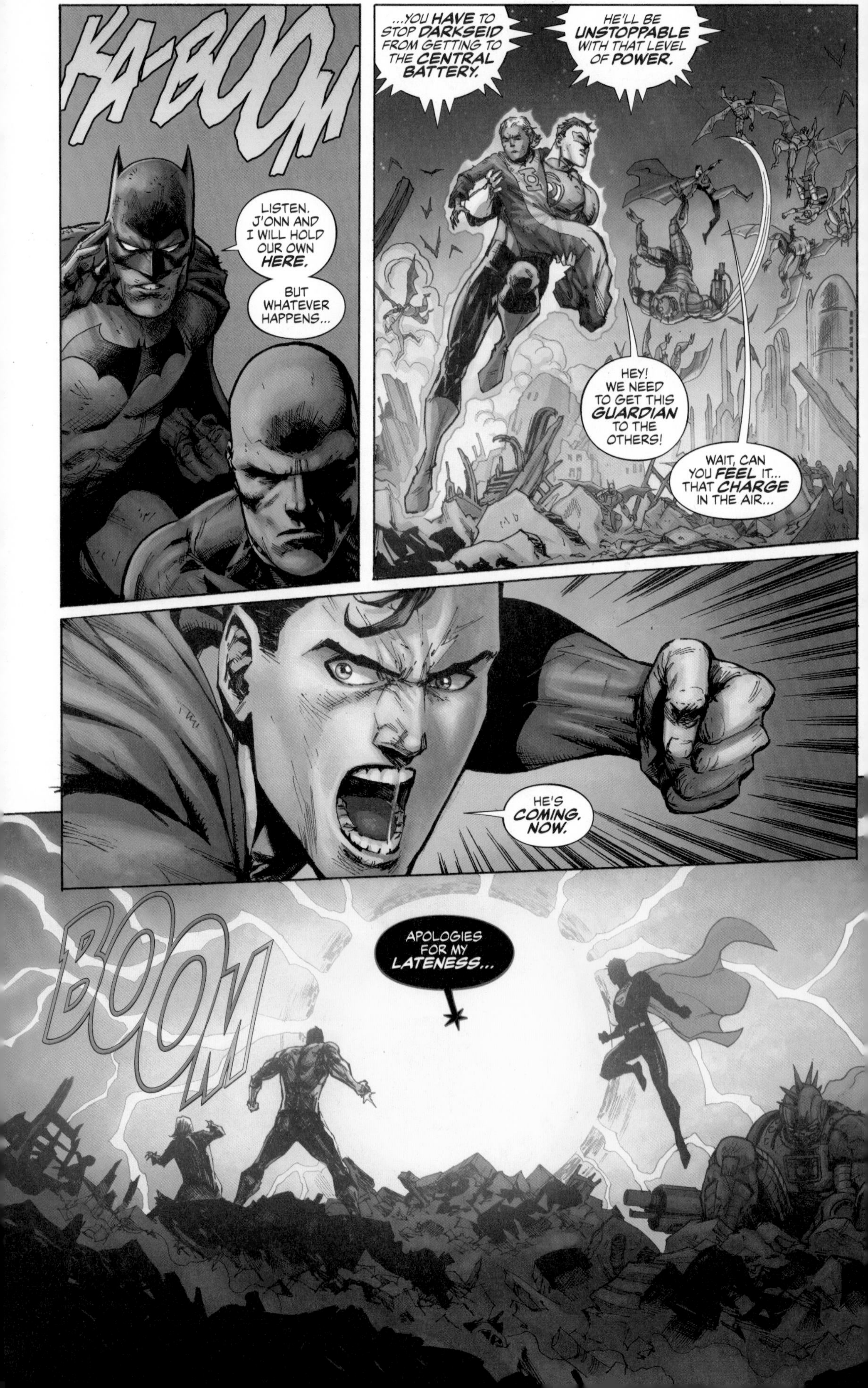
KA-BOOM
LISTEN. J'ONN AND I WILL HOLD OUR OWN HERE.
BUT WHATEVER HAPPENS...
...YOU HAVE TO STOP DARKSEID FROM GETTING TO THE CENTRAL BATTERY.
HE'LL BE UNSTOPPABLE WITH THAT LEVEL OF POWER.
HEY! WE NEED TO GET THIS GUARDIAN TO THE OTHERS!
WAIT, CAN YOU FEEL IT... THAT CHARGE IN THE AIR...
HE'S COMING. NOW.
BOOM
APOLOGIES FOR MY LATENESS...

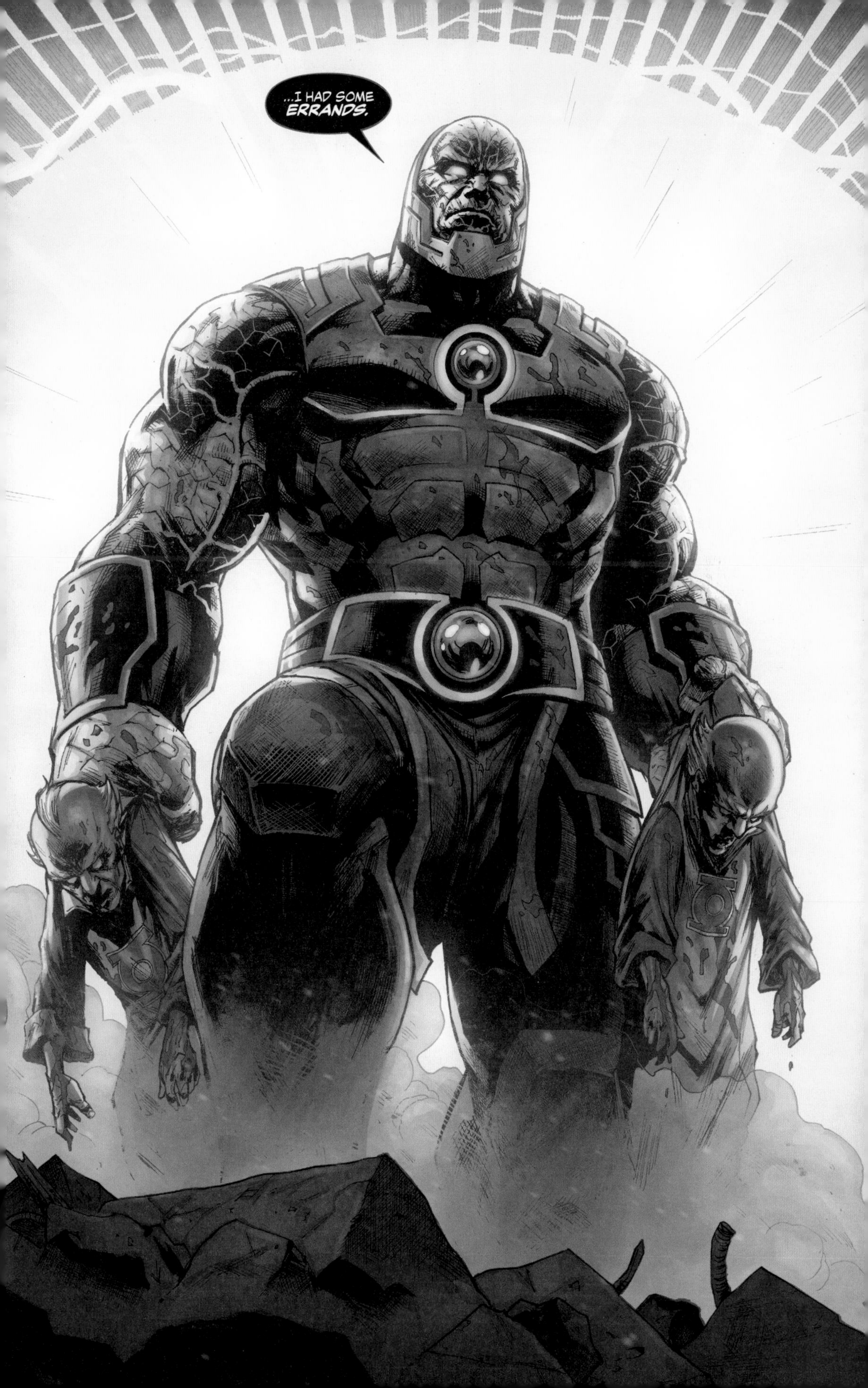
...I HAD SOME ERRANDS.

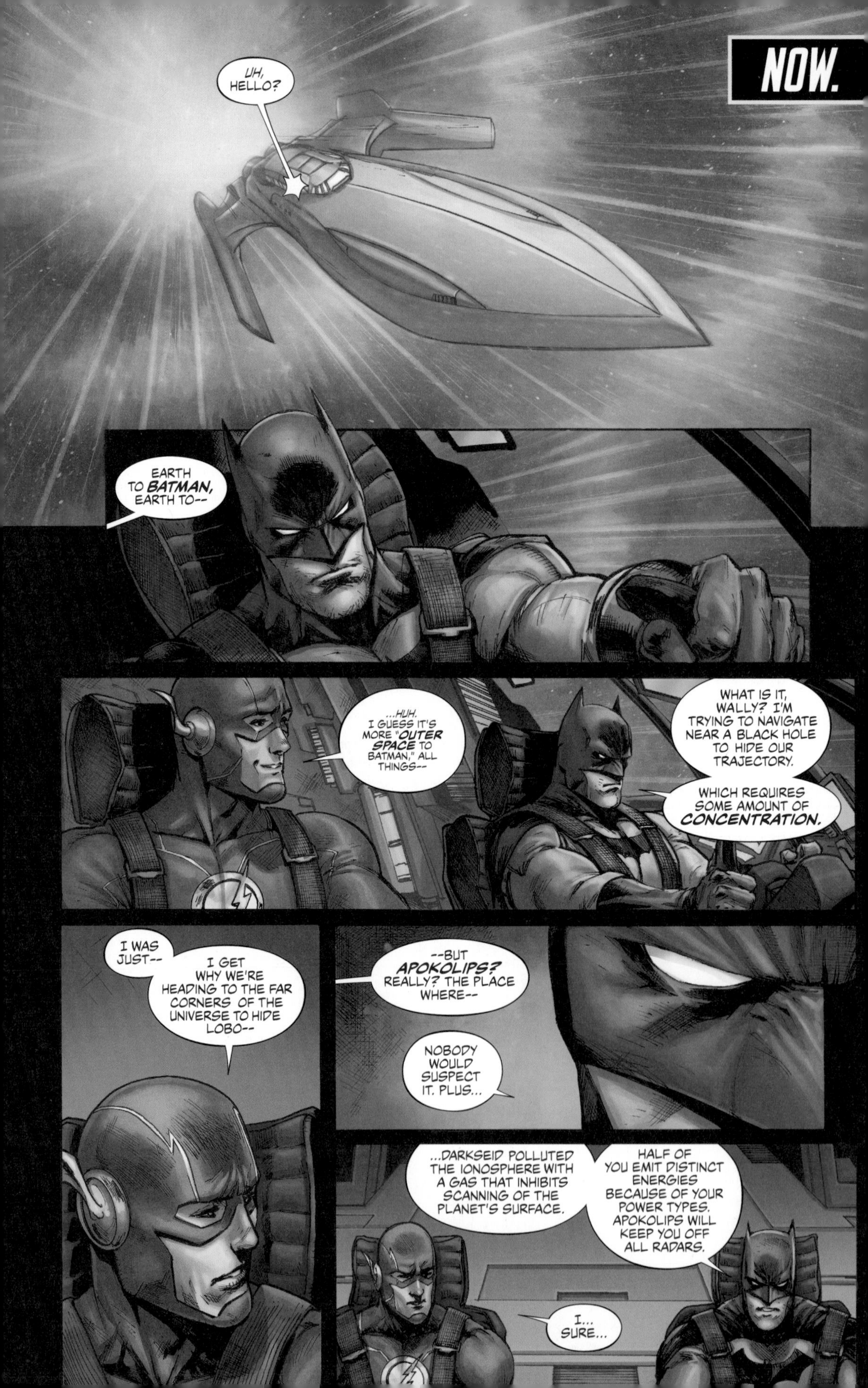
NOW.
UH, HELLO?
EARTH TO BATMAN, EARTH TO--
...HUH. I GUESS IT'S MORE "OUTER SPACE TO BATMAN," ALL THINGS--
WHAT IS IT, WALLY? I'M TRYING TO NAVIGATE NEAR A BLACK HOLE TO HIDE OUR TRAJECTORY.
WHICH REQUIRES SOME AMOUNT OF CONCENTRATION.
I WAS JUST--
I GET WHY WE'RE HEADING TO THE FAR CORNERS OF THE UNIVERSE TO HIDE LOBO--
--BUT APOKOLIPS? REALLY? THE PLACE WHERE--
NOBODY WOULD SUSPECT IT. PLUS...
...DARKSEID POLLUTED THE IONOSPHERE WITH A GAS THAT INHIBITS SCANNING OF THE PLANET'S SURFACE.
HALF OF YOU EMIT DISTINCT ENERGIES BECAUSE OF YOUR POWER TYPES. APOKOLIPS WILL KEEP YOU OFF ALL RADARS.
I... SURE...

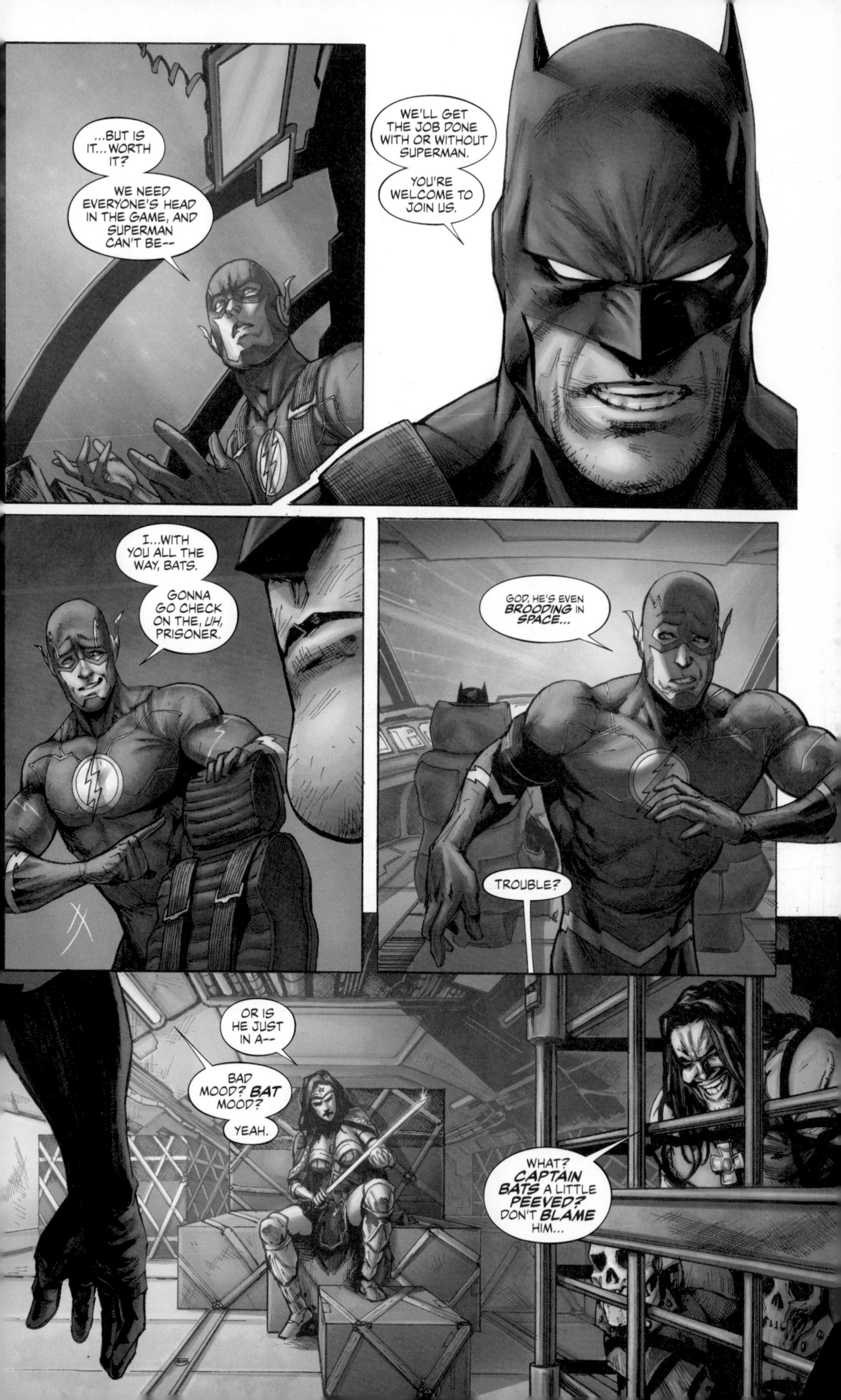
...BUT IS IT... WORTH IT?
WE NEED EVERYONE'S HEAD IN THE GAME, AND SUPERMAN CAN'T BE--
WE'LL GET THE JOB DONE WITH OR WITHOUT SUPERMAN.
YOU'RE WELCOME TO JOIN US.
I...WITH YOU ALL THE WAY, BATS.
GONNA GO CHECK ON THE, UH, PRISONER.
GOD, HE'S EVEN BROODING IN SPACE...
TROUBLE?
OR IS HE JUST IN A--
BAD MOOD? BAT MOOD?
YEAH.
WHAT? CAPTAIN BATS A LITTLE PEEVED? DON'T BLAME HIM...

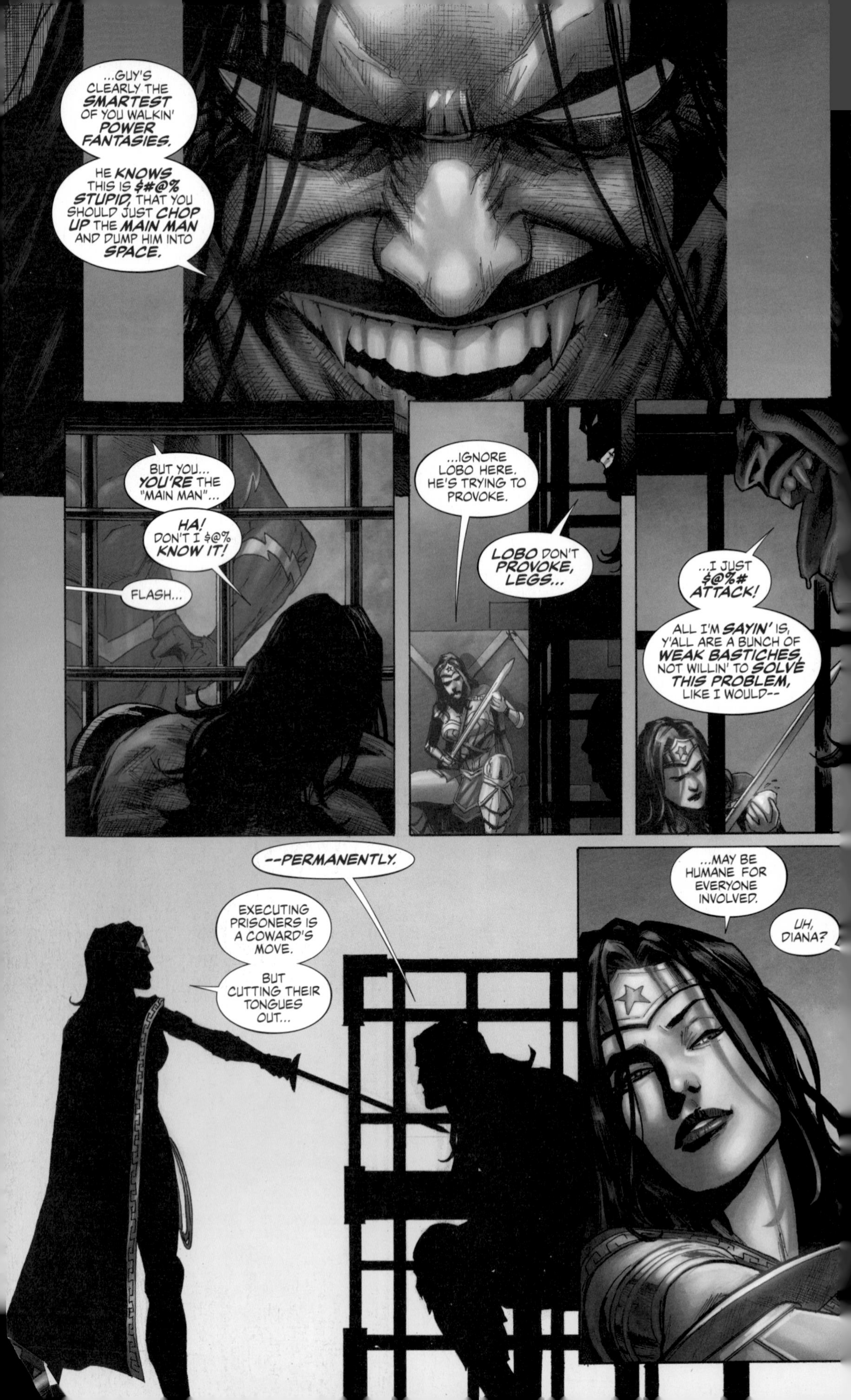
...GUY'S CLEARLY THE SMARTEST OF YOU WALKIN' POWER FANTASIES.
HE KNOWS THIS IS $#@% STUPID, THAT YOU SHOULD JUST CHOP UP THE MAIN MAN AND DUMP HIM INTO SPACE.
BUT YOU... YOU'RE THE "MAIN MAN"...
HA! DON'T I $@% KNOW IT!
FLASH...
...IGNORE LOBO HERE. HE'S TRYING TO PROVOKE.
LOBO DON'T PROVOKE, LEGS...
...I JUST $@%# ATTACK!
ALL I'M SAYIN' IS, Y'ALL ARE A BUNCH OF WEAK BASTICHES, NOT WILLIN' TO SOLVE THIS PROBLEM, LIKE I WOULD--
--PERMANENTLY.
EXECUTING PRISONERS IS A COWARD'S MOVE.
BUT CUTTING THEIR TONGUES OUT...
...MAY BE HUMANE FOR EVERYONE INVOLVED.
UH, DIANA?

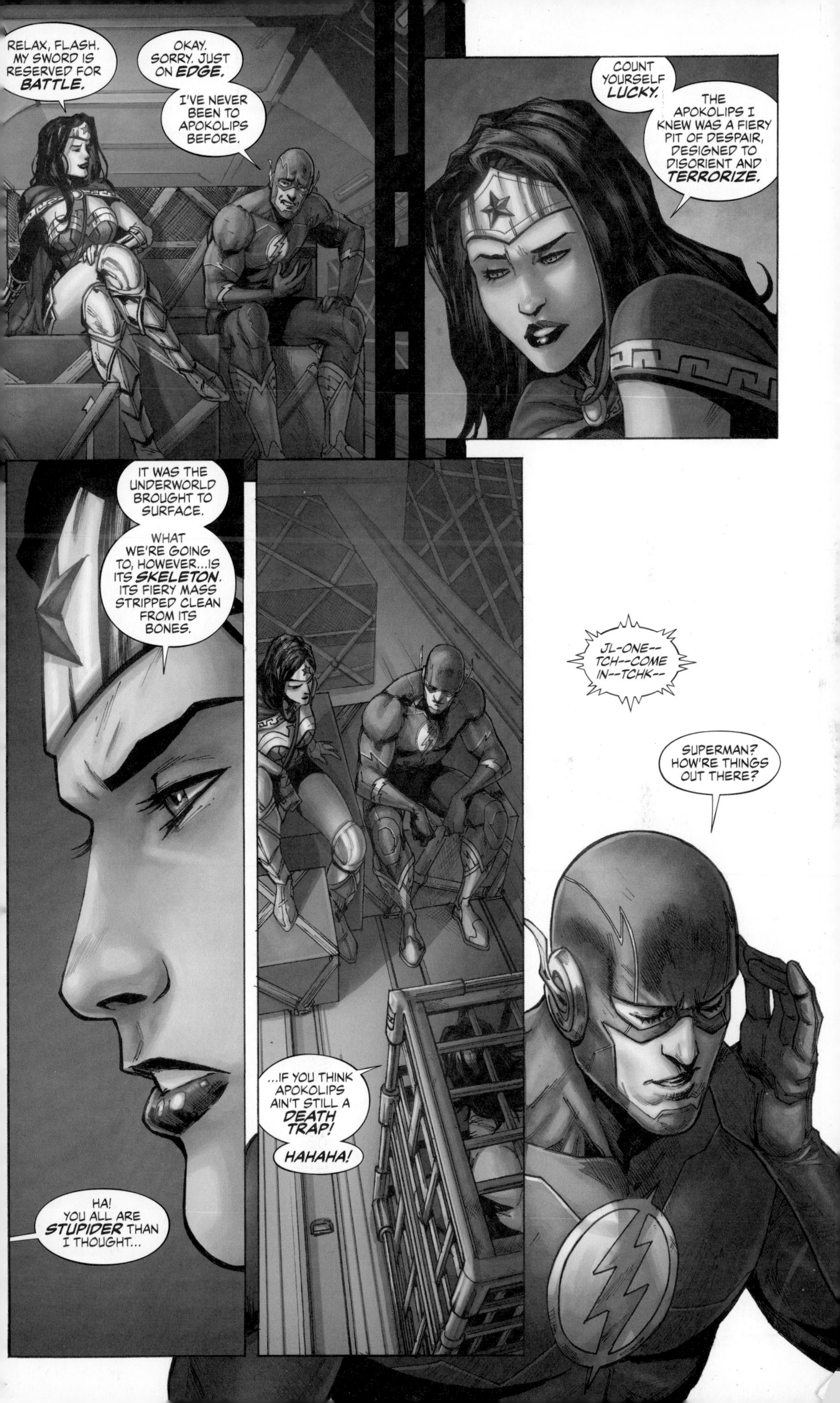
RELAX, FLASH. MY SWORD IS RESERVED FOR BATTLE.
OKAY. SORRY. JUST ON EDGE.
I'VE NEVER BEEN TO APOKOLIPS BEFORE.
COUNT YOURSELF LUCKY.
THE APOKOLIPS I KNEW WAS A FIERY PIT OF DESPAIR, DESIGNED TO DISORIENT AND TERRORIZE.
IT WAS THE UNDERWORLD BROUGHT TO SURFACE.
WHAT WE'RE GOING TO, HOWEVER...IS ITS SKELETON. ITS FIERY MASS STRIPPED CLEAN FROM ITS BONES.
HA! YOU ALL ARE STUPIDER THAN I THOUGHT...
...IF YOU THINK APOKOLIPS AIN'T STILL A DEATH TRAP!
HAHAHA!
JL-ONE--TCH--COME IN--TCHK--
SUPERMAN? HOW'RE THINGS OUT THERE?

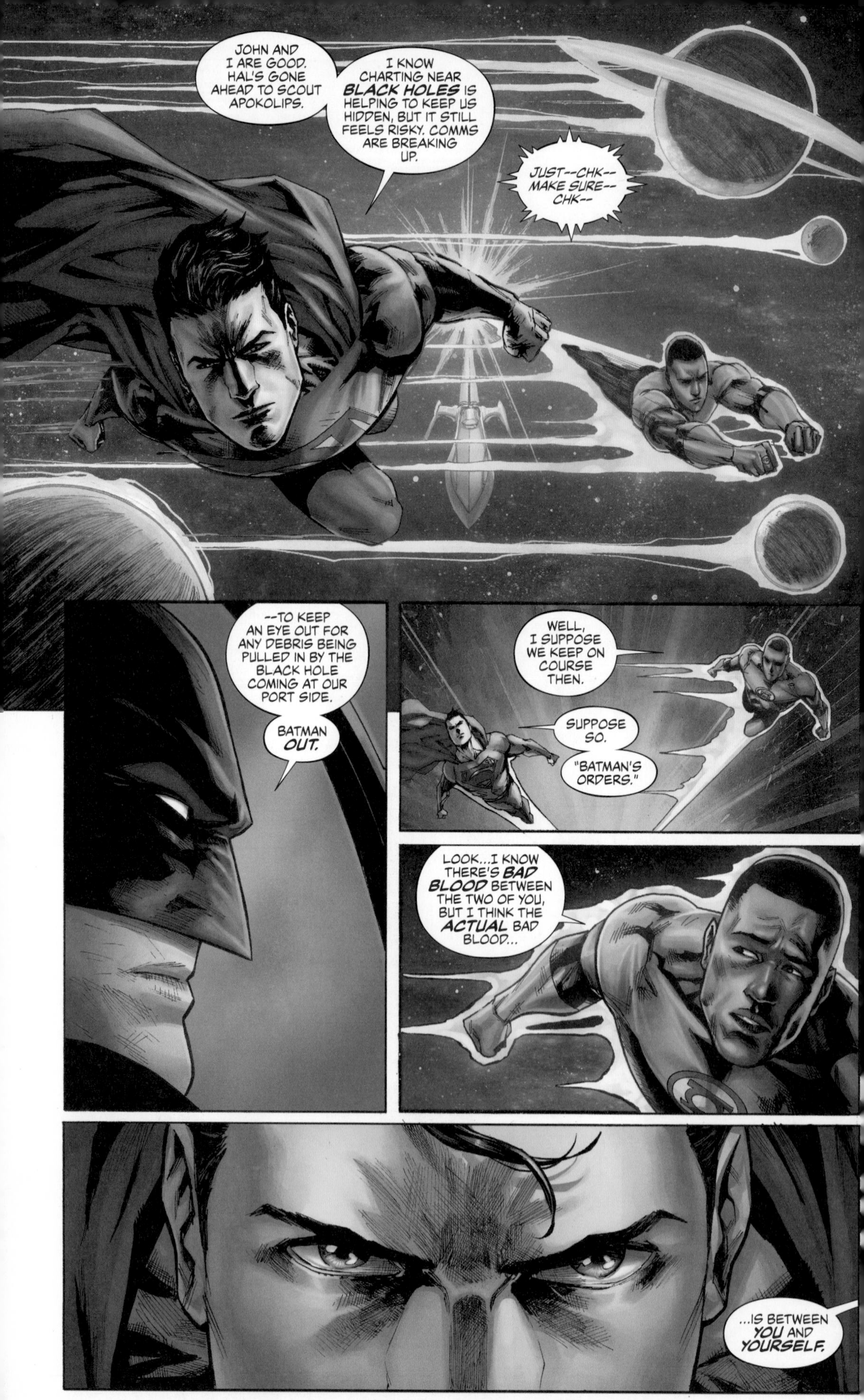

JOHN AND I ARE GOOD. HAL'S GONE AHEAD TO SCOUT APOKOLIPS.
I KNOW CHARTING NEAR BLACK HOLES IS HELPING TO KEEP US HIDDEN, BUT IT STILL FEELS RISKY. COMMS ARE BREAKING UP.
JUST--CHK--MAKE SURE--CHK--
--TO KEEP AN EYE OUT FOR ANY DEBRIS BEING PULLED IN BY THE BLACK HOLE COMING AT OUR PORT SIDE.
BATMAN OUT.
WELL, I SUPPOSE WE KEEP ON COURSE THEN.
SUPPOSE SO.
"BATMAN'S ORDERS."
LOOK...I KNOW THERE'S BAD BLOOD BETWEEN THE TWO OF YOU, BUT I THINK THE ACTUAL BAD BLOOD...
...IS BETWEEN YOU AND YOURSELF.

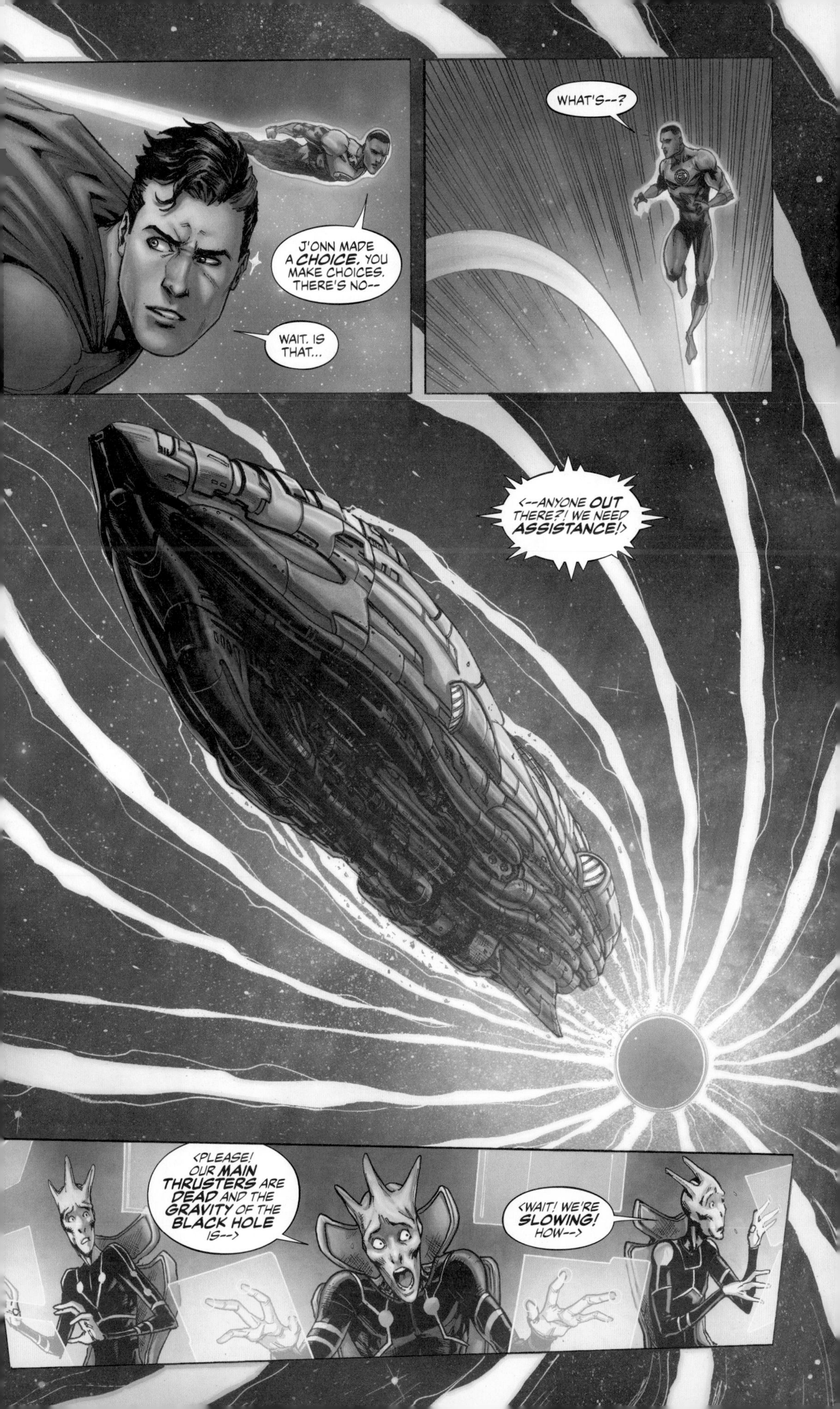
J'ONN MADE A CHOICE. YOU MAKE CHOICES. THERE'S NO--
WAIT. IS THAT...
WHAT'S--?
<--ANYONE OUT THERE?! WE NEED ASSISTANCE!>
<PLEASE! OUR MAIN THRUSTERS ARE DEAD AND THE GRAVITY OF THE BLACK HOLE IS-->
<WAIT! WE'RE SLOWING! HOW-->

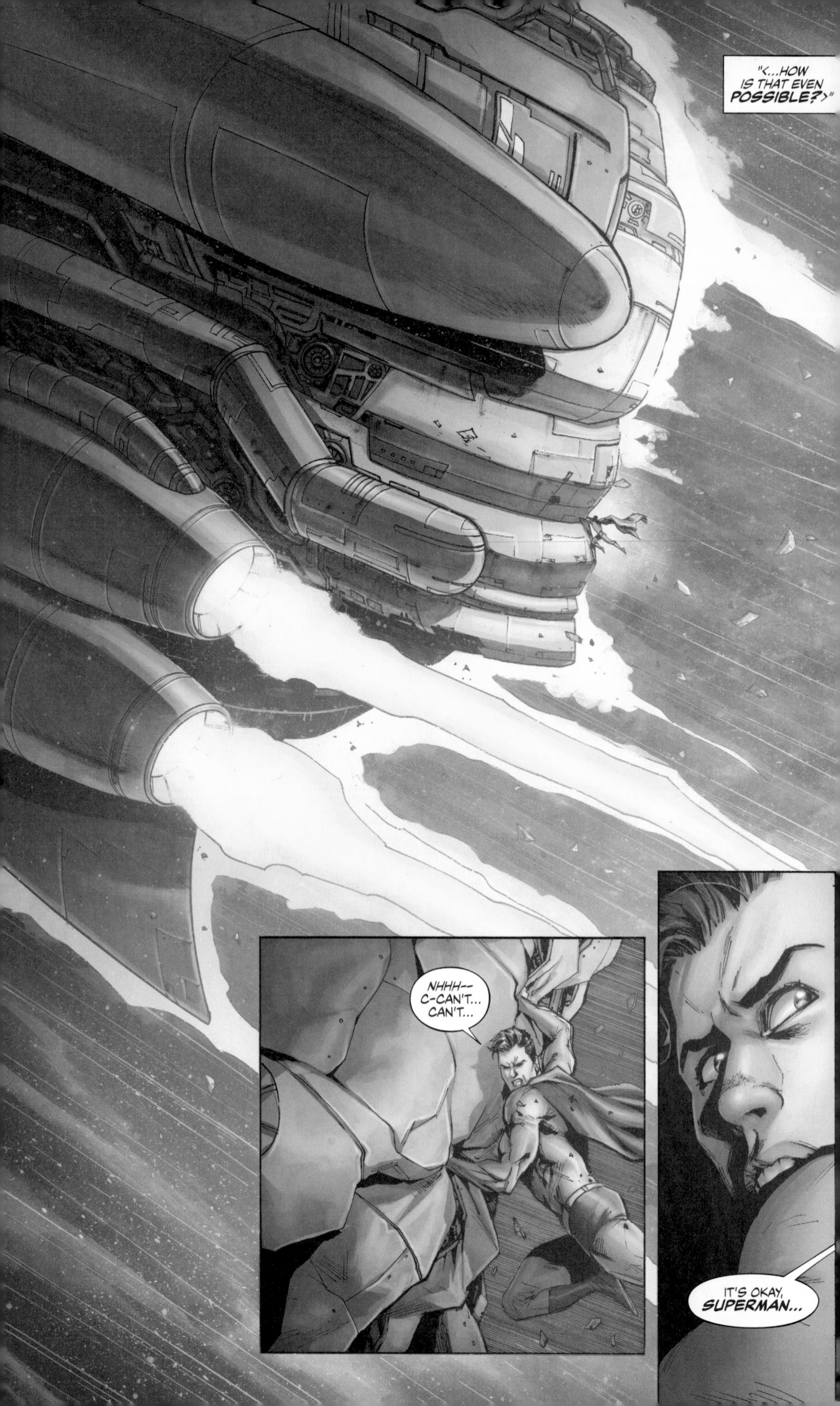
"<...HOW IS THAT EVEN POSSIBLE?>"
NHHH-- C-CAN'T... CAN'T...
IT'S OKAY, SUPERMAN...

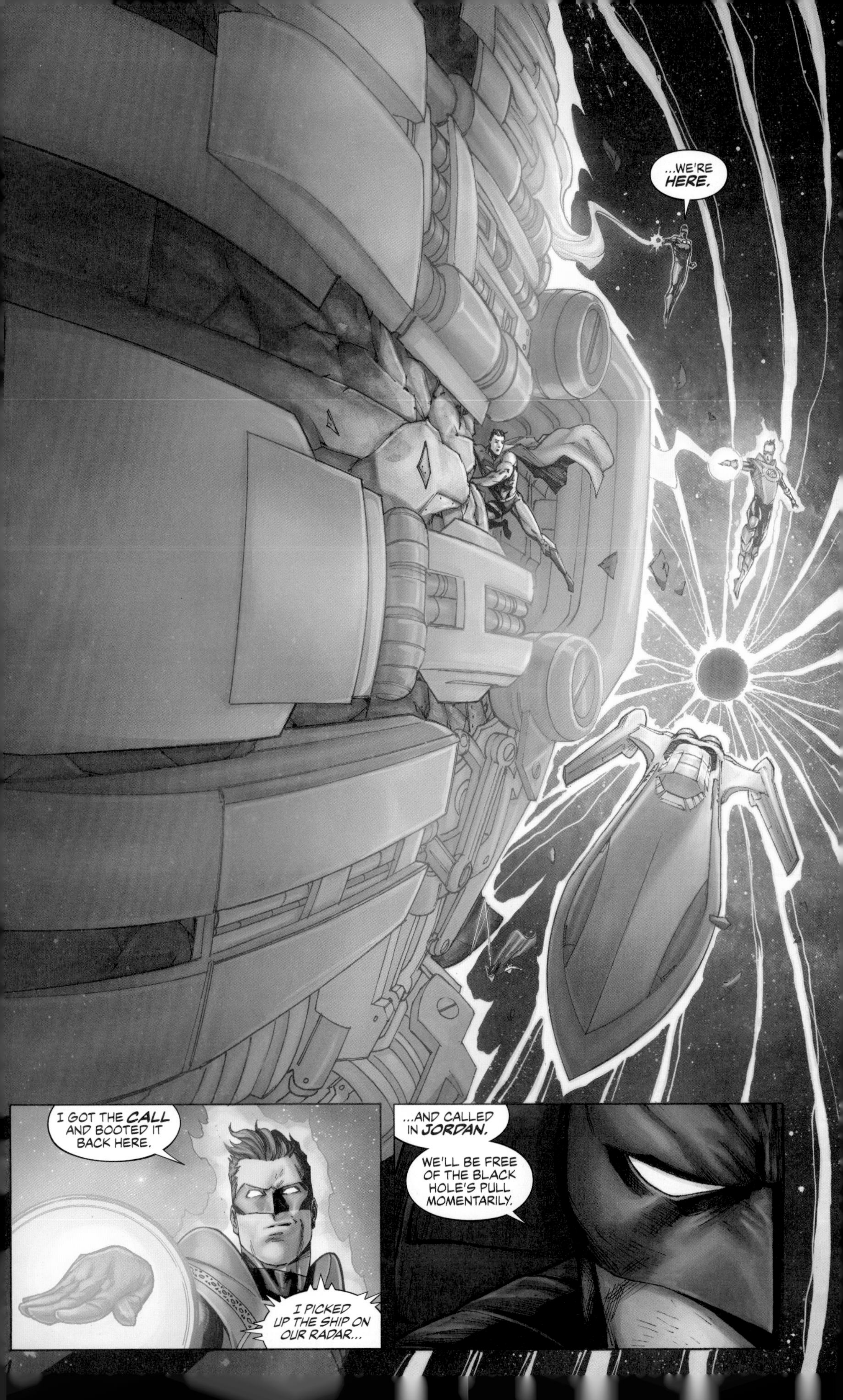
...WE'RE HERE.
I GOT THE CALL AND BOOTED IT BACK HERE.
I PICKED UP THE SHIP ON OUR RADAR...
...AND CALLED IN JORDAN.
WE'LL BE FREE OF THE BLACK HOLE'S PULL MOMENTARILY.

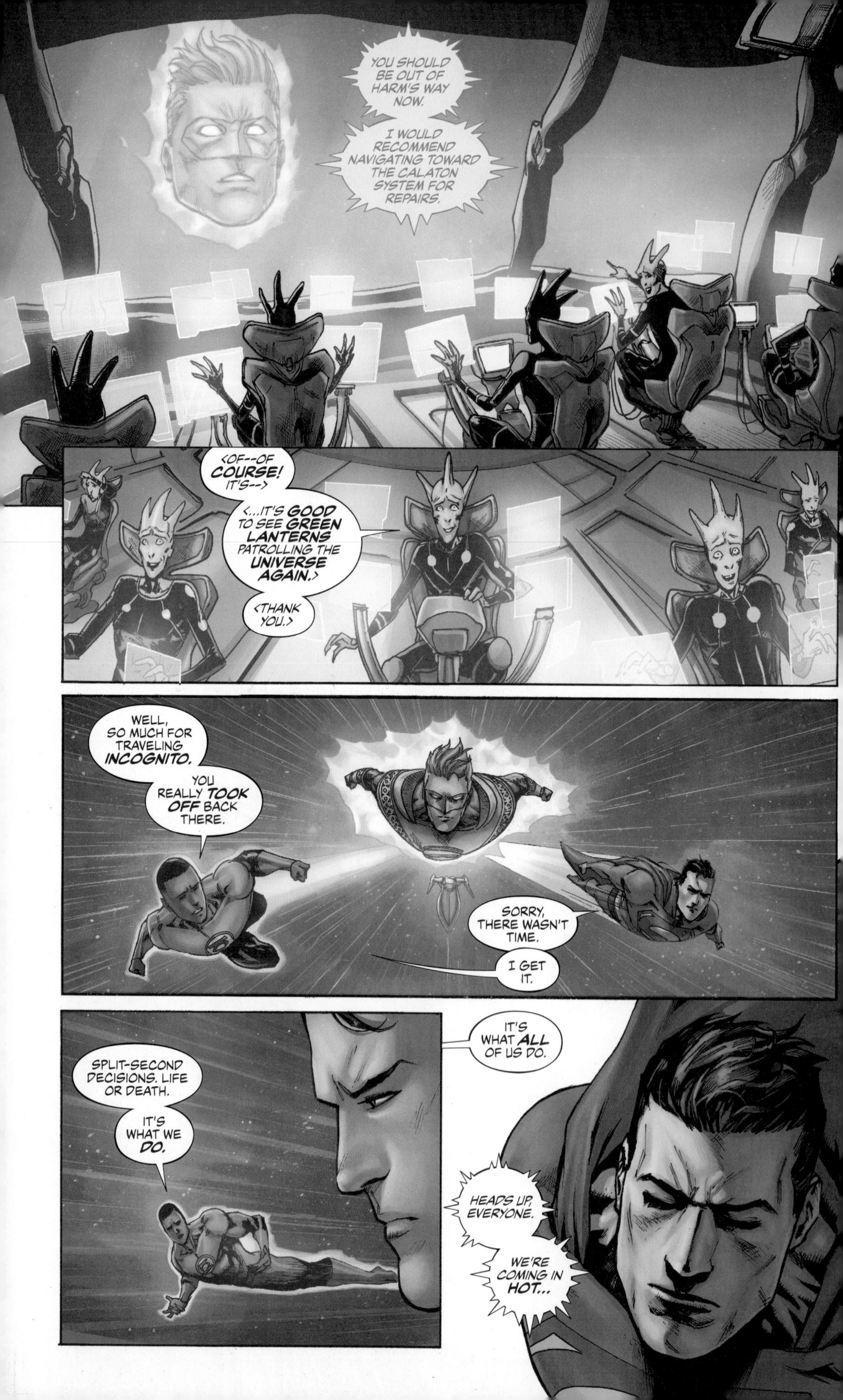
YOU SHOULD BE OUT OF HARM'S WAY NOW.
I WOULD RECOMMEND NAVIGATING TOWARD THE CALATON SYSTEM FOR REPAIRS.
<OF--OF COURSE! IT'S-->
<...IT'S GOOD TO SEE GREEN LANTERNS PATROLLING THE UNIVERSE AGAIN.>
<THANK YOU.>
WELL, SO MUCH FOR TRAVELING INCOGNITO.
YOU REALLY TOOK OFF BACK THERE.
SORRY, THERE WASN'T TIME.
I GET IT.
SPLIT-SECOND DECISIONS. LIFE OR DEATH.
IT'S WHAT WE DO.
IT'S WHAT ALL OF US DO.
HEADS UP, EVERYONE.
WE'RE COMING IN HOT...

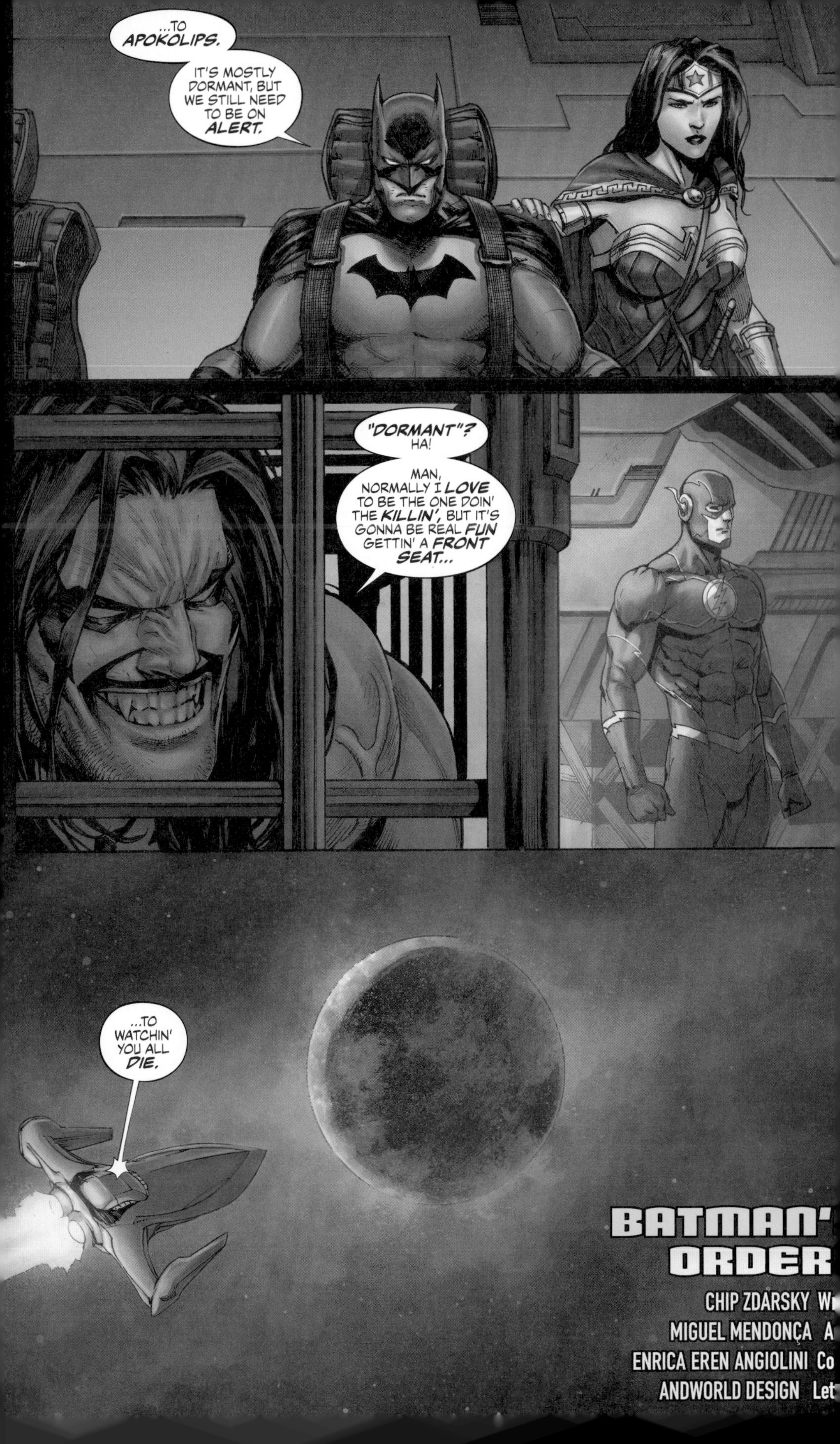
...TO APOKOLIPS.
IT'S MOSTLY DORMANT, BUT WE STILL NEED TO BE ON ALERT.
"DORMANT"? HA!
MAN, NORMALLY I LOVE TO BE THE ONE DOIN' THE KILLIN', BUT IT'S GONNA BE REAL FUN GETTIN' A FRONT SEAT...
...TO WATCHIN' YOU ALL DIE.
BATMAN'
ORDER
CHIP ZDARSKY
MIGUEL MENDONÇA
ENRICA EREN ANGIOLINI
ANDWORLD DESIGN

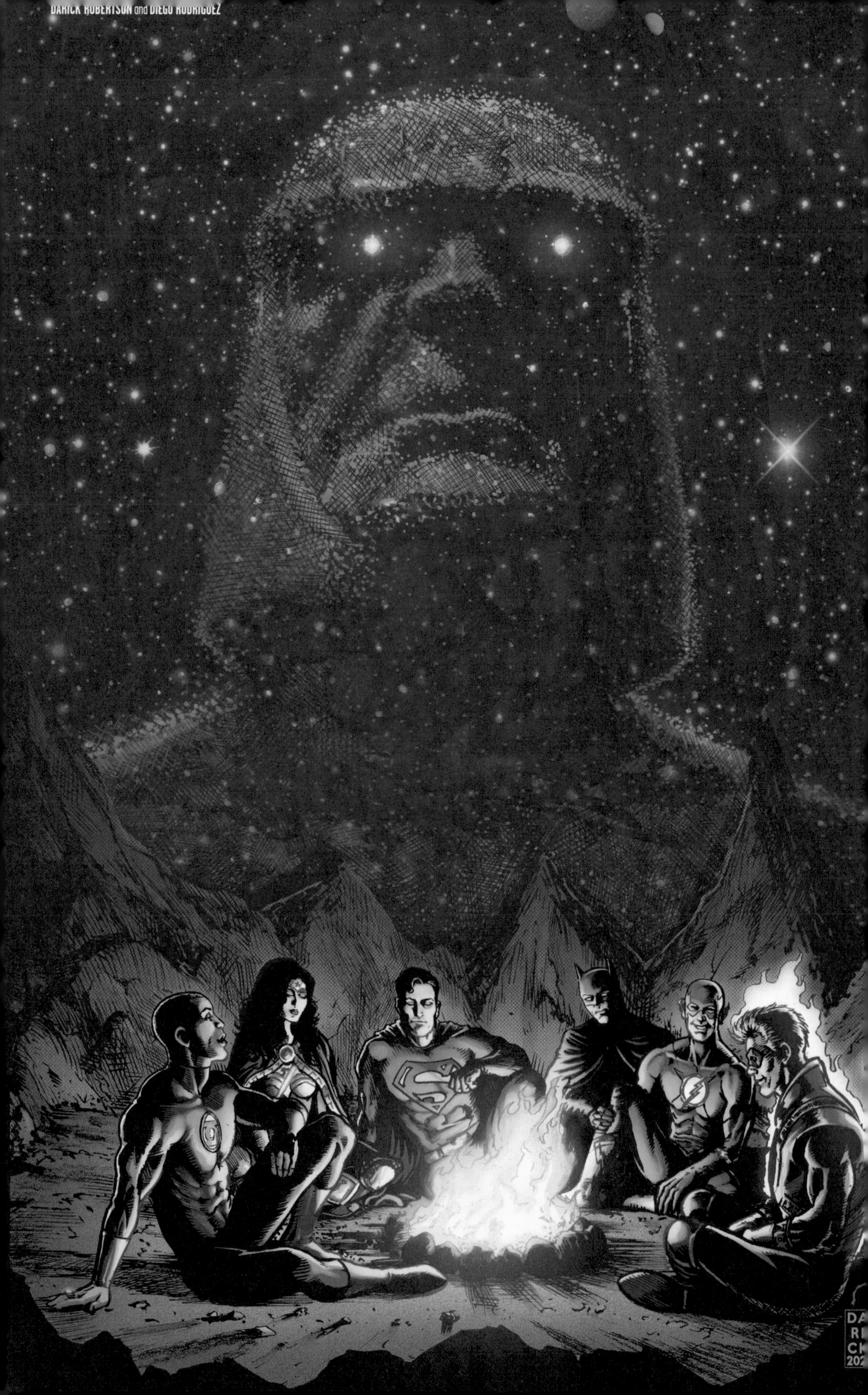
DARICK ROBERTSON and DIEGO RODRIGUEZ

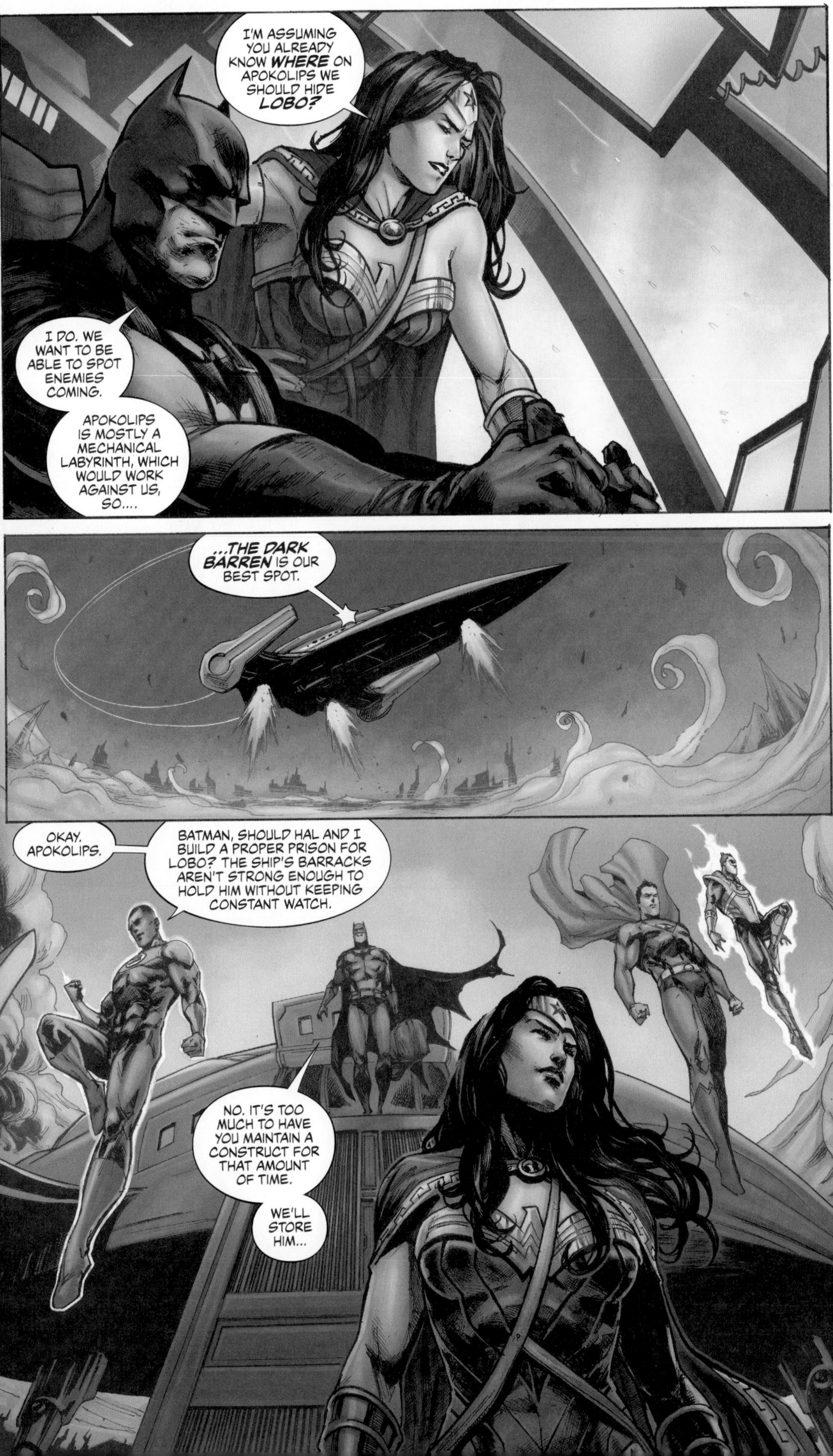
I'M ASSUMING YOU ALREADY KNOW WHERE ON APOKOLIPS WE SHOULD HIDE LOBO?
I DO. WE WANT TO BE ABLE TO SPOT ENEMIES COMING.
APOKOLIPS IS MOSTLY A MECHANICAL LABYRINTH, WHICH WOULD WORK AGAINST US, SO....
...THE DARK BARREN IS OUR BEST SPOT.
OKAY. APOKOLIPS.
BATMAN, SHOULD HAL AND I BUILD A PROPER PRISON FOR LOBO? THE SHIP'S BARRACKS AREN'T STRONG ENOUGH TO HOLD HIM WITHOUT KEEPING CONSTANT WATCH.
NO. IT'S TOO MUCH TO HAVE YOU MAINTAIN A CONSTRUCT FOR THAT AMOUNT OF TIME.
WE'LL STORE HIM...

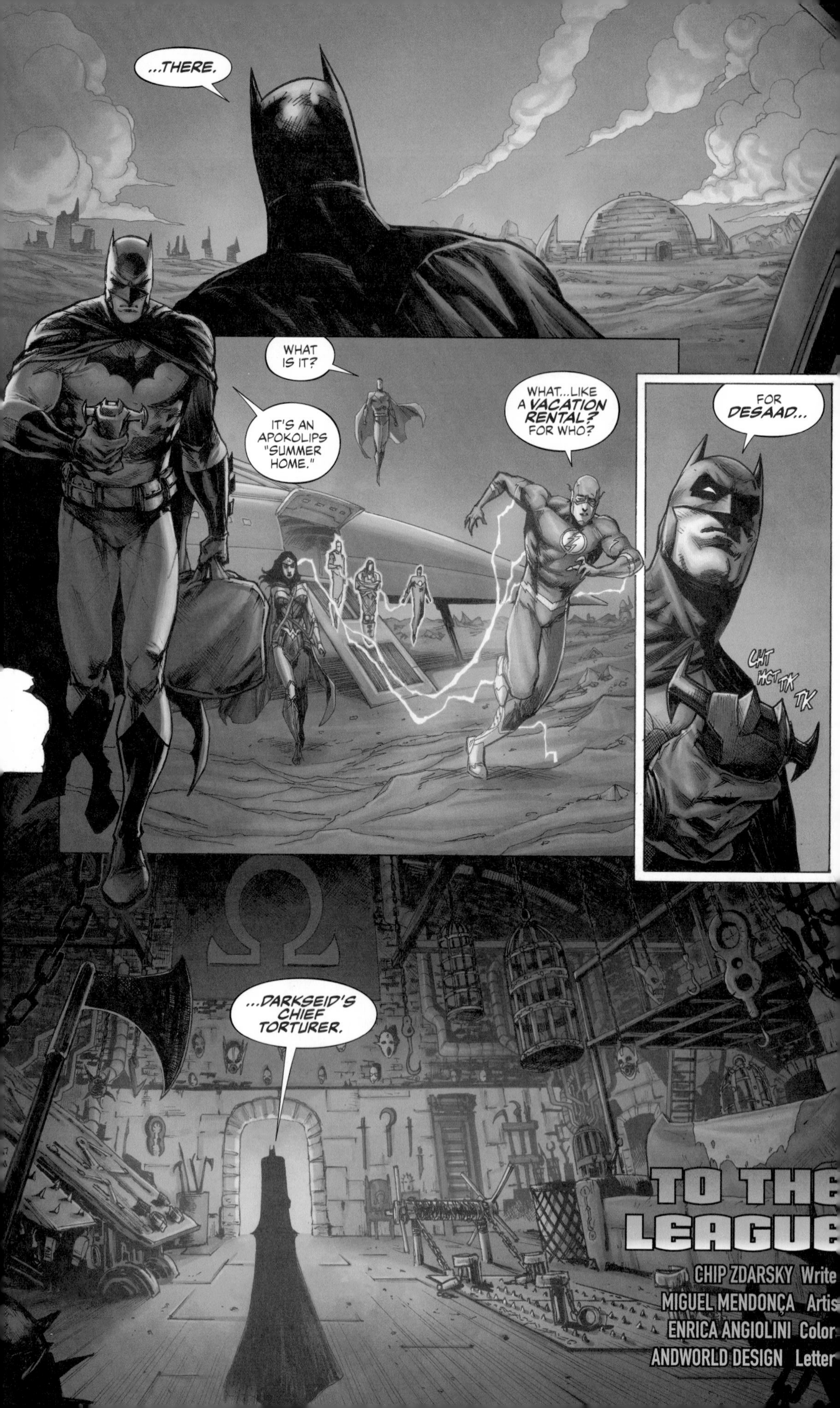
...THERE.
WHAT IS IT?
IT'S AN APOKOLIPS "SUMMER HOME."
WHAT...LIKE A VACATION RENTAL? FOR WHO?
FOR DESAAD...
CHT HCT TK TK
...DARKSEID'S CHIEF TORTURER.
TO THE LEAGUE
CHIP ZDARSKY Write
MIGUEL MENDONÇA Artis
ENRICA ANGIOLINI Color
ANDWORLD DESIGN Letter

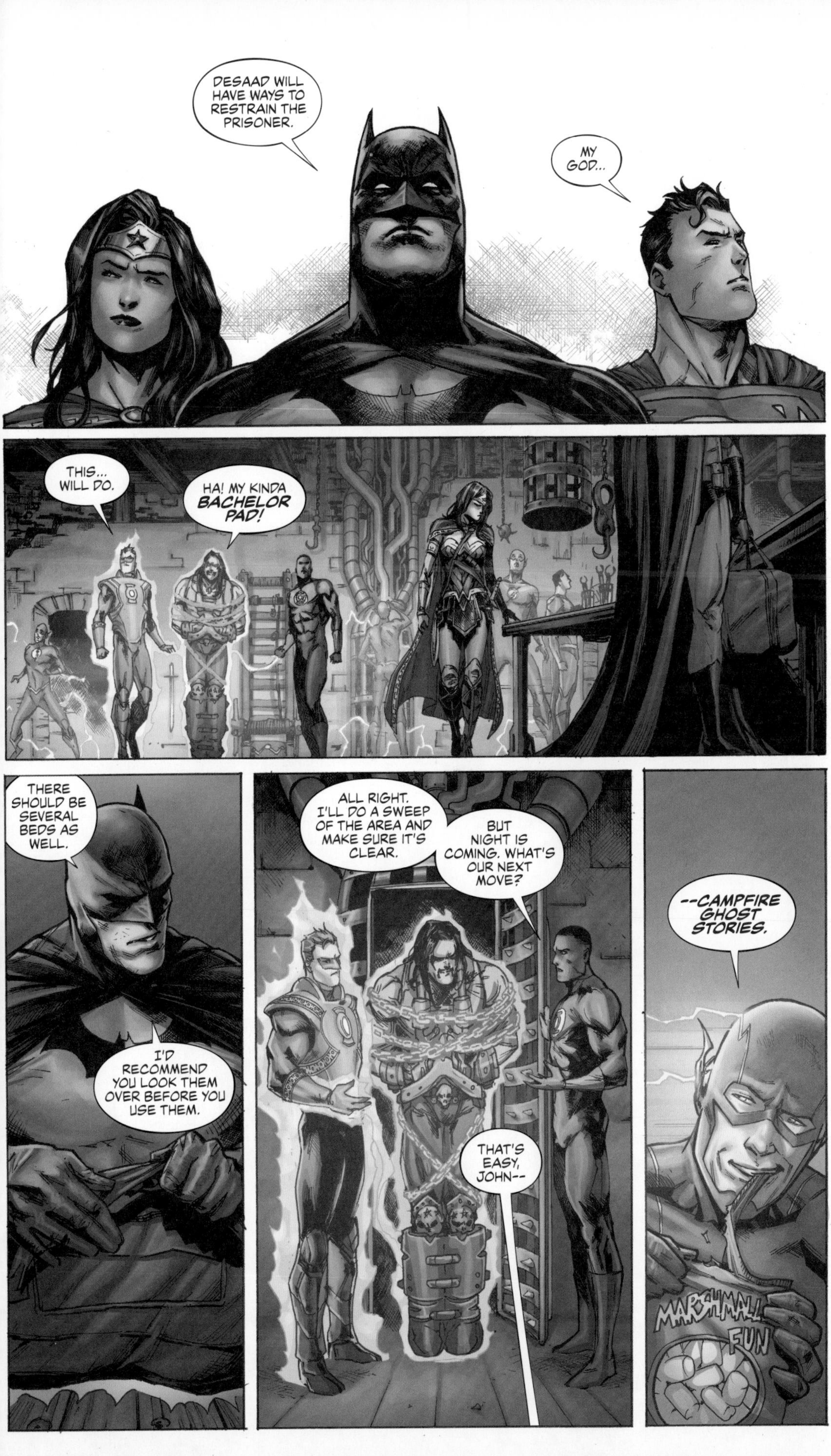
DESAAD WILL HAVE WAYS TO RESTRAIN THE PRISONER.
MY GOD...
THIS... WILL DO.
HA! MY KINDA BACHELOR PAD!
THERE SHOULD BE SEVERAL BEDS AS WELL.
I'D RECOMMEND YOU LOOK THEM OVER BEFORE YOU USE THEM.
ALL RIGHT. I'LL DO A SWEEP OF THE AREA AND MAKE SURE IT'S CLEAR.
BUT NIGHT IS COMING. WHAT'S OUR NEXT MOVE?
THAT'S EASY, JOHN--
--CAMPFIRE GHOST STORIES.
MARSHMALL FUN

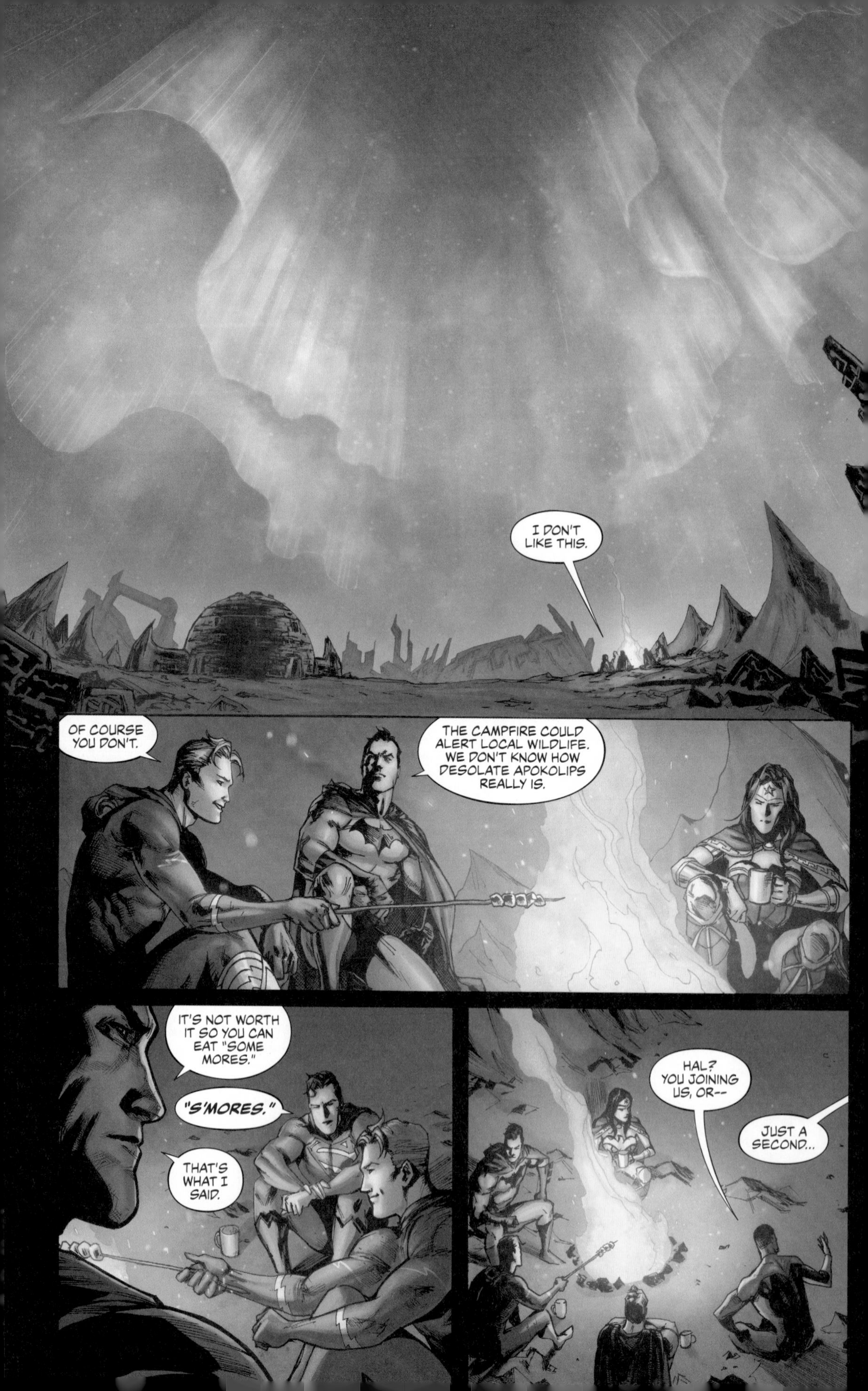
I DON'T LIKE THIS.
OF COURSE YOU DON'T.
THE CAMPFIRE COULD ALERT LOCAL WILDLIFE. WE DON'T KNOW HOW DESOLATE APOKOLIPS REALLY IS.
IT'S NOT WORTH IT SO YOU CAN EAT "SOME MORES."
"S'MORES."
THAT'S WHAT I SAID.
HAL? YOU JOINING US, OR--
JUST A SECOND...

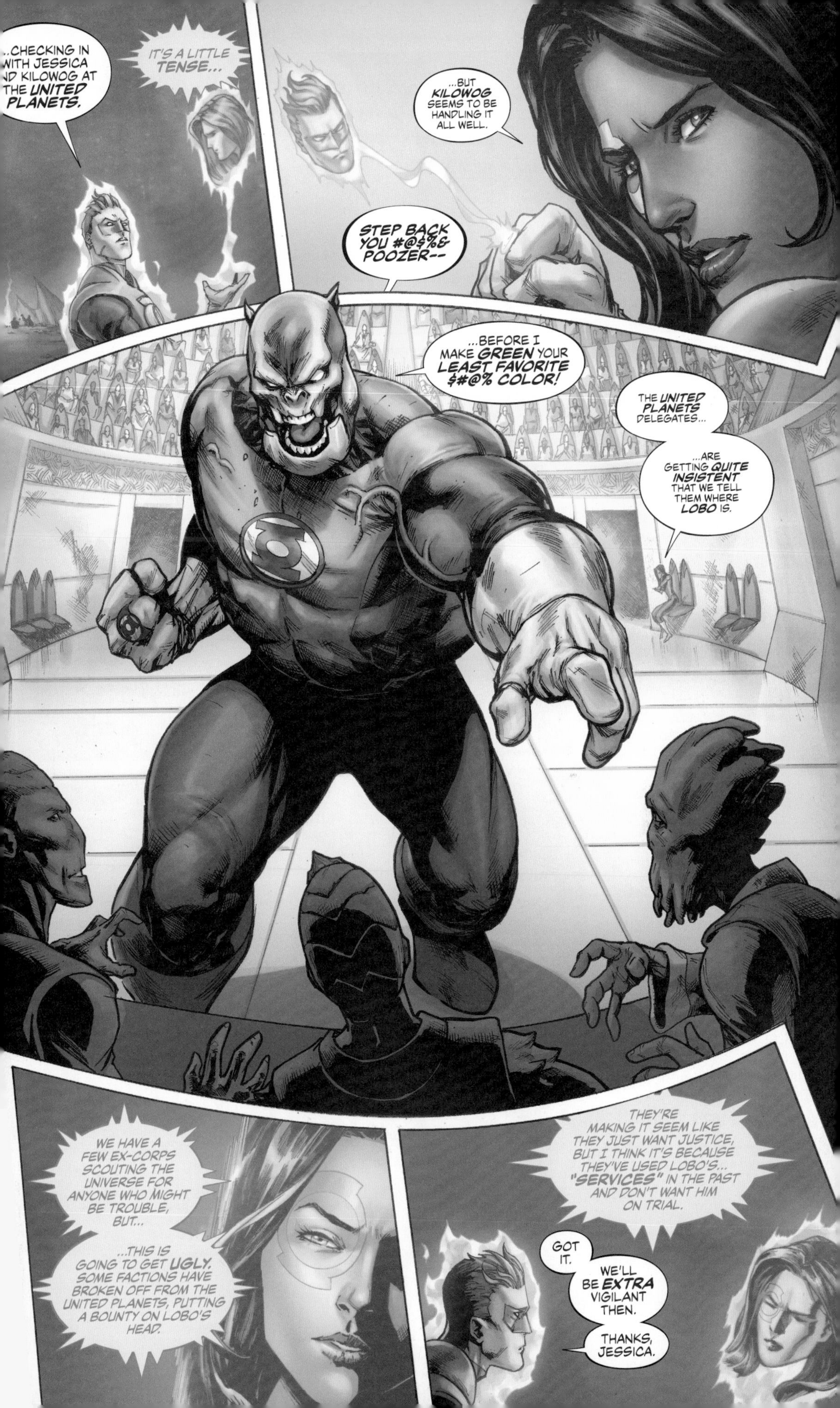
...CHECKING IN WITH JESSICA ND KILOWOG AT THE UNITED PLANETS.
IT'S A LITTLE TENSE...
...BUT KILOWOG SEEMS TO BE HANDLING IT ALL WELL.
STEP BACK YOU #@$%& POOZER--
...BEFORE I MAKE GREEN YOUR LEAST FAVORITE $#@% COLOR!
THE UNITED PLANETS DELEGATES...
...ARE GETTING QUITE INSISTENT THAT WE TELL THEM WHERE LOBO IS.
WE HAVE A FEW EX-CORPS SCOUTING THE UNIVERSE FOR ANYONE WHO MIGHT BE TROUBLE, BUT...
...THIS IS GOING TO GET UGLY. SOME FACTIONS HAVE BROKEN OFF FROM THE UNITED PLANETS, PUTTING A BOUNTY ON LOBO'S HEAD.
THEY'RE MAKING IT SEEM LIKE THEY JUST WANT JUSTICE, BUT I THINK IT'S BECAUSE THEY'VE USED LOBO'S... "SERVICES" IN THE PAST AND DON'T WANT HIM ON TRIAL.
GOT IT.
WE'LL BE EXTRA VIGILANT THEN.
THANKS, JESSICA.

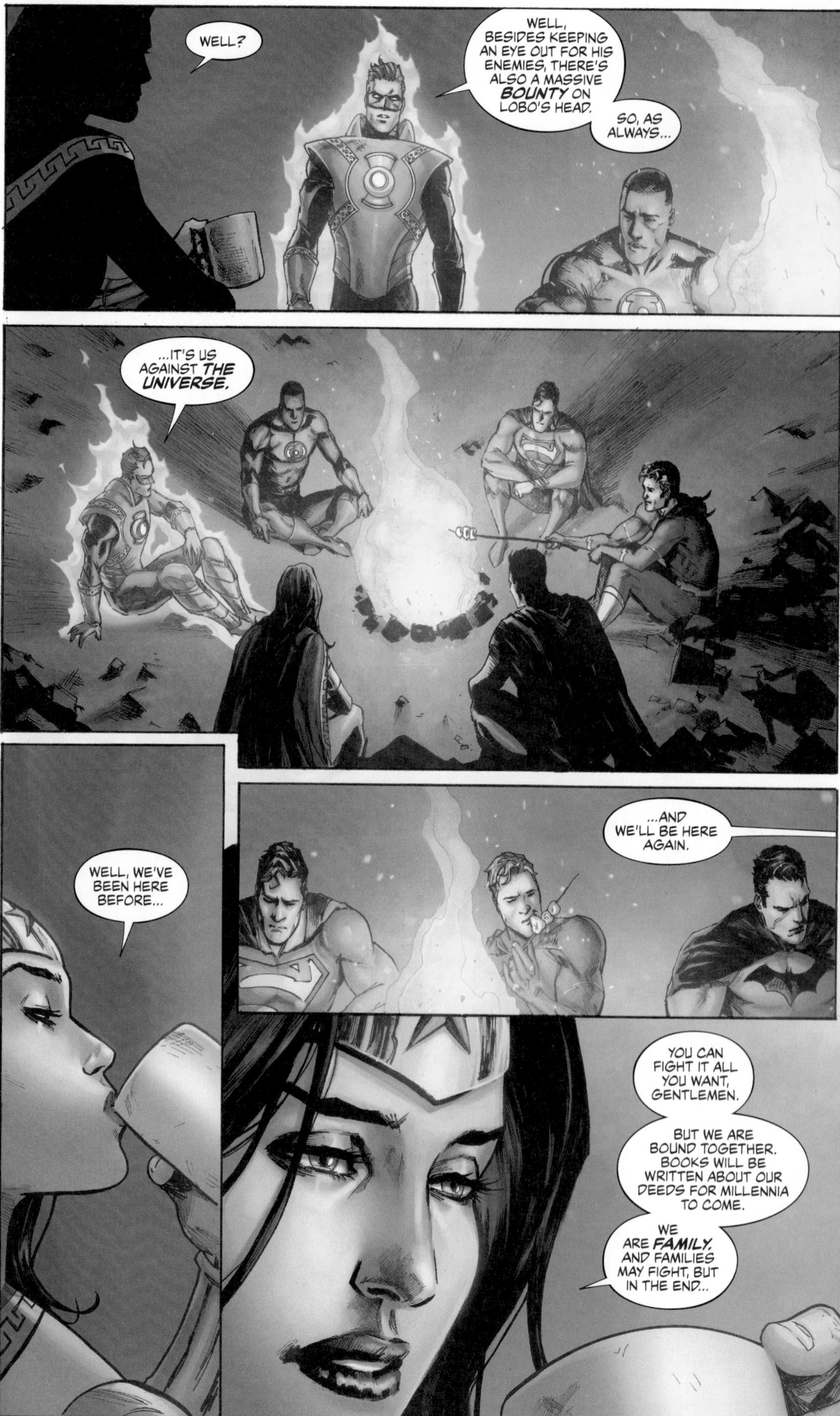
WELL?
WELL, BESIDES KEEPING AN EYE OUT FOR HIS ENEMIES, THERE'S ALSO A MASSIVE BOUNTY ON LOBO'S HEAD.
SO, AS ALWAYS...
...IT'S US AGAINST THE UNIVERSE.
WELL, WE'VE BEEN HERE BEFORE...
...AND WE'LL BE HERE AGAIN.
YOU CAN FIGHT IT ALL YOU WANT, GENTLEMEN.
BUT WE ARE BOUND TOGETHER. BOOKS WILL BE WRITTEN ABOUT OUR DEEDS FOR MILLENNIA TO COME.
WE ARE FAMILY. AND FAMILIES MAY FIGHT, BUT IN THE END...

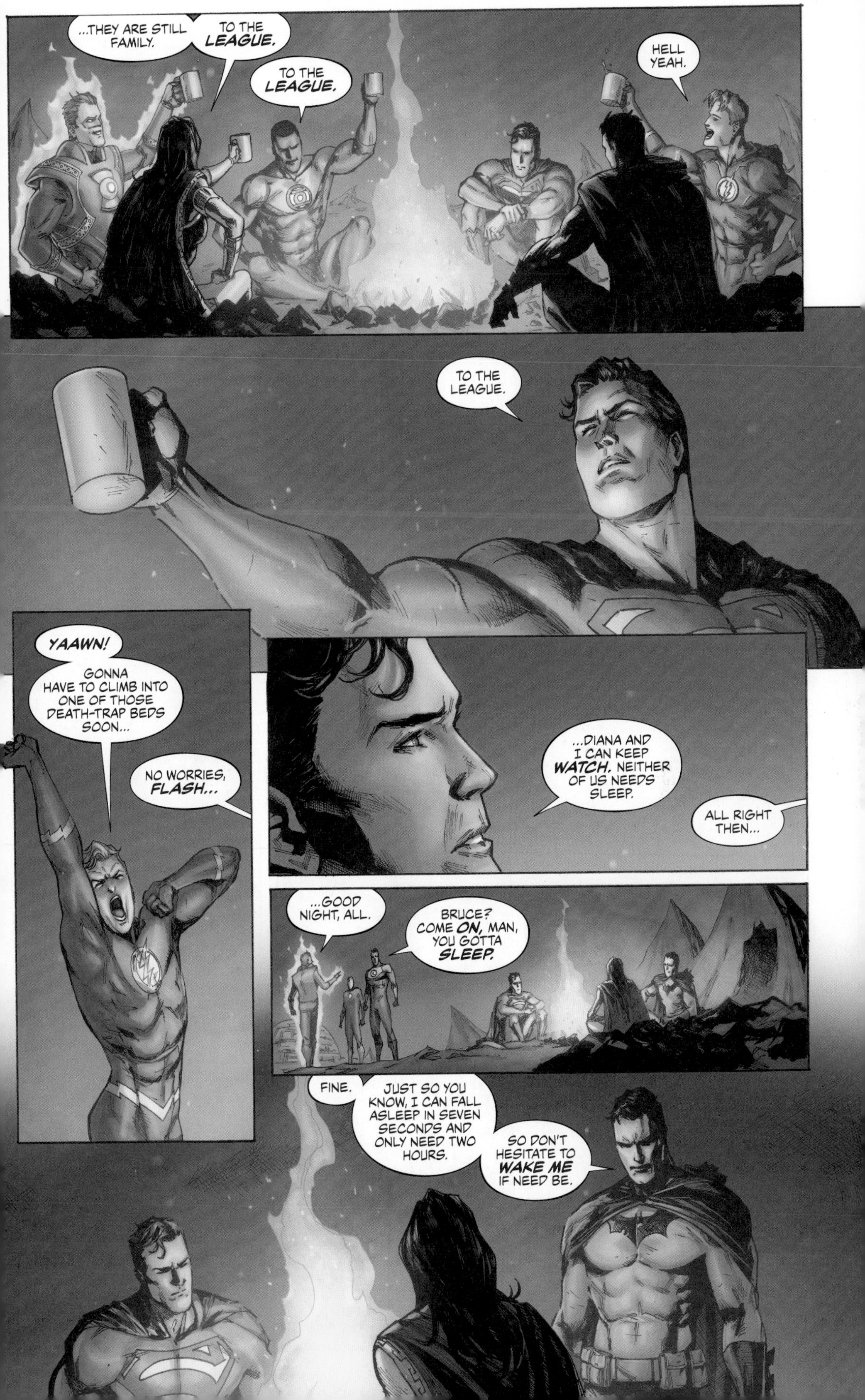

...THEY ARE STILL FAMILY.
TO THE LEAGUE.
TO THE LEAGUE.
HELL YEAH.
TO THE LEAGUE.
YAAWN!
GONNA HAVE TO CLIMB INTO ONE OF THOSE DEATH-TRAP BEDS SOON...
NO WORRIES, FLASH...
...DIANA AND I CAN KEEP WATCH. NEITHER OF US NEEDS SLEEP.
ALL RIGHT THEN...
...GOOD NIGHT, ALL.
BRUCE? COME ON, MAN, YOU GOTTA SLEEP.
FINE.
JUST SO YOU KNOW, I CAN FALL ASLEEP IN SEVEN SECONDS AND ONLY NEED TWO HOURS.
SO DON'T HESITATE TO WAKE ME IF NEED BE.

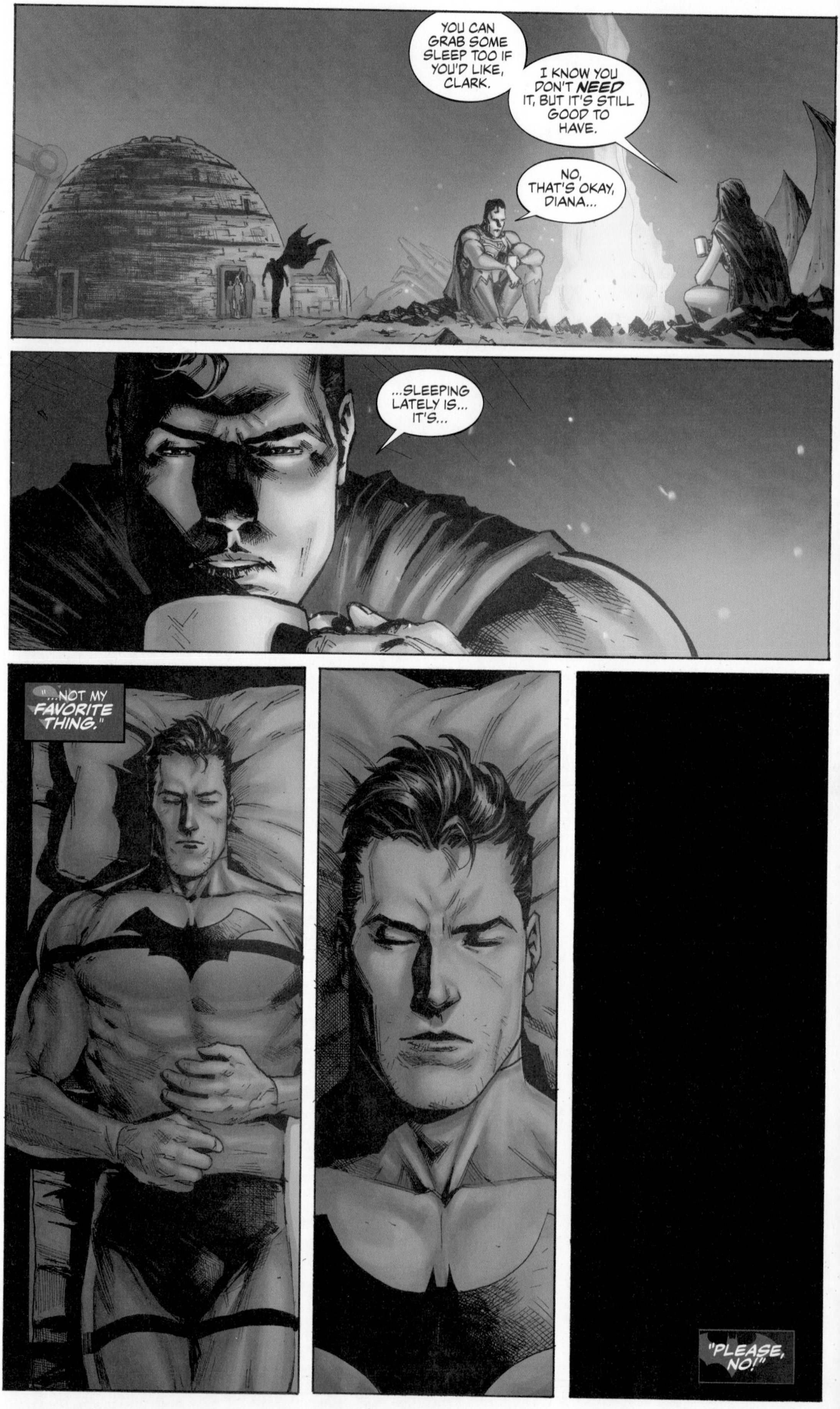

YOU CAN GRAB SOME SLEEP TOO IF YOU'D LIKE, CLARK.
I KNOW YOU DON'T NEED IT, BUT IT'S STILL GOOD TO HAVE.
NO, THAT'S OKAY, DIANA...
...SLEEPING LATELY IS... IT'S...
"...NOT MY FAVORITE THING."
"PLEASE, NO!"

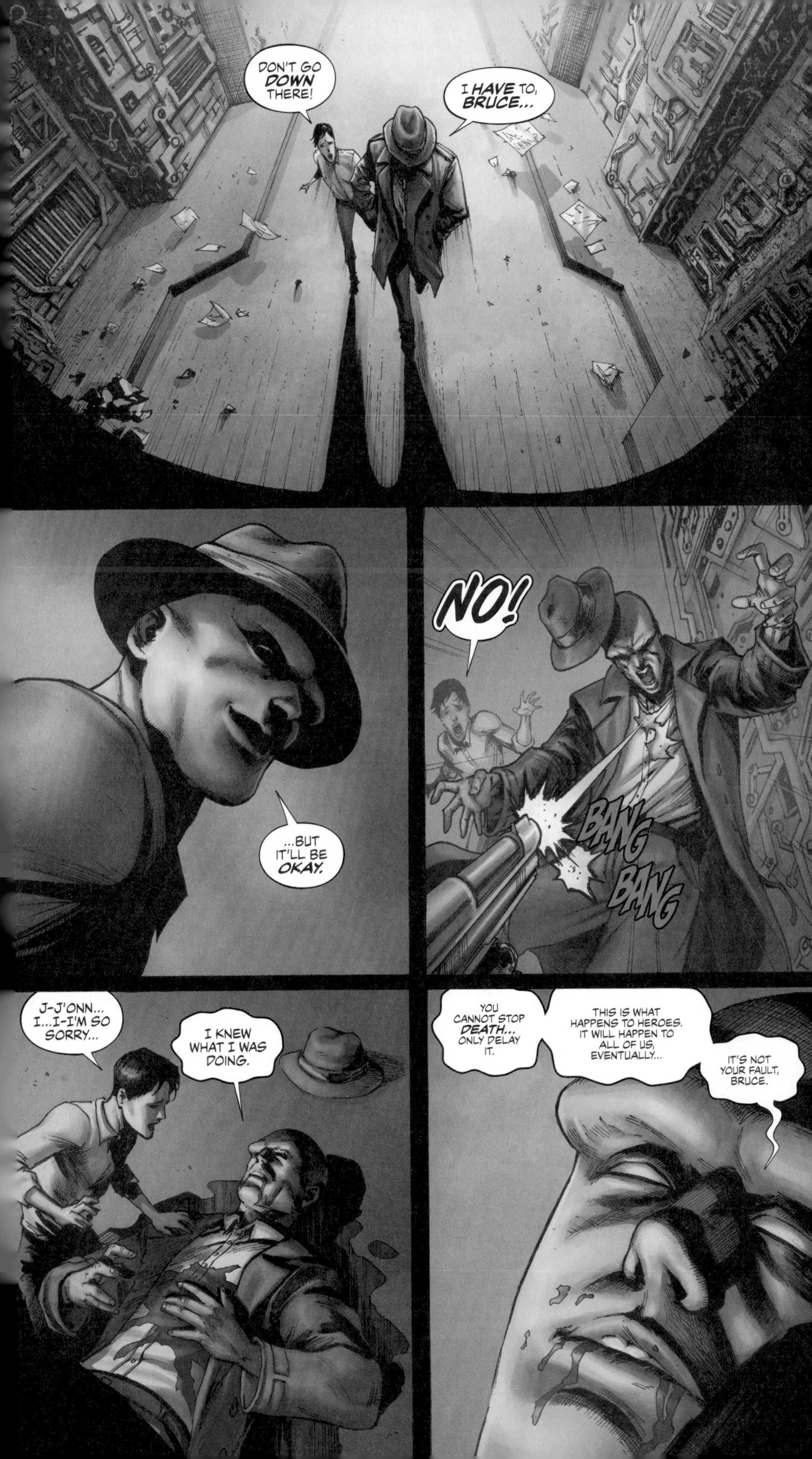
DON'T GO DOWN THERE!
I HAVE TO, BRUCE...
...BUT IT'LL BE OKAY.
NO!
BANG
BANG
J-J'ONN... I...I-I'M SO SORRY...
I KNEW WHAT I WAS DOING.
YOU CANNOT STOP DEATH... ONLY DELAY IT.
THIS IS WHAT HAPPENS TO HEROES. IT WILL HAPPEN TO ALL OF US, EVENTUALLY...
IT'S NOT YOUR FAULT, BRUCE.

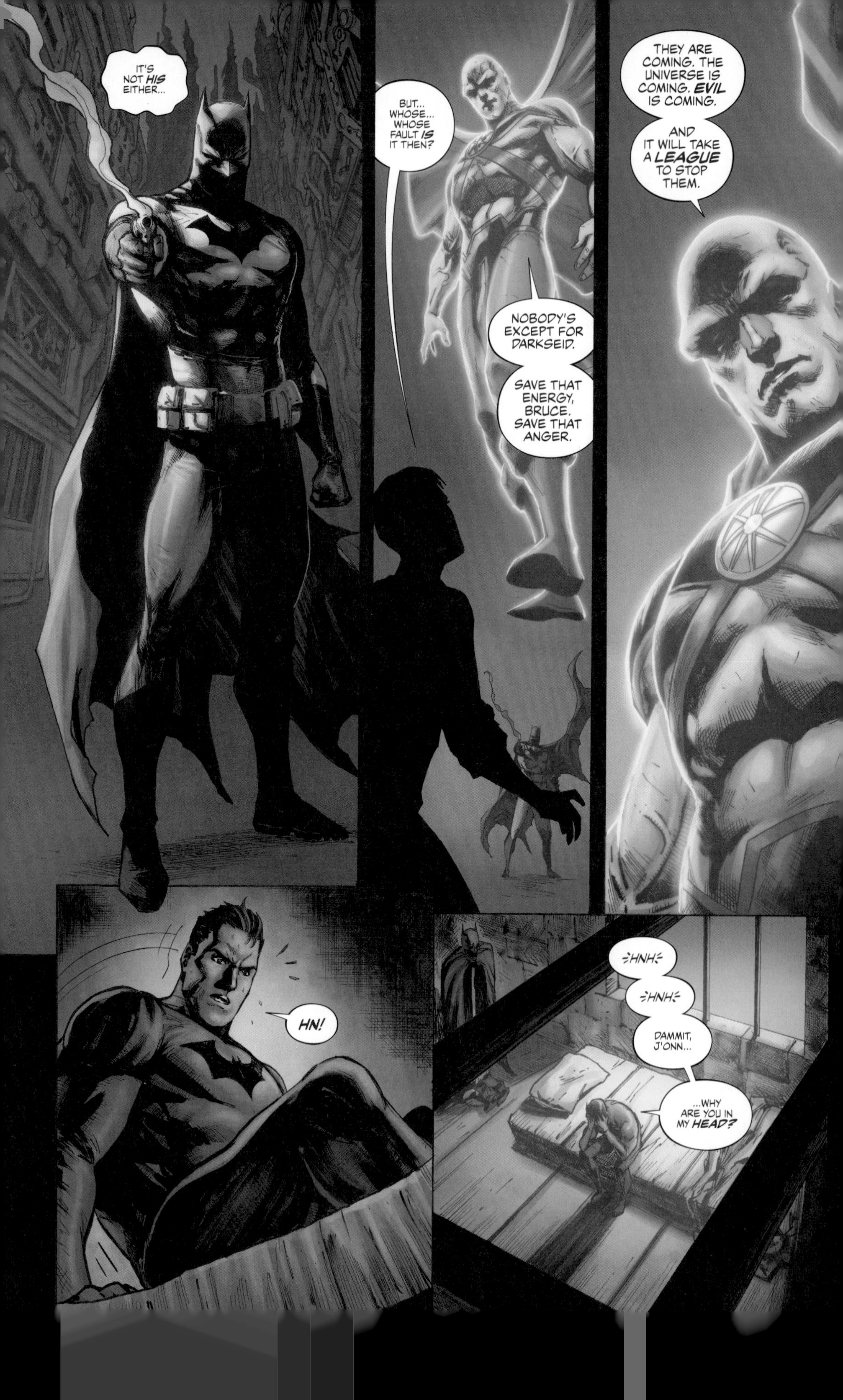
IT'S NOT HIS EITHER...
BUT... WHOSE... WHOSE FAULT IS IT THEN?
NOBODY'S EXCEPT FOR DARKSEID.
SAVE THAT ENERGY, BRUCE. SAVE THAT ANGER.
THEY ARE COMING. THE UNIVERSE IS COMING. EVIL IS COMING.
AND IT WILL TAKE A LEAGUE TO STOP THEM.
HN!
HNH
HNH
DAMMIT, J'ONN...
...WHY ARE YOU IN MY HEAD?

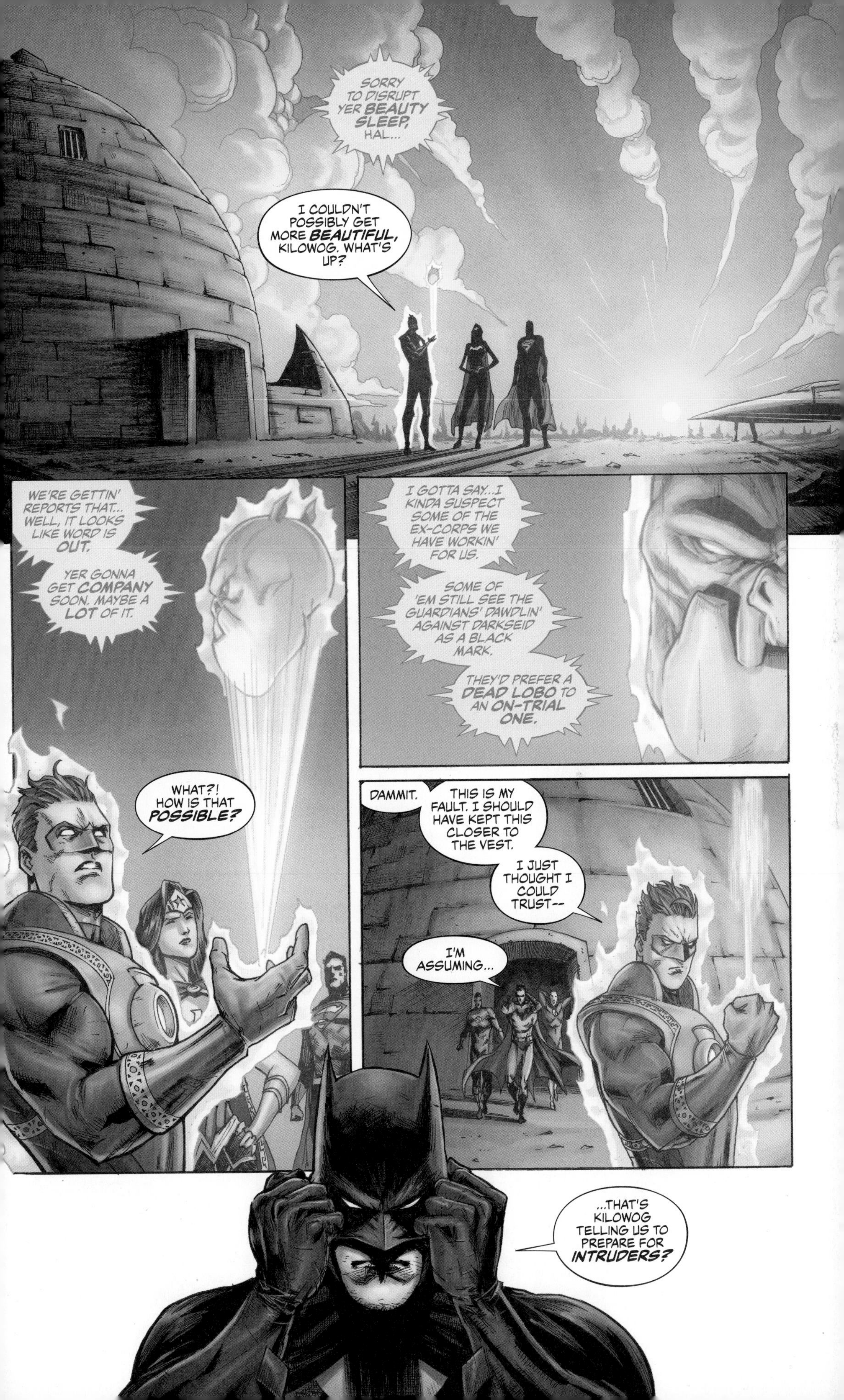
SORRY TO DISRUPT YER BEAUTY SLEEP, HAL...
I COULDN'T POSSIBLY GET MORE BEAUTIFUL, KILOWOG. WHAT'S UP?
WE'RE GETTIN' REPORTS THAT... WELL, IT LOOKS LIKE WORD IS OUT.
YER GONNA GET COMPANY SOON. MAYBE A LOT OF IT.
WHAT?! HOW IS THAT POSSIBLE?
I GOTTA SAY...I KINDA SUSPECT SOME OF THE EX-CORPS WE HAVE WORKIN' FOR US.
SOME OF 'EM STILL SEE THE GUARDIANS' DAWDLIN' AGAINST DARKSEID AS A BLACK MARK.
THEY'D PREFER A DEAD LOBO TO AN ON-TRIAL ONE.
DAMMIT.
THIS IS MY FAULT. I SHOULD HAVE KEPT THIS CLOSER TO THE VEST.
I JUST THOUGHT I COULD TRUST--
I'M ASSUMING...
...THAT'S KILOWOG TELLING US TO PREPARE FOR INTRUDERS?

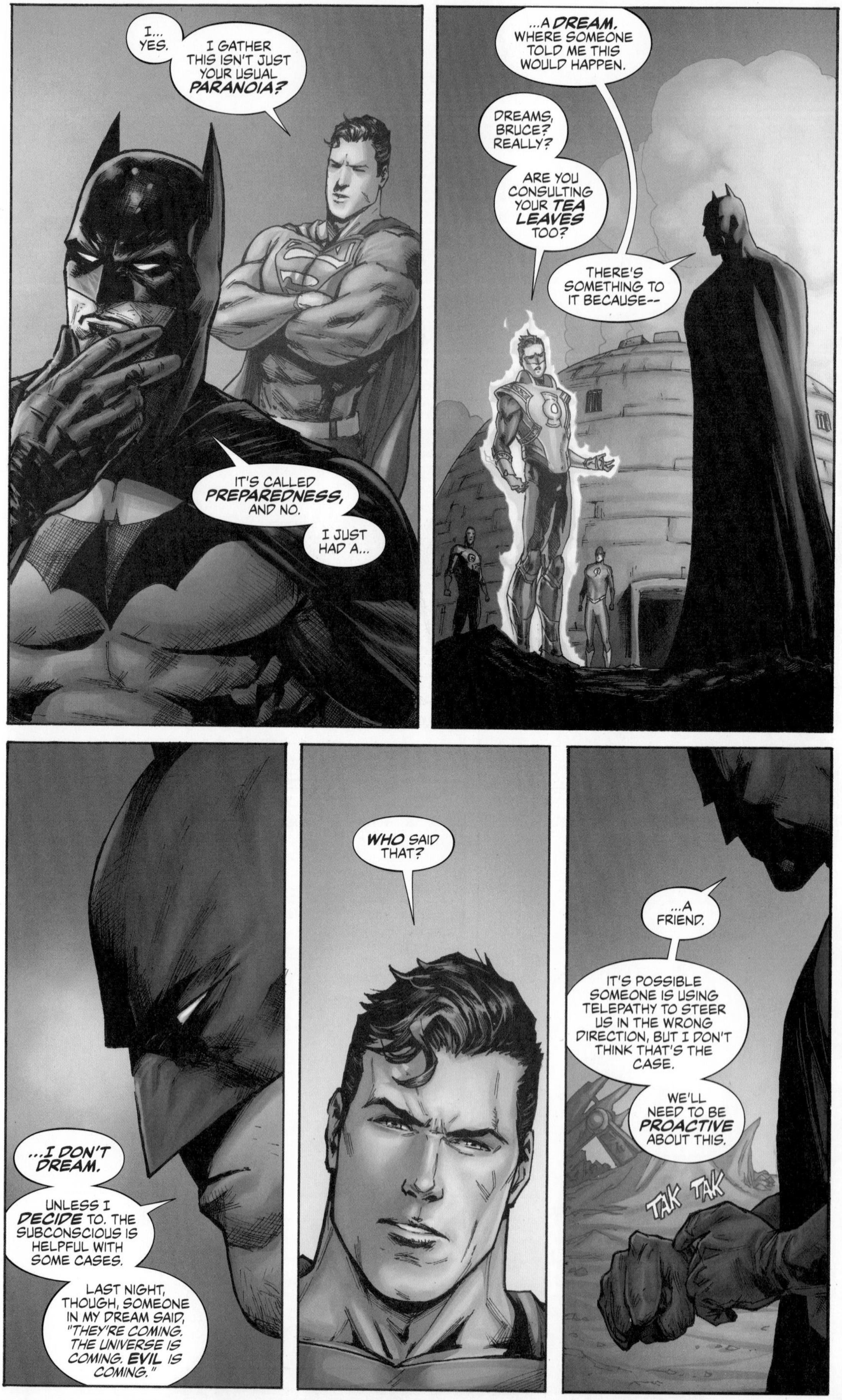
I... YES.
I GATHER THIS ISN'T JUST YOUR USUAL PARANOIA?
IT'S CALLED PREPAREDNESS, AND NO.
I JUST HAD A...
...A DREAM. WHERE SOMEONE TOLD ME THIS WOULD HAPPEN.
DREAMS, BRUCE? REALLY?
ARE YOU CONSULTING YOUR TEA LEAVES TOO?
THERE'S SOMETHING TO IT BECAUSE--
...I DON'T DREAM.
UNLESS I DECIDE TO. THE SUBCONSCIOUS IS HELPFUL WITH SOME CASES.
LAST NIGHT, THOUGH, SOMEONE IN MY DREAM SAID, "THEY'RE COMING. THE UNIVERSE IS COMING. EVIL IS COMING."
WHO SAID THAT?
...A FRIEND.
IT'S POSSIBLE SOMEONE IS USING TELEPATHY TO STEER US IN THE WRONG DIRECTION, BUT I DON'T THINK THAT'S THE CASE.
WE'LL NEED TO BE PROACTIVE ABOUT THIS.
TAK TAK

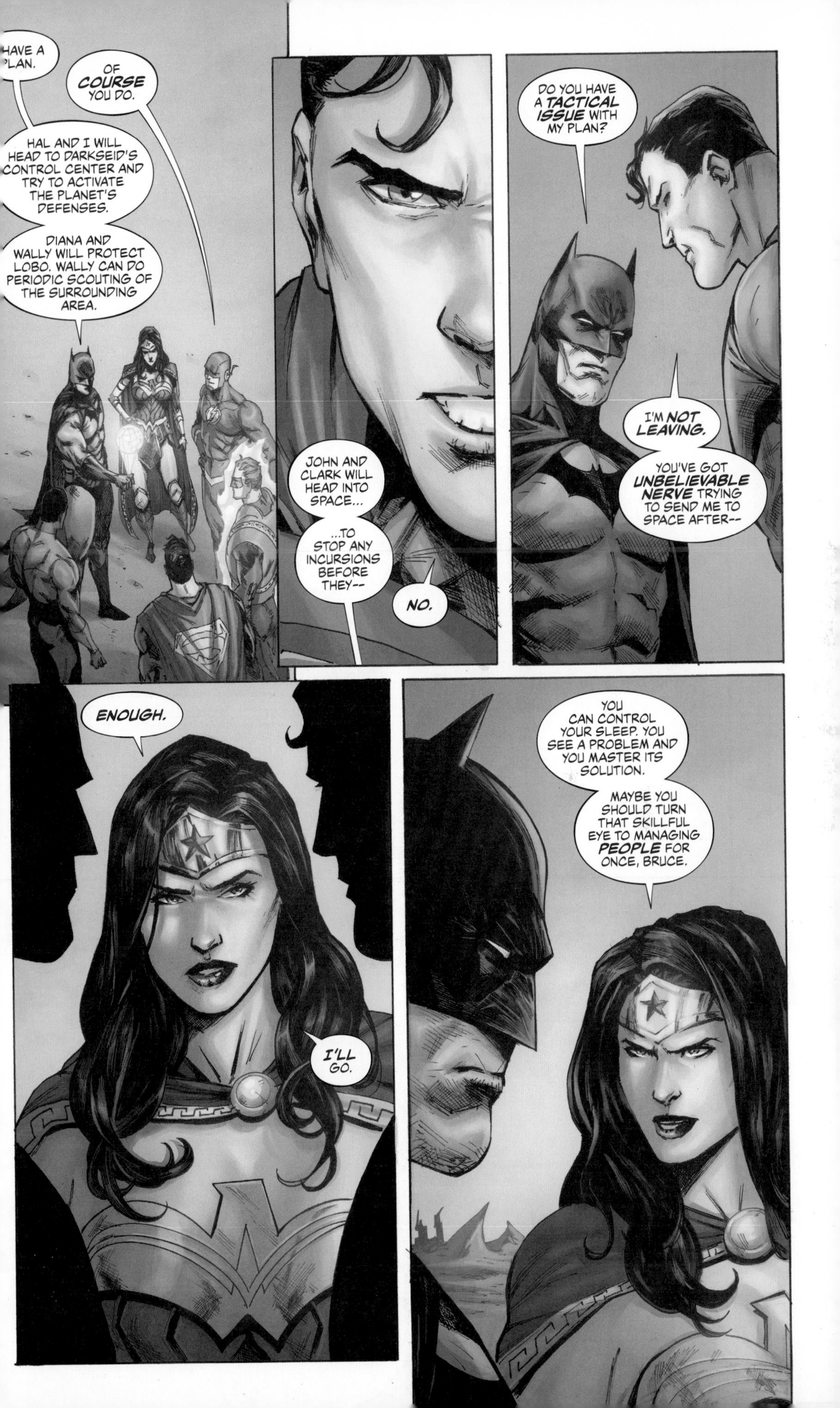

HAVE A PLAN.
OF COURSE YOU DO.
HAL AND I WILL HEAD TO DARKSEID'S CONTROL CENTER AND TRY TO ACTIVATE THE PLANET'S DEFENSES.
DIANA AND WALLY WILL PROTECT LOBO. WALLY CAN DO PERIODIC SCOUTING OF THE SURROUNDING AREA.
JOHN AND CLARK WILL HEAD INTO SPACE...
...TO STOP ANY INCURSIONS BEFORE THEY--
NO.
DO YOU HAVE A TACTICAL ISSUE WITH MY PLAN?
I'M NOT LEAVING.
YOU'VE GOT UNBELIEVABLE NERVE TRYING TO SEND ME TO SPACE AFTER--
ENOUGH.
I'LL GO.
YOU CAN CONTROL YOUR SLEEP. YOU SEE A PROBLEM AND YOU MASTER ITS SOLUTION.
MAYBE YOU SHOULD TURN THAT SKILLFUL EYE TO MANAGING PEOPLE FOR ONCE, BRUCE.

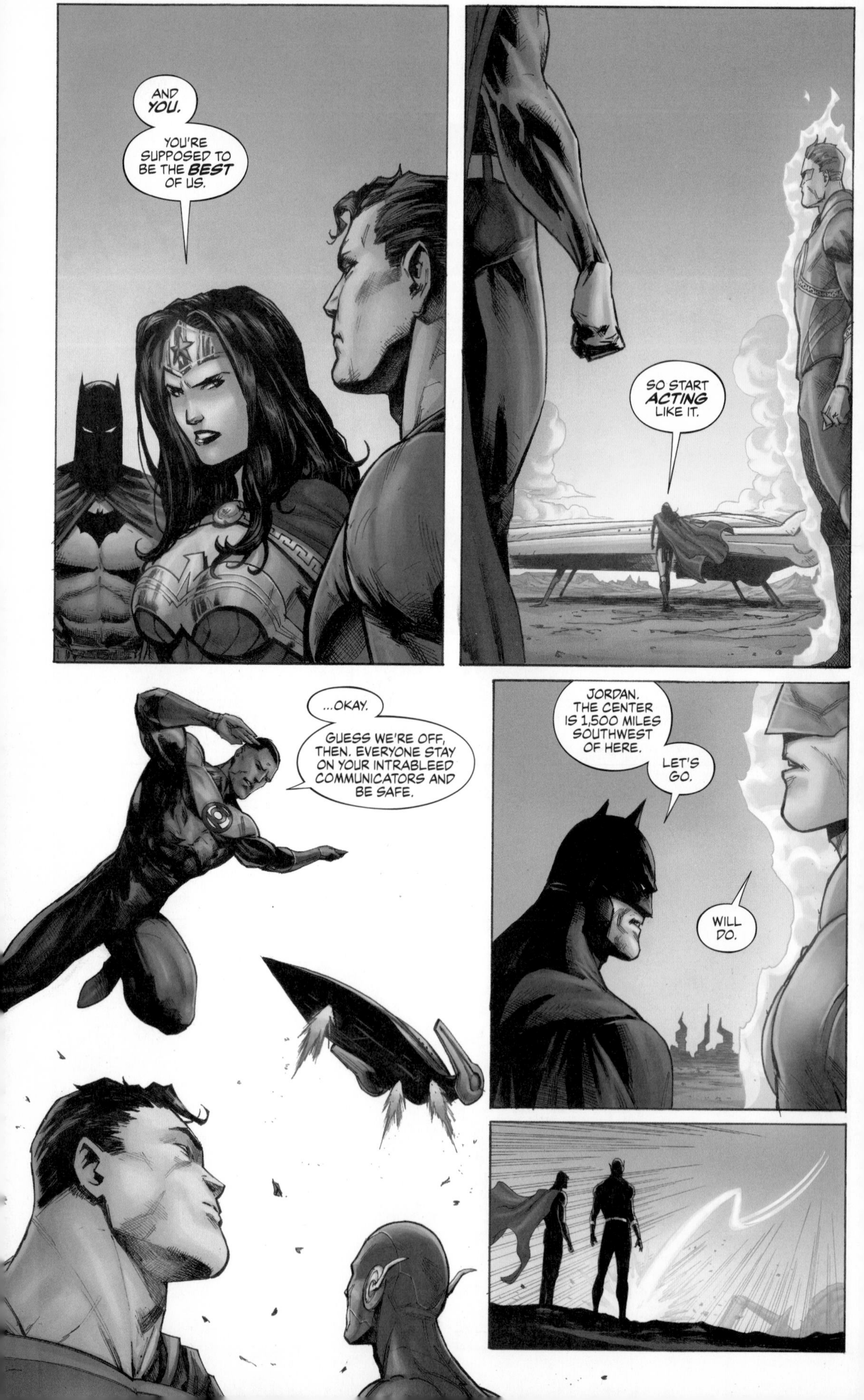
AND YOU.
YOU'RE SUPPOSED TO BE THE BEST OF US.
SO START ACTING LIKE IT.
...OKAY.
GUESS WE'RE OFF, THEN. EVERYONE STAY ON YOUR INTRABLEED COMMUNICATORS AND BE SAFE.
JORDAN. THE CENTER IS 1,500 MILES SOUTHWEST OF HERE.
LET'S GO.
WILL DO.

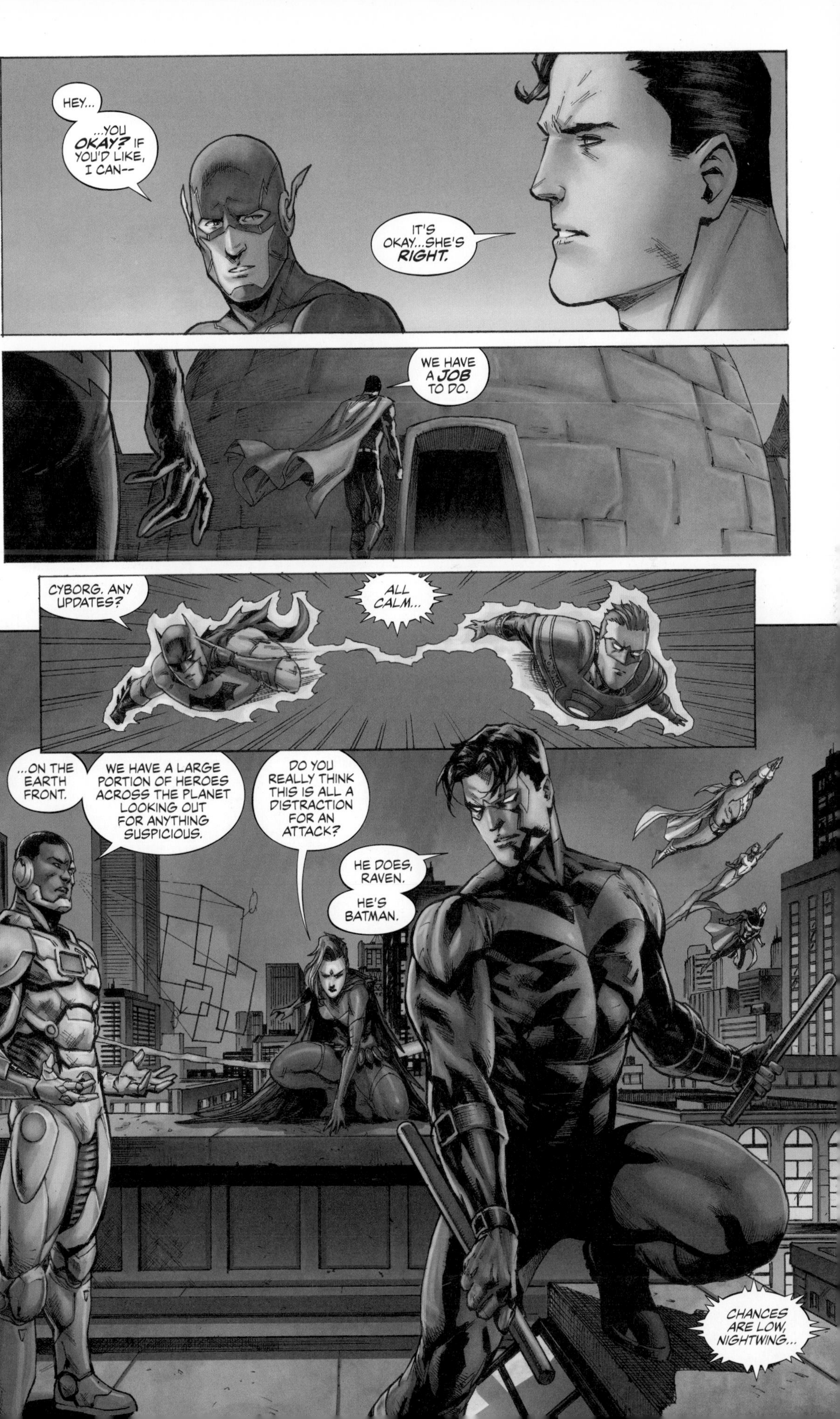

HEY...
...YOU OKAY? IF YOU'D LIKE, I CAN--
IT'S OKAY...SHE'S RIGHT.
WE HAVE A JOB TO DO.
CYBORG. ANY UPDATES?
ALL CALM...
...ON THE EARTH FRONT.
WE HAVE A LARGE PORTION OF HEROES ACROSS THE PLANET LOOKING OUT FOR ANYTHING SUSPICIOUS.
DO YOU REALLY THINK THIS IS ALL A DISTRACTION FOR AN ATTACK?
HE DOES, RAVEN.
HE'S BATMAN.
CHANCES ARE LOW, NIGHTWING...

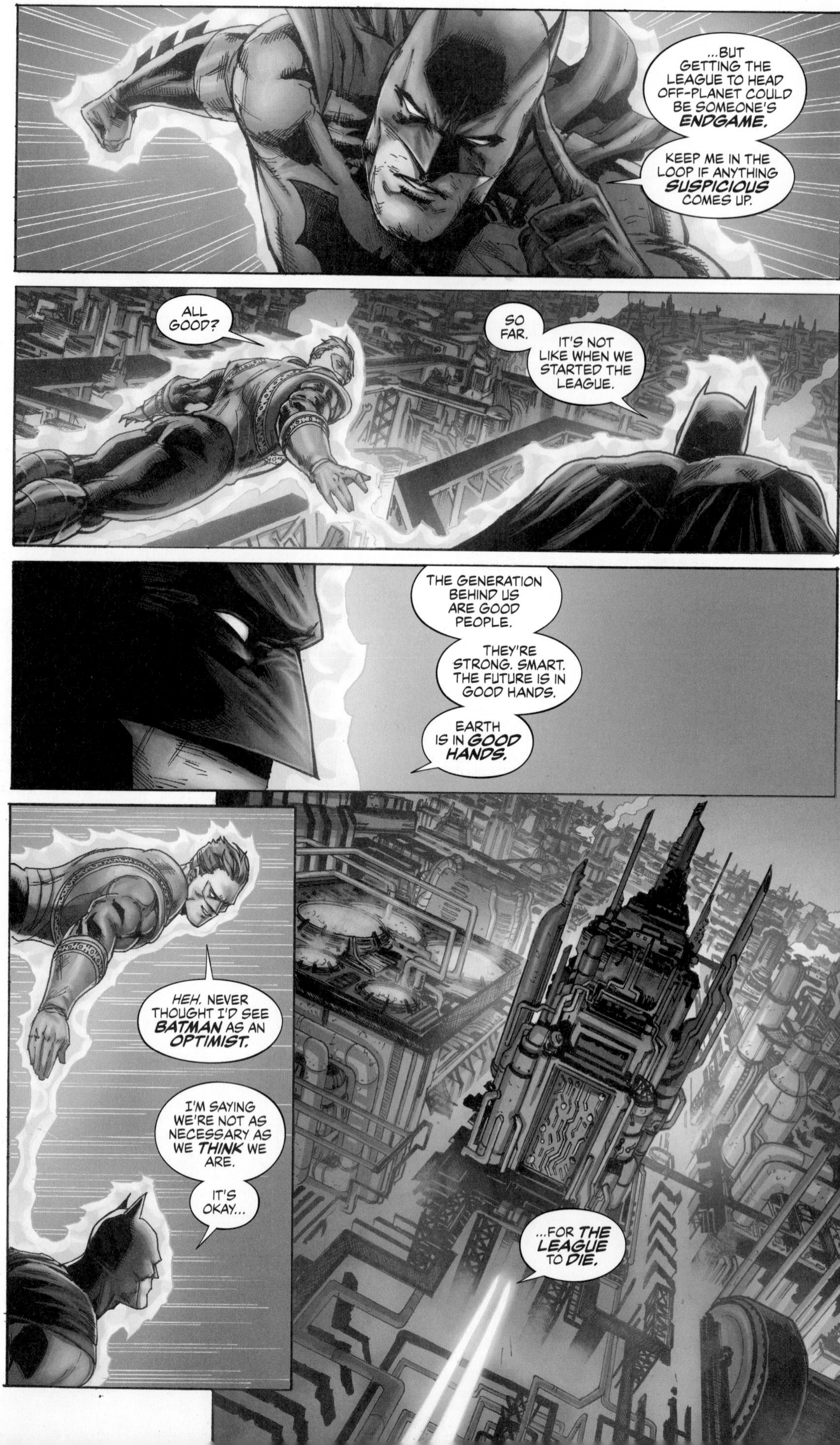
...BUT GETTING THE LEAGUE TO HEAD OFF-PLANET COULD BE SOMEONE'S ENDGAME.
KEEP ME IN THE LOOP IF ANYTHING SUSPICIOUS COMES UP.
ALL GOOD?
SO FAR.
IT'S NOT LIKE WHEN WE STARTED THE LEAGUE.
THE GENERATION BEHIND US ARE GOOD PEOPLE.
THEY'RE STRONG. SMART. THE FUTURE IS IN GOOD HANDS.
EARTH IS IN GOOD HANDS.
HEH. NEVER THOUGHT I'D SEE BATMAN AS AN OPTIMIST.
I'M SAYING WE'RE NOT AS NECESSARY AS WE THINK WE ARE.
IT'S OKAY...
...FOR THE LEAGUE TO DIE.

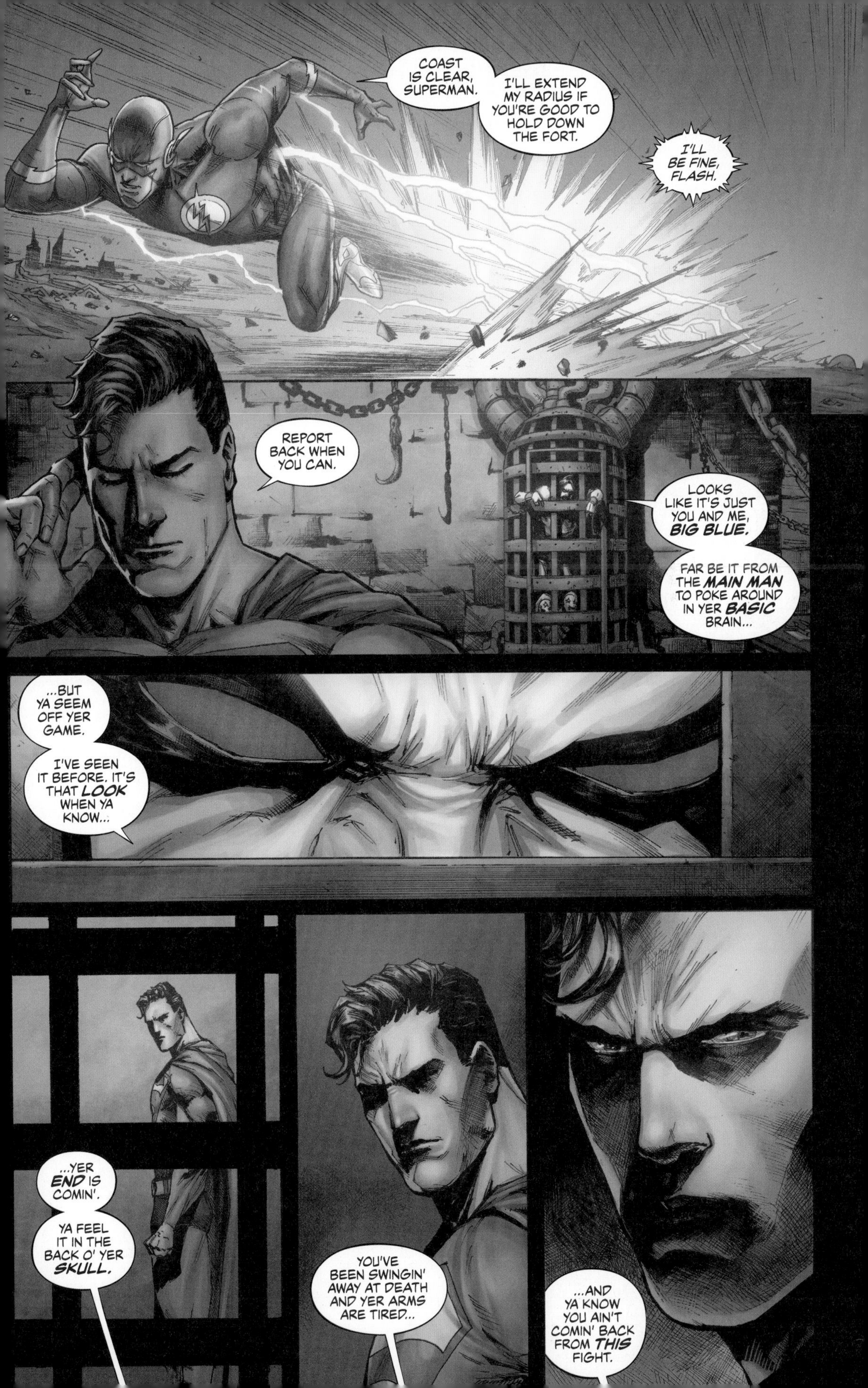
COAST IS CLEAR, SUPERMAN.
I'LL EXTEND MY RADIUS IF YOU'RE GOOD TO HOLD DOWN THE FORT.
I'LL BE FINE, FLASH.
REPORT BACK WHEN YOU CAN.
LOOKS LIKE IT'S JUST YOU AND ME, BIG BLUE.
FAR BE IT FROM THE MAIN MAN TO POKE AROUND IN YER BASIC BRAIN...
...BUT YA SEEM OFF YER GAME.
I'VE SEEN IT BEFORE. IT'S THAT LOOK WHEN YA KNOW...
...YER END IS COMIN'.
YA FEEL IT IN THE BACK O' YER SKULL.
YOU'VE BEEN SWINGIN' AWAY AT DEATH AND YER ARMS ARE TIRED...
...AND YA KNOW YOU AIN'T COMIN' BACK FROM THIS FIGHT.

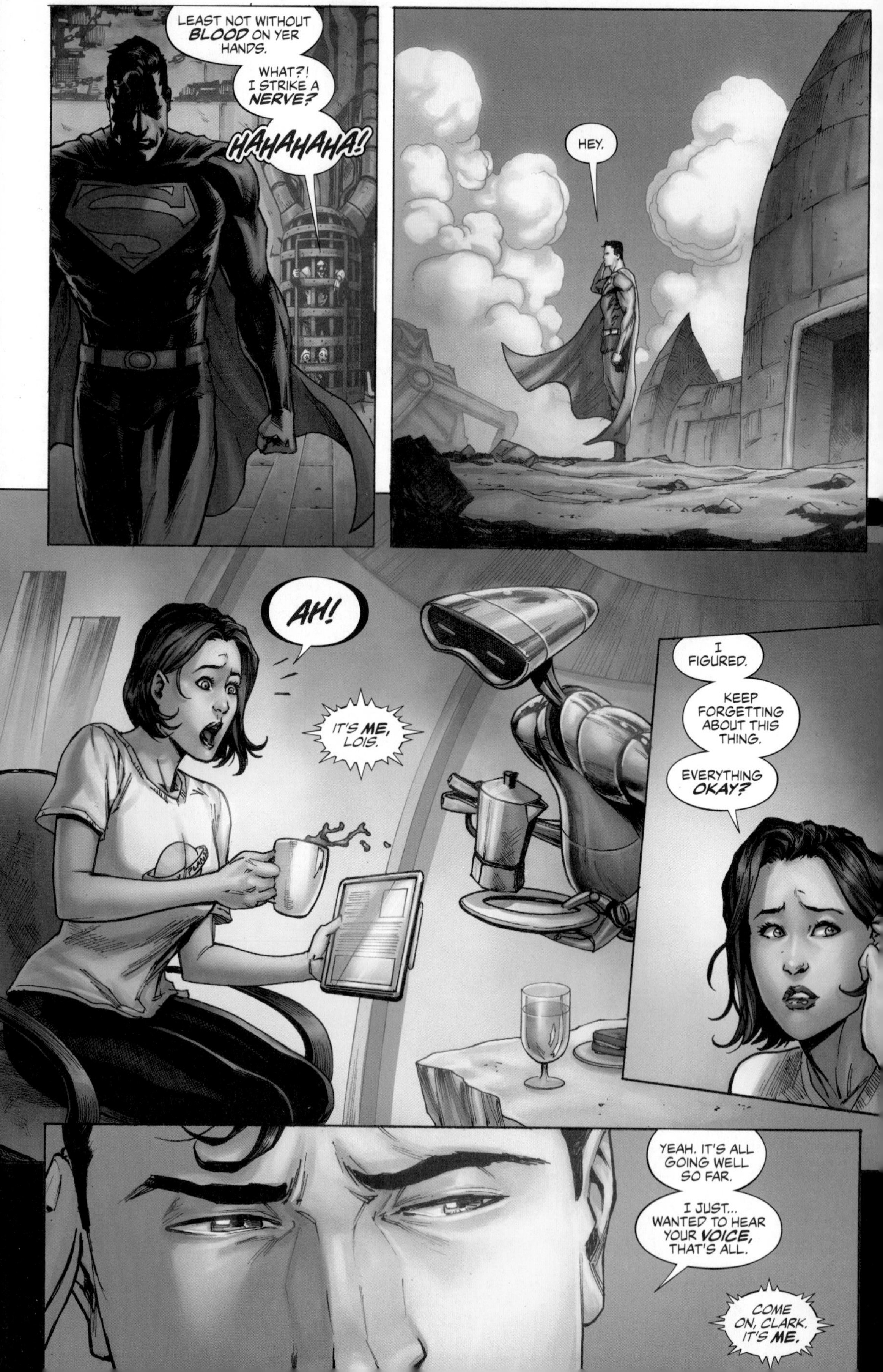
LEAST NOT WITHOUT BLOOD ON YER HANDS.
WHAT?! I STRIKE A NERVE?
HAHAHAHA!
HEY.
AH!
IT'S ME, LOIS.
I FIGURED.
KEEP FORGETTING ABOUT THIS THING.
EVERYTHING OKAY?
YEAH. IT'S ALL GOING WELL SO FAR.
I JUST... WANTED TO HEAR YOUR VOICE, THAT'S ALL.
COME ON, CLARK. IT'S ME.

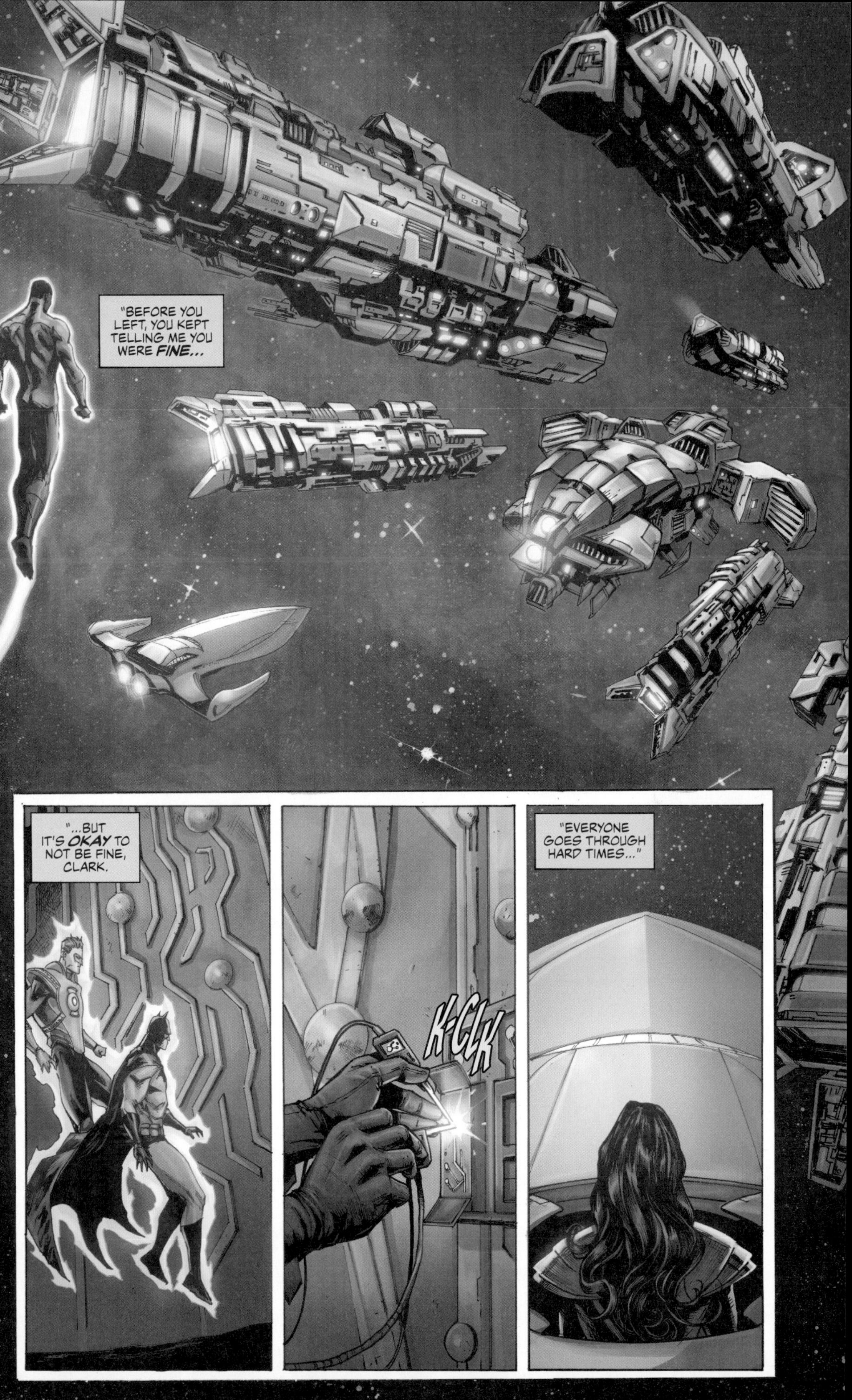
"BEFORE YOU LEFT, YOU KEPT TELLING ME YOU WERE FINE...
"...BUT IT'S OKAY TO NOT BE FINE, CLARK.
K-CLK
"EVERYONE GOES THROUGH HARD TIMES..."

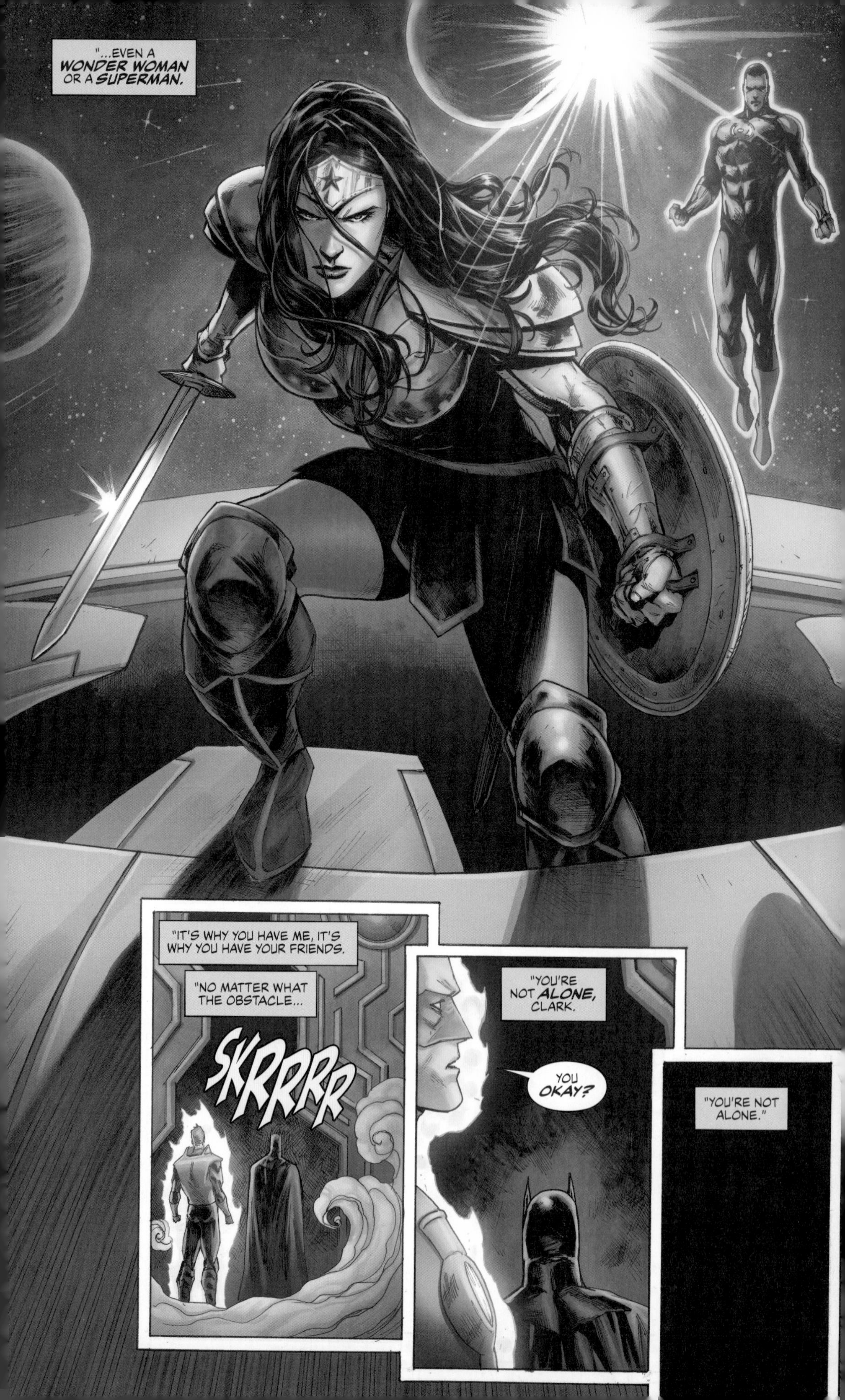
"...EVEN A WONDER WOMAN OR A SUPERMAN.
"IT'S WHY YOU HAVE ME, IT'S WHY YOU HAVE YOUR FRIENDS.
"NO MATTER WHAT THE OBSTACLE...
SKRRRR
"YOU'RE NOT ALONE, CLARK.
YOU OKAY?
"YOU'RE NOT ALONE."

Justice League: Last Ride #4 cover art by
DARICK ROBERTSON and **DIEGO RODRIGUEZ**

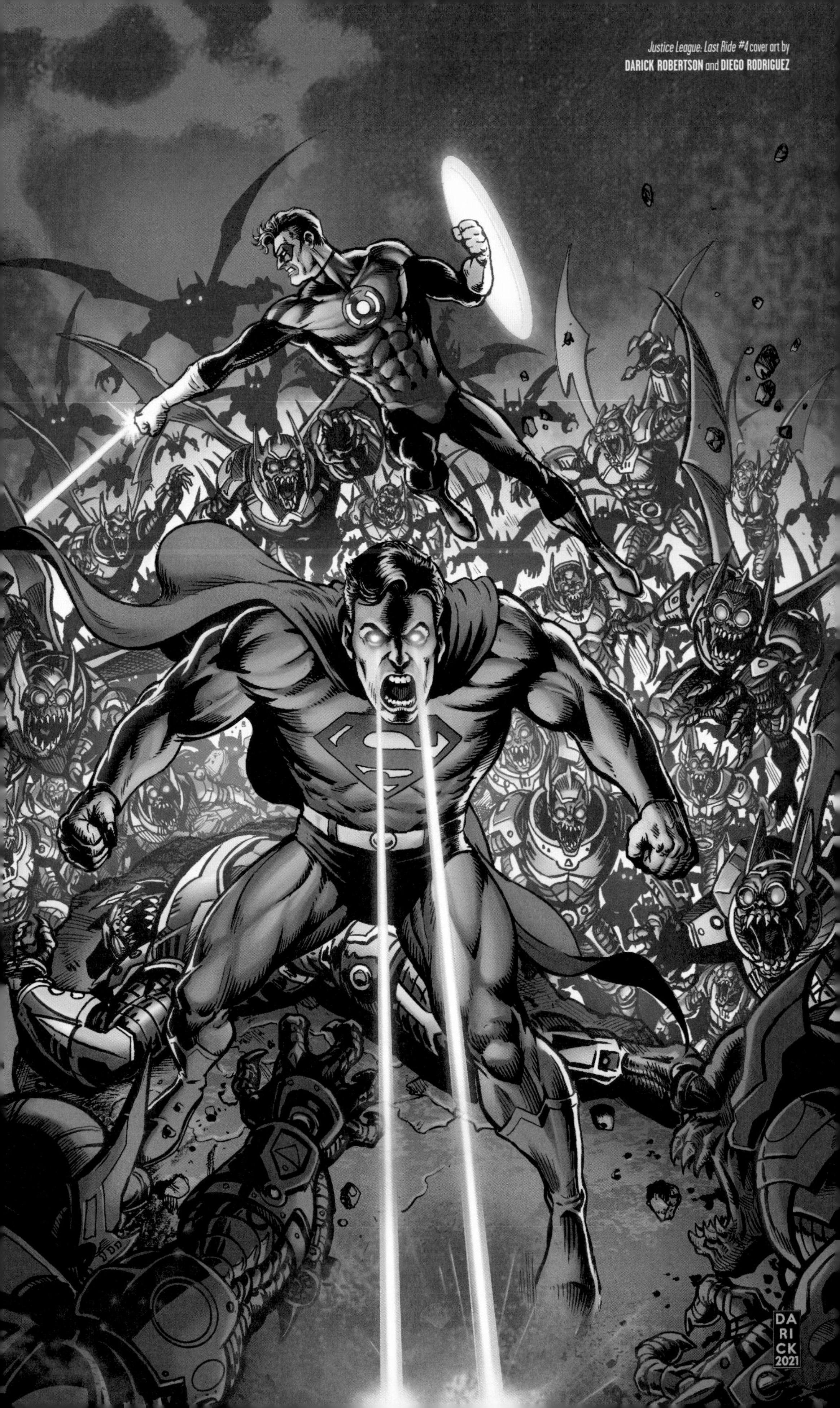
DA
RI
CK
2021

BEFORE.

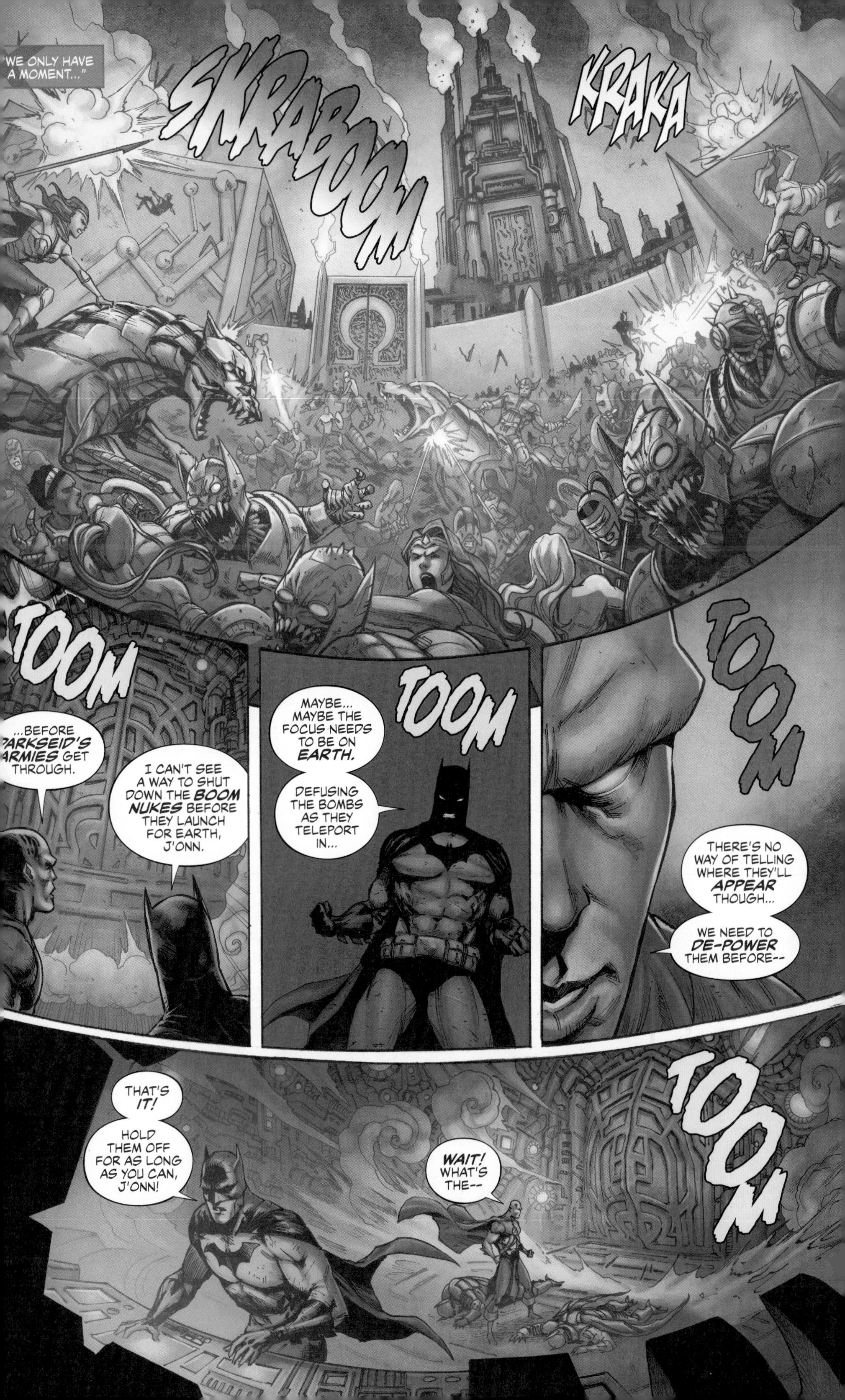
"WE ONLY HAVE A MOMENT..."
SKRABOOOM
KRAKA
TOOM
...BEFORE DARKSEID'S ARMIES GET THROUGH.
I CAN'T SEE A WAY TO SHUT DOWN THE BOOM NUKES BEFORE THEY LAUNCH FOR EARTH, J'ONN.
TOOM
MAYBE... MAYBE THE FOCUS NEEDS TO BE ON EARTH.
DEFUSING THE BOMBS AS THEY TELEPORT IN...
TOOM
THERE'S NO WAY OF TELLING WHERE THEY'LL APPEAR THOUGH...
WE NEED TO DE-POWER THEM BEFORE--
TOOM
THAT'S IT!
HOLD THEM OFF FOR AS LONG AS YOU CAN, J'ONN!
WAIT! WHAT'S THE--

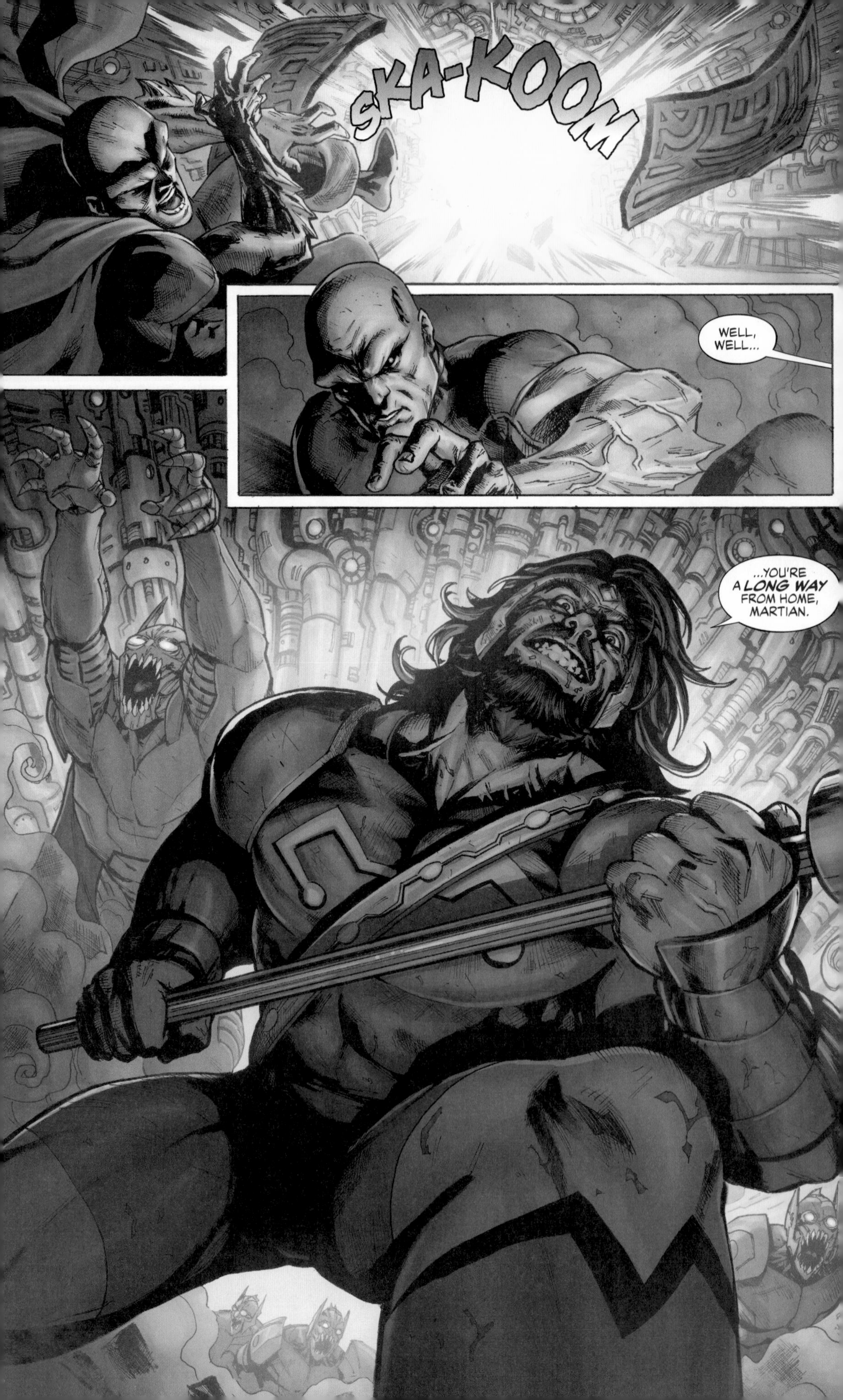
SKA-KOOM
WELL, WELL...
...YOU'RE A LONG WAY FROM HOME, MARTIAN.

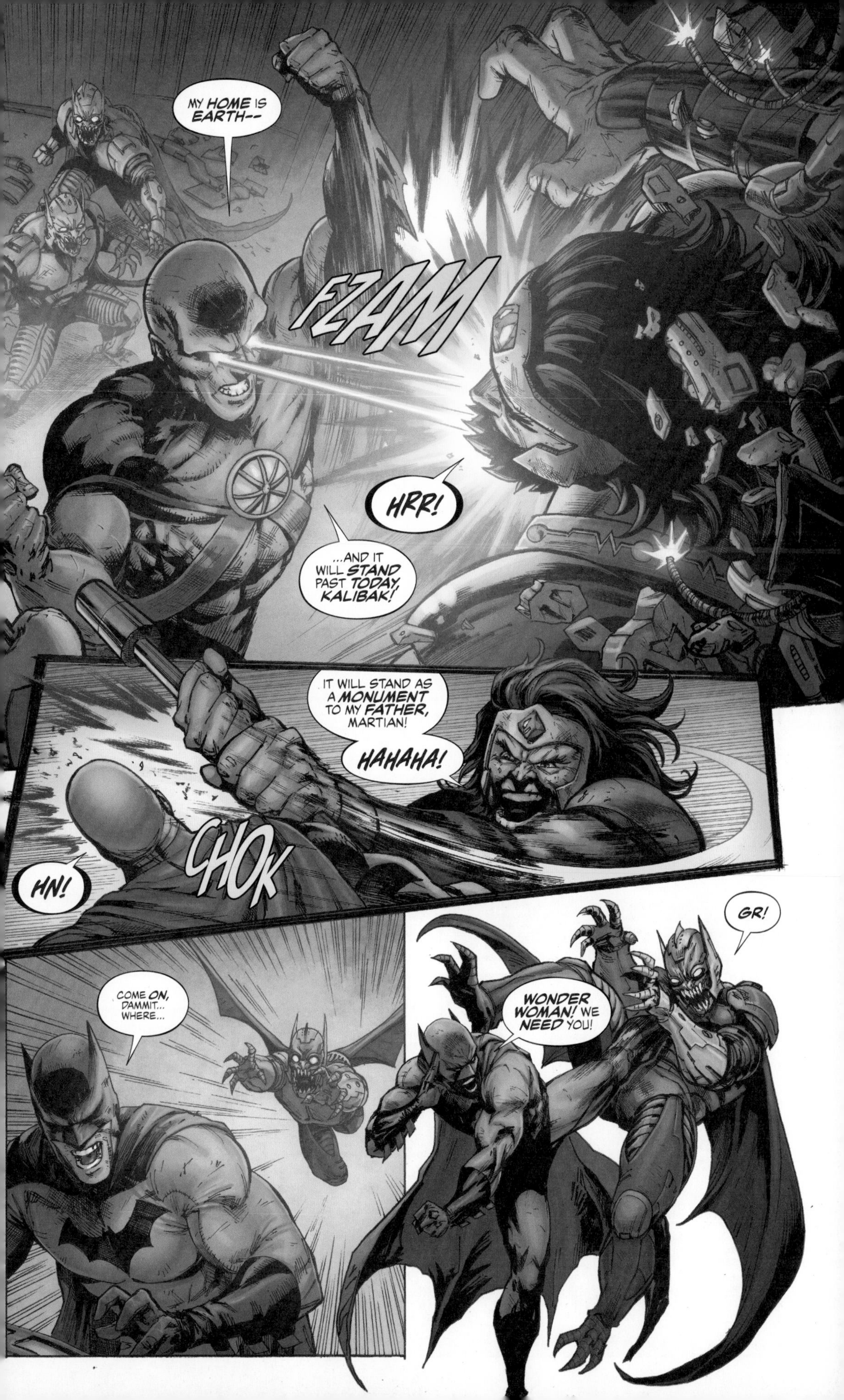

MY HOME IS EARTH--
FZAM
HRR!
...AND IT WILL STAND PAST TODAY, KALIBAK!
IT WILL STAND AS A MONUMENT TO MY FATHER, MARTIAN!
HAHAHA!
CHOK
HN!
COME ON, DAMMIT... WHERE...
GR!
WONDER WOMAN! WE NEED YOU!

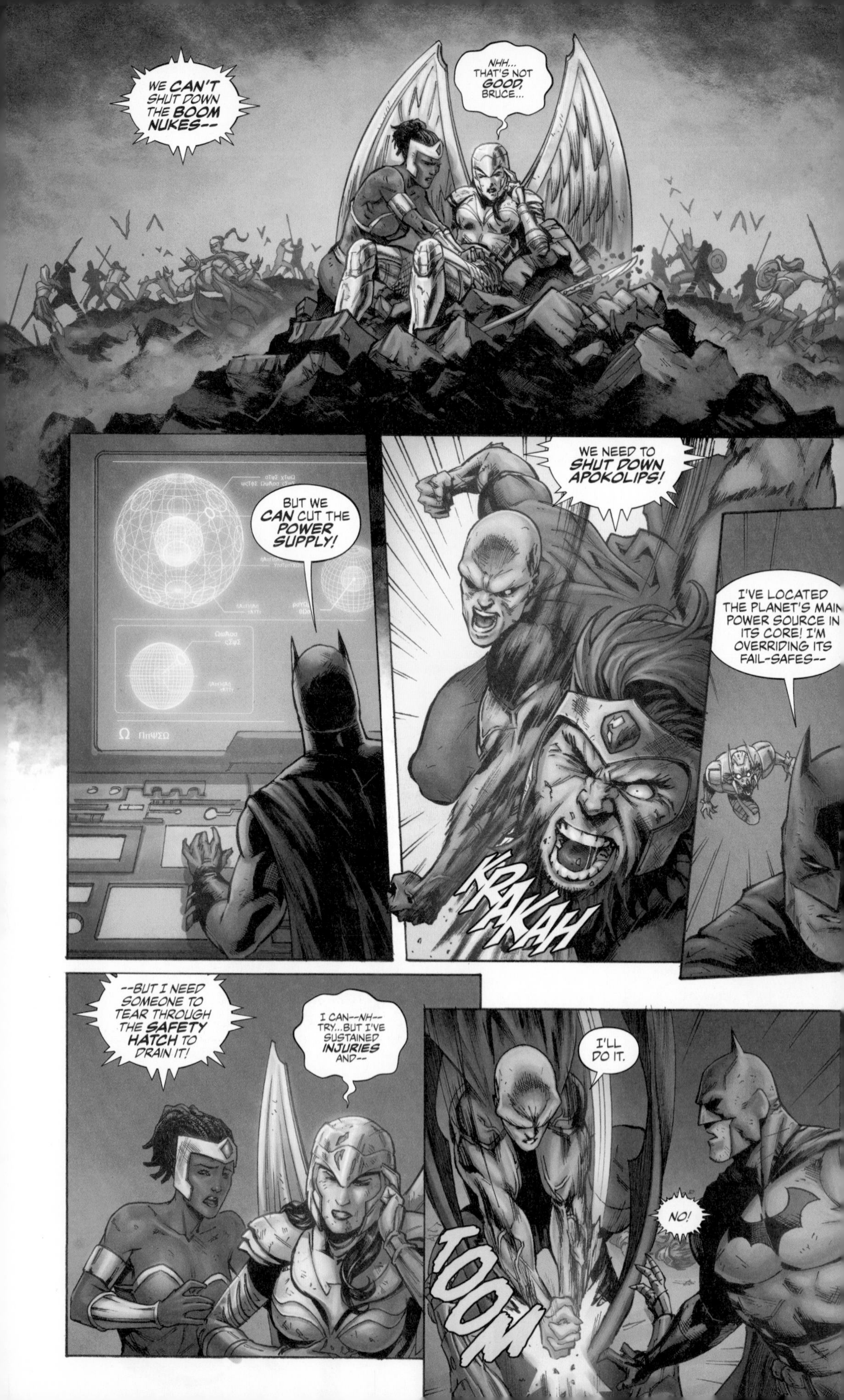
WE CAN'T SHUT DOWN THE BOOM NUKES--
NHH... THAT'S NOT GOOD, BRUCE...
BUT WE CAN CUT THE POWER SUPPLY!
WE NEED TO SHUT DOWN APOKOLIPS!
KRAKAH
I'VE LOCATED THE PLANET'S MAIN POWER SOURCE IN ITS CORE! I'M OVERRIDING ITS FAIL-SAFES--
--BUT I NEED SOMEONE TO TEAR THROUGH THE SAFETY HATCH TO DRAIN IT!
I CAN--NH-- TRY...BUT I'VE SUSTAINED INJURIES AND--
I'LL DO IT.
NO!
TOOOM

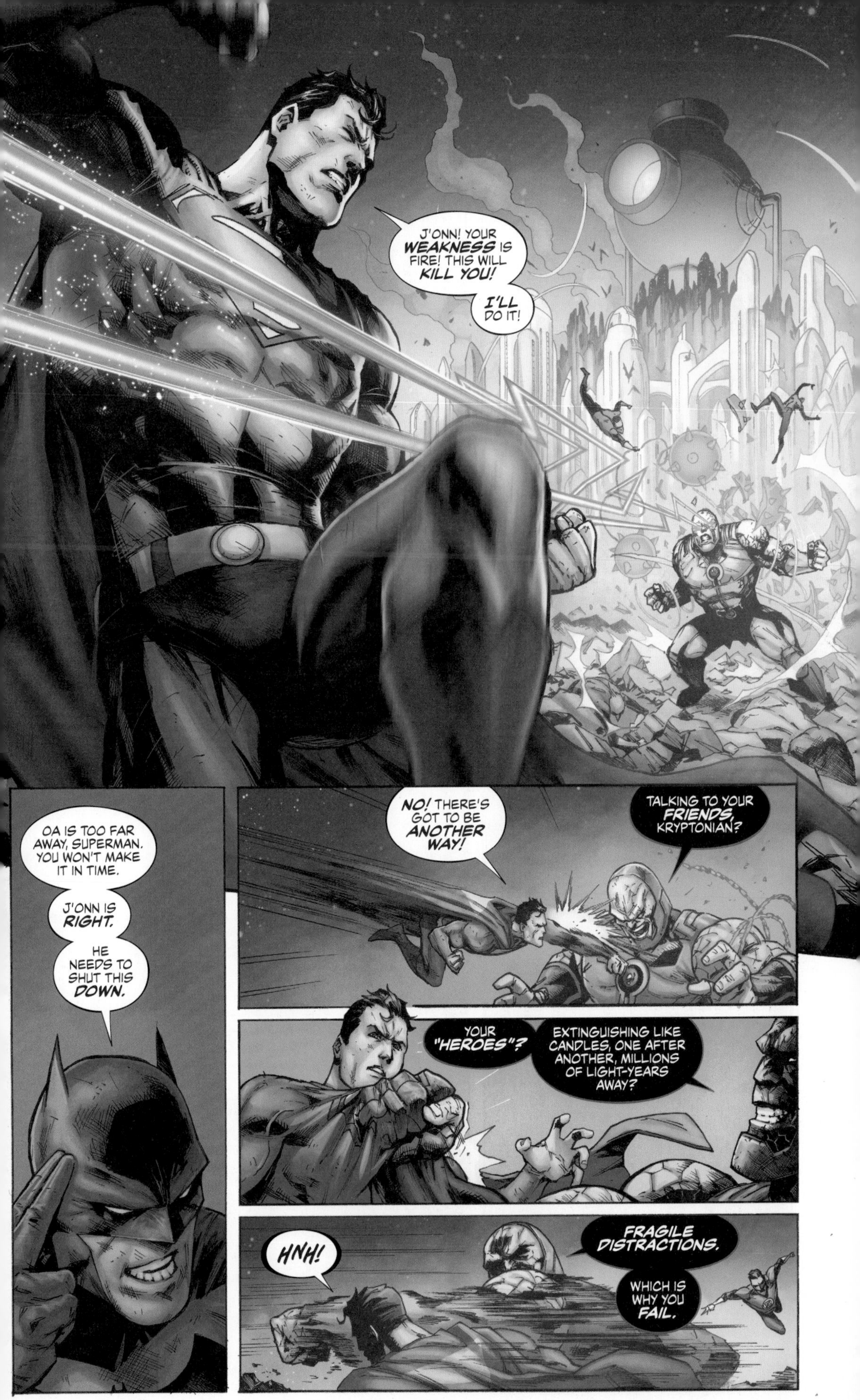
J'ONN! YOUR WEAKNESS IS FIRE! THIS WILL KILL YOU!
I'LL DO IT!
OA IS TOO FAR AWAY, SUPERMAN. YOU WON'T MAKE IT IN TIME.
J'ONN IS RIGHT.
HE NEEDS TO SHUT THIS DOWN.
NO! THERE'S GOT TO BE ANOTHER WAY!
TALKING TO YOUR FRIENDS, KRYPTONIAN?
YOUR "HEROES"?
EXTINGUISHING LIKE CANDLES, ONE AFTER ANOTHER, MILLIONS OF LIGHT-YEARS AWAY?
HNH!
FRAGILE DISTRACTIONS.
WHICH IS WHY YOU FAIL.

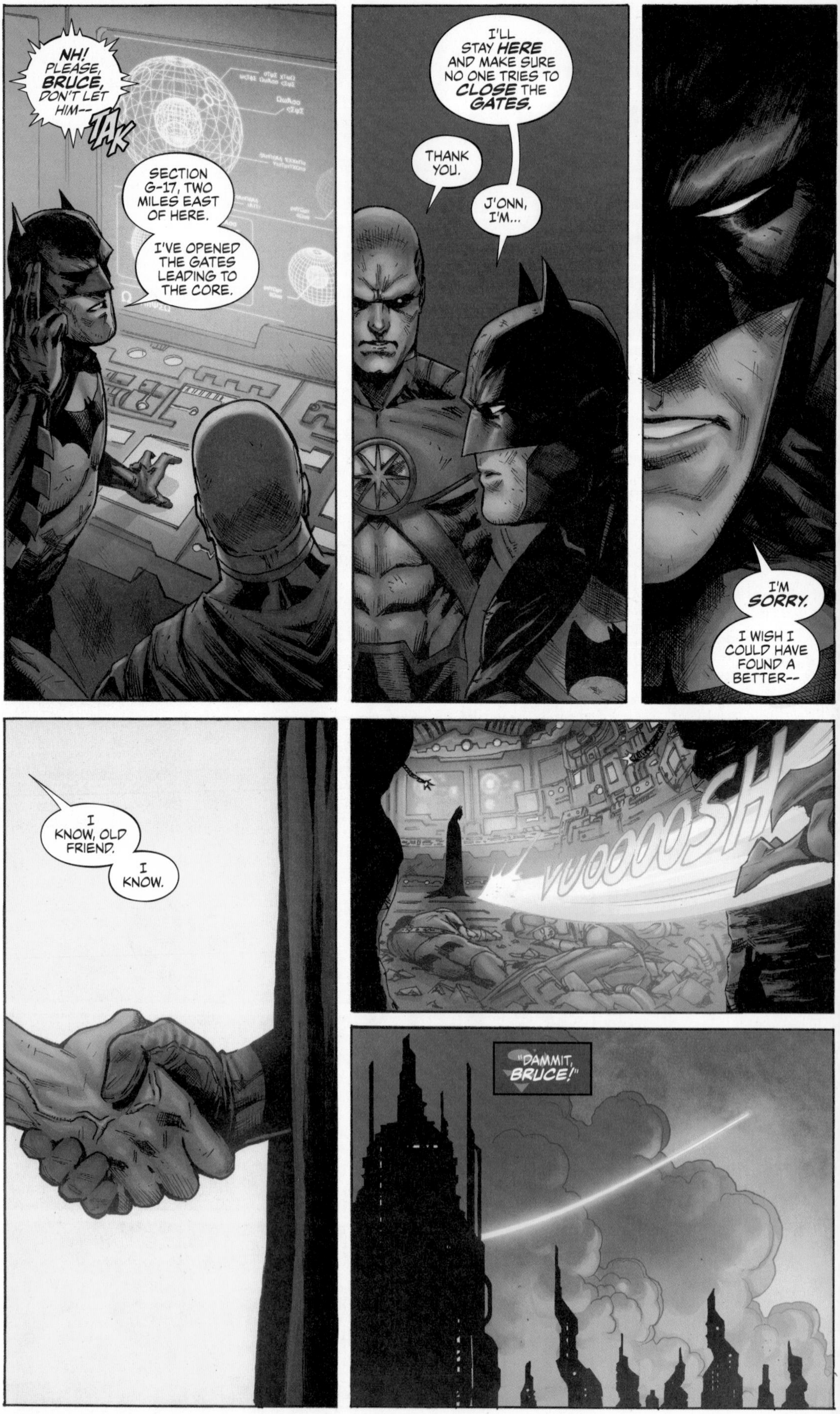

NH! PLEASE, BRUCE, DON'T LET HIM--
TAK
SECTION G-17, TWO MILES EAST OF HERE.
I'VE OPENED THE GATES LEADING TO THE CORE.
I'LL STAY HERE AND MAKE SURE NO ONE TRIES TO CLOSE THE GATES.
THANK YOU.
J'ONN, I'M...
I'M SORRY.
I WISH I COULD HAVE FOUND A BETTER--
I KNOW, OLD FRIEND.
I KNOW.
VOOOOOSH
"DAMMIT, BRUCE!"

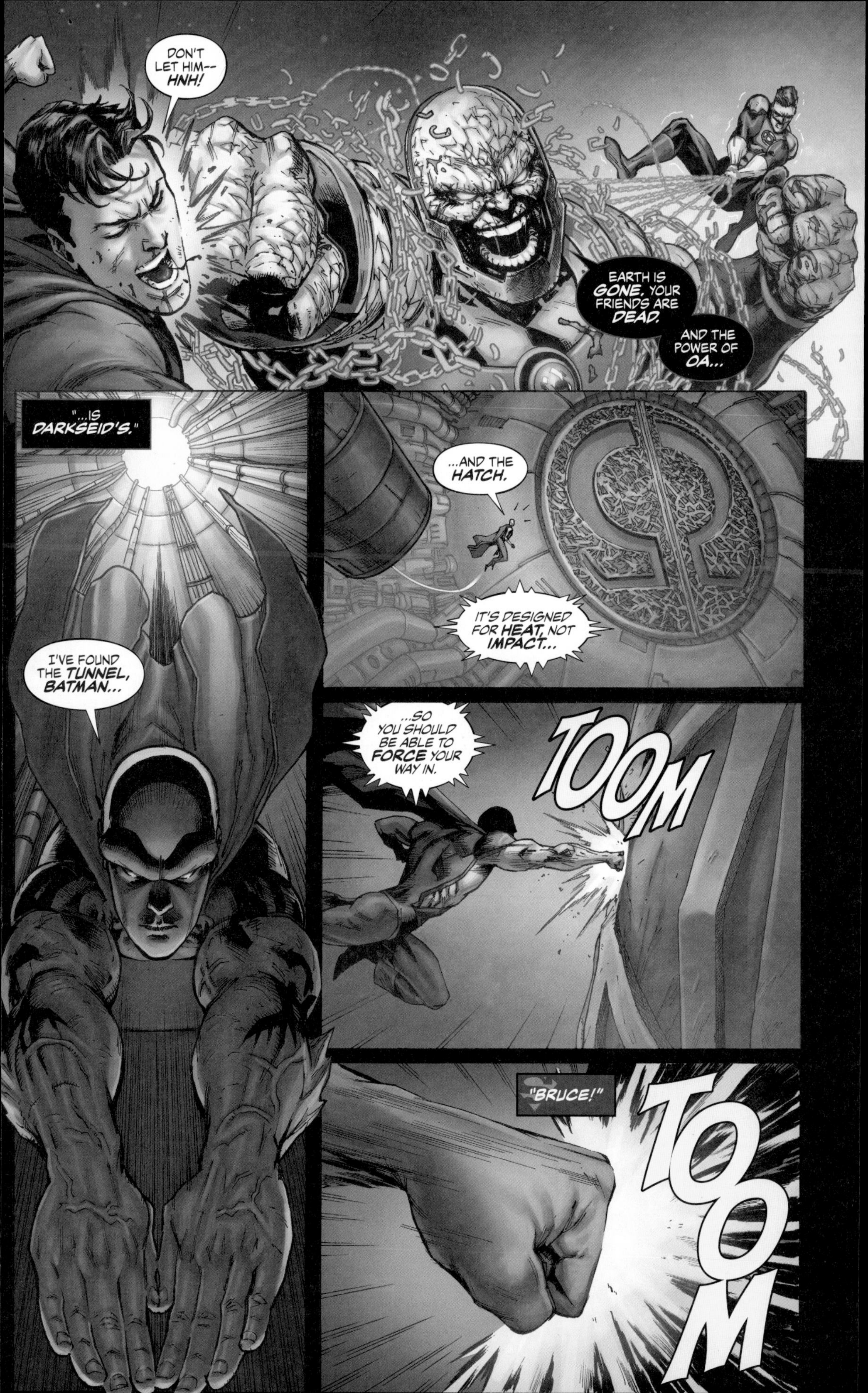
DON'T LET HIM-- HNH!
EARTH IS GONE. YOUR FRIENDS ARE DEAD.
AND THE POWER OF OA...
"...IS DARKSEID'S."
...AND THE HATCH.
IT'S DESIGNED FOR HEAT, NOT IMPACT...
I'VE FOUND THE TUNNEL, BATMAN...
...SO YOU SHOULD BE ABLE TO FORCE YOUR WAY IN.
TOOM
"BRUCE!"
TOOOM

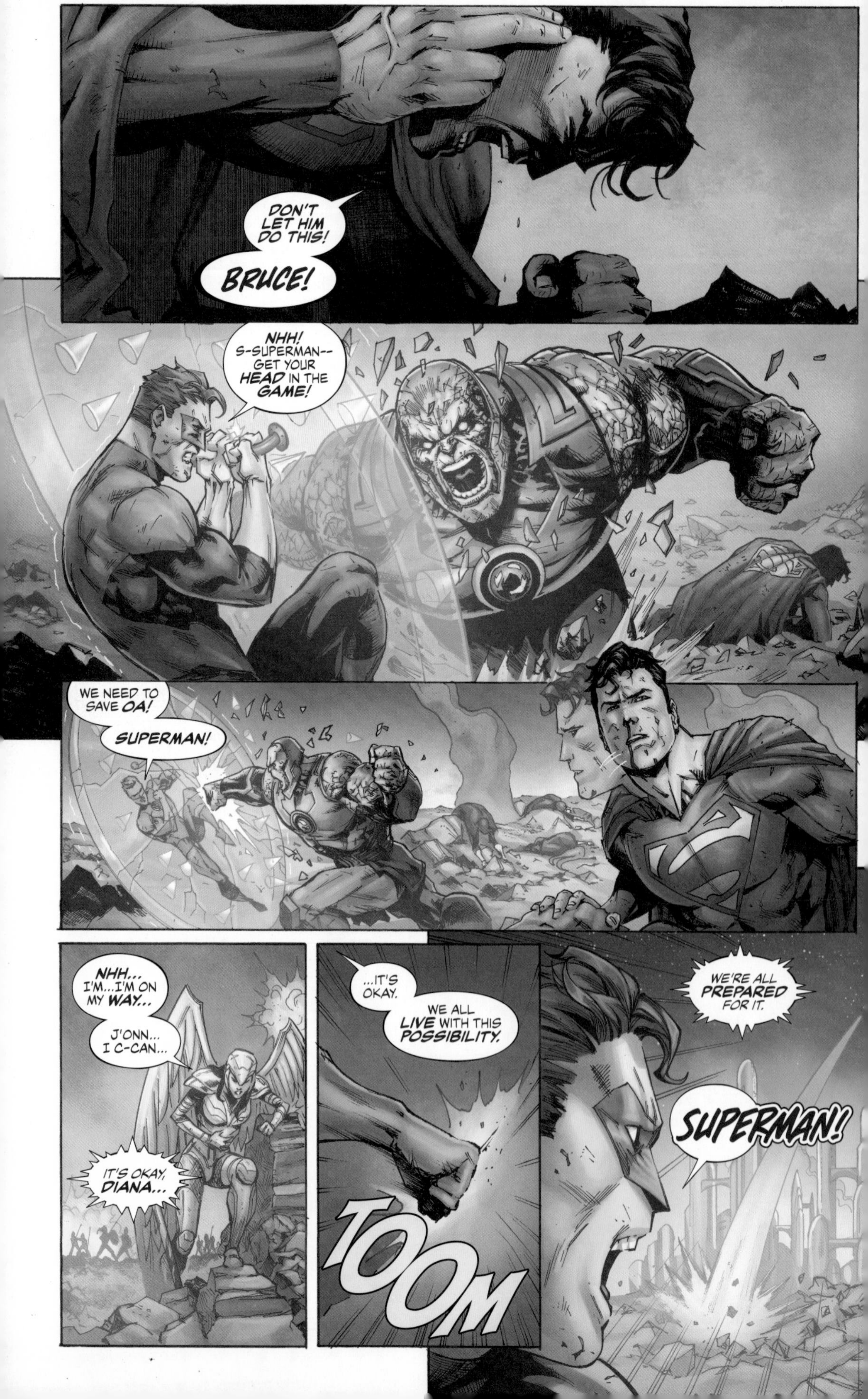
DON'T LET HIM DO THIS!
BRUCE!
NHH! S-SUPERMAN-- GET YOUR HEAD IN THE GAME!
WE NEED TO SAVE OA!
SUPERMAN!
NHH... I'M...I'M ON MY WAY...
J'ONN... I C-CAN...
IT'S OKAY, DIANA...
...IT'S OKAY.
WE ALL LIVE WITH THIS POSSIBILITY.
TOOM
WE'RE ALL PREPARED FOR IT.
SUPERMAN!

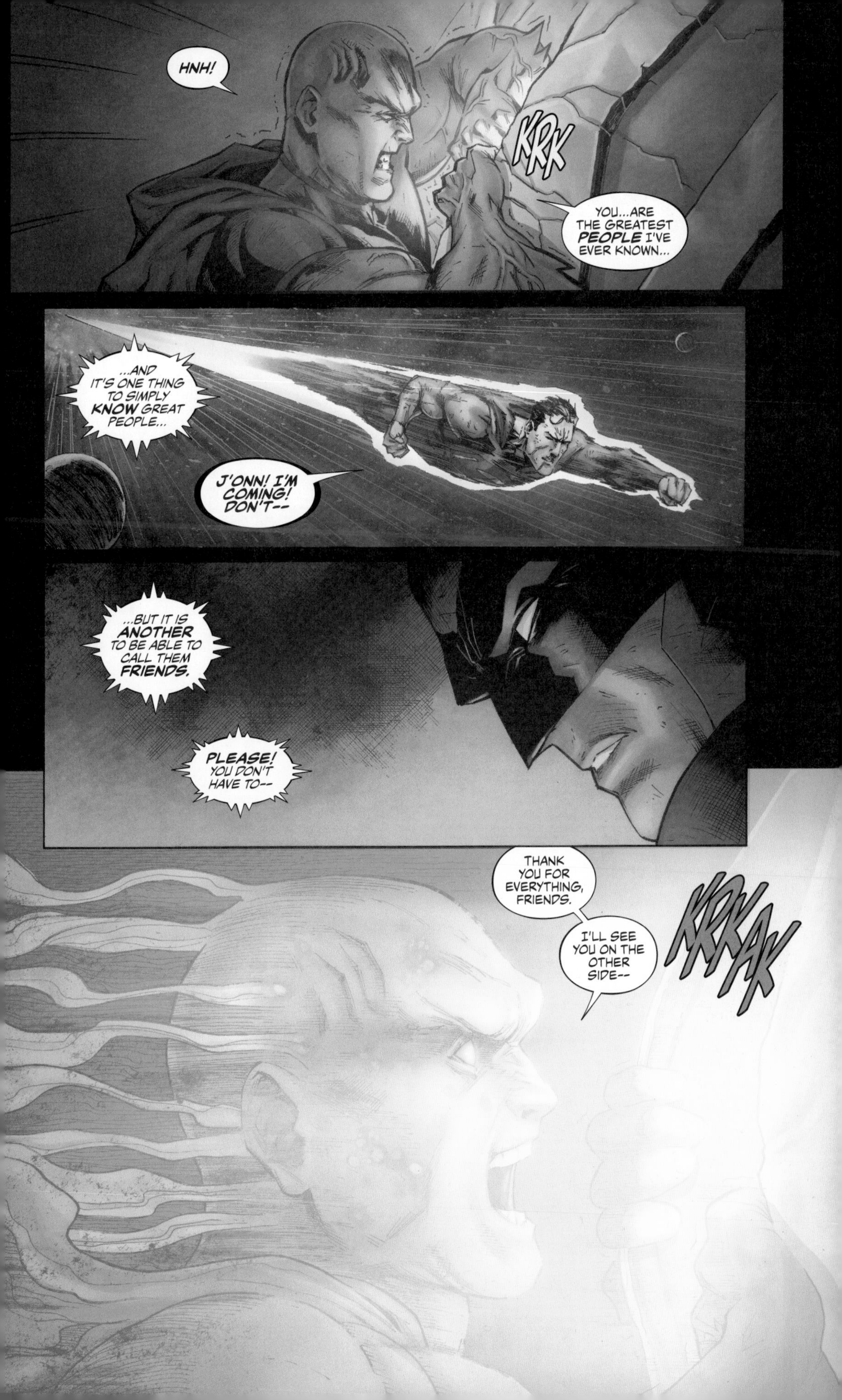
HNH!
KRK
YOU...ARE THE GREATEST PEOPLE I'VE EVER KNOWN...
...AND IT'S ONE THING TO SIMPLY KNOW GREAT PEOPLE...
J'ONN! I'M COMING! DON'T--
...BUT IT IS ANOTHER TO BE ABLE TO CALL THEM FRIENDS.
PLEASE! YOU DON'T HAVE TO--
THANK YOU FOR EVERYTHING, FRIENDS.
I'LL SEE YOU ON THE OTHER SIDE--
KRKAK

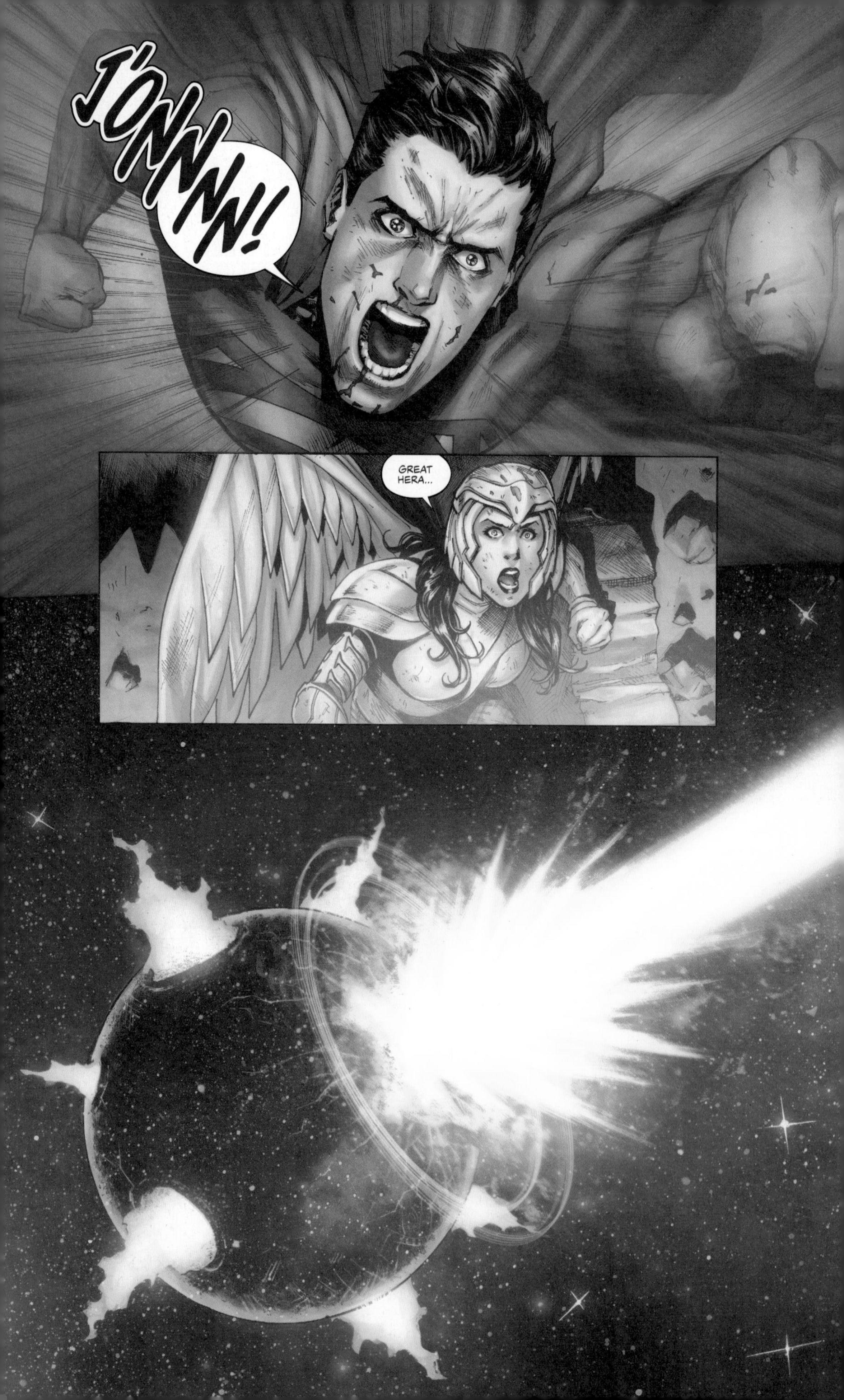
J'ONNNN!
GREAT HERA...

NOW.

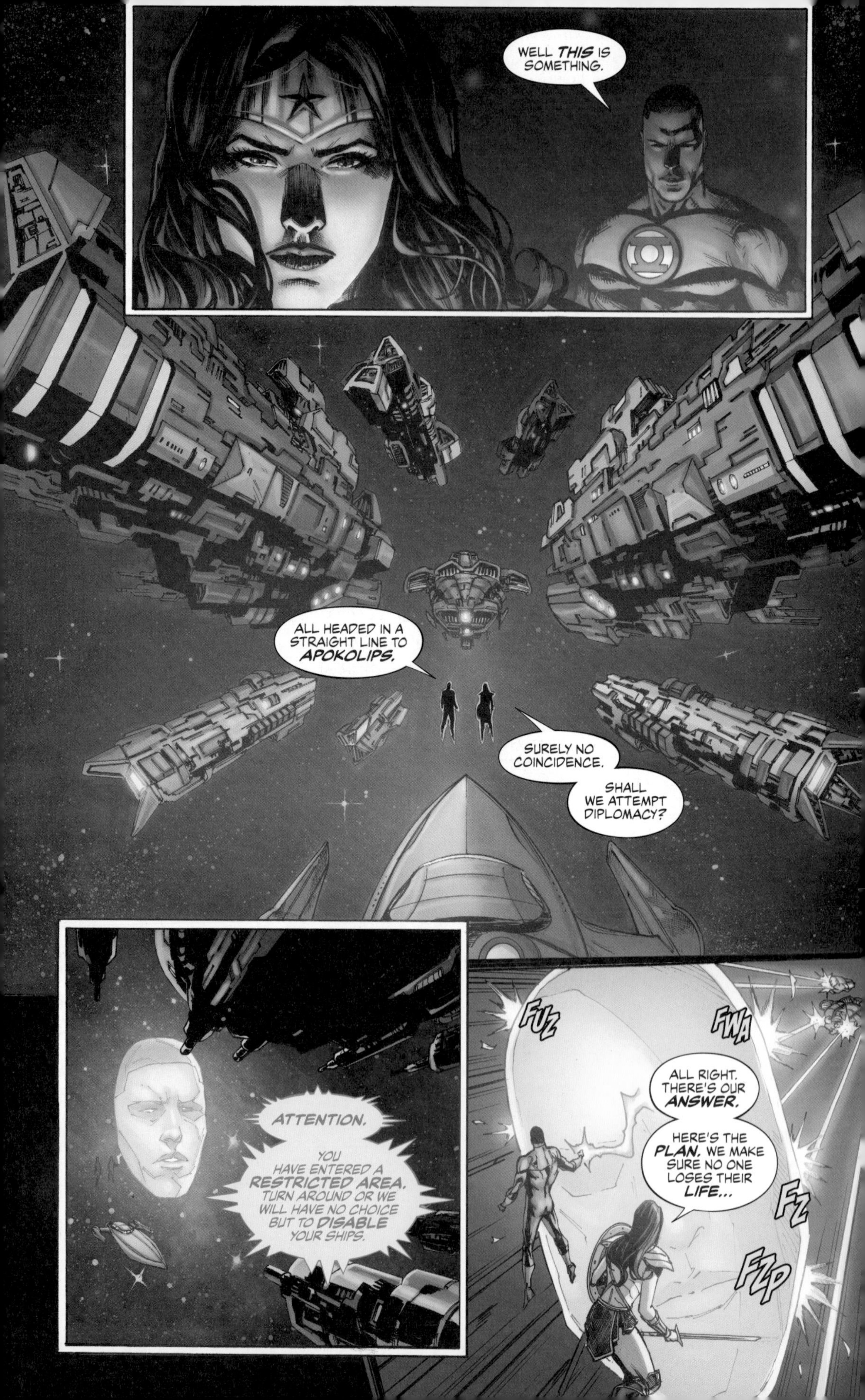
WELL THIS IS SOMETHING.
ALL HEADED IN A STRAIGHT LINE TO APOKOLIPS.
SURELY NO COINCIDENCE.
SHALL WE ATTEMPT DIPLOMACY?
ATTENTION.
YOU HAVE ENTERED A RESTRICTED AREA. TURN AROUND OR WE WILL HAVE NO CHOICE BUT TO DISABLE YOUR SHIPS.
FUZ
FWA
ALL RIGHT. THERE'S OUR ANSWER.
HERE'S THE PLAN. WE MAKE SURE NO ONE LOSES THEIR LIFE...
FZ
FZP

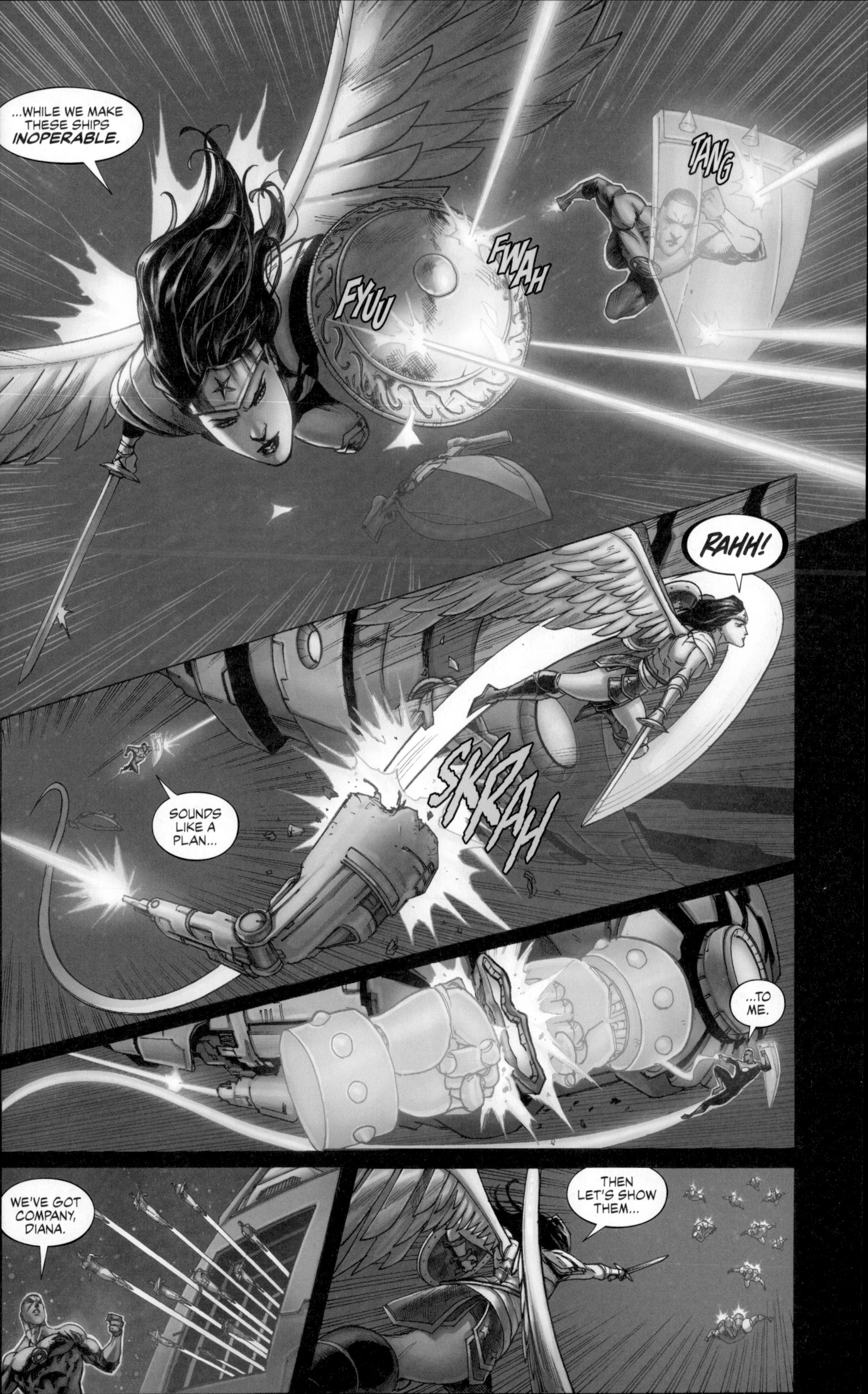
...WHILE WE MAKE THESE SHIPS *INOPERABLE.*
TANG
FWAH
FYUU
RAHH!
SOUNDS LIKE A PLAN...
SKRAH
...TO ME.
WE'VE GOT COMPANY, DIANA.
THEN LET'S SHOW THEM...

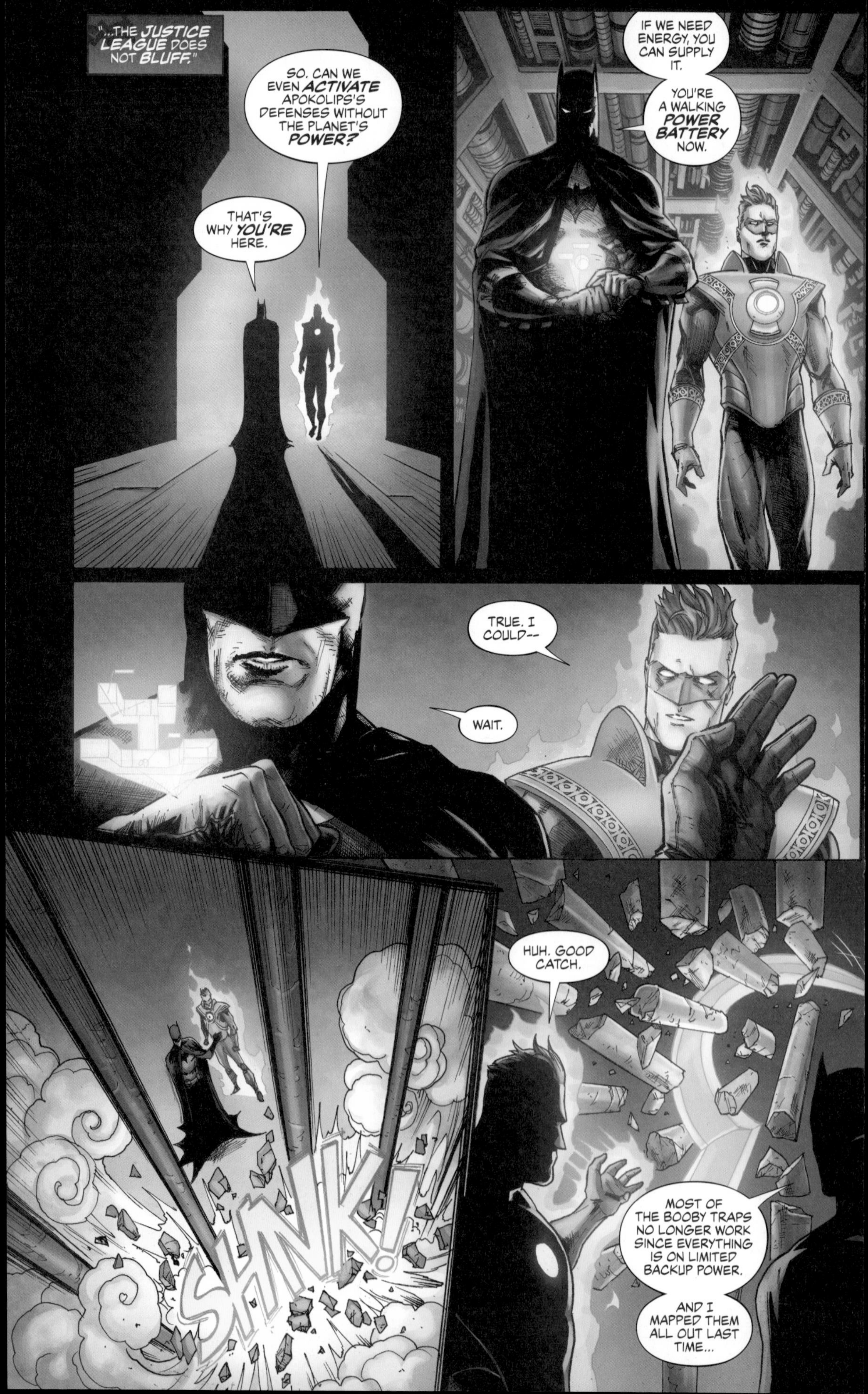
"...THE JUSTICE LEAGUE DOES NOT BLUFF."
SO. CAN WE EVEN ACTIVATE APOKOLIPS'S DEFENSES WITHOUT THE PLANET'S POWER?
THAT'S WHY YOU'RE HERE.
IF WE NEED ENERGY, YOU CAN SUPPLY IT.
YOU'RE A WALKING POWER BATTERY NOW.
TRUE. I COULD--
WAIT.
SHNK!
HUH. GOOD CATCH.
MOST OF THE BOOBY TRAPS NO LONGER WORK SINCE EVERYTHING IS ON LIMITED BACKUP POWER.
AND I MAPPED THEM ALL OUT LAST TIME...

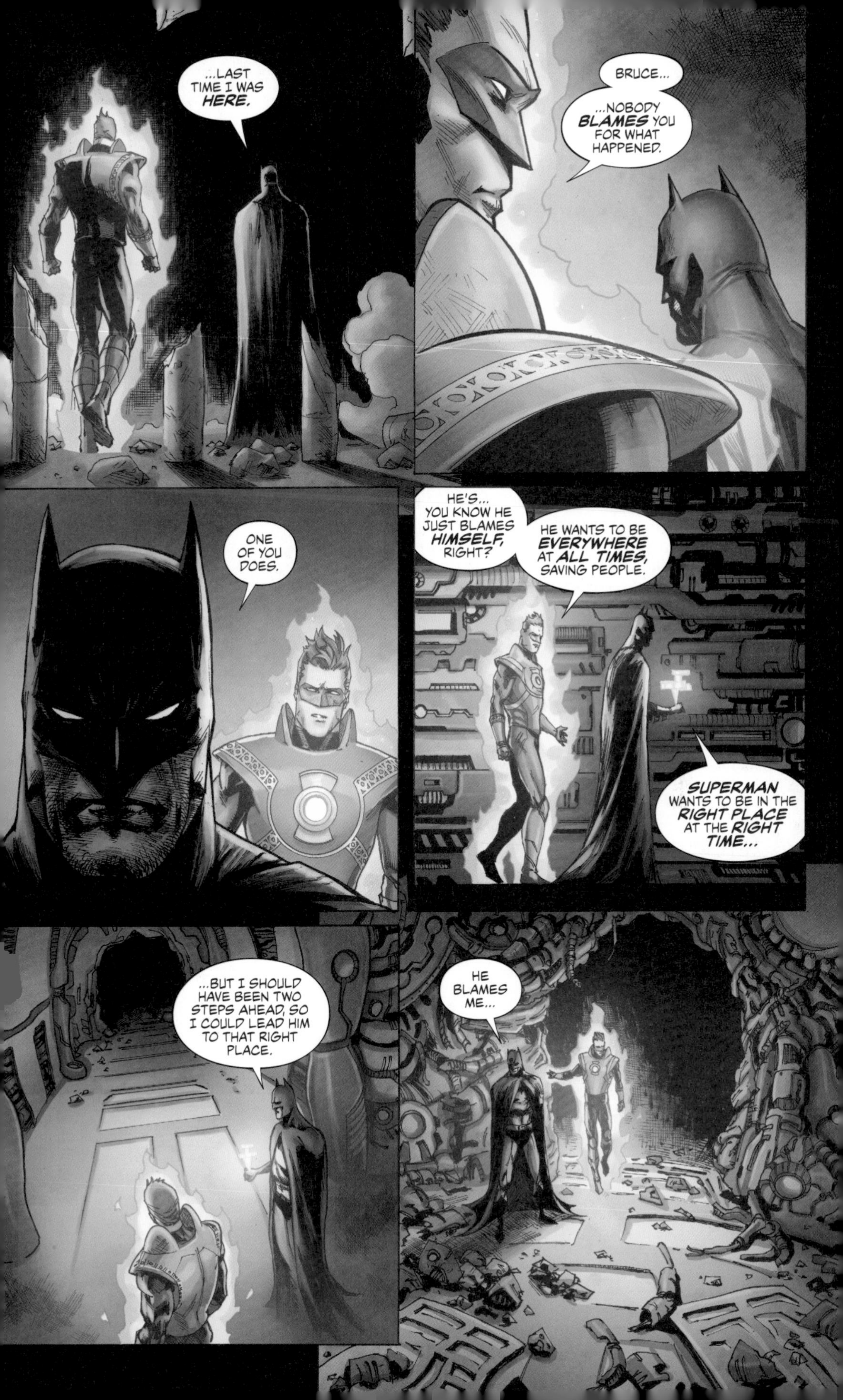
...LAST TIME I WAS HERE.
BRUCE...
...NOBODY BLAMES YOU FOR WHAT HAPPENED.
ONE OF YOU DOES.
HE'S... YOU KNOW HE JUST BLAMES HIMSELF, RIGHT?
HE WANTS TO BE EVERYWHERE AT ALL TIMES, SAVING PEOPLE.
SUPERMAN WANTS TO BE IN THE RIGHT PLACE AT THE RIGHT TIME...
...BUT I SHOULD HAVE BEEN TWO STEPS AHEAD, SO I COULD LEAD HIM TO THAT RIGHT PLACE.
HE BLAMES ME...

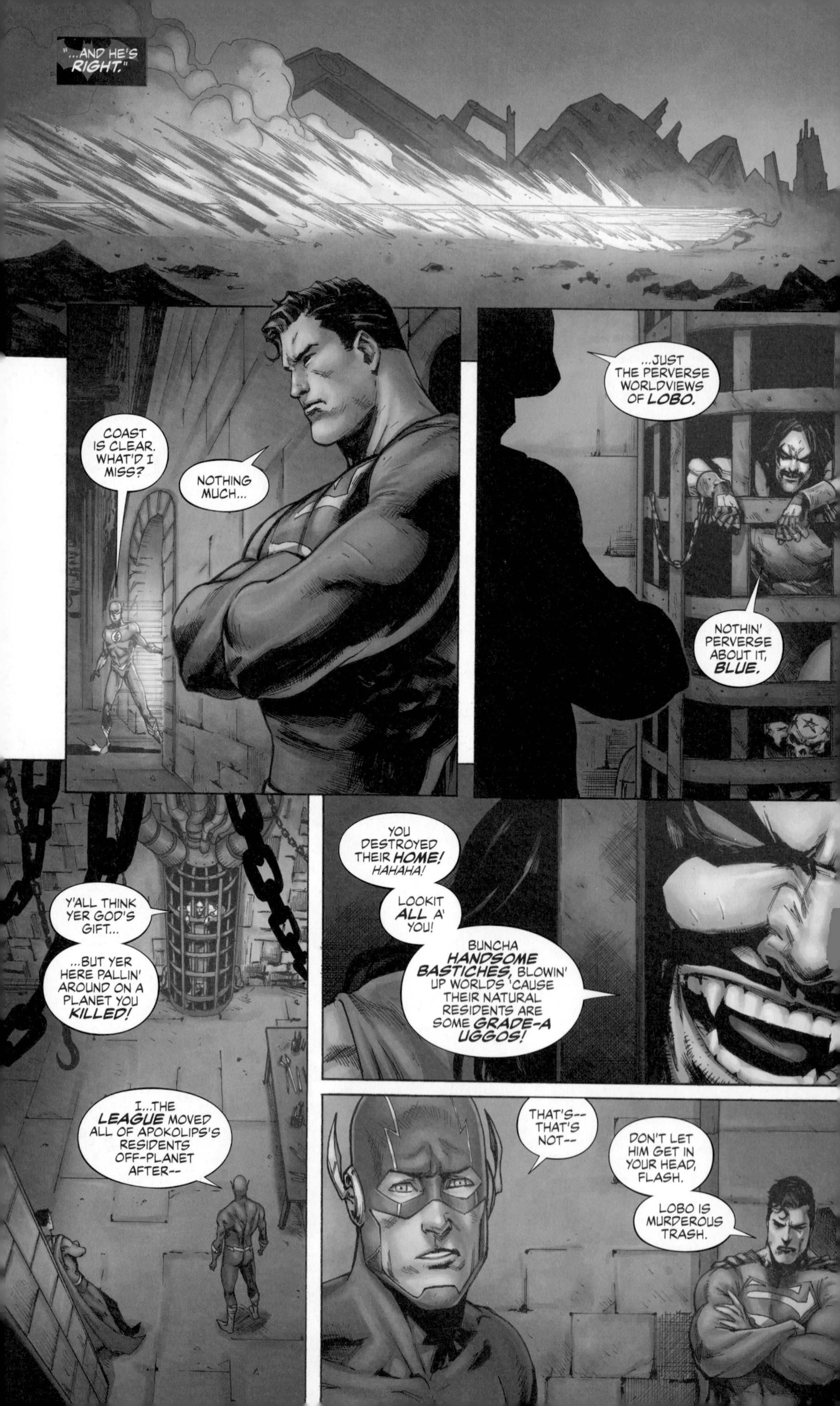
"...AND HE'S RIGHT."
COAST IS CLEAR. WHAT'D I MISS?
NOTHING MUCH...
...JUST THE PERVERSE WORLDVIEWS OF LOBO.
NOTHIN' PERVERSE ABOUT IT, BLUE.
Y'ALL THINK YER GOD'S GIFT...
...BUT YER HERE PALLIN' AROUND ON A PLANET YOU KILLED!
YOU DESTROYED THEIR HOME! HAHAHA!
LOOKIT ALL A' YOU!
BUNCHA HANDSOME BASTICHES, BLOWIN' UP WORLDS 'CAUSE THEIR NATURAL RESIDENTS ARE SOME GRADE-A UGGOS!
I...THE LEAGUE MOVED ALL OF APOKOLIPS'S RESIDENTS OFF-PLANET AFTER--
THAT'S--THAT'S NOT--
DON'T LET HIM GET IN YOUR HEAD, FLASH.
LOBO IS MURDEROUS TRASH.

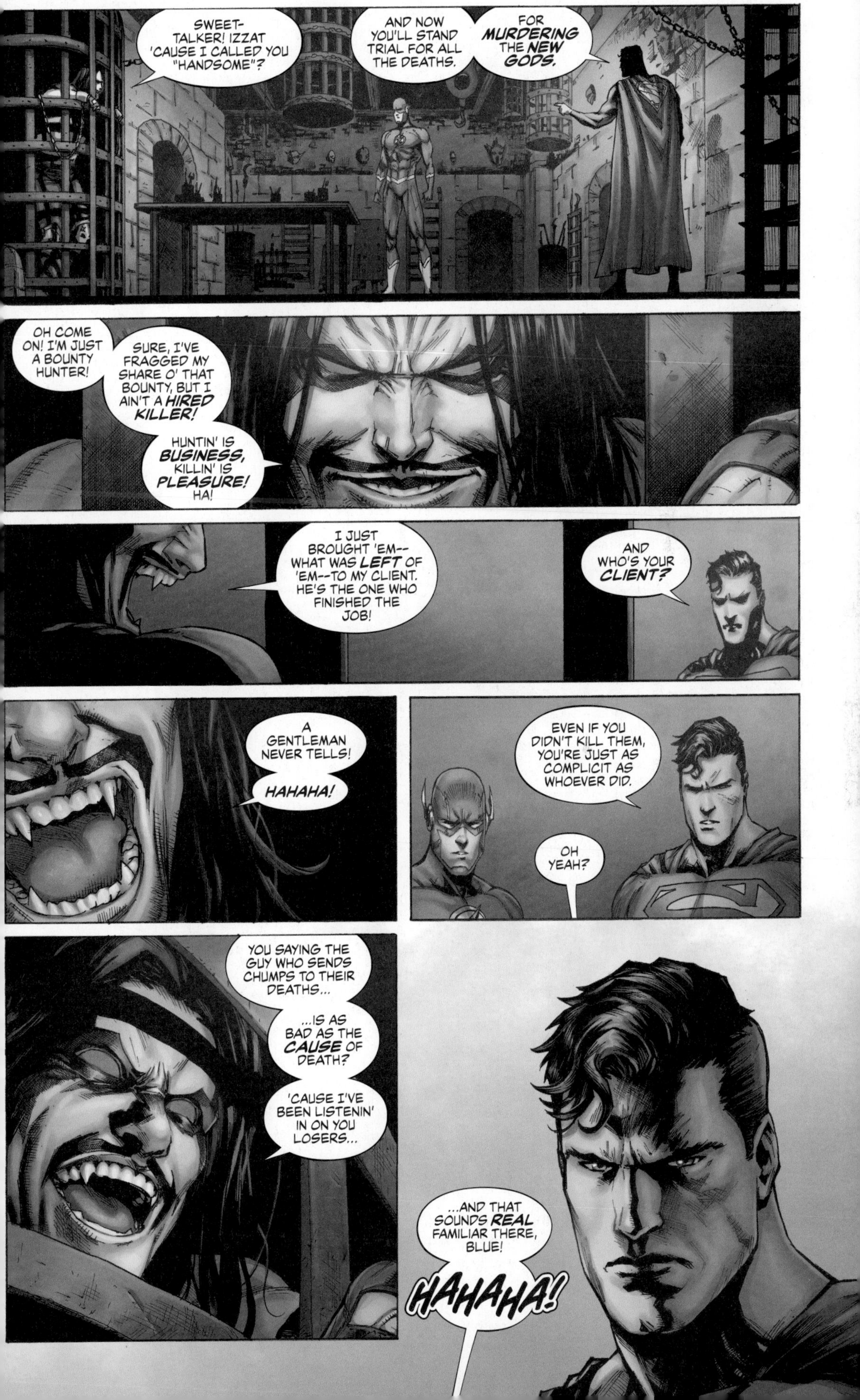
SWEET-TALKER! IZZAT 'CAUSE I CALLED YOU "HANDSOME"?
AND NOW YOU'LL STAND TRIAL FOR ALL THE DEATHS.
FOR MURDERING THE NEW GODS.
OH COME ON! I'M JUST A BOUNTY HUNTER!
SURE, I'VE FRAGGED MY SHARE O' THAT BOUNTY, BUT I AIN'T A HIRED KILLER!
HUNTIN' IS BUSINESS, KILLIN' IS PLEASURE! HA!
I JUST BROUGHT 'EM--WHAT WAS LEFT OF 'EM--TO MY CLIENT. HE'S THE ONE WHO FINISHED THE JOB!
AND WHO'S YOUR CLIENT?
A GENTLEMAN NEVER TELLS!
HAHAHA!
EVEN IF YOU DIDN'T KILL THEM, YOU'RE JUST AS COMPLICIT AS WHOEVER DID.
OH YEAH?
YOU SAYING THE GUY WHO SENDS CHUMPS TO THEIR DEATHS...
...IS AS BAD AS THE CAUSE OF DEATH?
'CAUSE I'VE BEEN LISTENIN' IN ON YOU LOSERS...
...AND THAT SOUNDS REAL FAMILIAR THERE, BLUE!
HAHAHA!

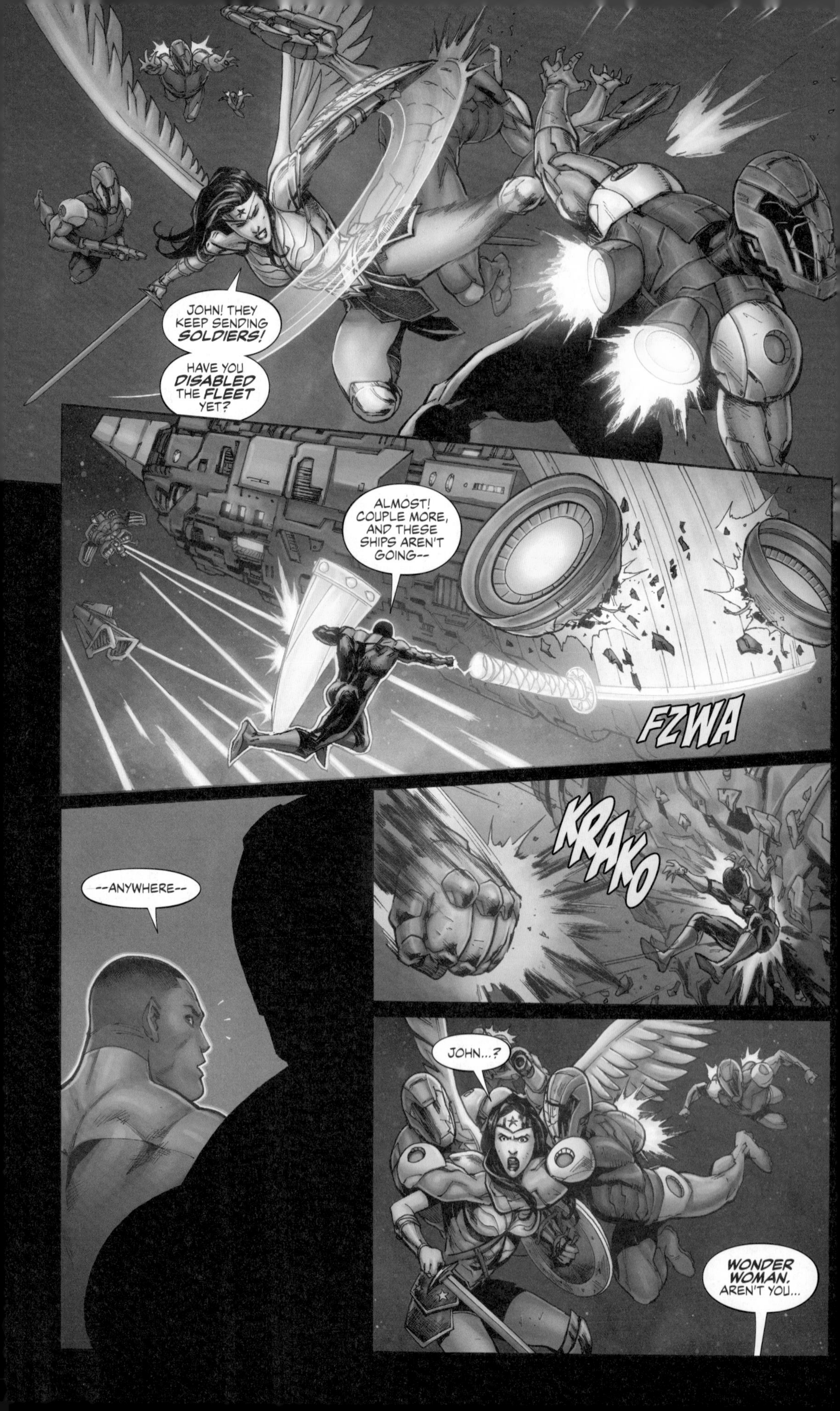
JOHN! THEY KEEP SENDING SOLDIERS!
HAVE YOU DISABLED THE FLEET YET?
ALMOST! COUPLE MORE, AND THESE SHIPS AREN'T GOING--
FZWA
--ANYWHERE--
KRAKO
JOHN...?
WONDER WOMAN. AREN'T YOU...

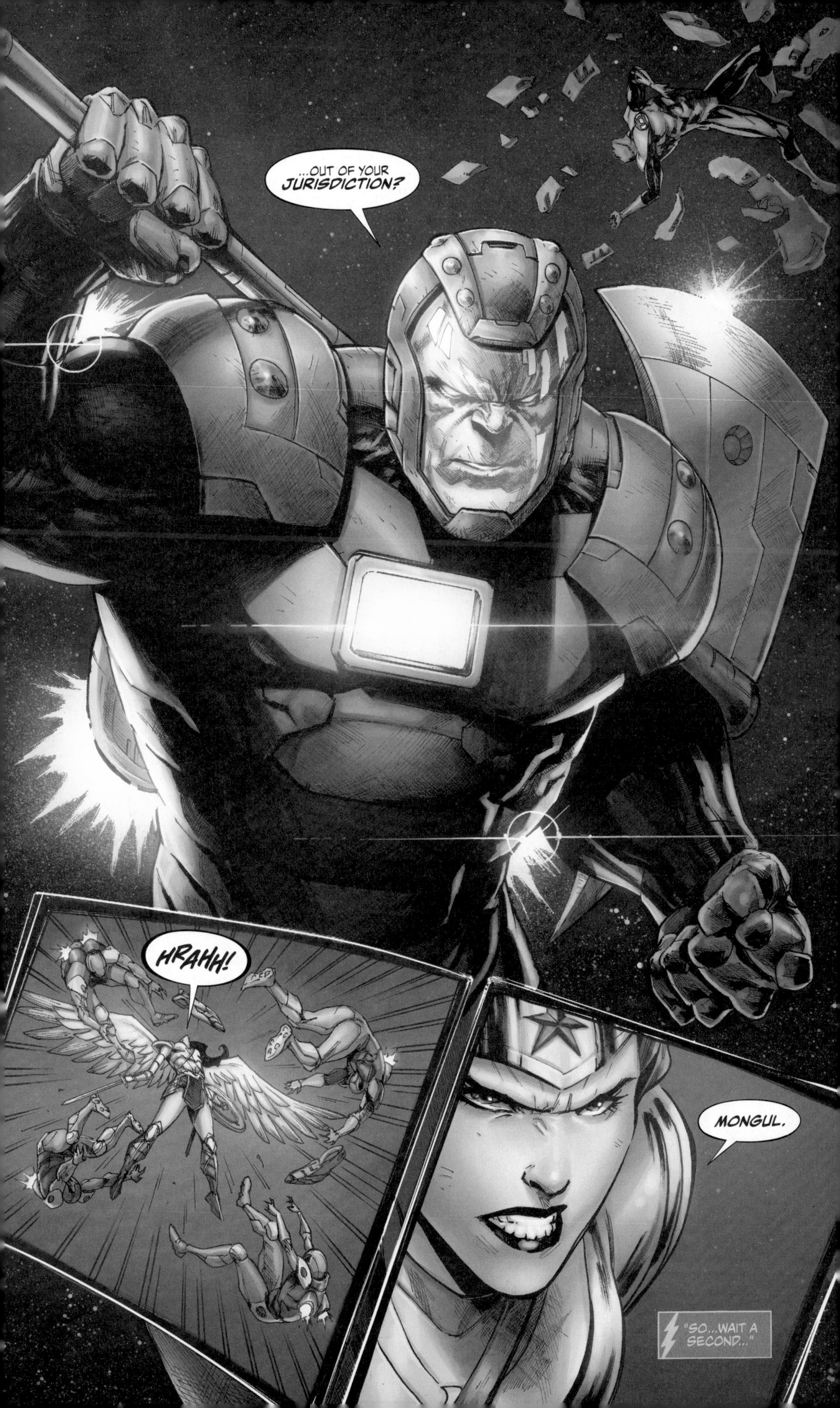
...OUT OF YOUR JURISDICTION?
HRAHH!
MONGUL.
"SO...WAIT A SECOND..."

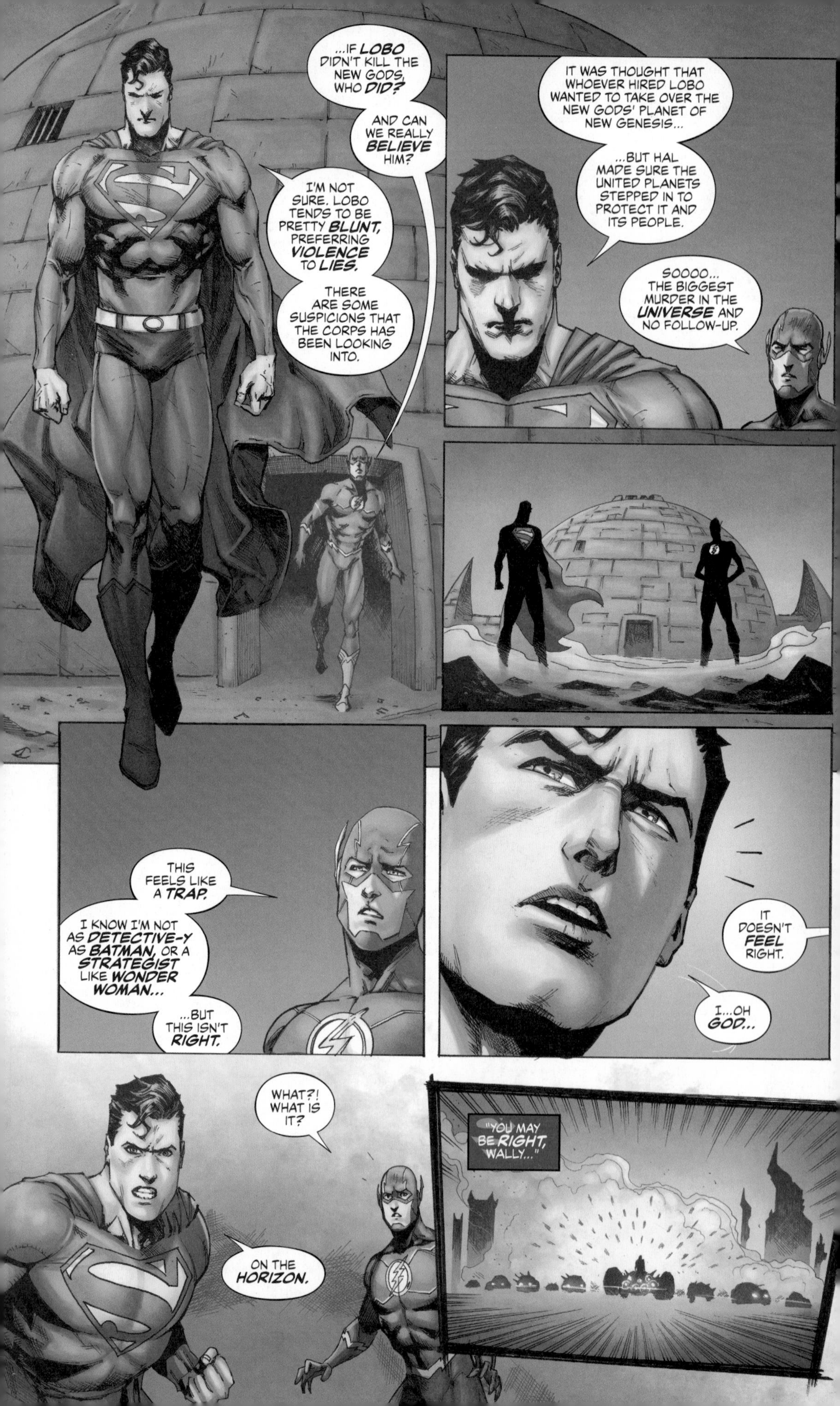

...IF LOBO DIDN'T KILL THE NEW GODS, WHO DID?
AND CAN WE REALLY BELIEVE HIM?
I'M NOT SURE. LOBO TENDS TO BE PRETTY BLUNT, PREFERRING VIOLENCE TO LIES.
THERE ARE SOME SUSPICIONS THAT THE CORPS HAS BEEN LOOKING INTO.
IT WAS THOUGHT THAT WHOEVER HIRED LOBO WANTED TO TAKE OVER THE NEW GODS' PLANET OF NEW GENESIS...
...BUT HAL MADE SURE THE UNITED PLANETS STEPPED IN TO PROTECT IT AND ITS PEOPLE.
SOOOO... THE BIGGEST MURDER IN THE UNIVERSE AND NO FOLLOW-UP.
THIS FEELS LIKE A TRAP.
I KNOW I'M NOT AS DETECTIVE-Y AS BATMAN, OR A STRATEGIST LIKE WONDER WOMAN...
...BUT THIS ISN'T RIGHT.
IT DOESN'T FEEL RIGHT.
I...OH GOD...
WHAT?! WHAT IS IT?
ON THE HORIZON.
"YOU MAY BE RIGHT, WALLY..."

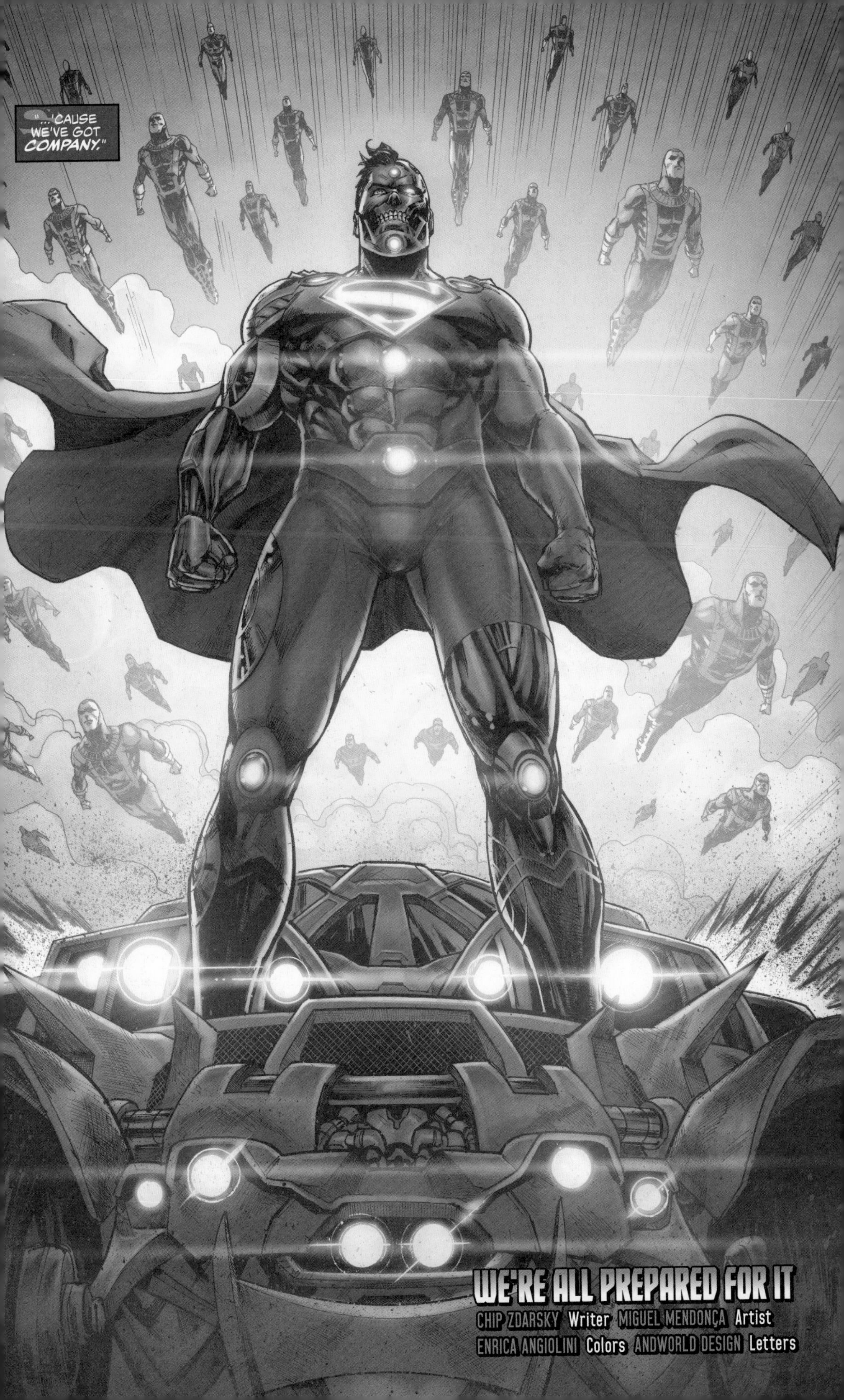
"...'CAUSE WE'VE GOT COMPANY."
WE'RE ALL PREPARED FOR IT
CHIP ZDARSKY Writer MIGUEL MENDONÇA Artist
ENRICA ANGIOLINI Colors ANDWORLD DESIGN Letters

Justice League: Last Ride #5 cover art by
DARICK ROBERTSON and **DIEGO RODRIGUEZ**

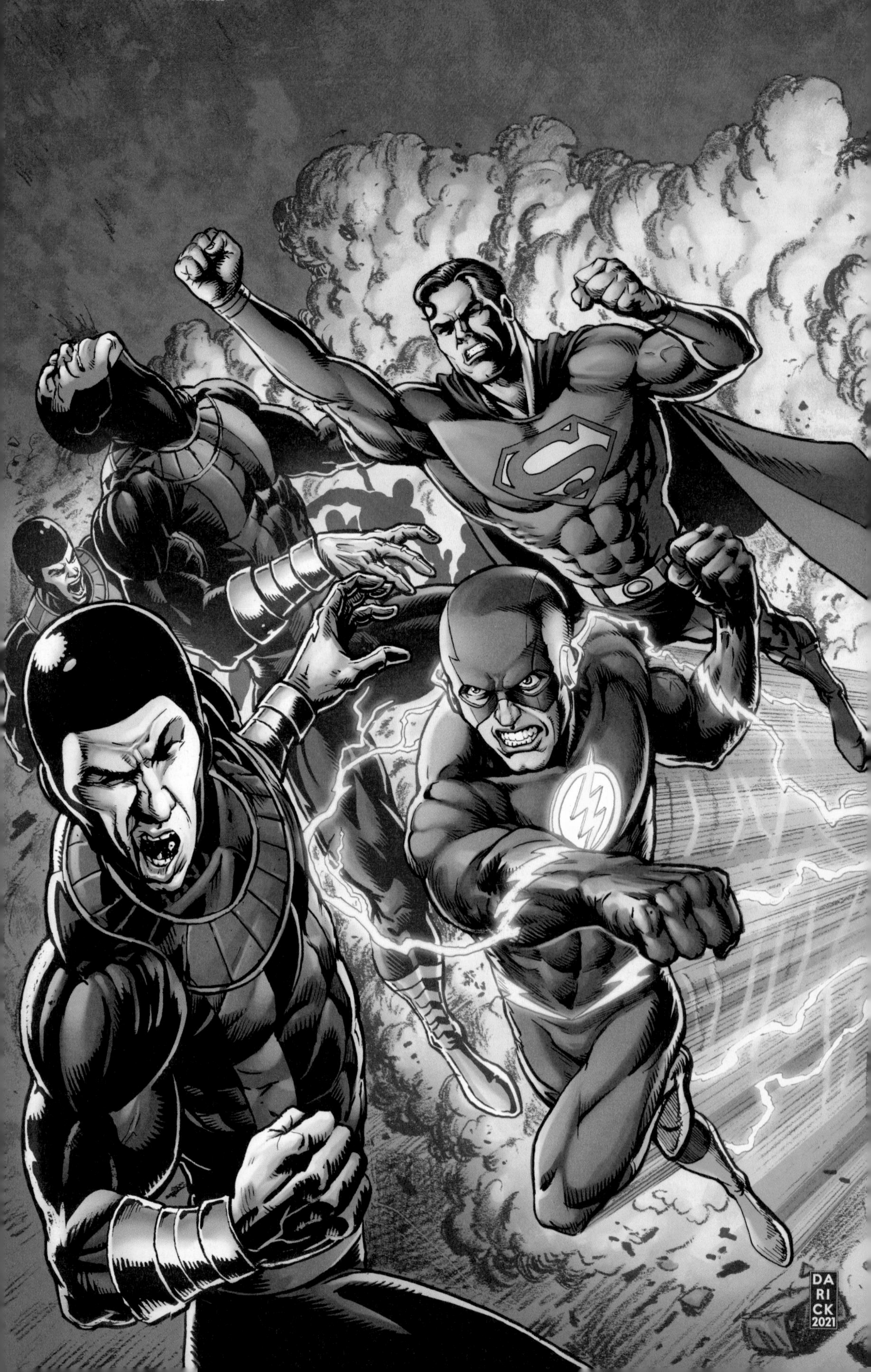
DA
RI
CK
2021

NOW.

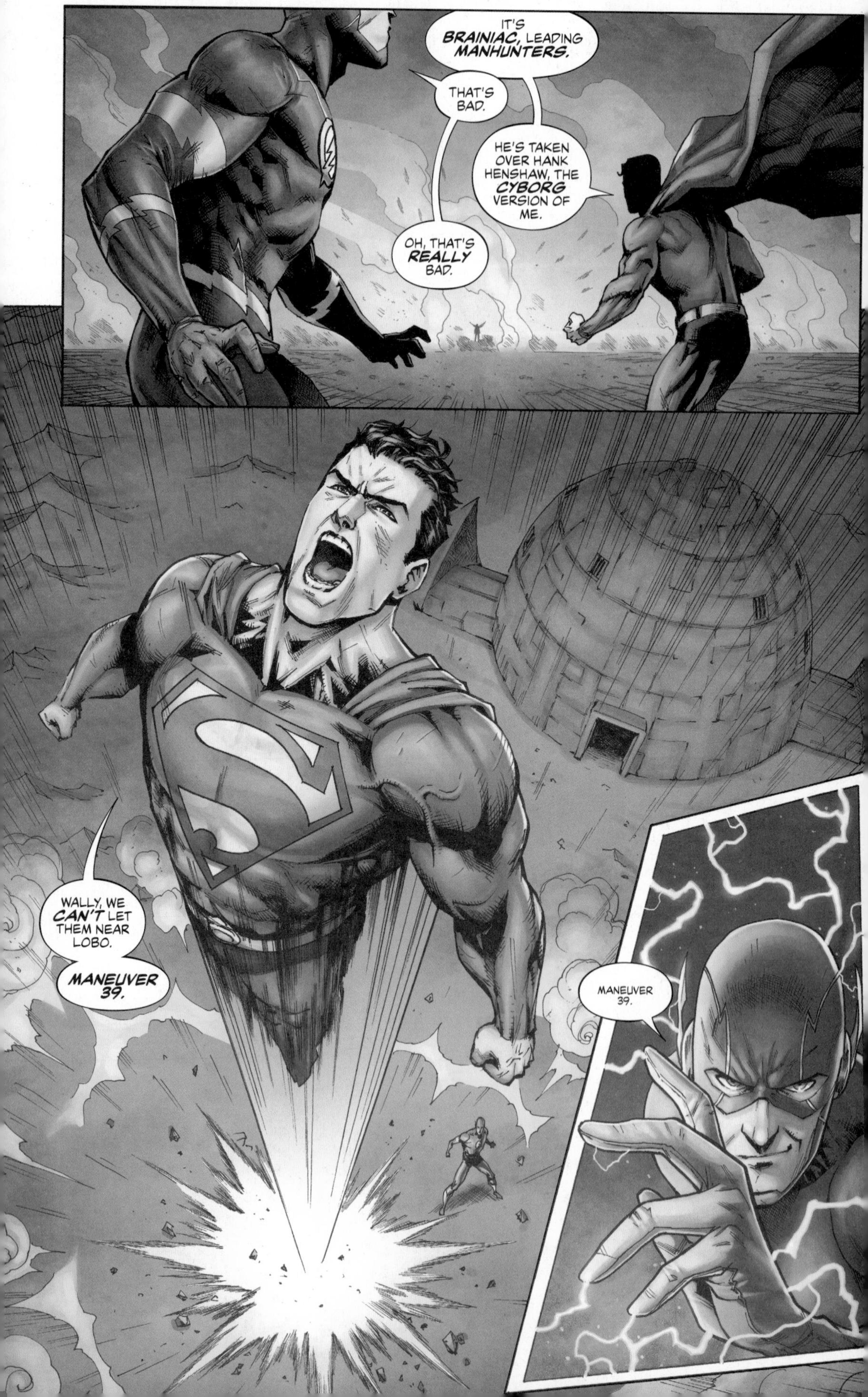

IT'S BRAINIAC, LEADING MANHUNTERS.
THAT'S BAD.
HE'S TAKEN OVER HANK HENSHAW, THE CYBORG VERSION OF ME.
OH, THAT'S REALLY BAD.
WALLY, WE CAN'T LET THEM NEAR LOBO.
MANEUVER 39.
MANEUVER 39.

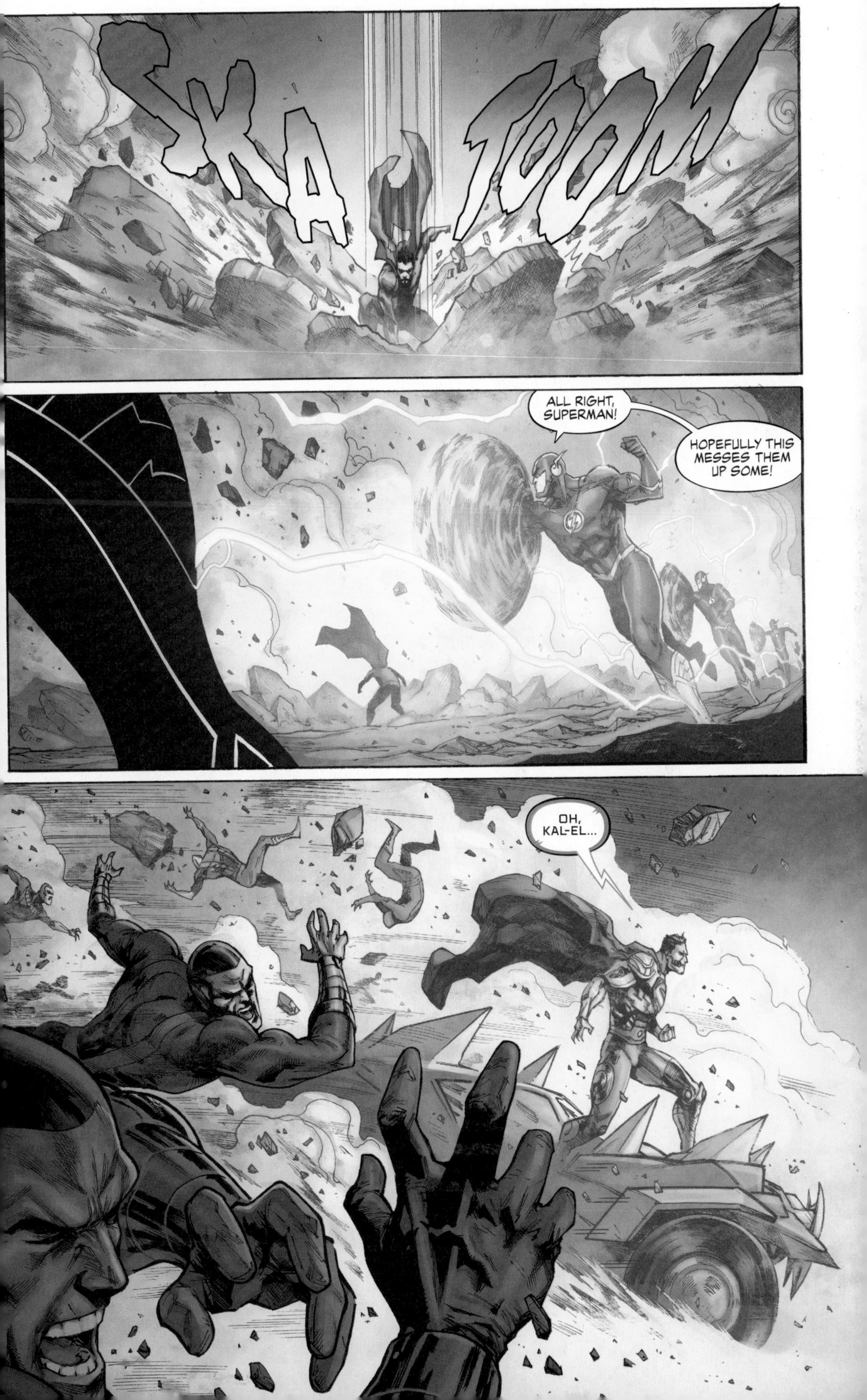
SKA TOOM
ALL RIGHT, SUPERMAN!
HOPEFULLY THIS MESSES THEM UP SOME!
OH, KAL-EL...

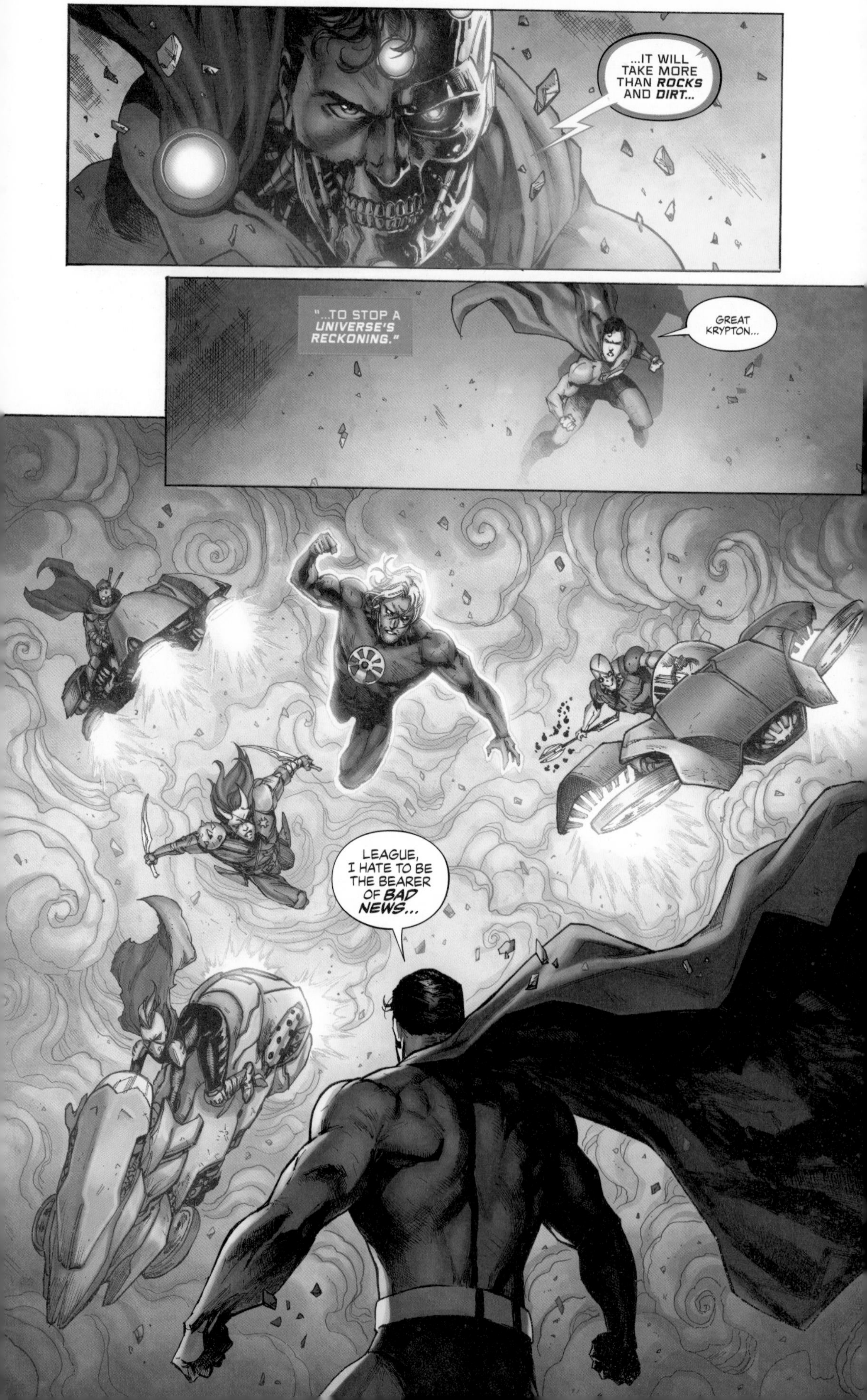
...IT WILL TAKE MORE THAN ROCKS AND DIRT...
"...TO STOP A UNIVERSE'S RECKONING."
GREAT KRYPTON...
LEAGUE, I HATE TO BE THE BEARER OF BAD NEWS...

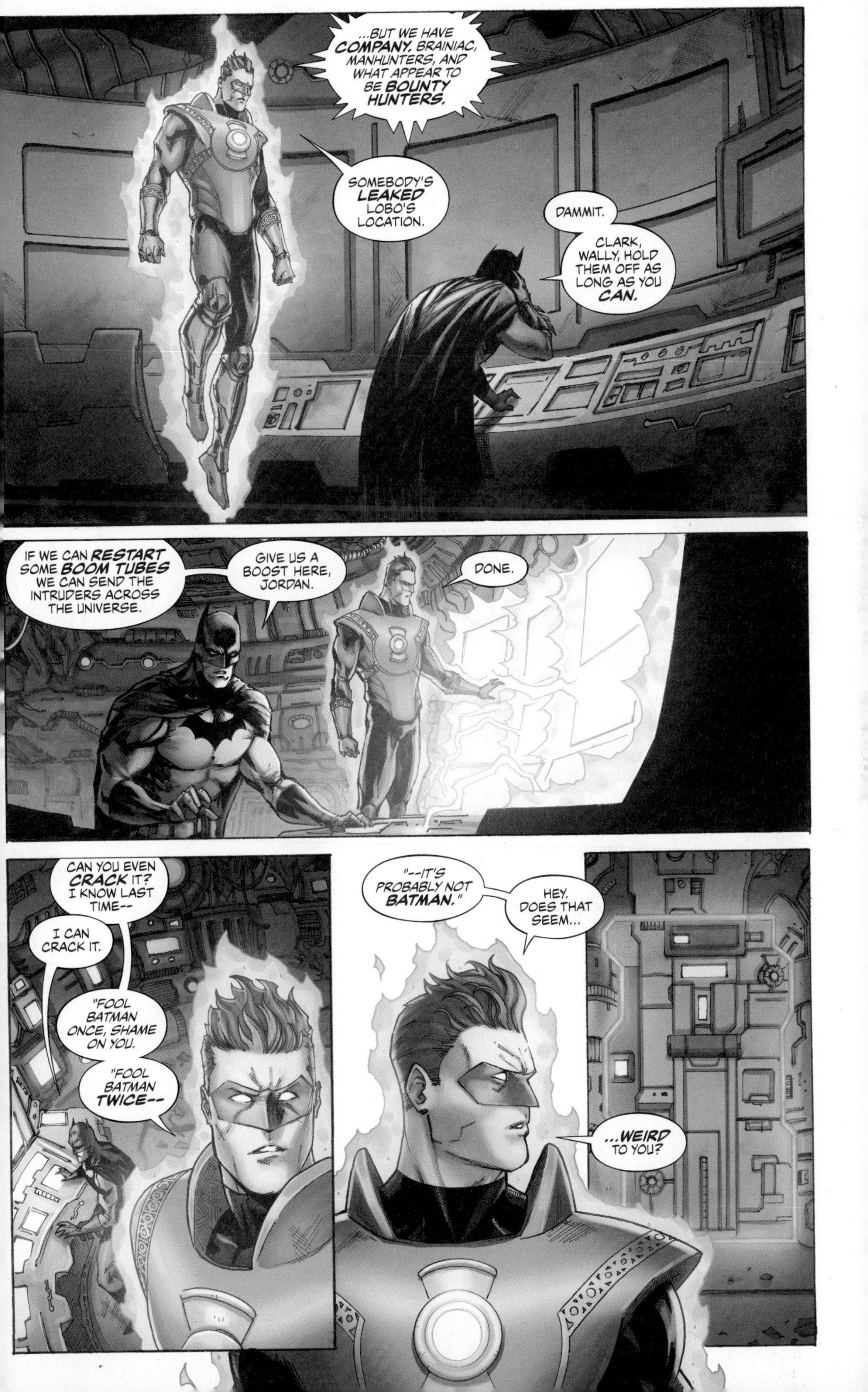
...BUT WE HAVE COMPANY. BRAINIAC, MANHUNTERS, AND WHAT APPEAR TO BE BOUNTY HUNTERS.
SOMEBODY'S LEAKED LOBO'S LOCATION.
DAMMIT.
CLARK, WALLY, HOLD THEM OFF AS LONG AS YOU CAN.
IF WE CAN RESTART SOME BOOM TUBES WE CAN SEND THE INTRUDERS ACROSS THE UNIVERSE.
GIVE US A BOOST HERE, JORDAN.
DONE.
CAN YOU EVEN CRACK IT? I KNOW LAST TIME--
I CAN CRACK IT.
"FOOL BATMAN ONCE, SHAME ON YOU.
"FOOL BATMAN TWICE--
"--IT'S PROBABLY NOT BATMAN."
HEY. DOES THAT SEEM...
...WEIRD TO YOU?

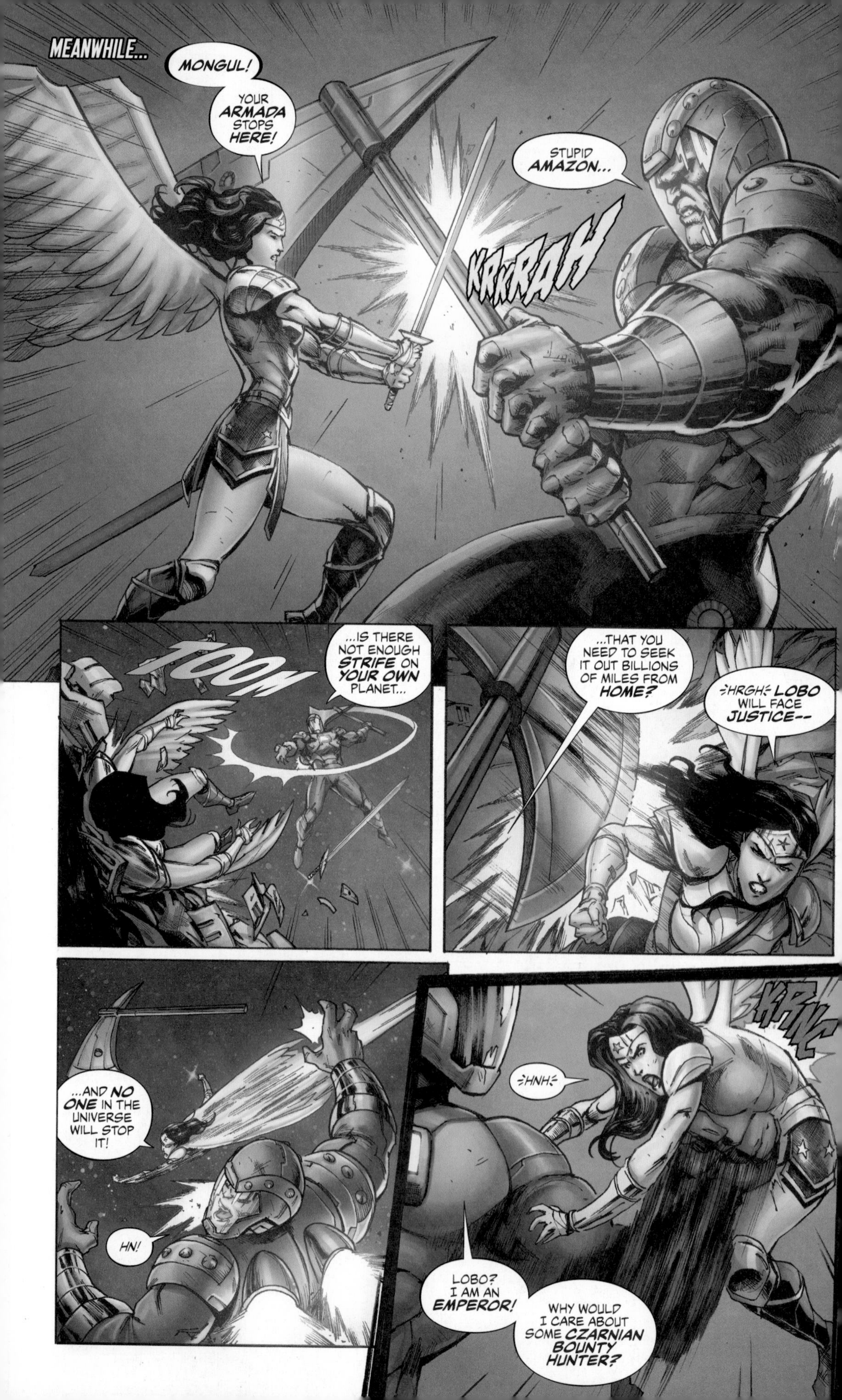
MEANWHILE...
MONGUL!
YOUR ARMADA STOPS HERE!
STUPID AMAZON...
KRKRAAH
TOOM
...IS THERE NOT ENOUGH STRIFE ON YOUR OWN PLANET...
...THAT YOU NEED TO SEEK IT OUT BILLIONS OF MILES FROM HOME?
HRGH LOBO WILL FACE JUSTICE--
...AND NO ONE IN THE UNIVERSE WILL STOP IT!
HN!
KRNC
HNH
LOBO? I AM AN EMPEROR!
WHY WOULD I CARE ABOUT SOME CZARNIAN BOUNTY HUNTER?

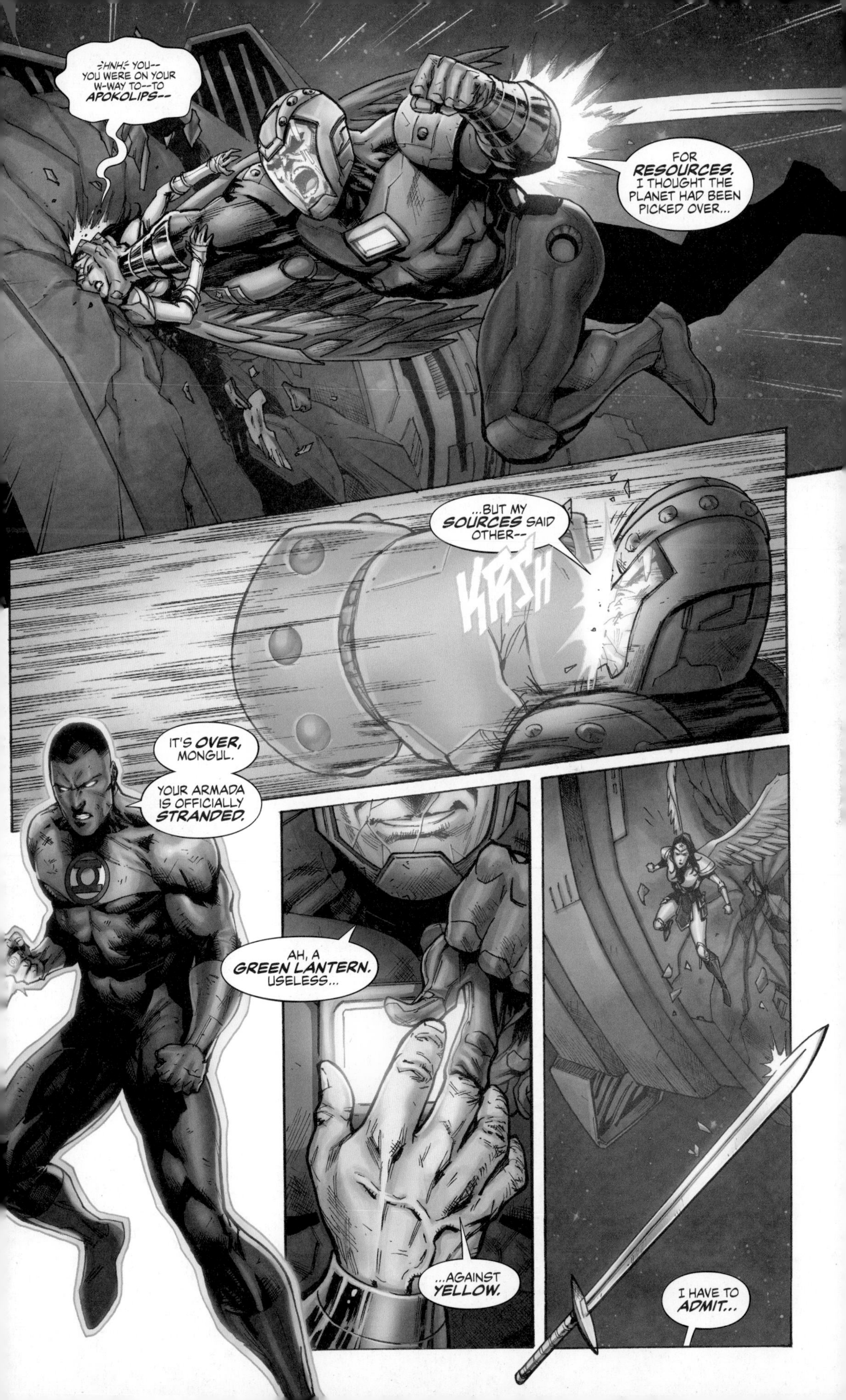

≈HNH≈ YOU--
YOU WERE ON YOUR
W-WAY TO--TO
APOKOLIPS--
FOR
RESOURCES.
I THOUGHT THE
PLANET HAD BEEN
PICKED OVER...
...BUT MY
SOURCES SAID
OTHER--
KRSH
IT'S OVER,
MONGUL.
YOUR ARMADA
IS OFFICIALLY
STRANDED.
AH, A
GREEN LANTERN.
USELESS...
...AGAINST
YELLOW.
I HAVE TO
ADMIT...

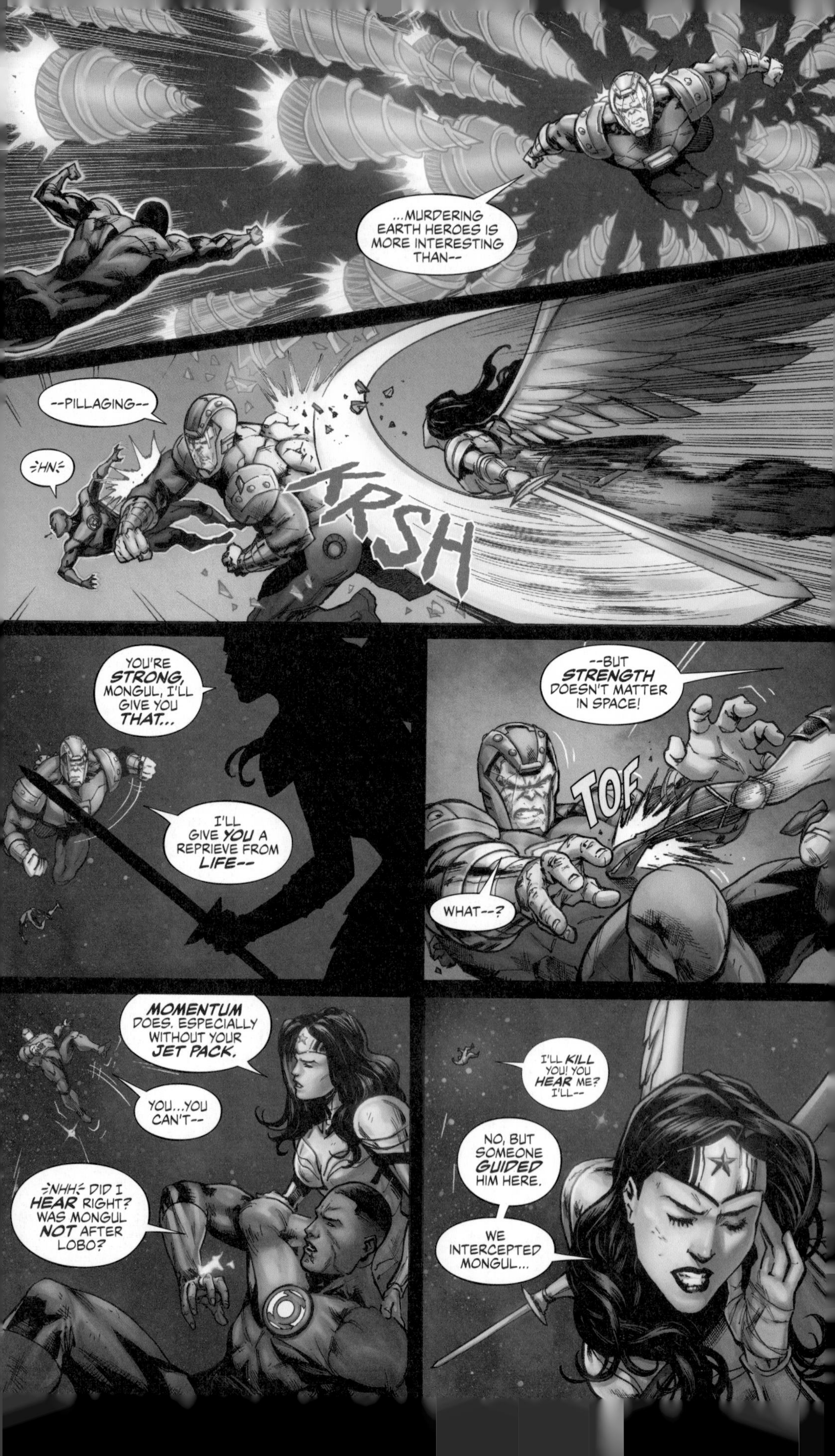
...MURDERING EARTH HEROES IS MORE INTERESTING THAN--
--PILLAGING--
HN
KRSH
YOU'RE STRONG, MONGUL, I'LL GIVE YOU THAT...
I'LL GIVE YOU A REPRIEVE FROM LIFE--
--BUT STRENGTH DOESN'T MATTER IN SPACE!
TOF
WHAT--?
MOMENTUM DOES, ESPECIALLY WITHOUT YOUR JET PACK.
YOU...YOU CAN'T--
NHH DID I HEAR RIGHT? WAS MONGUL NOT AFTER LOBO?
I'LL KILL YOU! YOU HEAR ME? I'LL--
NO, BUT SOMEONE GUIDED HIM HERE.
WE INTERCEPTED MONGUL...

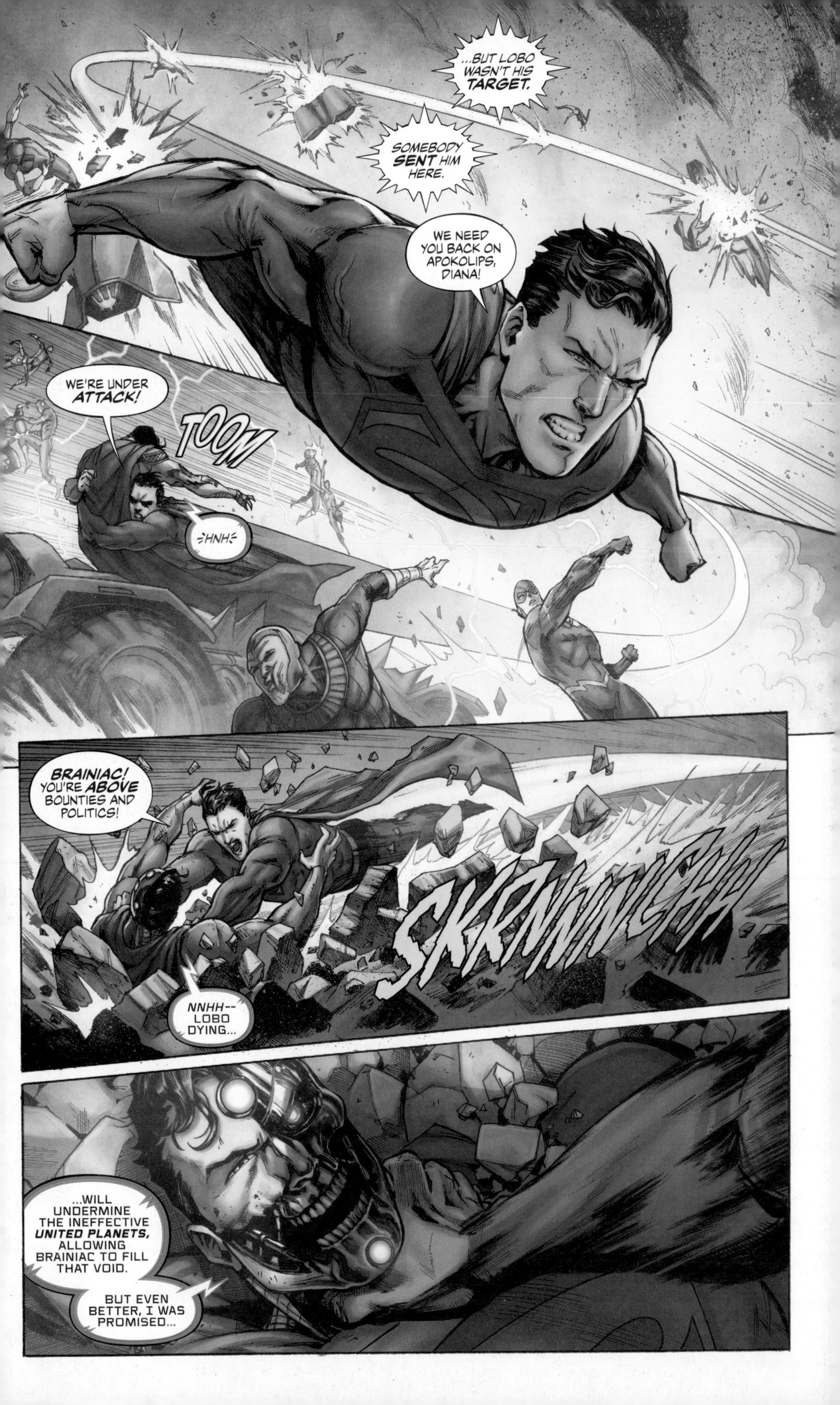

...BUT LOBO WASN'T HIS TARGET.
SOMEBODY SENT HIM HERE.
WE NEED YOU BACK ON APOKOLIPS, DIANA!
WE'RE UNDER ATTACK!
TOOM
HNH
BRAINIAC! YOU'RE ABOVE BOUNTIES AND POLITICS!
SKRNNNCHH
NNHH-- LOBO DYING...
...WILL UNDERMINE THE INEFFECTIVE UNITED PLANETS, ALLOWING BRAINIAC TO FILL THAT VOID.
BUT EVEN BETTER, I WAS PROMISED...

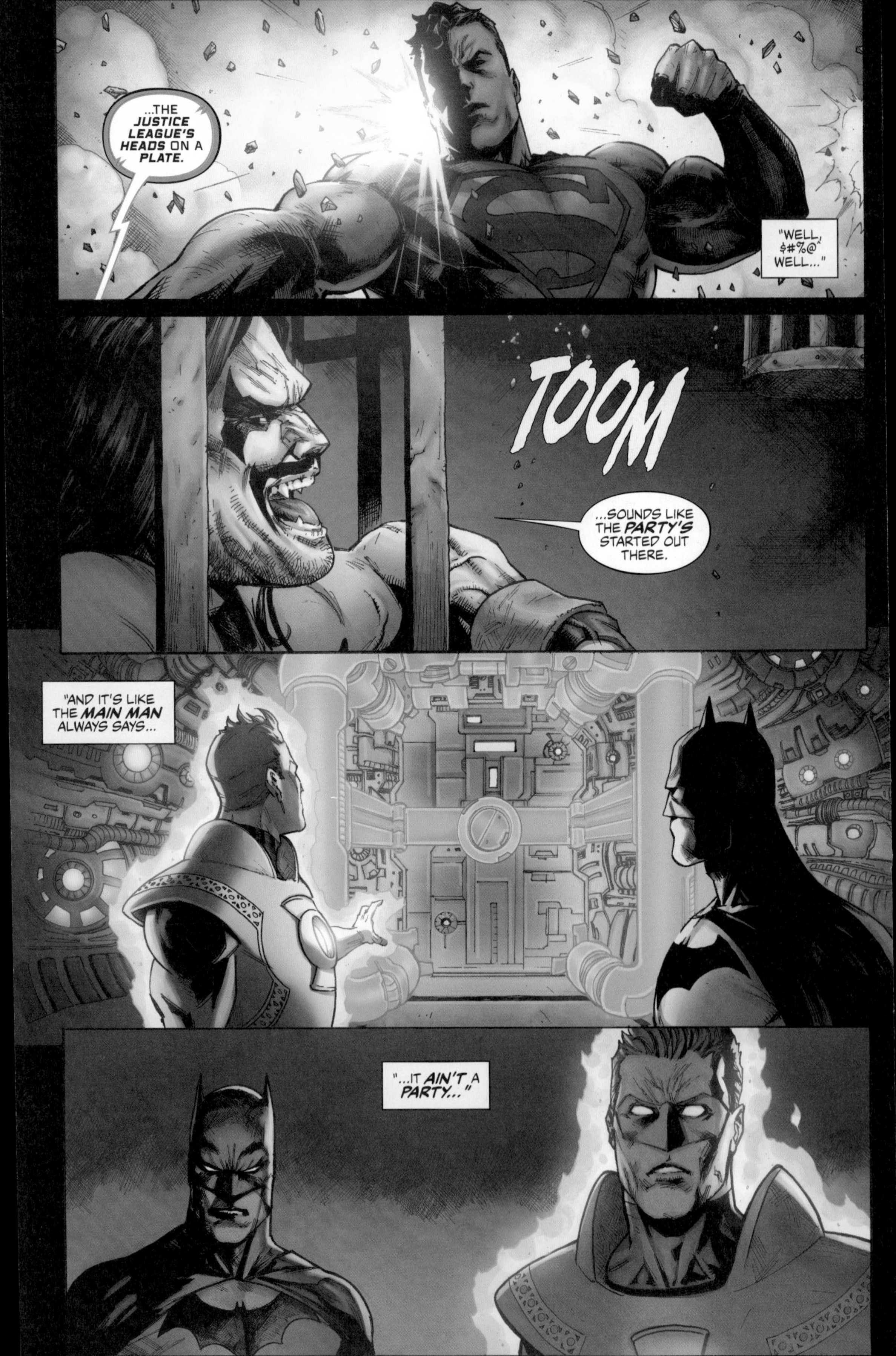

...THE JUSTICE LEAGUE'S HEADS ON A PLATE.
"WELL, $#%@^ WELL..."
TOOM
...SOUNDS LIKE THE PARTY'S STARTED OUT THERE.
"AND IT'S LIKE THE MAIN MAN ALWAYS SAYS...
"...IT AIN'T A PARTY..."

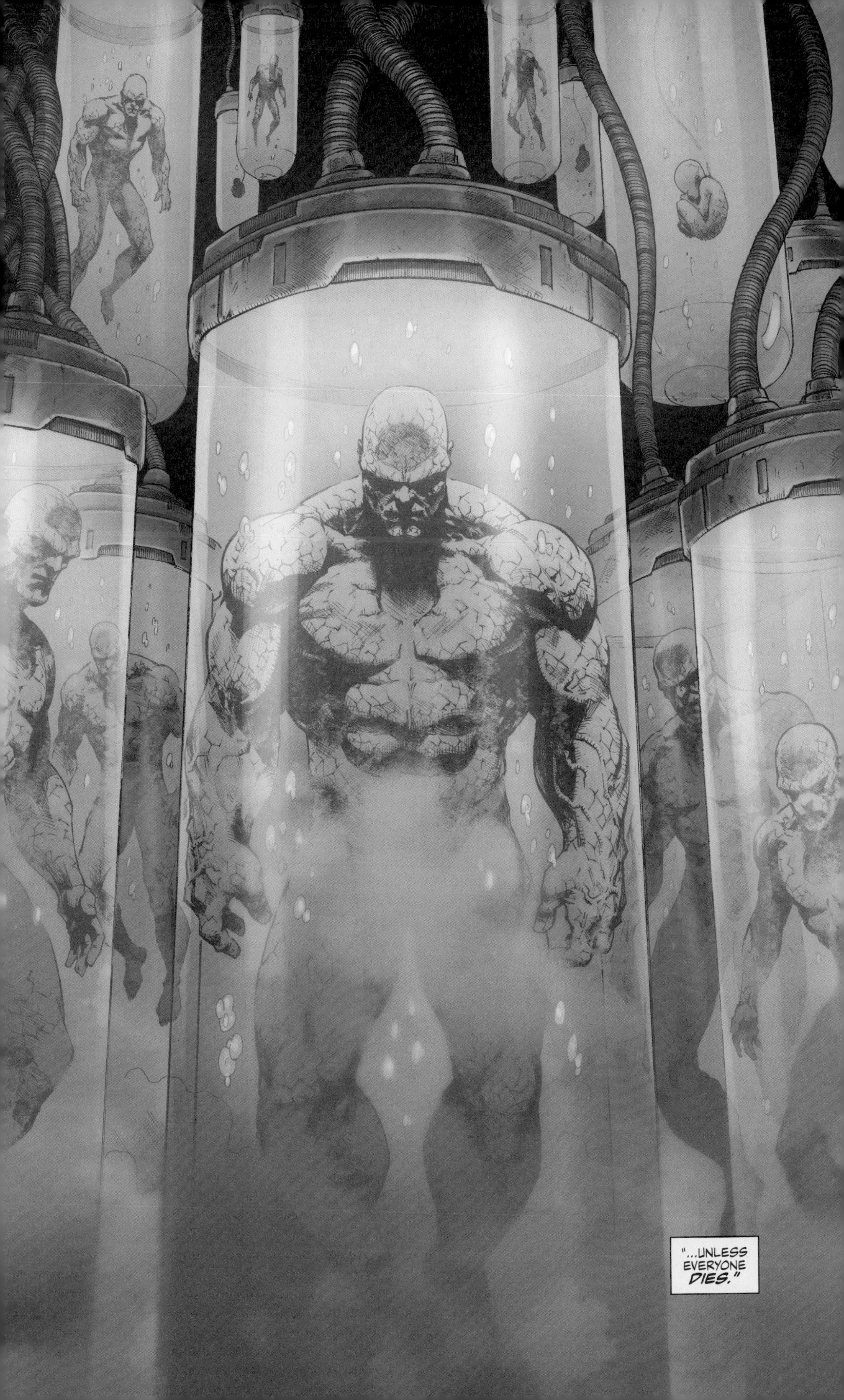
"...UNLESS EVERYONE *DIES*."

THEN.

"HOPELESS."

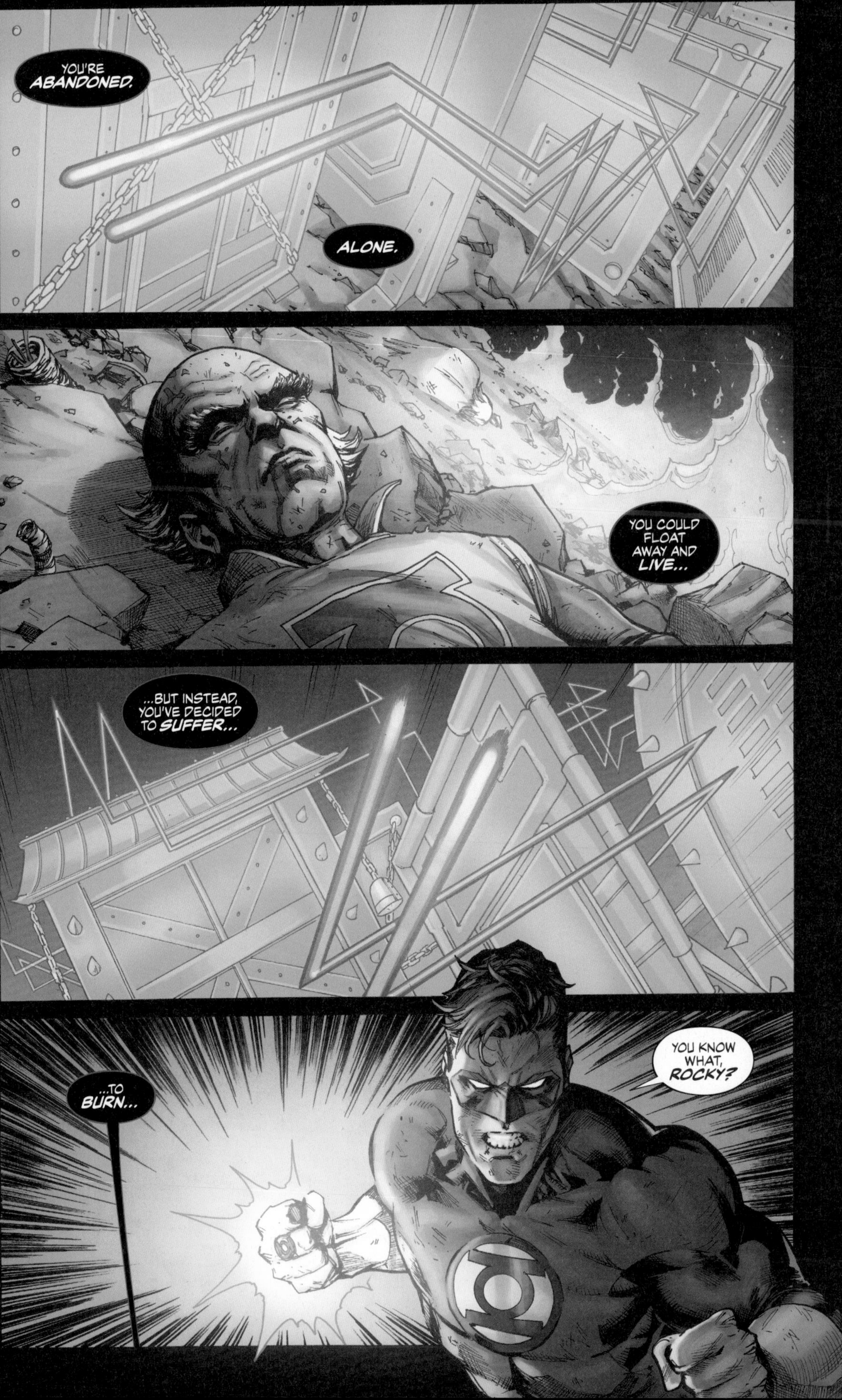
YOU'RE ABANDONED.
ALONE.
YOU COULD FLOAT AWAY AND LIVE...
...BUT INSTEAD, YOU'VE DECIDED TO SUFFER...
...TO BURN...
YOU KNOW WHAT, ROCKY?

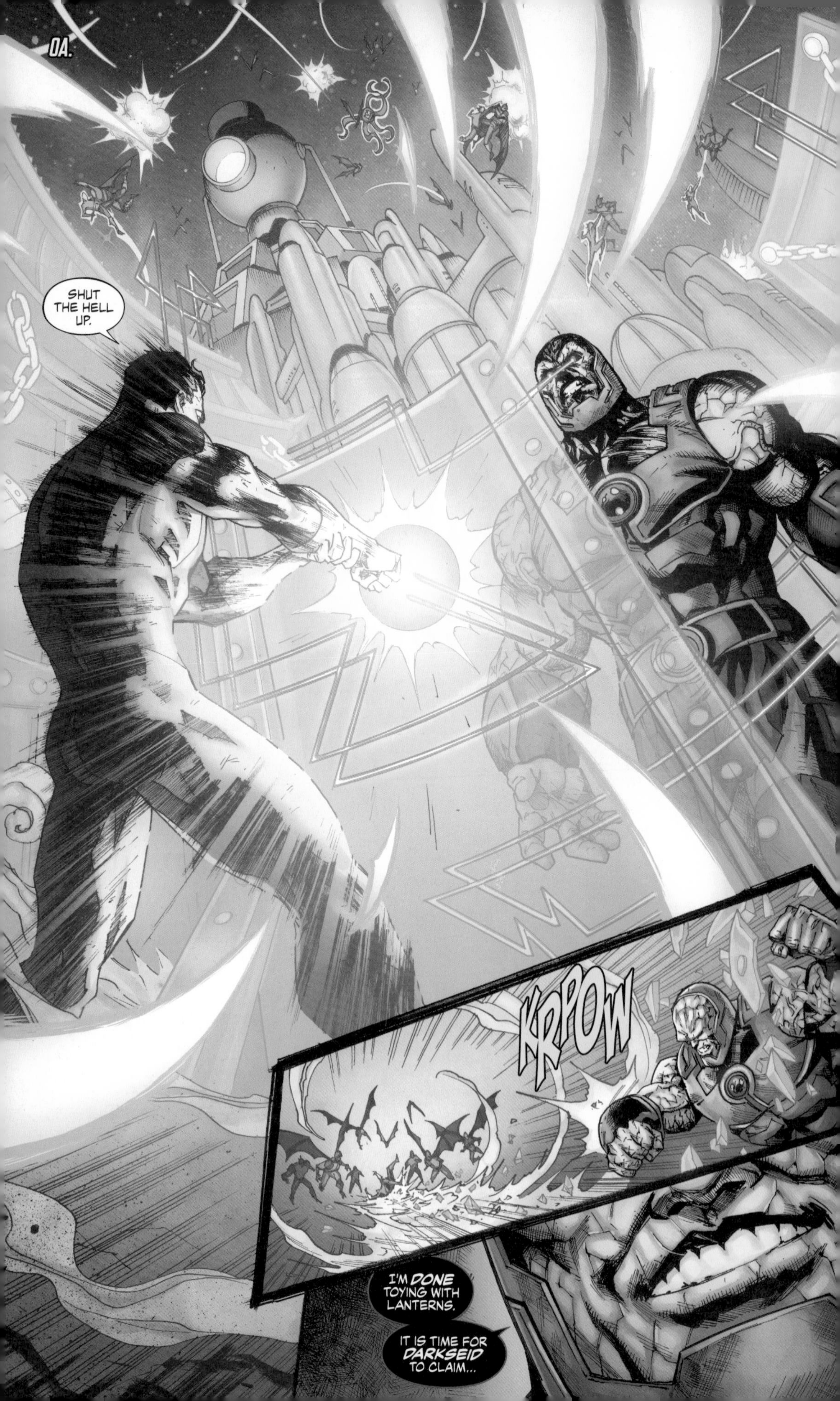
OA.
SHUT THE HELL UP.
KRPOW
I'M DONE TOYING WITH LANTERNS.
IT IS TIME FOR DARKSEID TO CLAIM...

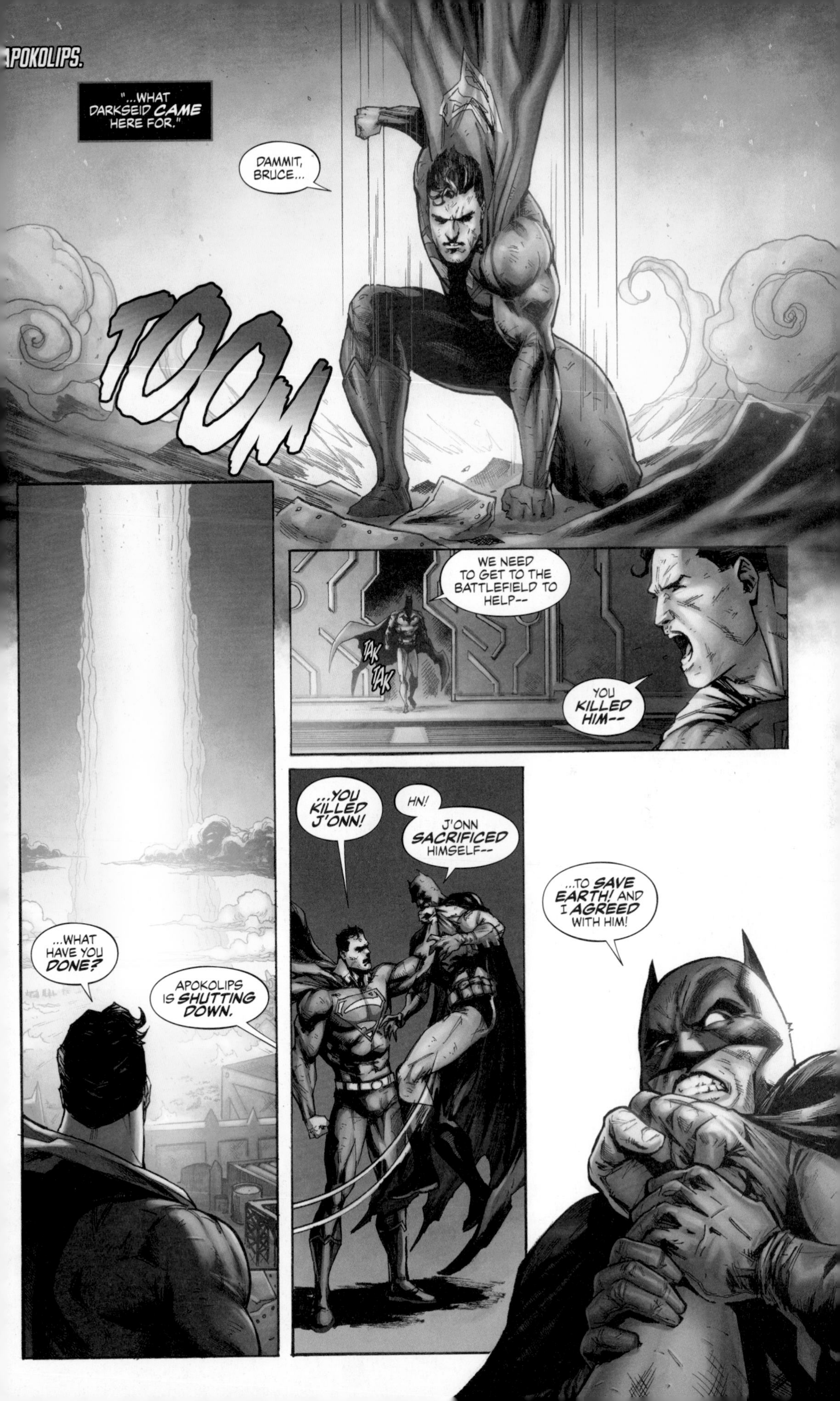
APOKOLIPS.
"...WHAT DARKSEID CAME HERE FOR."
DAMMIT, BRUCE...
TOOM
...WHAT HAVE YOU DONE?
APOKOLIPS IS SHUTTING DOWN.
WE NEED TO GET TO THE BATTLEFIELD TO HELP--
TAK TAK
YOU KILLED HIM--
...YOU KILLED J'ONN!
HN!
J'ONN SACRIFICED HIMSELF--
...TO SAVE EARTH! AND I AGREED WITH HIM!

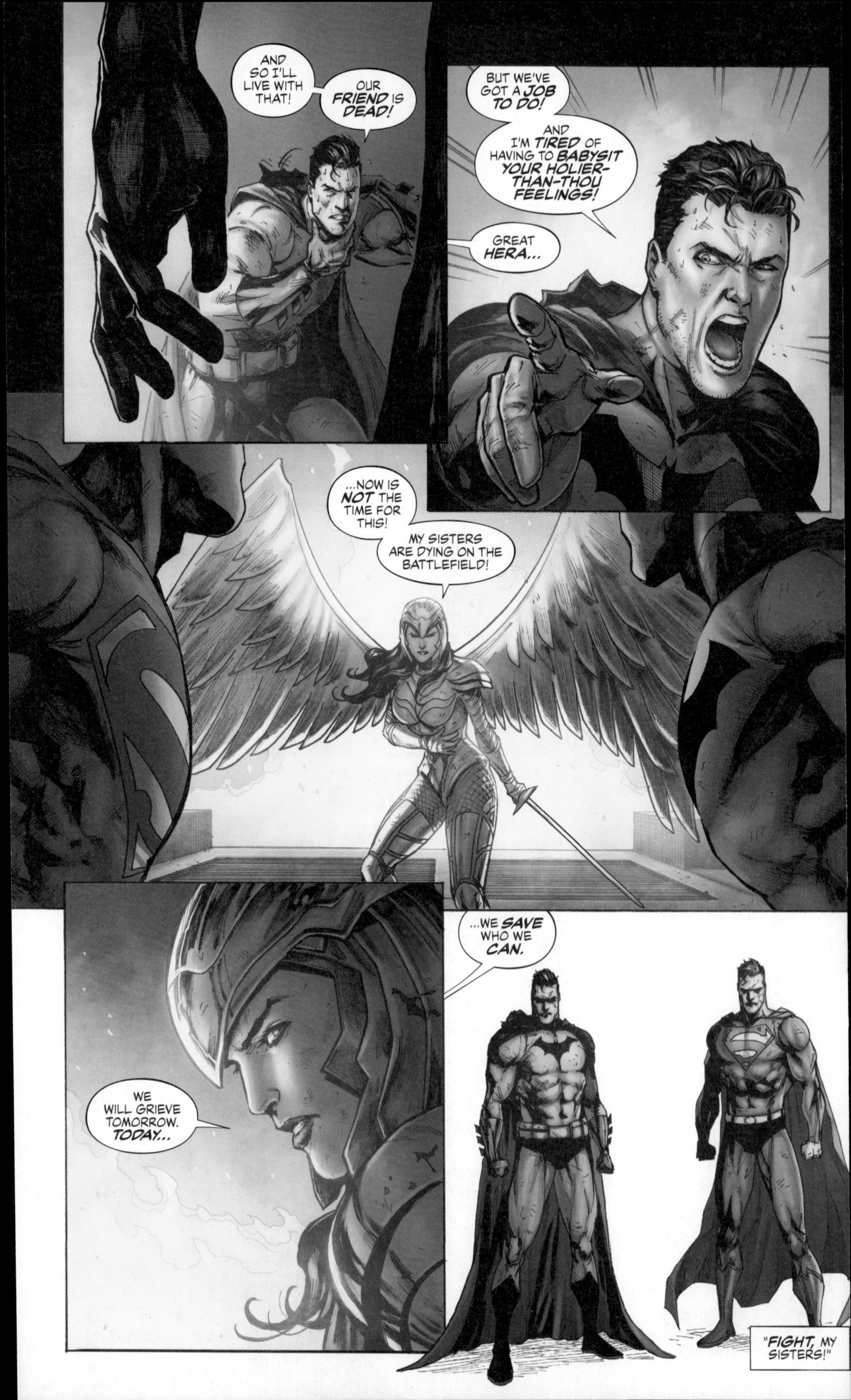

AND SO I'LL LIVE WITH THAT!
OUR FRIEND IS DEAD!
BUT WE'VE GOT A JOB TO DO!
AND I'M TIRED OF HAVING TO BABYSIT YOUR HOLIER-THAN-THOU FEELINGS!
GREAT HERA...
...NOW IS NOT THE TIME FOR THIS!
MY SISTERS ARE DYING ON THE BATTLEFIELD!
WE WILL GRIEVE TOMORROW. TODAY...
...WE SAVE WHO WE CAN.
"FIGHT, MY SISTERS!"

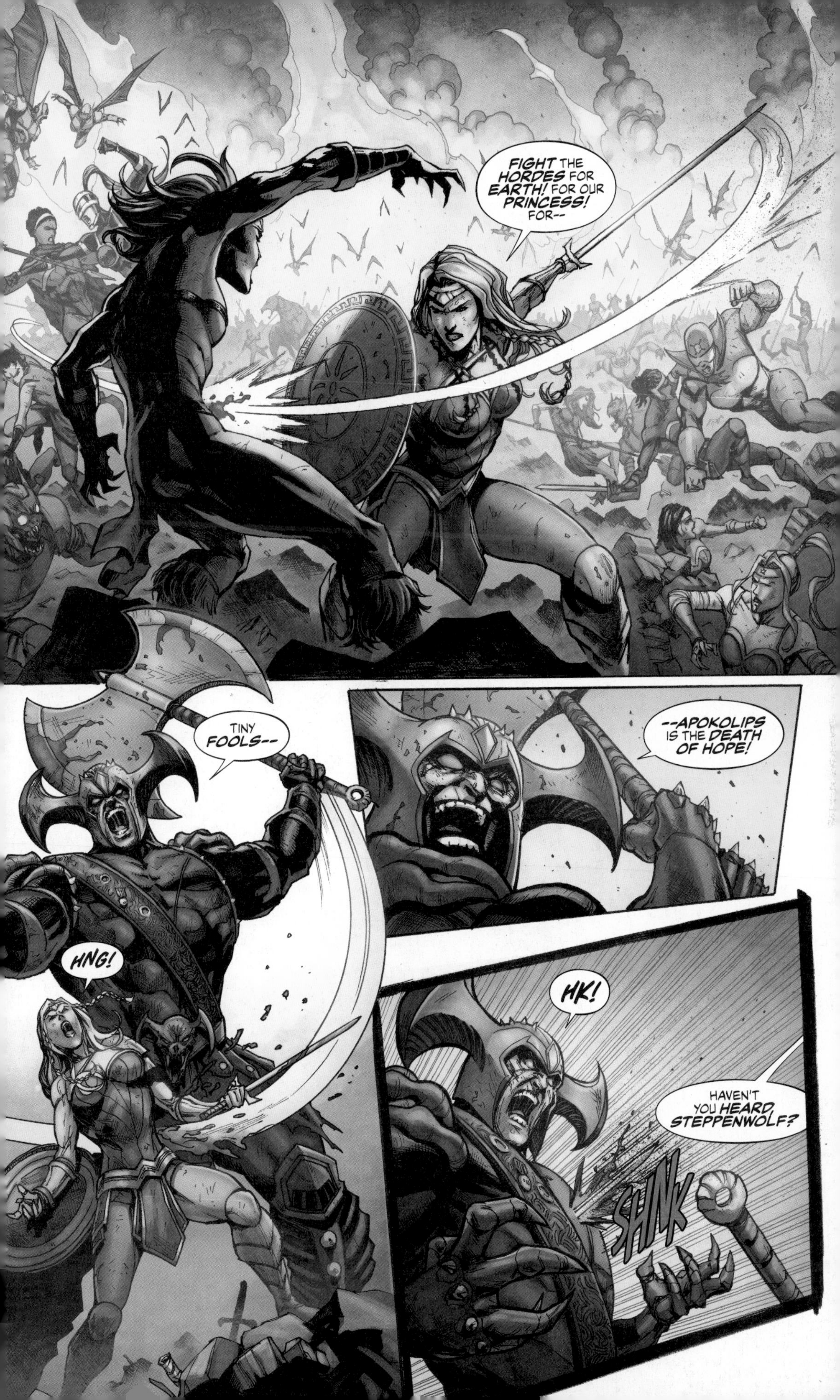

FIGHT THE HORDES FOR EARTH! FOR OUR PRINCESS! FOR--
TINY FOOLS--
--APOKOLIPS IS THE DEATH OF HOPE!
HNG!
HK!
HAVEN'T YOU HEARD, STEPPENWOLF?
SHINK

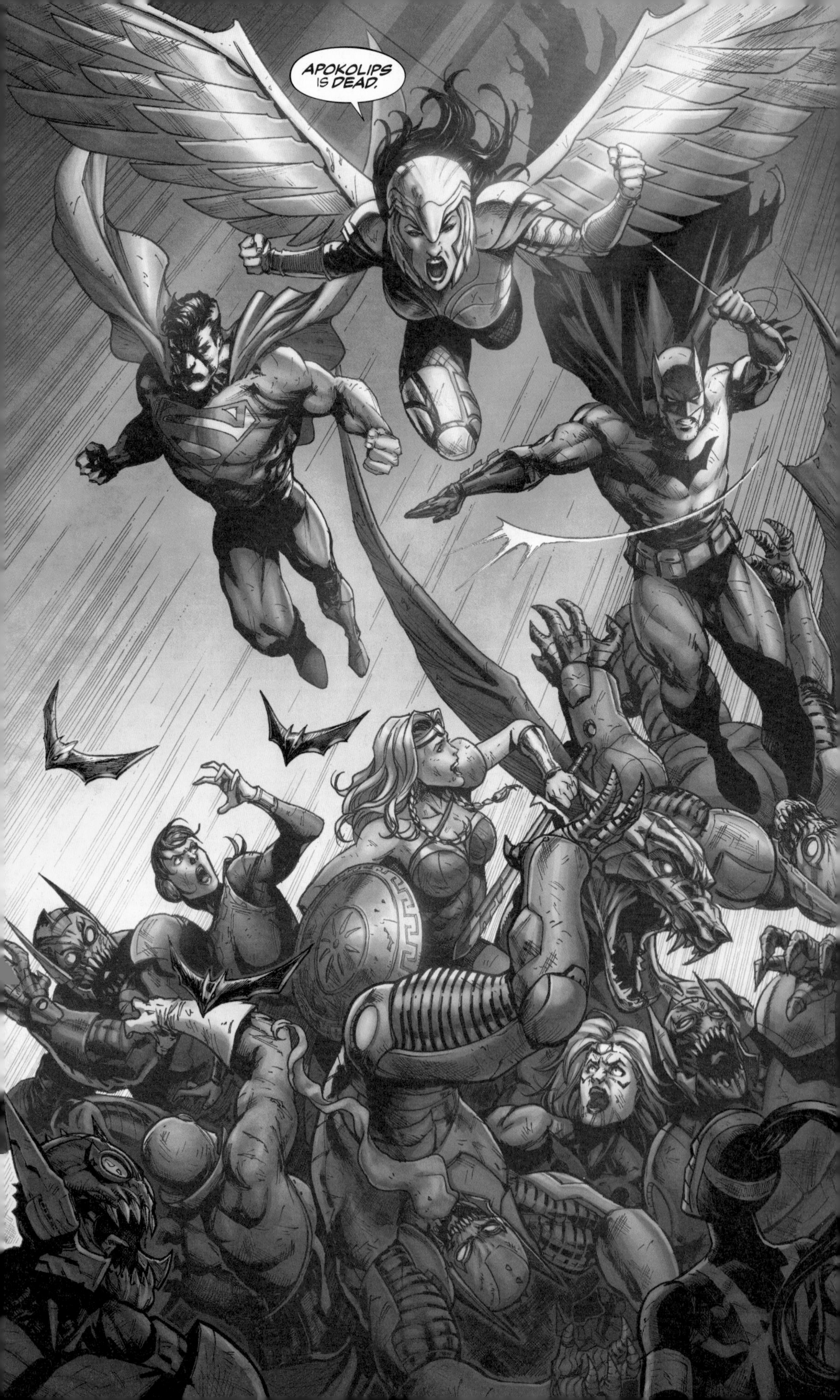
APOKOLIPS IS DEAD.

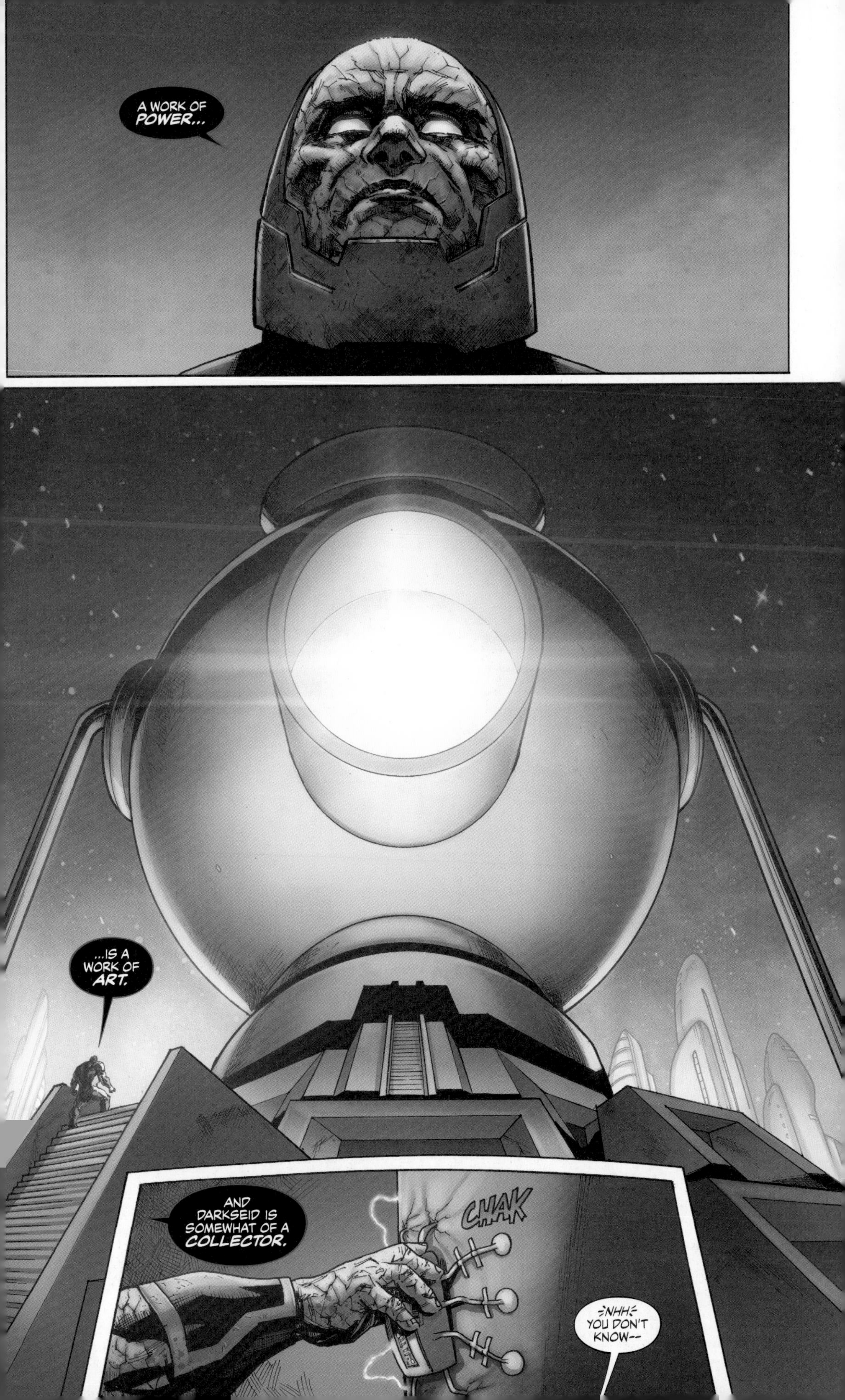
A WORK OF POWER...
...IS A WORK OF ART.
AND DARKSEID IS SOMEWHAT OF A COLLECTOR.
CHAK
NHH. YOU DON'T KNOW--

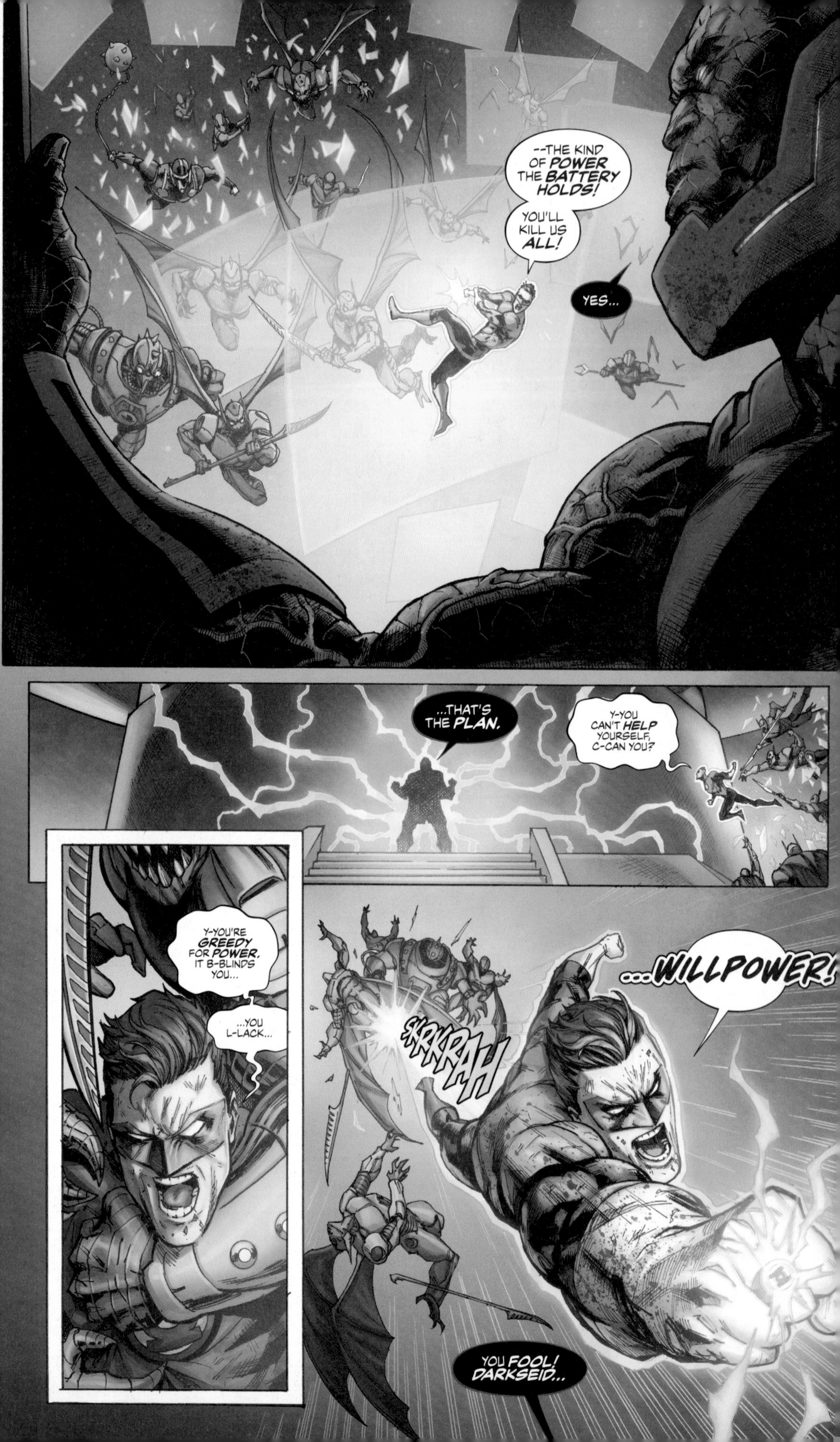
--THE KIND OF POWER THE BATTERY HOLDS!
YOU'LL KILL US ALL!
YES...
...THAT'S THE PLAN.
Y-YOU CAN'T HELP YOURSELF, C-CAN YOU?
Y-YOU'RE GREEDY FOR POWER. IT B-BLINDS YOU...
...YOU L-LACK...
...WILLPOWER!
SKRKRAH
YOU FOOL! DARKSEID...

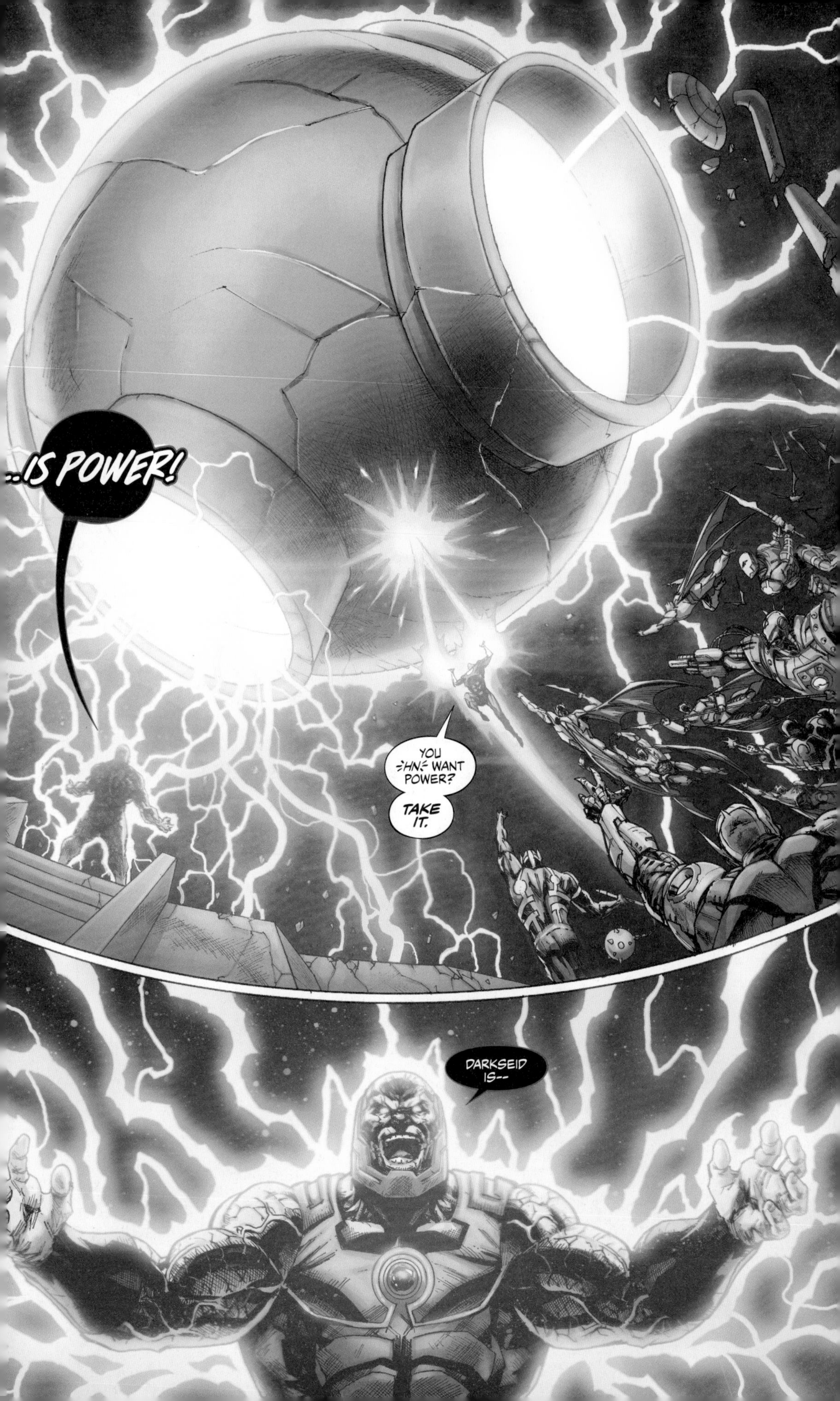

..IS POWER!
YOU =HN= WANT POWER?
TAKE IT.
DARKSEID IS--

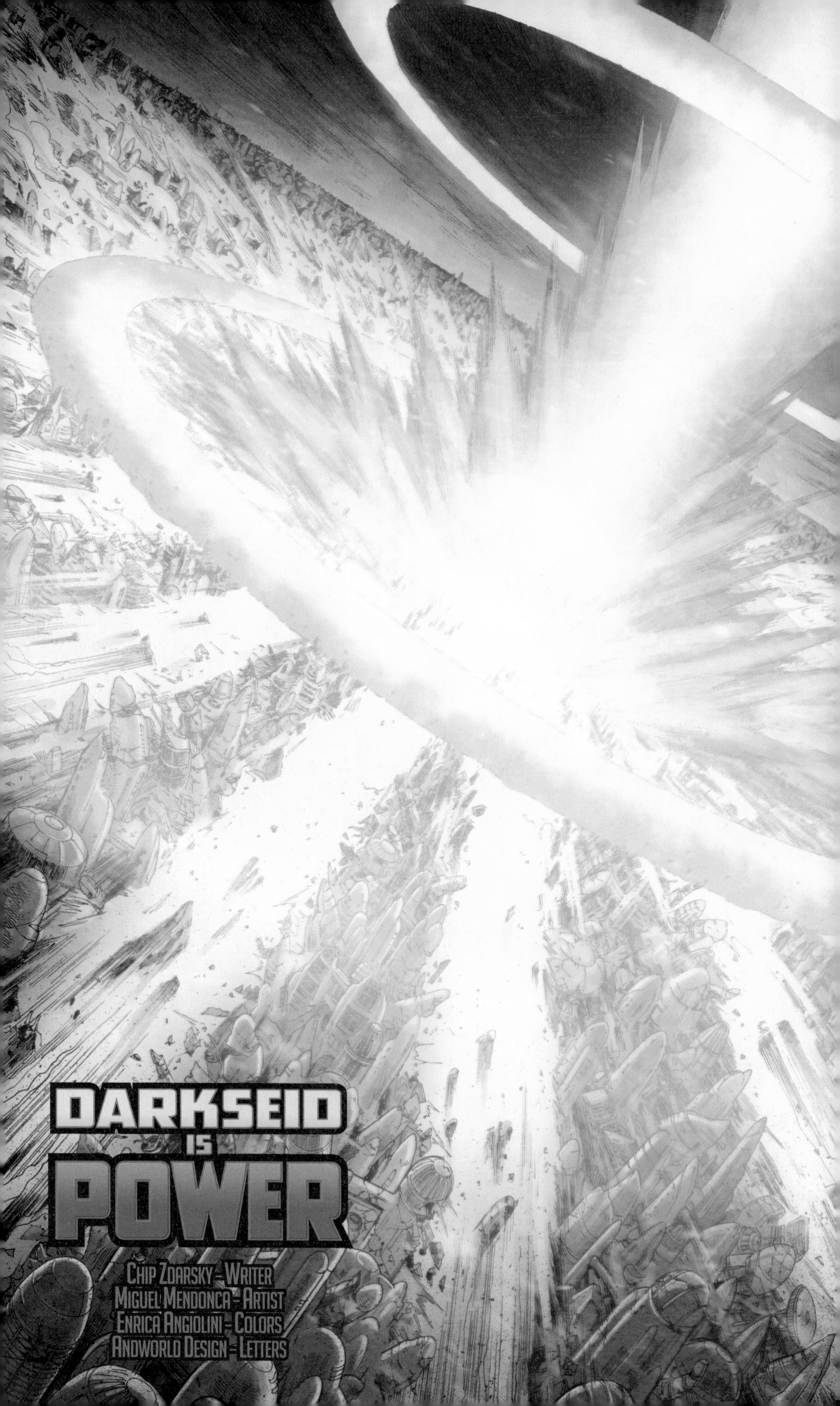
DARKSEID IS POWER
CHIP ZDARSKY - WRITER
MIGUEL MENDONCA - ARTIST
ENRICA ANGIOLINI - COLORS
ANDWORLD DESIGN - LETTERS

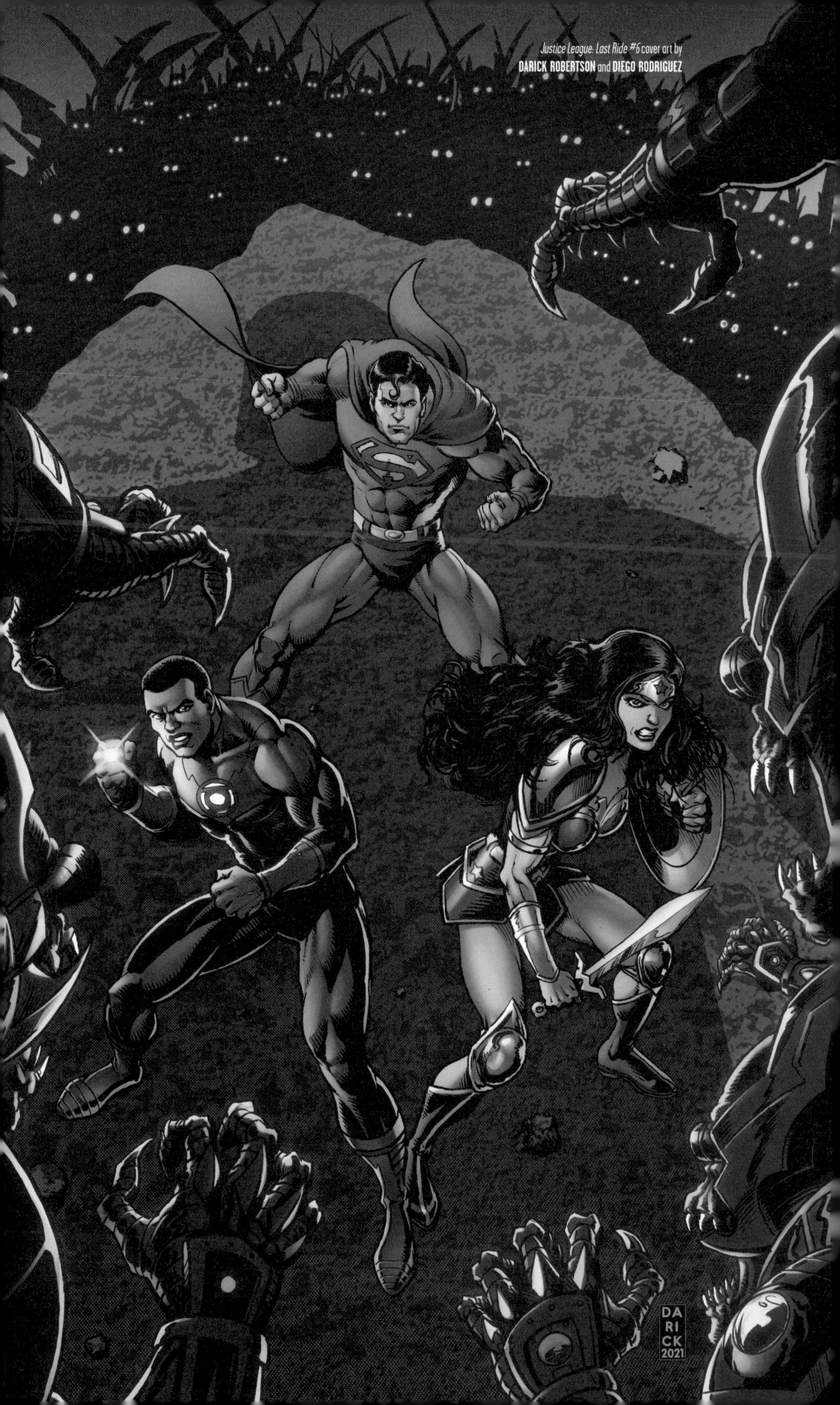
DA
RI
CK
2021

Justice League: Last Ride #6 cover art by
DARICK ROBERTSON and **DIEGO RODRIGUEZ**

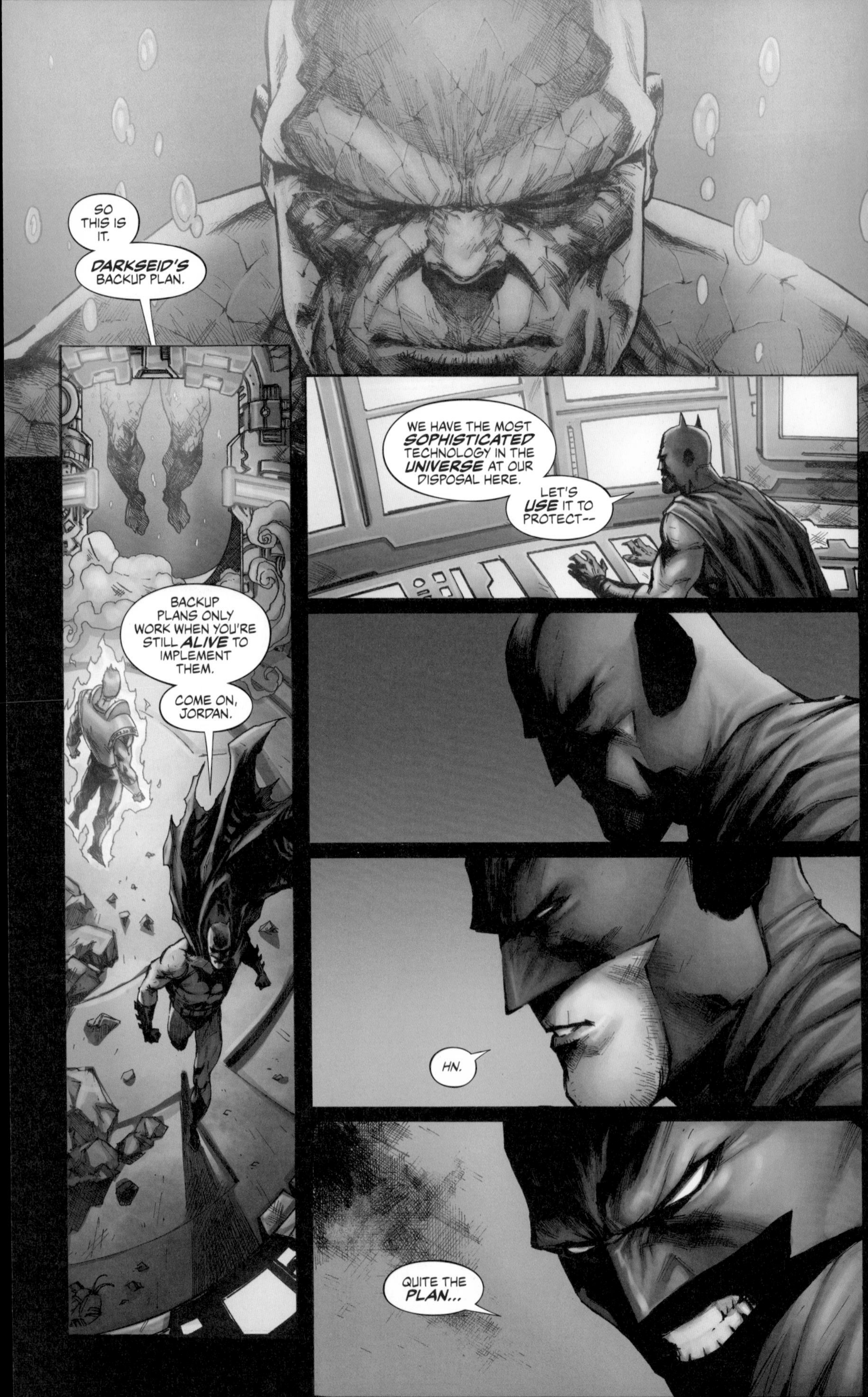
SO THIS IS IT.
DARKSEID'S BACKUP PLAN.
WE HAVE THE MOST SOPHISTICATED TECHNOLOGY IN THE UNIVERSE AT OUR DISPOSAL HERE.
LET'S USE IT TO PROTECT--
BACKUP PLANS ONLY WORK WHEN YOU'RE STILL ALIVE TO IMPLEMENT THEM.
COME ON, JORDAN.
HN.
QUITE THE PLAN...

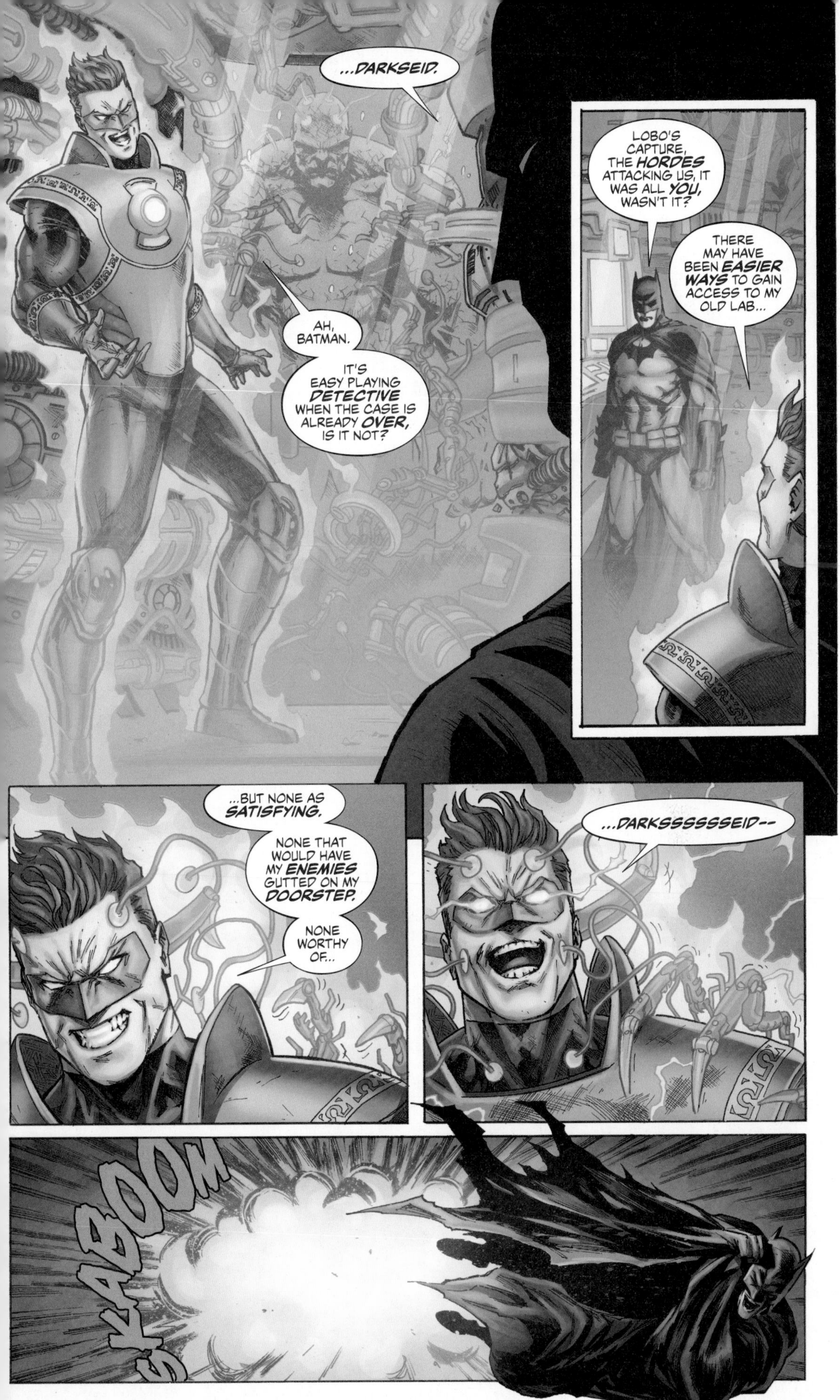
...DARKSEID.
LOBO'S CAPTURE, THE HORDES ATTACKING US, IT WAS ALL YOU, WASN'T IT?
AH, BATMAN.
IT'S EASY PLAYING DETECTIVE WHEN THE CASE IS ALREADY OVER, IS IT NOT?
THERE MAY HAVE BEEN EASIER WAYS TO GAIN ACCESS TO MY OLD LAB...
...BUT NONE AS SATISFYING.
NONE THAT WOULD HAVE MY ENEMIES GUTTED ON MY DOORSTEP.
NONE WORTHY OF...
...DARKSSSSSSEID--
SKABOOM

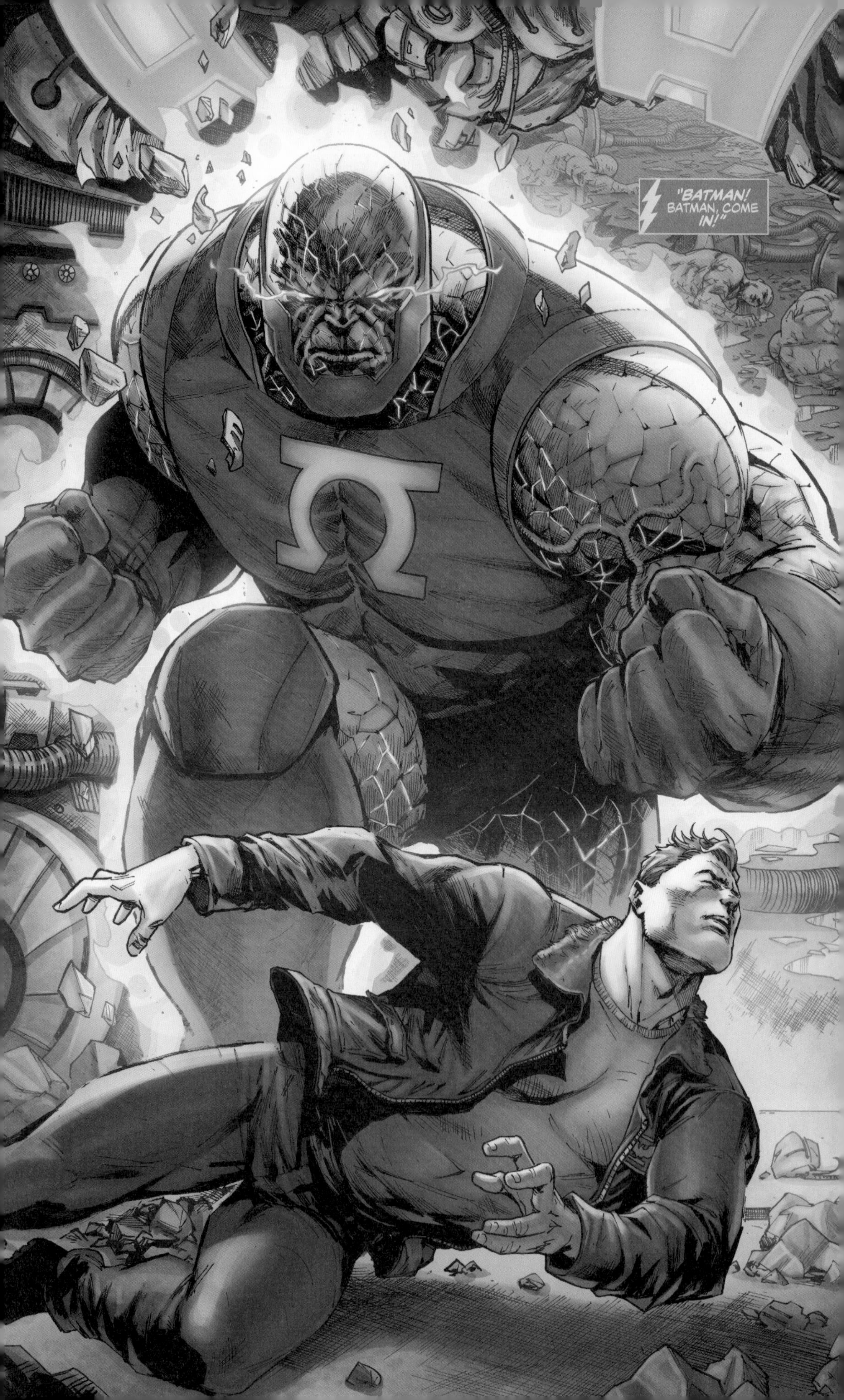
"BATMAN! BATMAN, COME IN!"

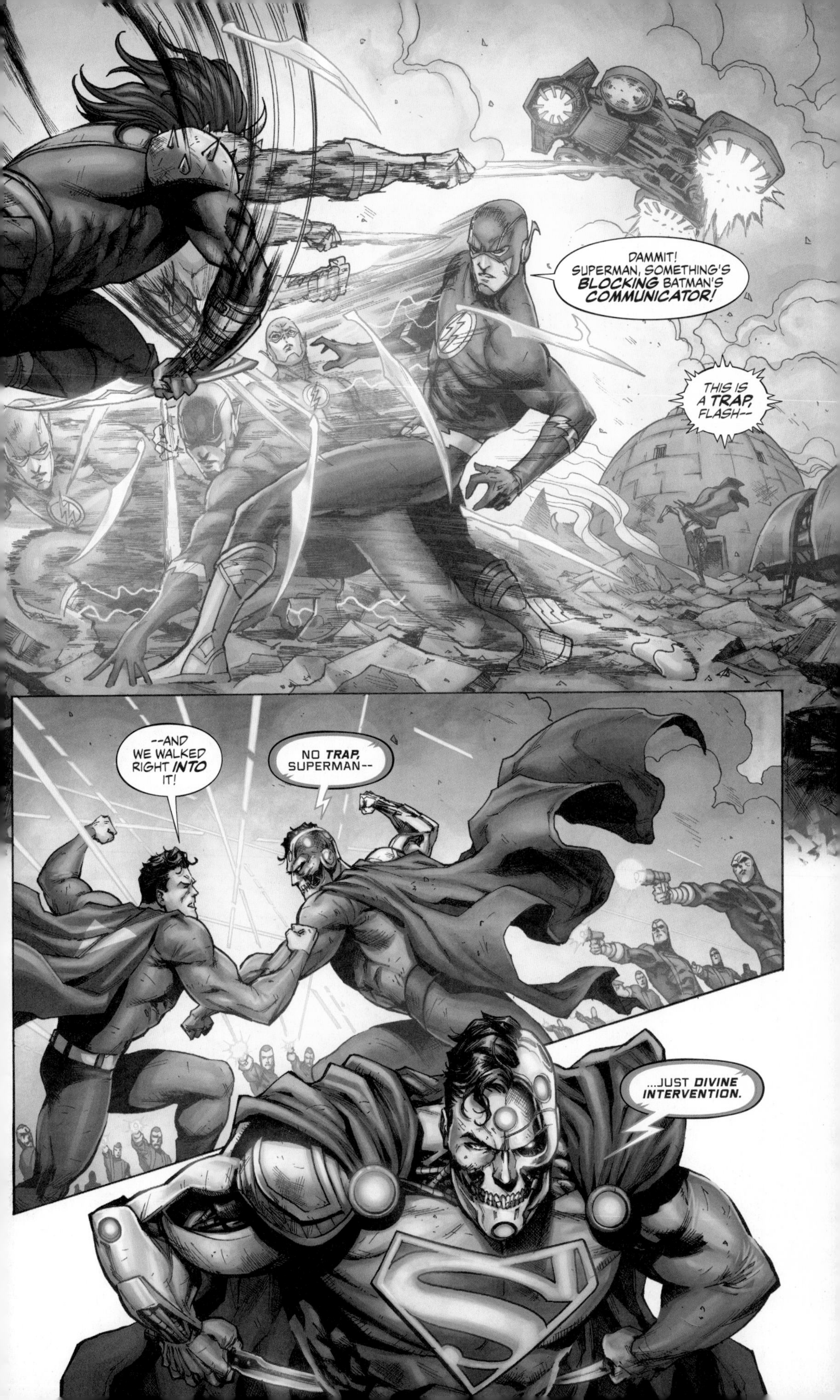
DAMMIT! SUPERMAN, SOMETHING'S BLOCKING BATMAN'S COMMUNICATOR!
THIS IS A TRAP, FLASH--
--AND WE WALKED RIGHT INTO IT!
NO TRAP, SUPERMAN--
...JUST DIVINE INTERVENTION.

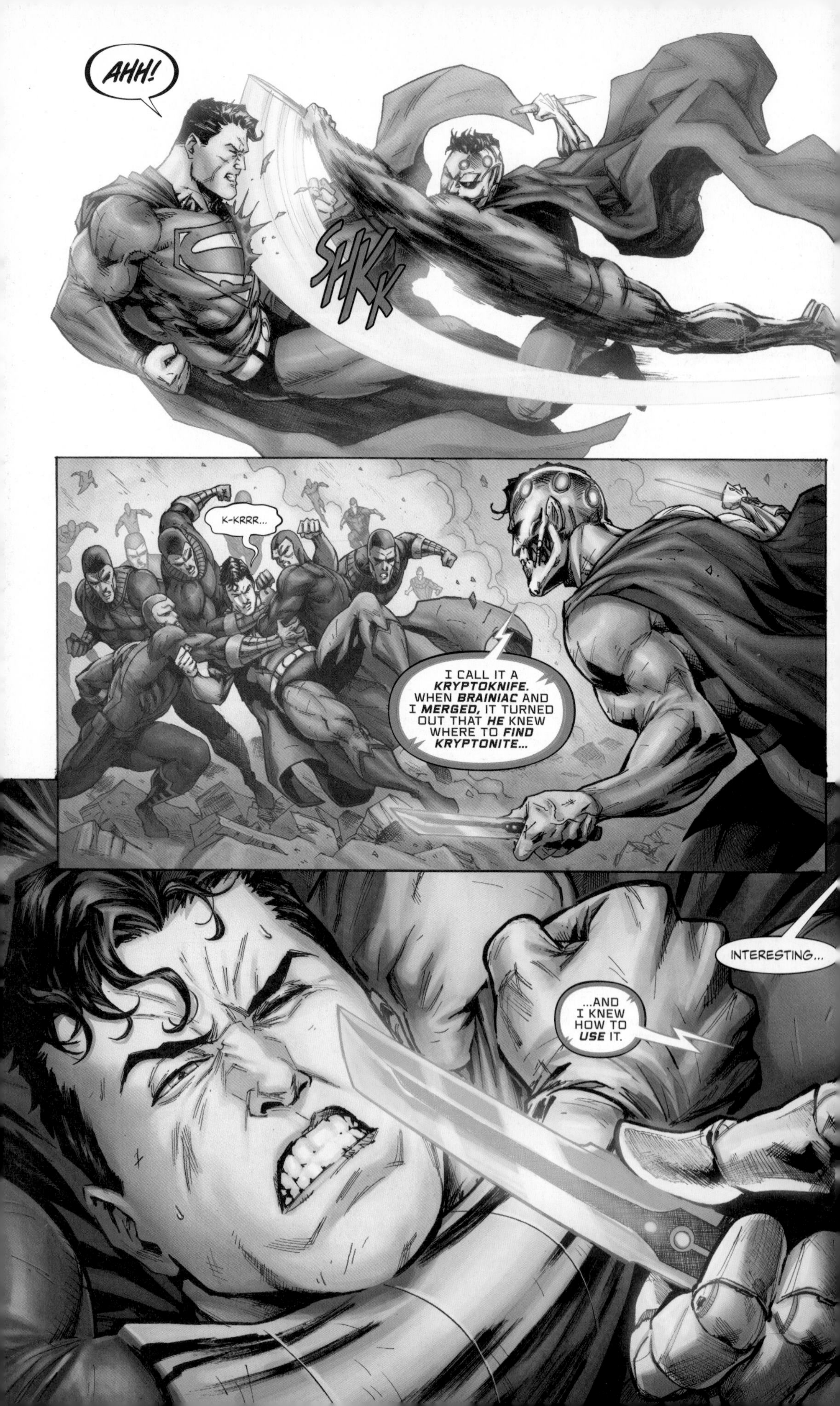

AHH!
SHKK
K-KRRR...
I CALL IT A KRYPTOKNIFE. WHEN BRAINIAC AND I MERGED, IT TURNED OUT THAT HE KNEW WHERE TO FIND KRYPTONITE...
INTERESTING...
...AND I KNEW HOW TO USE IT.

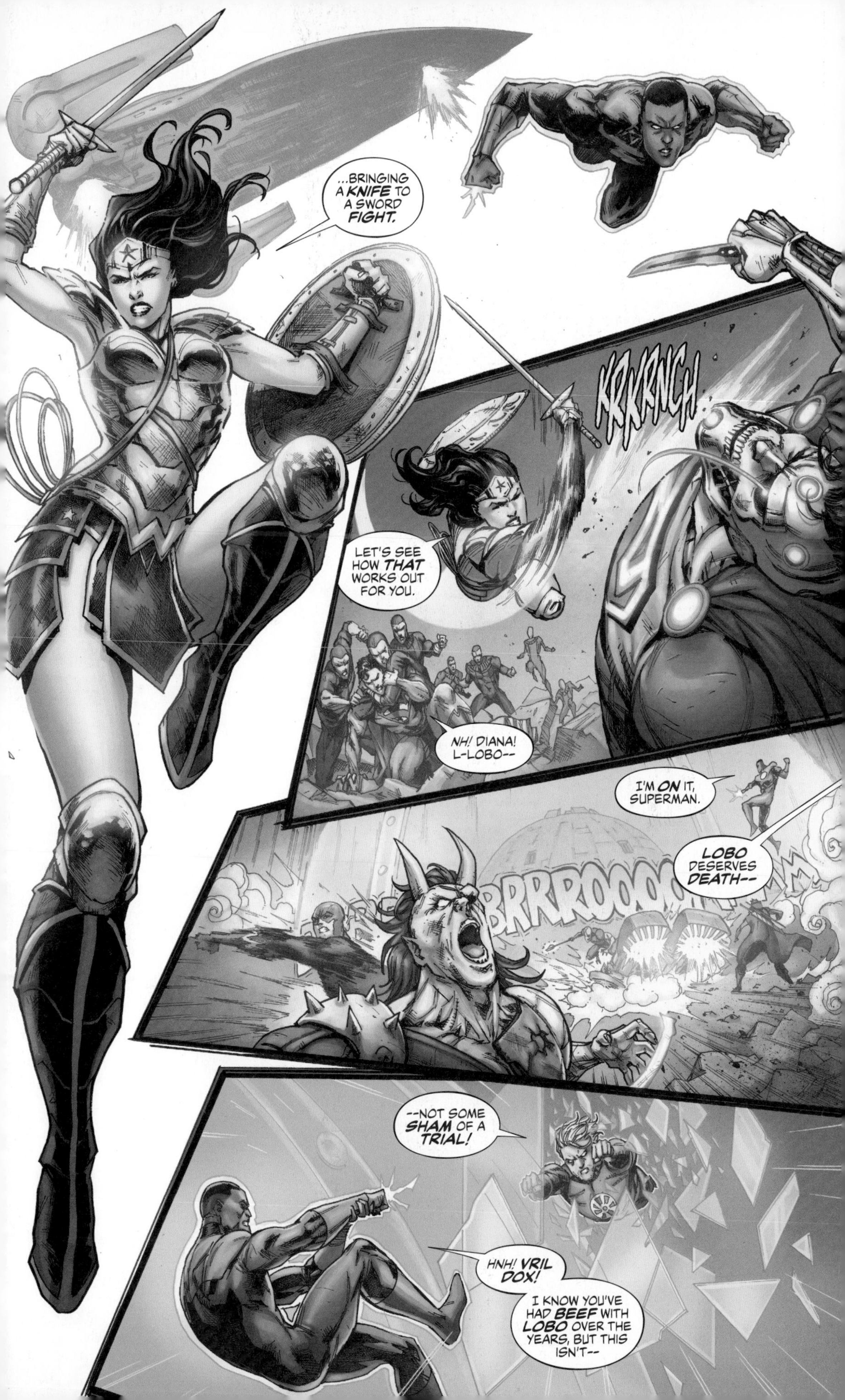
...BRINGING A KNIFE TO A SWORD FIGHT.
LET'S SEE HOW THAT WORKS OUT FOR YOU.
KRKRNCH
NH! DIANA! L-LOBO--
I'M ON IT, SUPERMAN.
LOBO DESERVES DEATH--
--NOT SOME SHAM OF A TRIAL!
HNH! VRIL DOX!
I KNOW YOU'VE HAD BEEF WITH LOBO OVER THE YEARS, BUT THIS ISN'T--

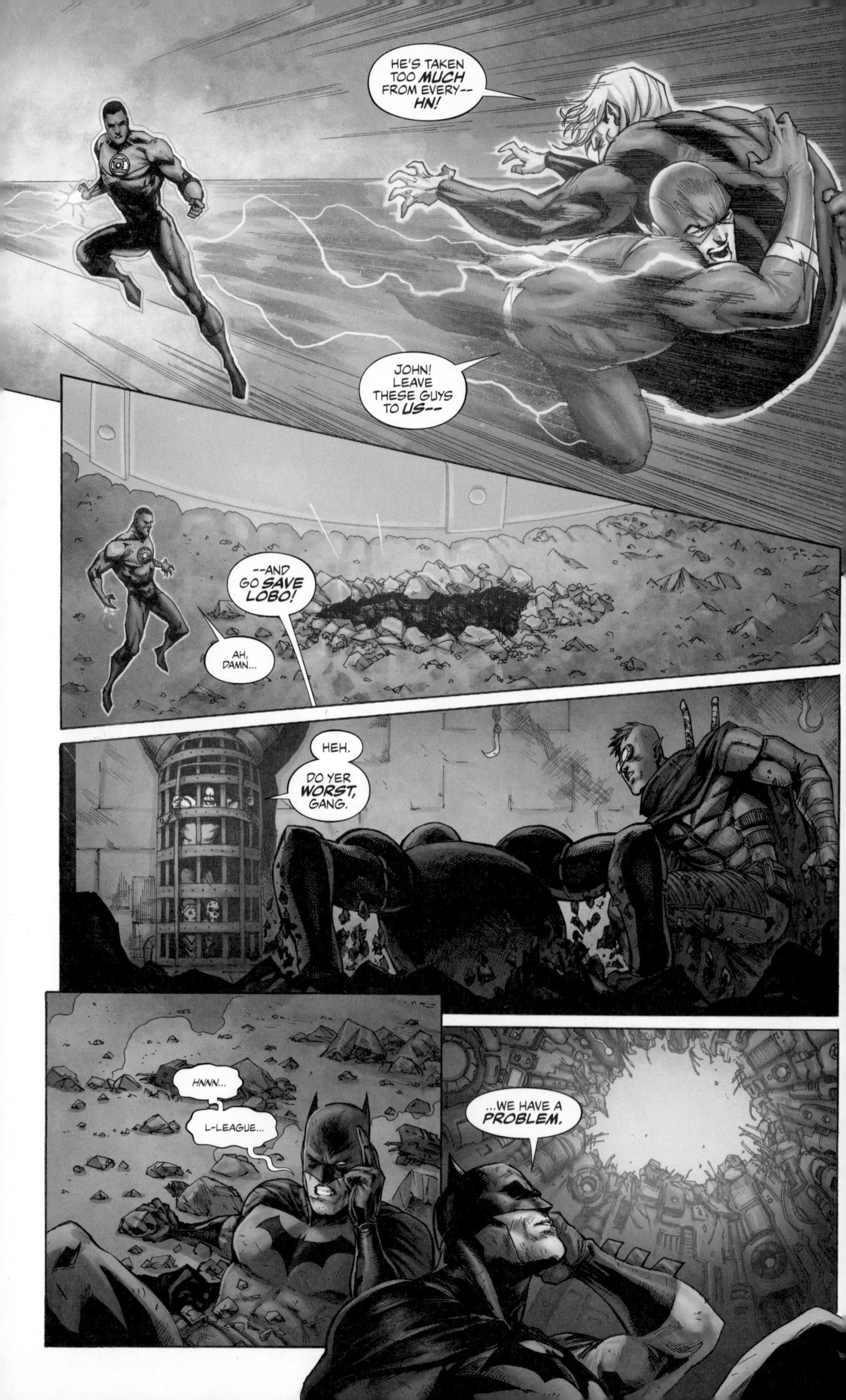
HE'S TAKEN TOO MUCH FROM EVERY-- HN!
JOHN! LEAVE THESE GUYS TO US--
--AND GO SAVE LOBO!
AH, DAMN...
HEH.
DO YER WORST, GANG.
HNNN...
L-LEAGUE...
...WE HAVE A PROBLEM.

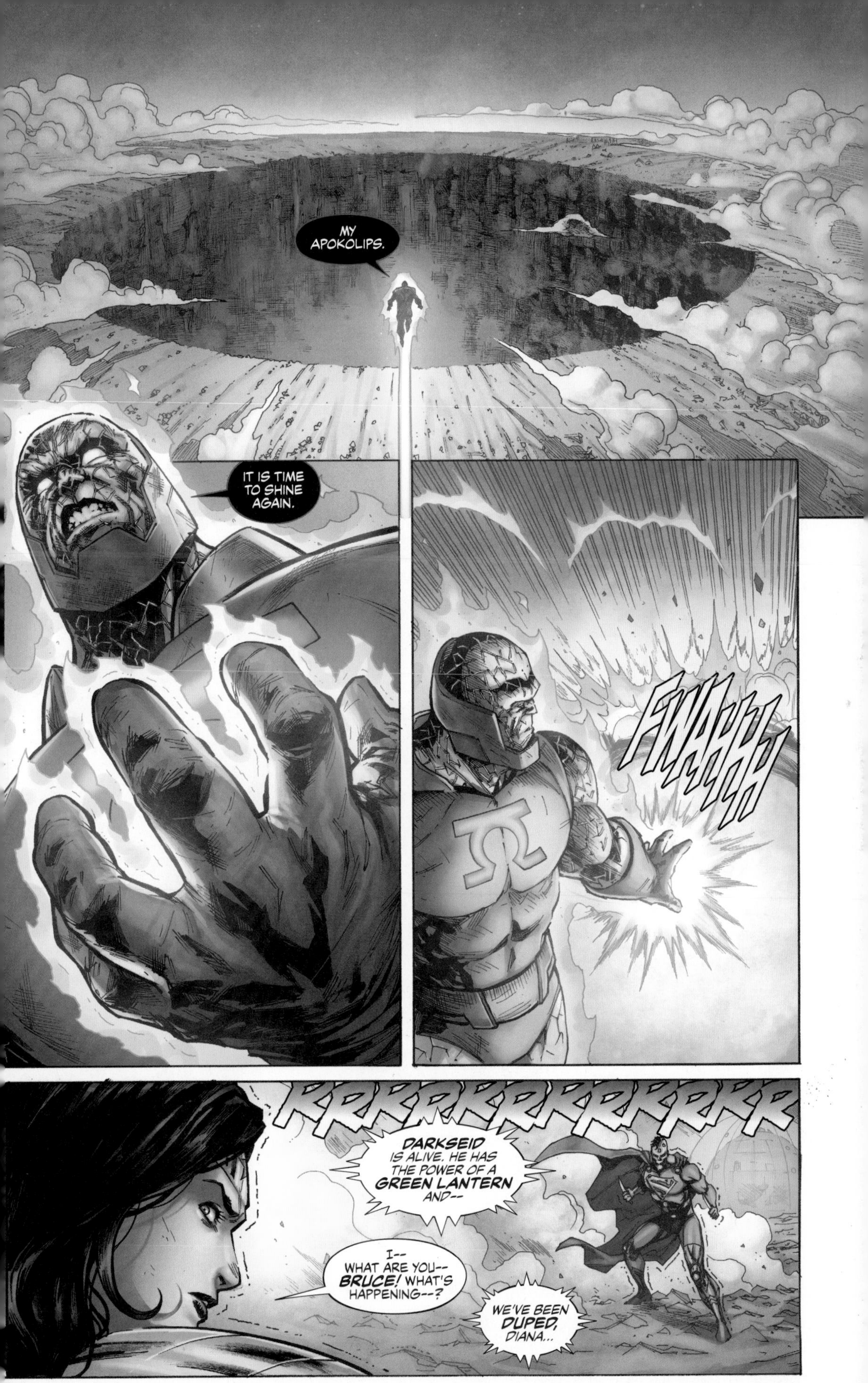
MY APOKOLIPS.
IT IS TIME TO SHINE AGAIN.
FWAHHH
KRRKRKRKRKRKRKRR
DARKSEID IS ALIVE. HE HAS THE POWER OF A GREEN LANTERN AND--
I-- WHAT ARE YOU-- BRUCE! WHAT'S HAPPENING--?
WE'VE BEEN DUPED, DIANA...

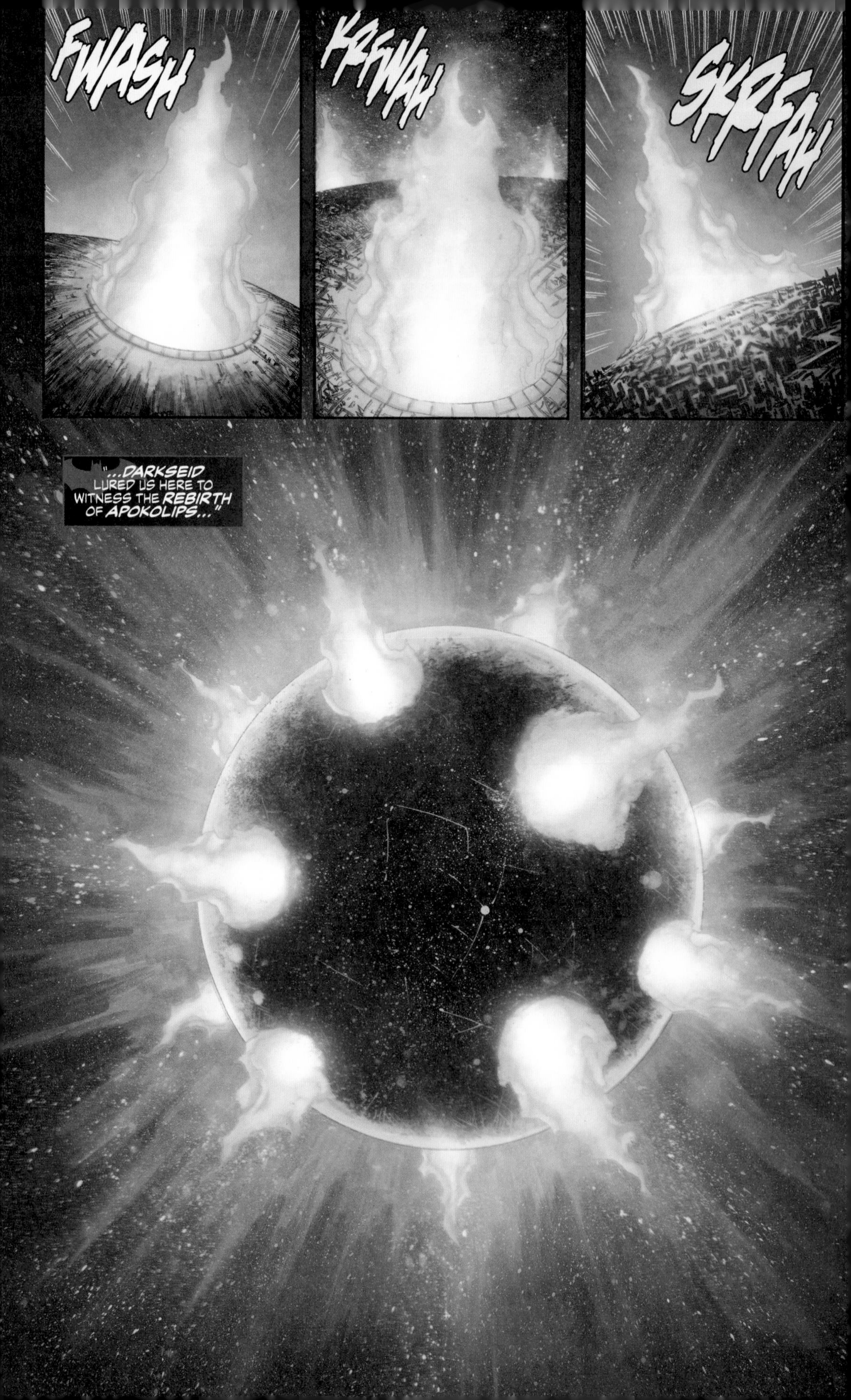
FWASH
KRFWAH
SKRFAH
"...DARKSEID LURED US HERE TO WITNESS THE REBIRTH OF APOKOLIPS..."

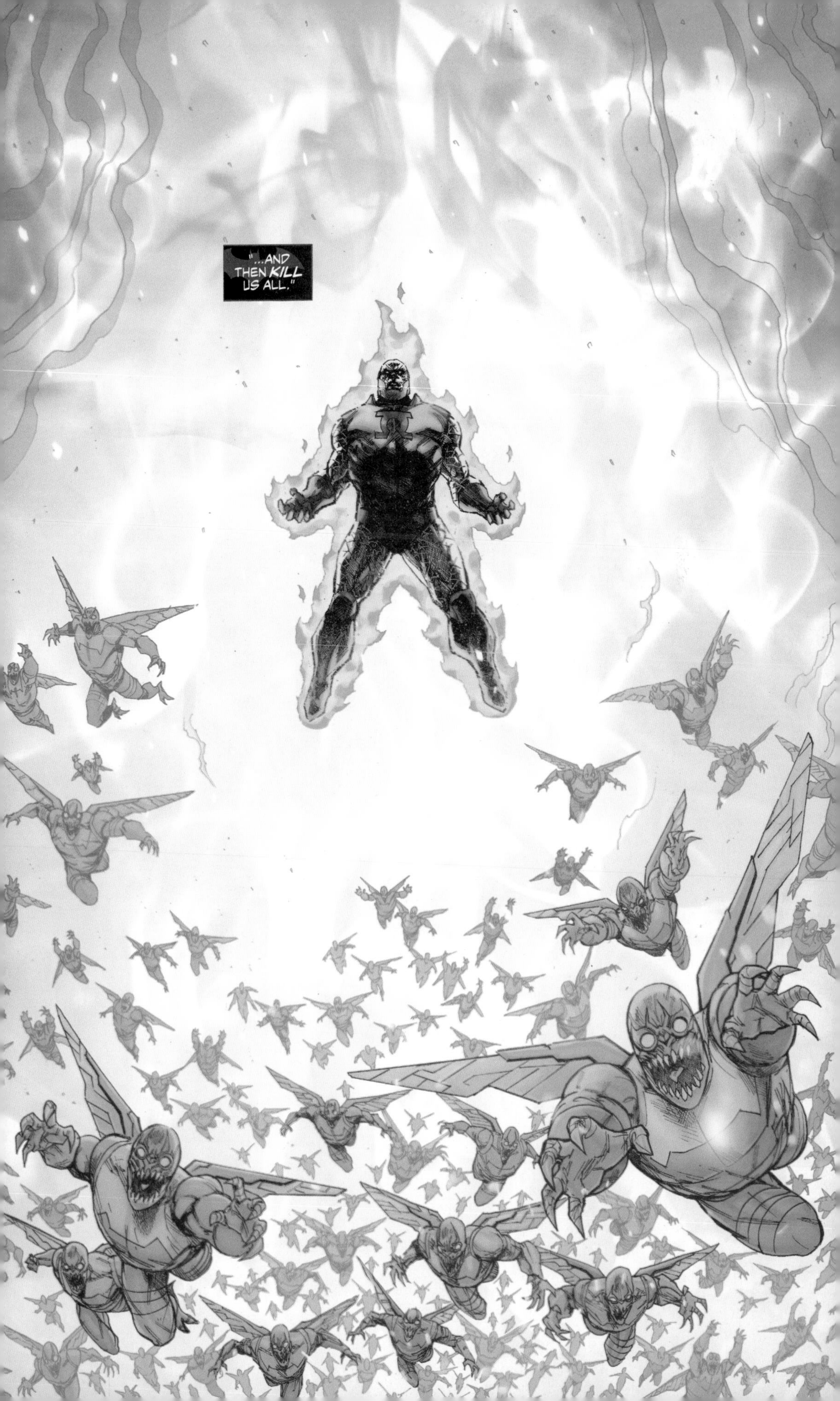
"...AND THEN KILL US ALL."

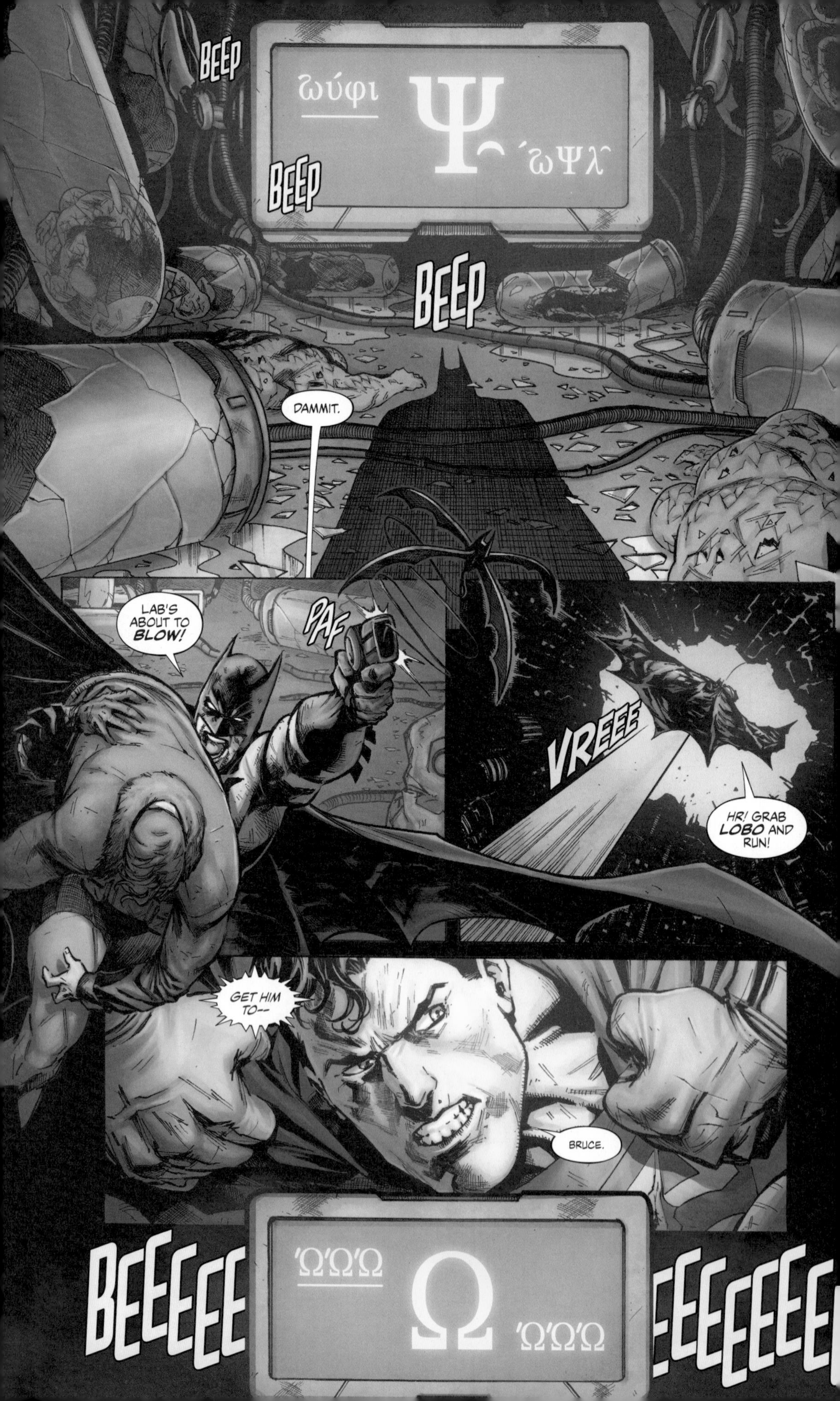

BEEP
ωύφι Ψ ´ωΨλ
BEEP
BEEP
DAMMIT.
LAB'S ABOUT TO BLOW!
PAF
VREEE
HR! GRAB LOBO AND RUN!
GET HIM TO--
BRUCE.
BEEEEE
'Ω'Ω'Ω Ω 'Ω'Ω'Ω
EEEEEEEE

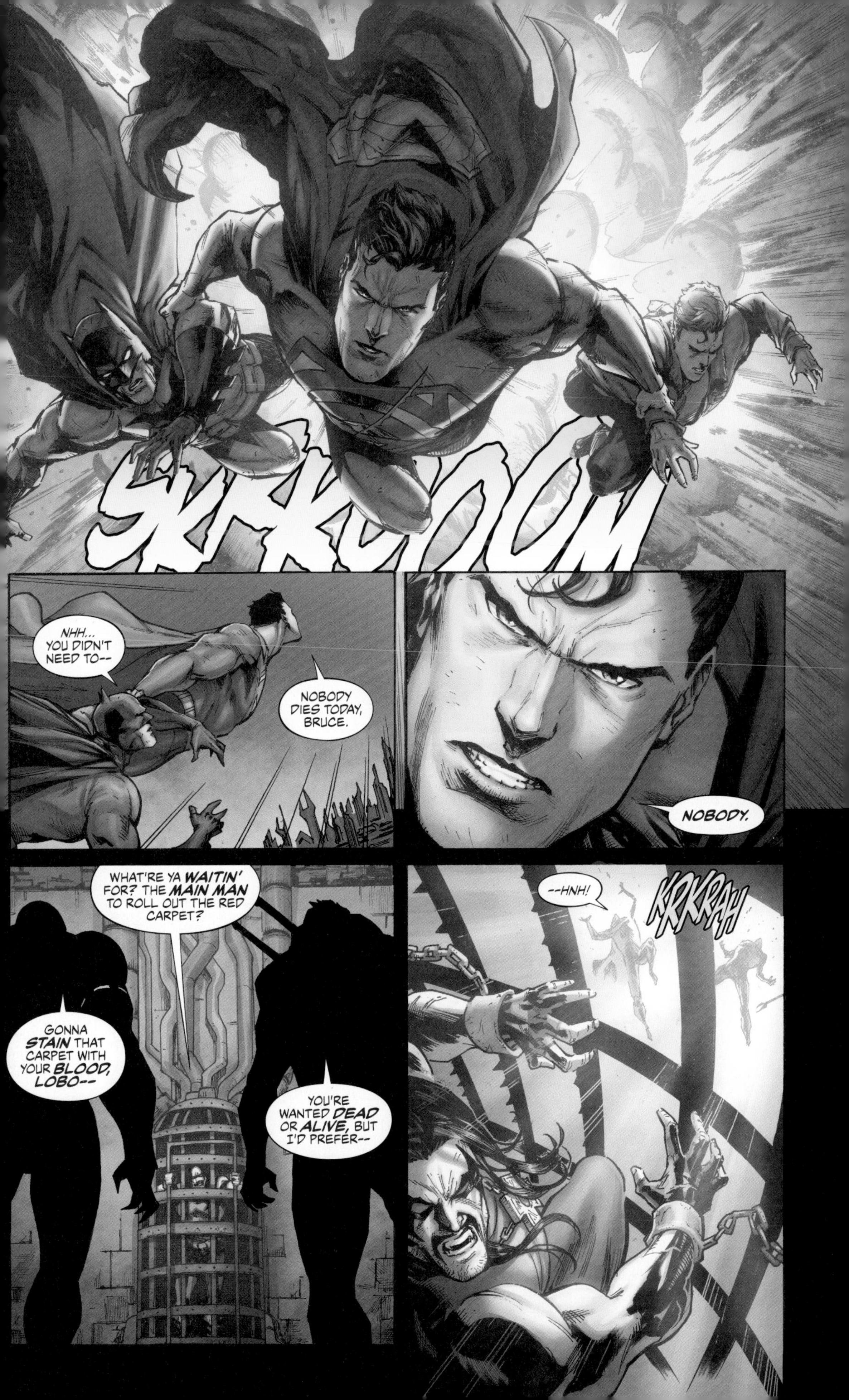
SKRAKOOOM
NHH... YOU DIDN'T NEED TO--
NOBODY DIES TODAY, BRUCE.
NOBODY.
WHAT'RE YA WAITIN' FOR? THE MAIN MAN TO ROLL OUT THE RED CARPET?
GONNA STAIN THAT CARPET WITH YOUR BLOOD, LOBO--
YOU'RE WANTED DEAD OR ALIVE, BUT I'D PREFER--
--HNH!
KRKRAH

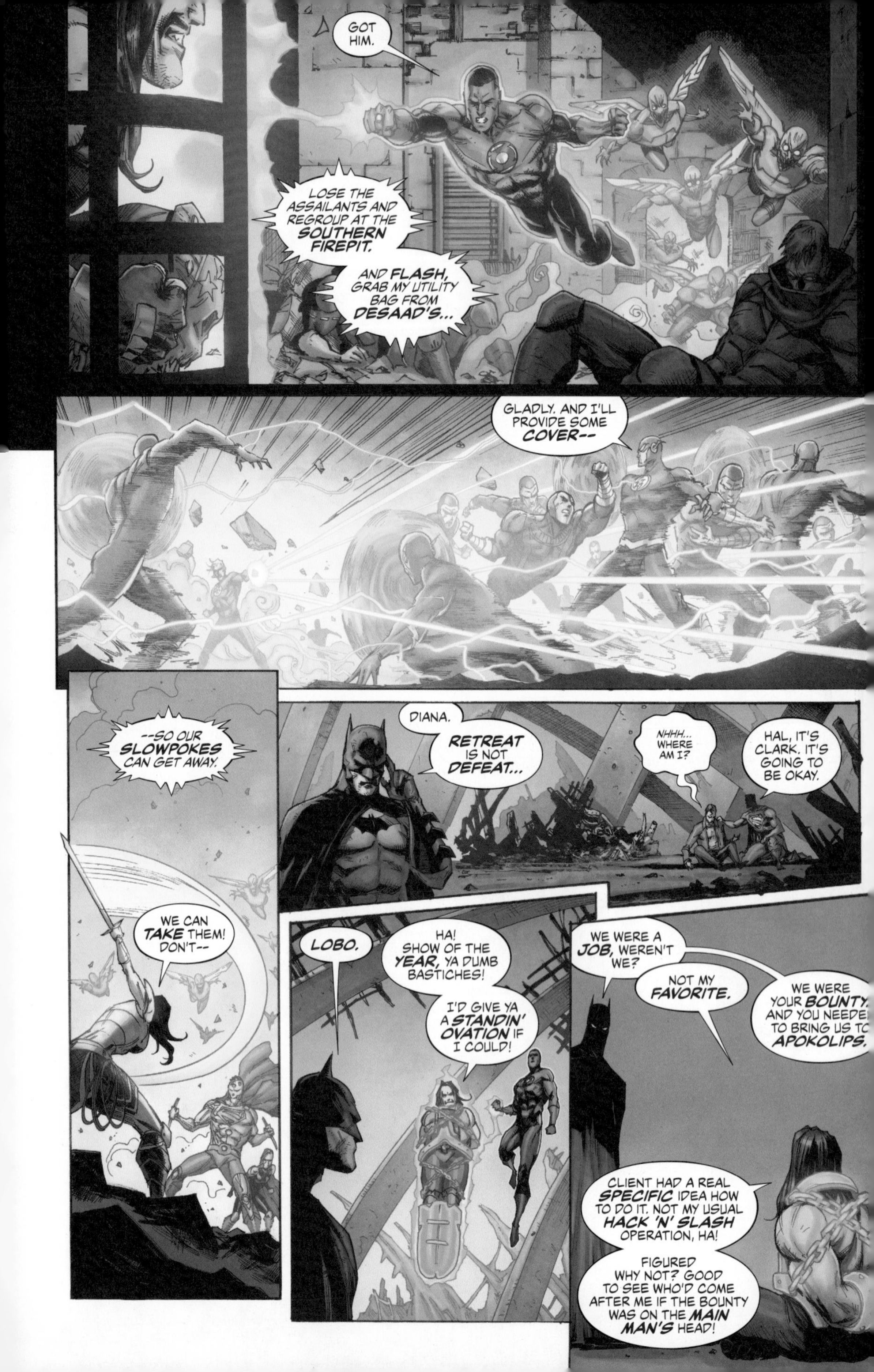
GOT HIM.
LOSE THE ASSAILANTS AND REGROUP AT THE SOUTHERN FIREPIT.
AND FLASH, GRAB MY UTILITY BAG FROM DESAAD'S...
GLADLY. AND I'LL PROVIDE SOME COVER--
--SO OUR SLOWPOKES CAN GET AWAY.
WE CAN TAKE THEM! DON'T--
DIANA.
RETREAT IS NOT DEFEAT...
NHHH... WHERE AM I?
HAL, IT'S CLARK. IT'S GOING TO BE OKAY.
LOBO.
HA! SHOW OF THE YEAR, YA DUMB BASTICHES!
I'D GIVE YA A STANDIN' OVATION IF I COULD!
WE WERE A JOB, WEREN'T WE?
NOT MY FAVORITE.
WE WERE YOUR BOUNTY. AND YOU NEEDE TO BRING US TO APOKOLIPS.
CLIENT HAD A REAL SPECIFIC IDEA HOW TO DO IT. NOT MY USUAL HACK 'N' SLASH OPERATION, HA!
FIGURED WHY NOT? GOOD TO SEE WHO'D COME AFTER ME IF THE BOUNTY WAS ON THE MAIN MAN'S HEAD!

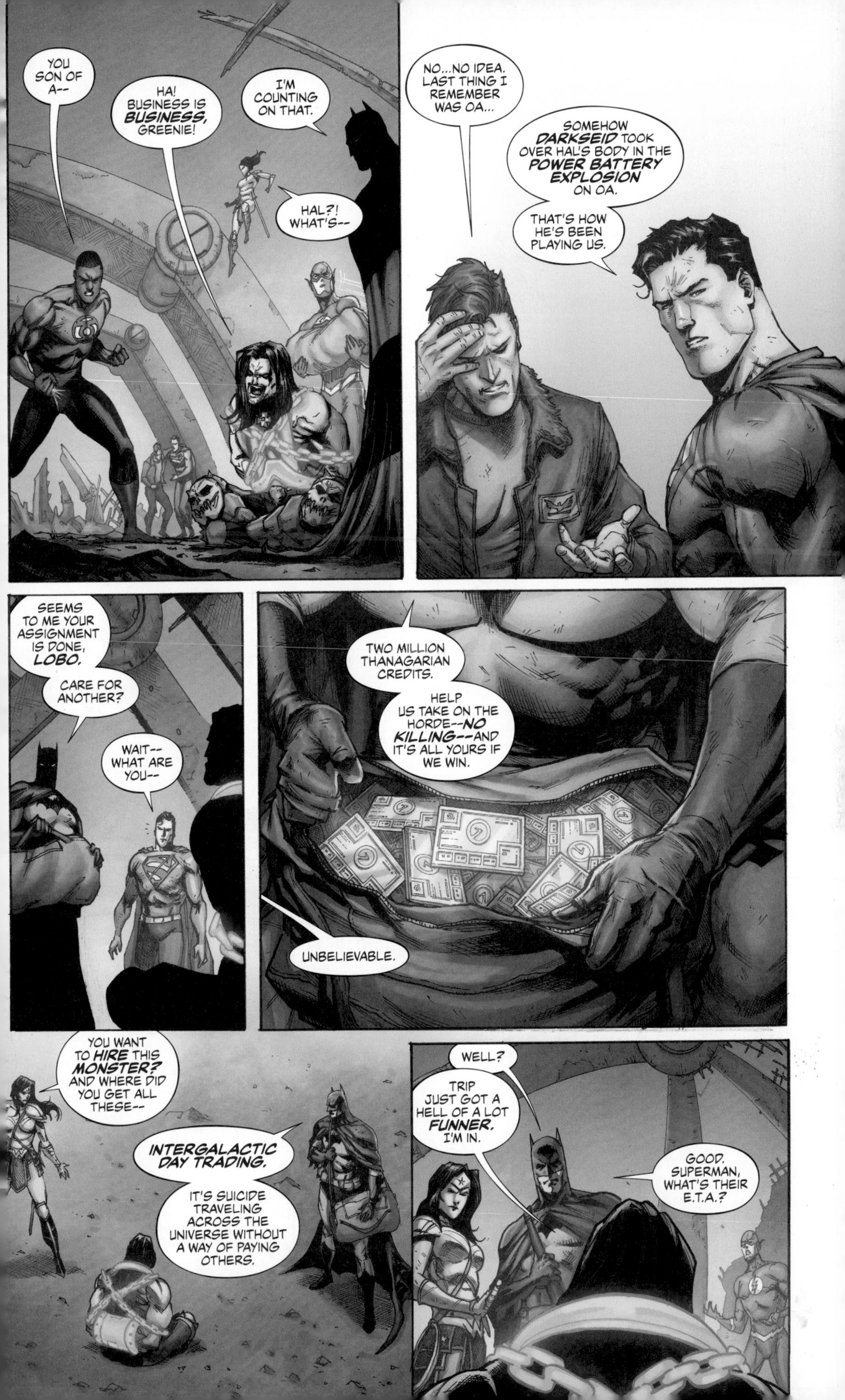
YOU SON OF A--
HA! BUSINESS IS BUSINESS, GREENIE!
I'M COUNTING ON THAT.
HAL?! WHAT'S--
NO...NO IDEA. LAST THING I REMEMBER WAS OA...
SOMEHOW DARKSEID TOOK OVER HAL'S BODY IN THE POWER BATTERY EXPLOSION ON OA.
THAT'S HOW HE'S BEEN PLAYING US.
SEEMS TO ME YOUR ASSIGNMENT IS DONE, LOBO.
CARE FOR ANOTHER?
WAIT-- WHAT ARE YOU--
TWO MILLION THANAGARIAN CREDITS.
HELP US TAKE ON THE HORDE--NO KILLING--AND IT'S ALL YOURS IF WE WIN.
UNBELIEVABLE.
YOU WANT TO HIRE THIS MONSTER? AND WHERE DID YOU GET ALL THESE--
INTERGALACTIC DAY TRADING.
IT'S SUICIDE TRAVELING ACROSS THE UNIVERSE WITHOUT A WAY OF PAYING OTHERS.
WELL?
TRIP JUST GOT A HELL OF A LOT FUNNER. I'M IN.
GOOD. SUPERMAN, WHAT'S THEIR E.T.A.?

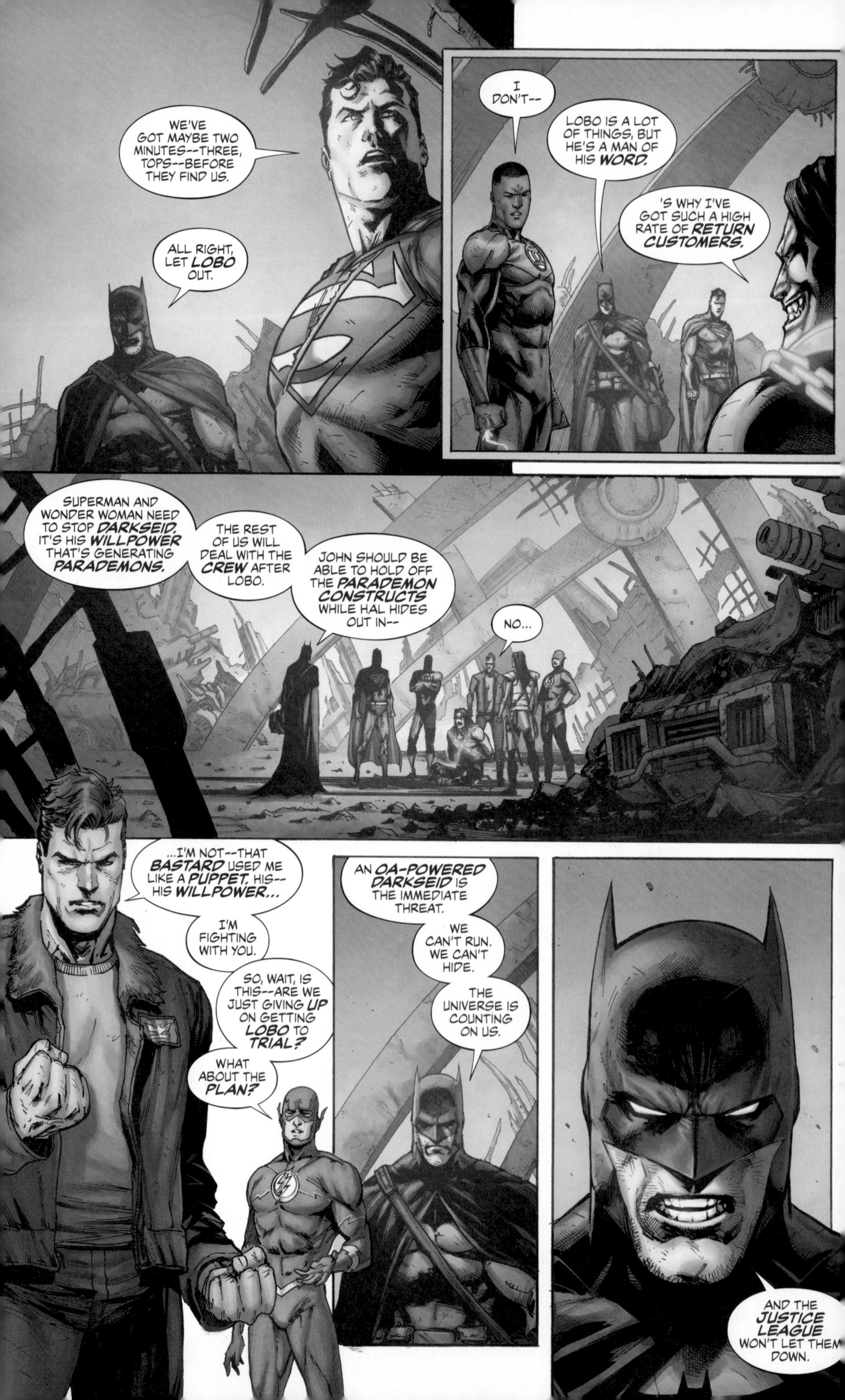

WE'VE GOT MAYBE TWO MINUTES--THREE, TOPS--BEFORE THEY FIND US.
ALL RIGHT, LET LOBO OUT.
I DON'T--
LOBO IS A LOT OF THINGS, BUT HE'S A MAN OF HIS WORD.
'S WHY I'VE GOT SUCH A HIGH RATE OF RETURN CUSTOMERS.
SUPERMAN AND WONDER WOMAN NEED TO STOP DARKSEID. IT'S HIS WILLPOWER THAT'S GENERATING PARADEMONS.
THE REST OF US WILL DEAL WITH THE CREW AFTER LOBO.
JOHN SHOULD BE ABLE TO HOLD OFF THE PARADEMON CONSTRUCTS WHILE HAL HIDES OUT IN--
NO...
...I'M NOT--THAT BASTARD USED ME LIKE A PUPPET. HIS--HIS WILLPOWER...
I'M FIGHTING WITH YOU.
SO, WAIT, IS THIS--ARE WE JUST GIVING UP ON GETTING LOBO TO TRIAL?
WHAT ABOUT THE PLAN?
AN OA-POWERED DARKSEID IS THE IMMEDIATE THREAT.
WE CAN'T RUN. WE CAN'T HIDE.
THE UNIVERSE IS COUNTING ON US.
AND THE JUSTICE LEAGUE WON'T LET THEM DOWN.

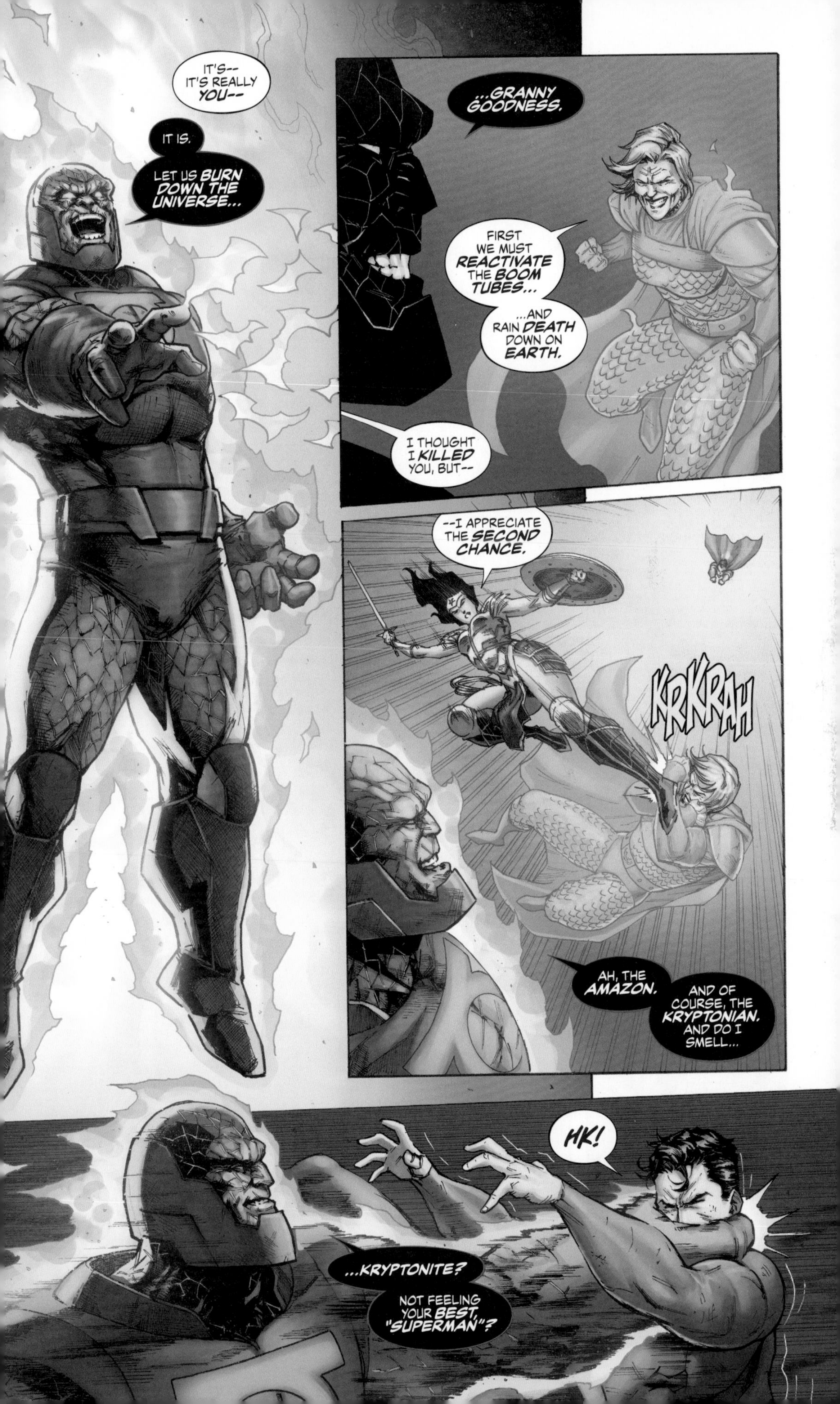

IT'S-- IT'S REALLY YOU--
IT IS.
LET US BURN DOWN THE UNIVERSE...
...GRANNY GOODNESS.
FIRST WE MUST REACTIVATE THE BOOM TUBES...
...AND RAIN DEATH DOWN ON EARTH.
I THOUGHT I KILLED YOU, BUT--
--I APPRECIATE THE SECOND CHANCE.
KRKRAH
AH, THE AMAZON.
AND OF COURSE, THE KRYPTONIAN. AND DO I SMELL...
HK!
...KRYPTONITE?
NOT FEELING YOUR BEST, "SUPERMAN"?

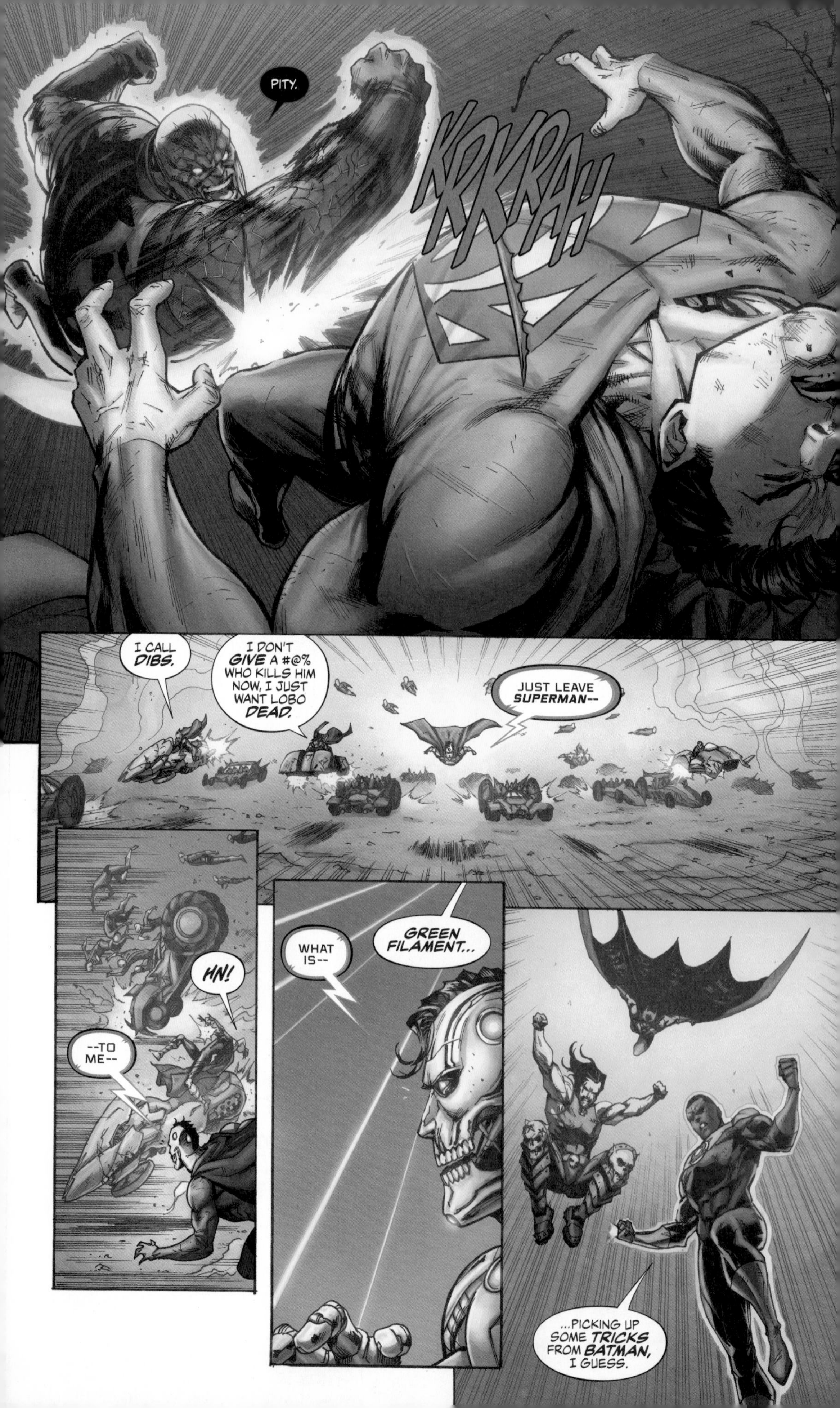
PITY.
KRKRAH
I CALL DIBS.
I DON'T GIVE A #@% WHO KILLS HIM NOW, I JUST WANT LOBO DEAD.
JUST LEAVE SUPERMAN--
HN!
--TO ME--
WHAT IS--
GREEN FILAMENT...
...PICKING UP SOME TRICKS FROM BATMAN, I GUESS.

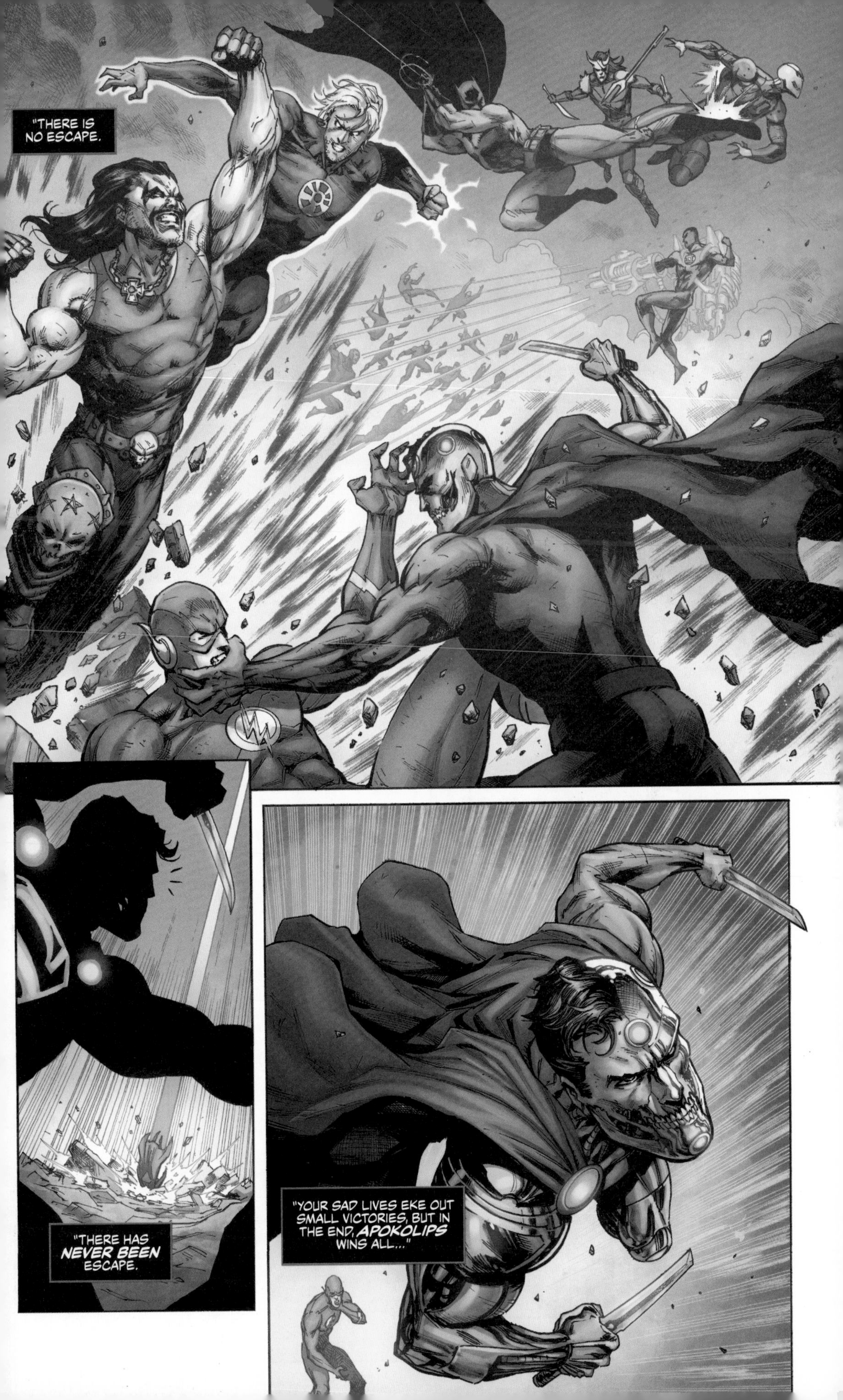
"THERE IS NO ESCAPE.
"THERE HAS NEVER BEEN ESCAPE.
"YOUR SAD LIVES EKE OUT SMALL VICTORIES, BUT IN THE END, APOKOLIPS WINS ALL..."

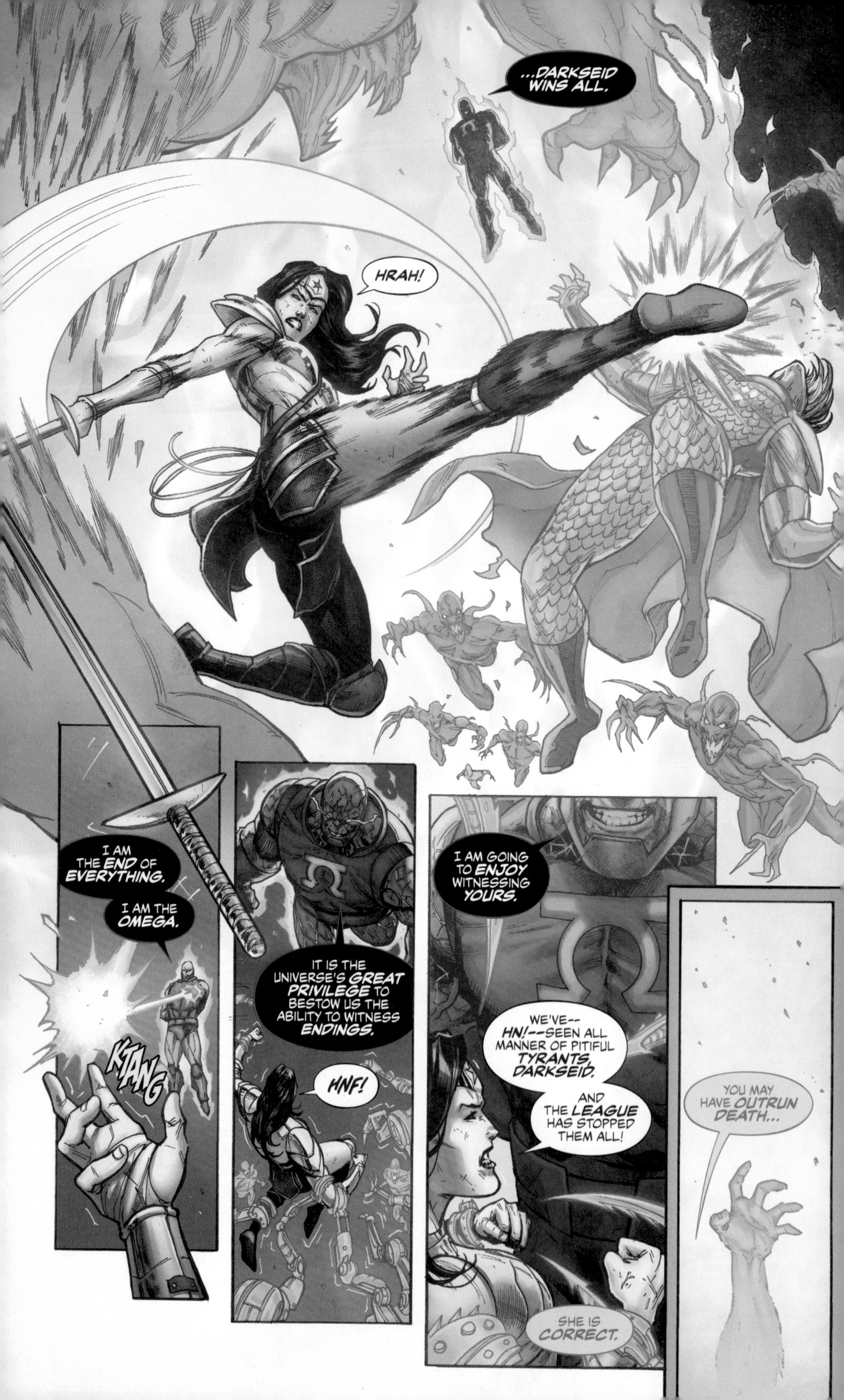
...DARKSEID WINS ALL.
HRAH!
I AM THE END OF EVERYTHING.
I AM THE OMEGA.
KTANG
IT IS THE UNIVERSE'S GREAT PRIVILEGE TO BESTOW US THE ABILITY TO WITNESS ENDINGS.
HNF!
I AM GOING TO ENJOY WITNESSING YOURS.
WE'VE-- HN!--SEEN ALL MANNER OF PITIFUL TYRANTS, DARKSEID.
AND THE LEAGUE HAS STOPPED THEM ALL!
SHE IS CORRECT.
YOU MAY HAVE OUTRUN DEATH...

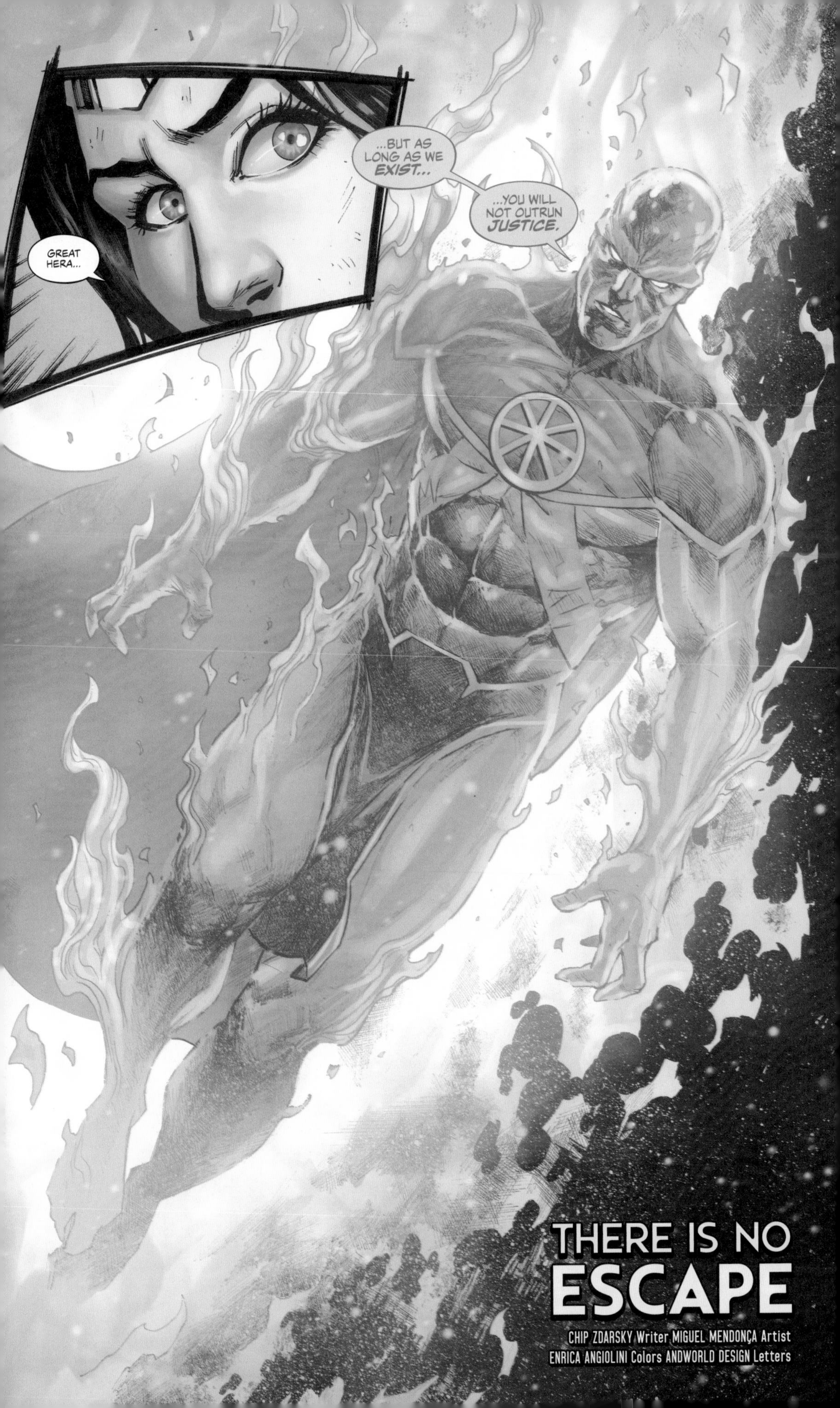
GREAT HERA...
...BUT AS LONG AS WE EXIST...
...YOU WILL NOT OUTRUN JUSTICE.
THERE IS NO ESCAPE
CHIP ZDARSKY Writer MIGUEL MENDONÇA Artist
ENRICA ANGIOLINI Colors ANDWORLD DESIGN Letters

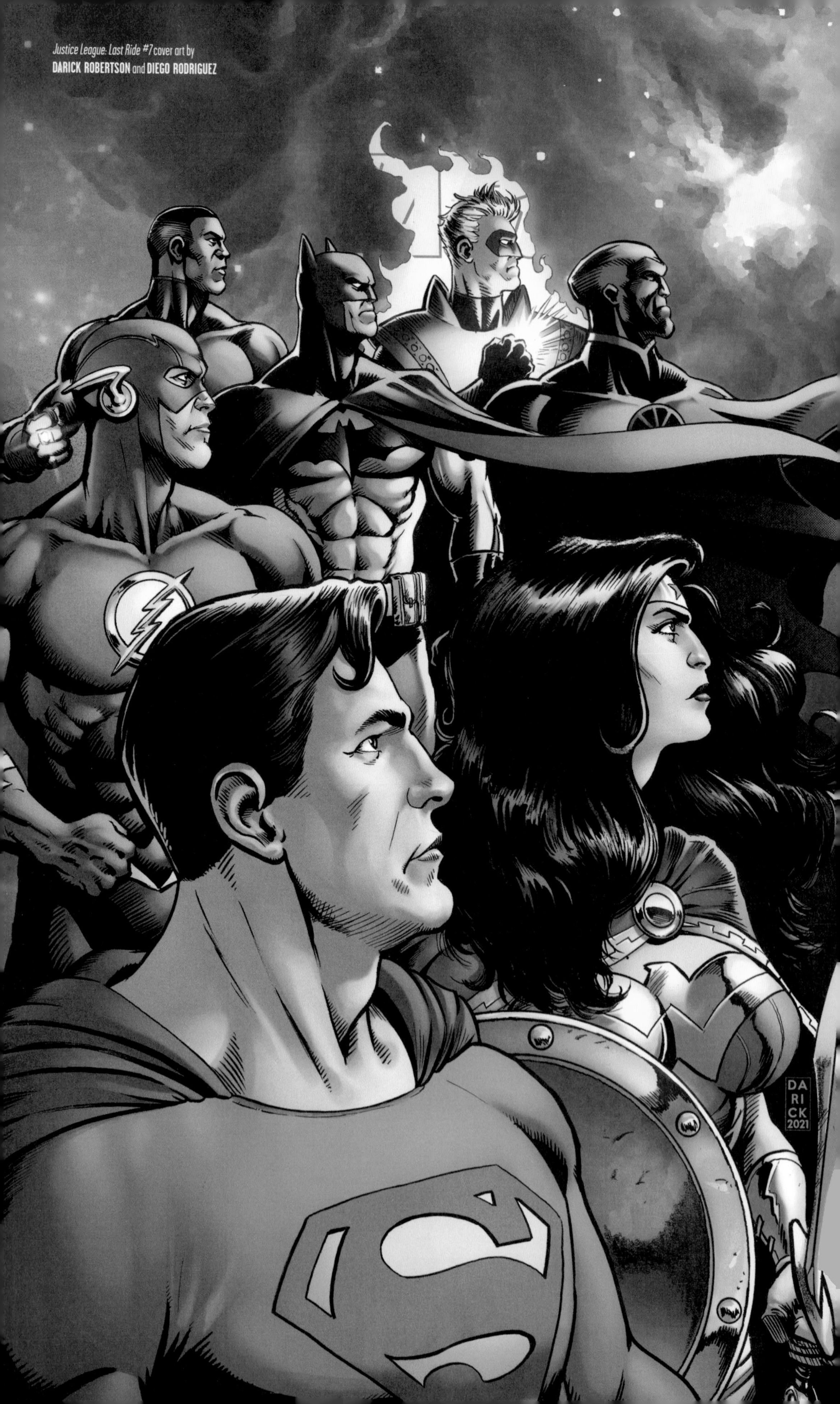
DA
RI
CK
2021

Justice League: Last Ride #7 cover art by
DARICK ROBERTSON and **DIEGO RODRIGUEZ**

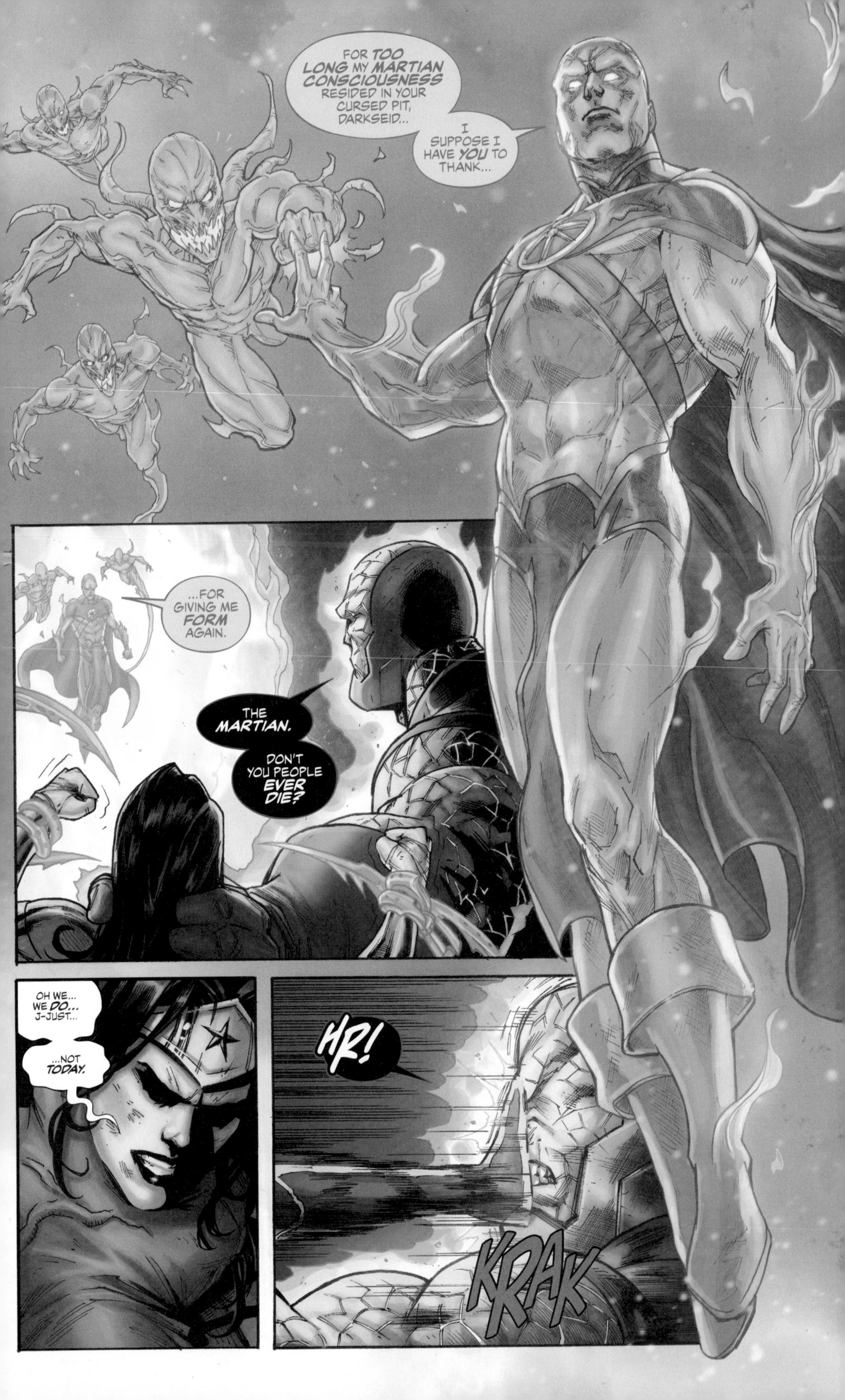
FOR TOO LONG MY MARTIAN CONSCIOUSNESS RESIDED IN YOUR CURSED PIT, DARKSEID...
I SUPPOSE I HAVE YOU TO THANK...
...FOR GIVING ME FORM AGAIN.
THE MARTIAN.
DON'T YOU PEOPLE EVER DIE?
OH WE... WE DO... J-JUST...
...NOT TODAY.
HR!
KRAK

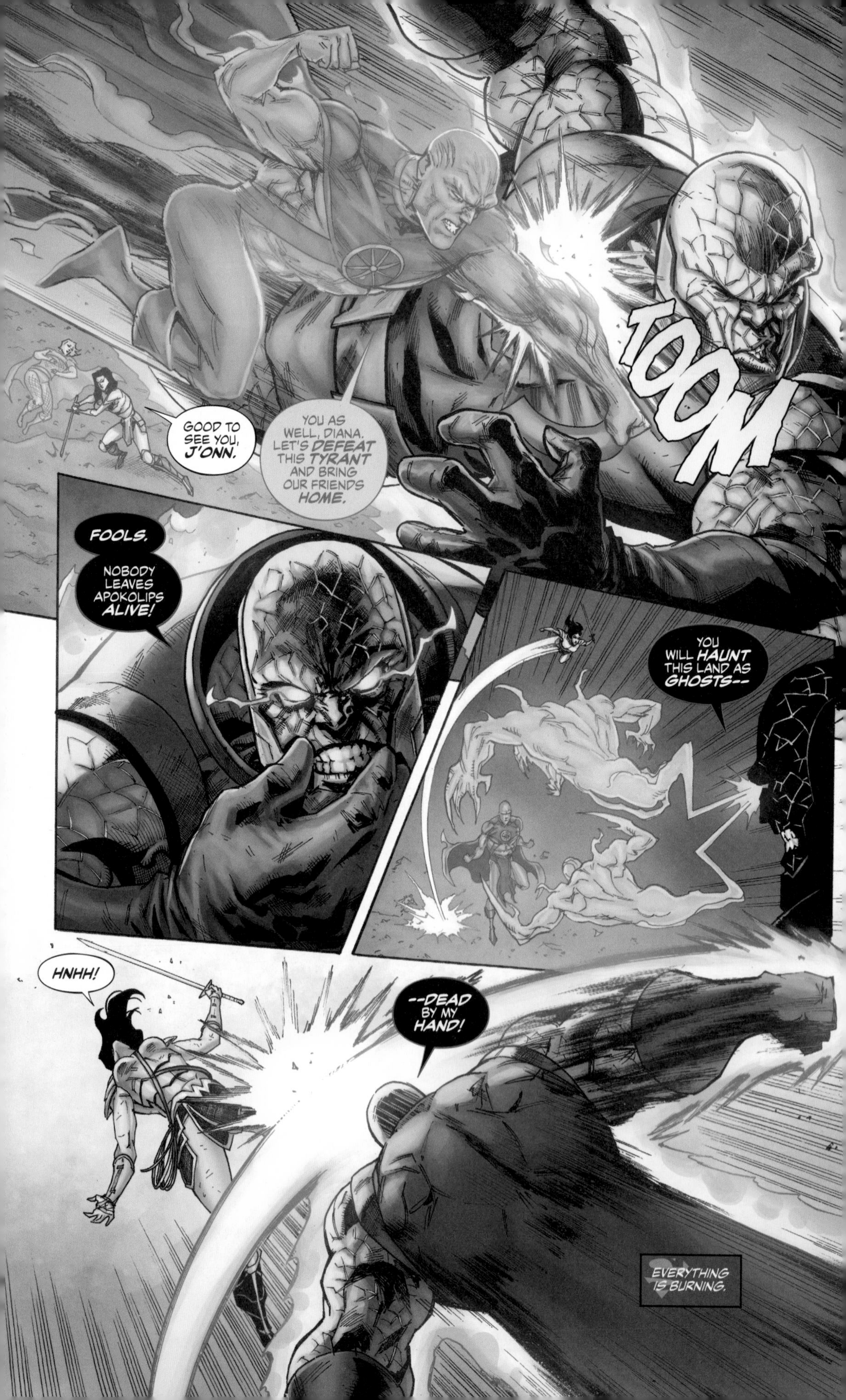
TOOM
GOOD TO SEE YOU, J'ONN.
YOU AS WELL, DIANA. LET'S DEFEAT THIS TYRANT AND BRING OUR FRIENDS HOME.
FOOLS.
NOBODY LEAVES APOKOLIPS ALIVE!
YOU WILL HAUNT THIS LAND AS GHOSTS--
HNHH!
--DEAD BY MY HAND!
EVERYTHING IS BURNING.

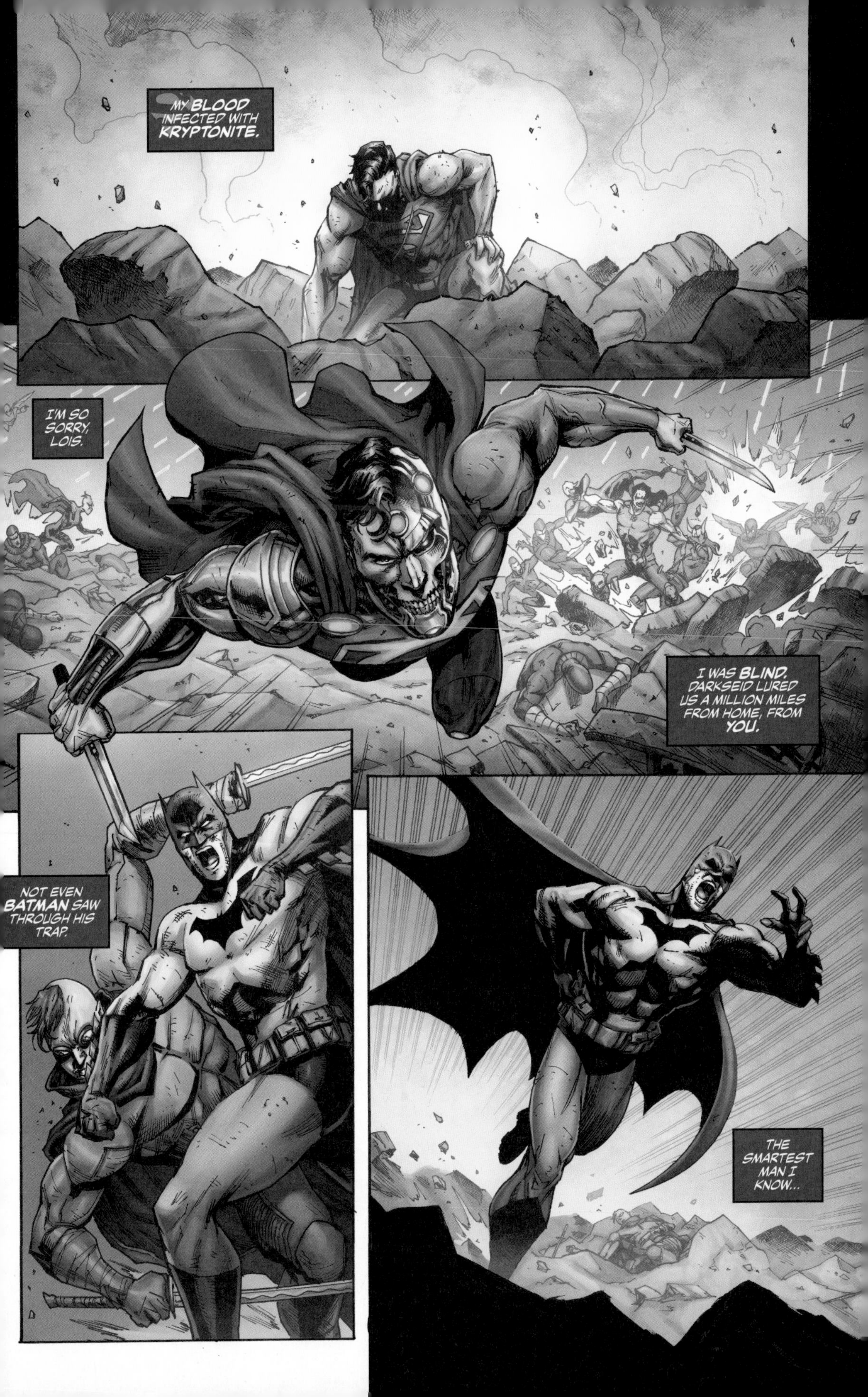
MY BLOOD INFECTED WITH KRYPTONITE.
I'M SO SORRY, LOIS.
I WAS BLIND. DARKSEID LURED US A MILLION MILES FROM HOME, FROM YOU.
NOT EVEN BATMAN SAW THROUGH HIS TRAP.
THE SMARTEST MAN I KNOW...

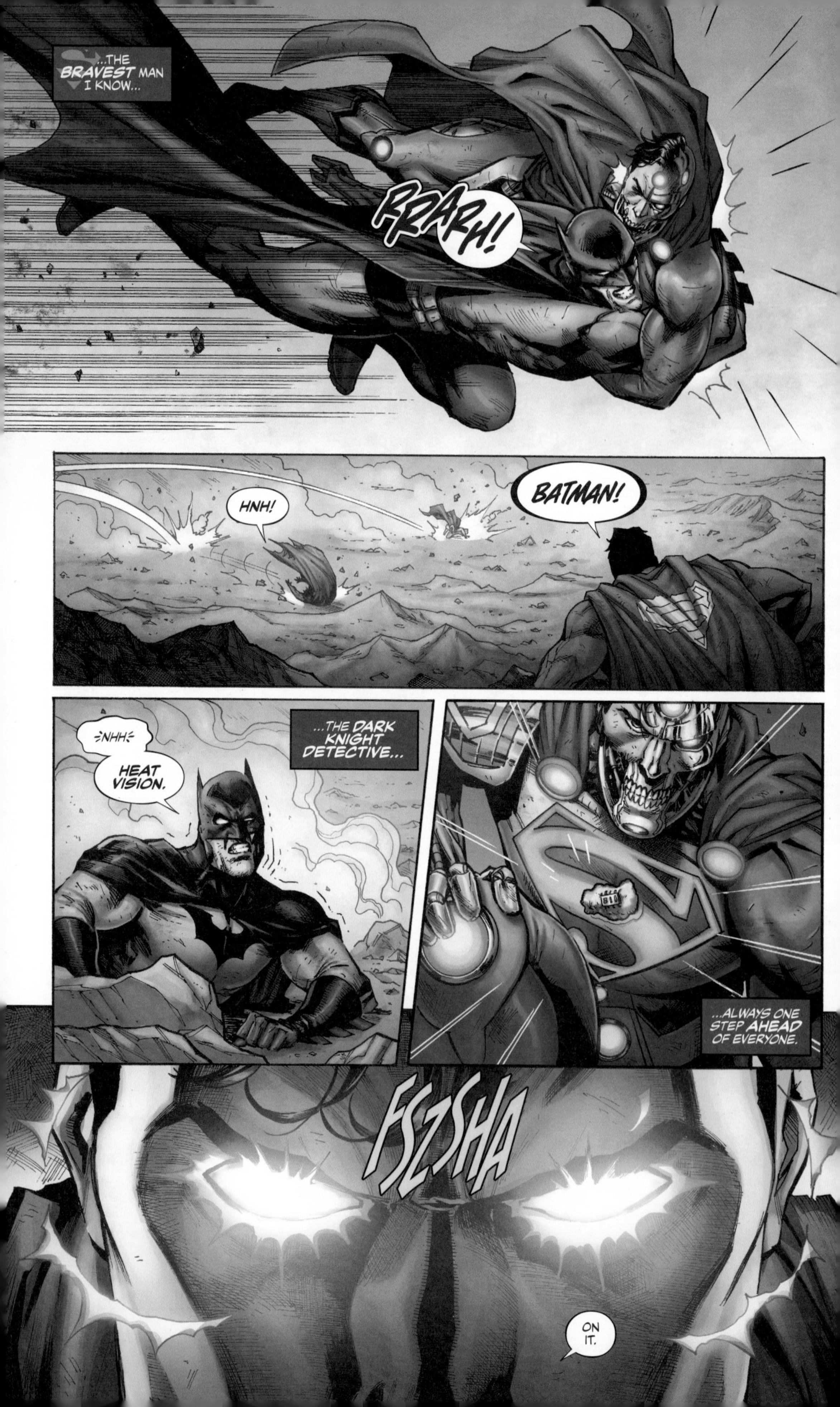

...THE BRAVEST MAN I KNOW...
RRARH!
HNH!
BATMAN!
NHH
HEAT VISION.
...THE DARK KNIGHT DETECTIVE...
...ALWAYS ONE STEP AHEAD OF EVERYONE.
FSZSHA
ON IT.

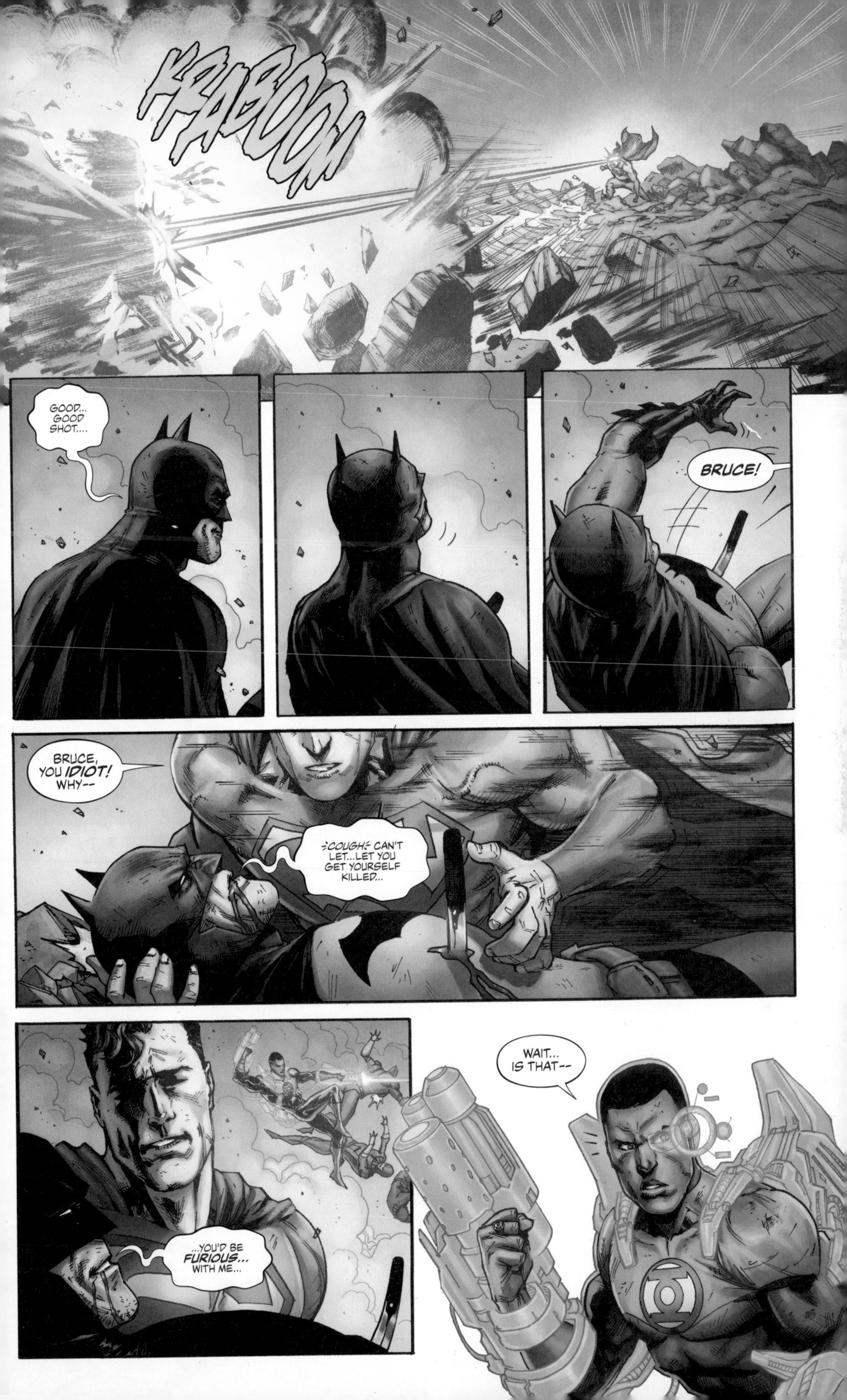
KRABOOM
GOOD... GOOD SHOT....
BRUCE!
BRUCE, YOU IDIOT! WHY--
=COUGH= CAN'T LET...LET YOU GET YOURSELF KILLED...
...YOU'D BE FURIOUS... WITH ME...
WAIT... IS THAT--

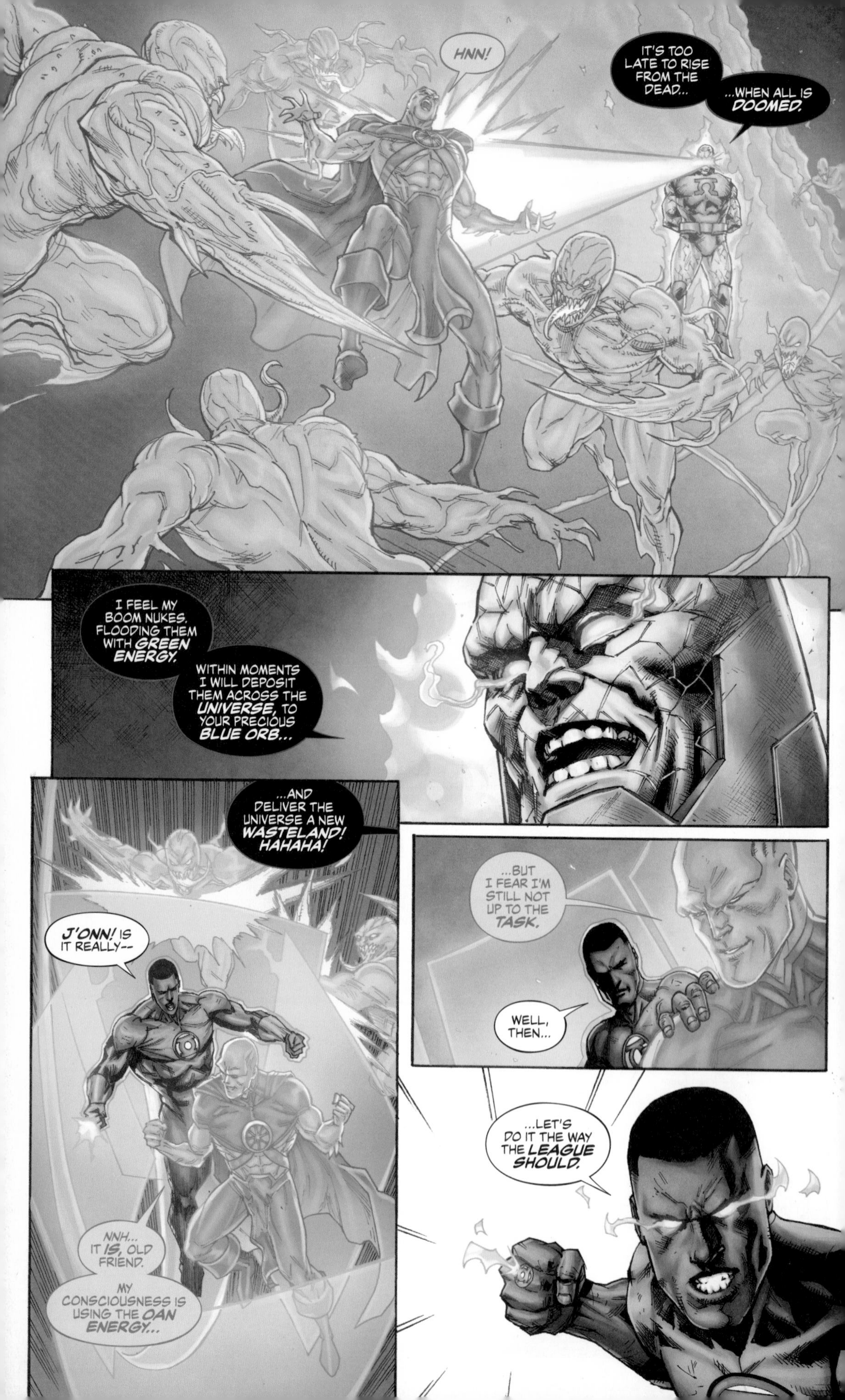
HNN!
IT'S TOO LATE TO RISE FROM THE DEAD...
...WHEN ALL IS DOOMED.
I FEEL MY BOOM NUKES. FLOODING THEM WITH GREEN ENERGY.
WITHIN MOMENTS I WILL DEPOSIT THEM ACROSS THE UNIVERSE, TO YOUR PRECIOUS BLUE ORB...
...AND DELIVER THE UNIVERSE A NEW WASTELAND! HAHAHA!
J'ONN! IS IT REALLY--
NNH... IT IS, OLD FRIEND.
MY CONSCIOUSNESS IS USING THE OAN ENERGY...
...BUT I FEAR I'M STILL NOT UP TO THE TASK.
WELL, THEN...
...LET'S DO IT THE WAY THE LEAGUE SHOULD.

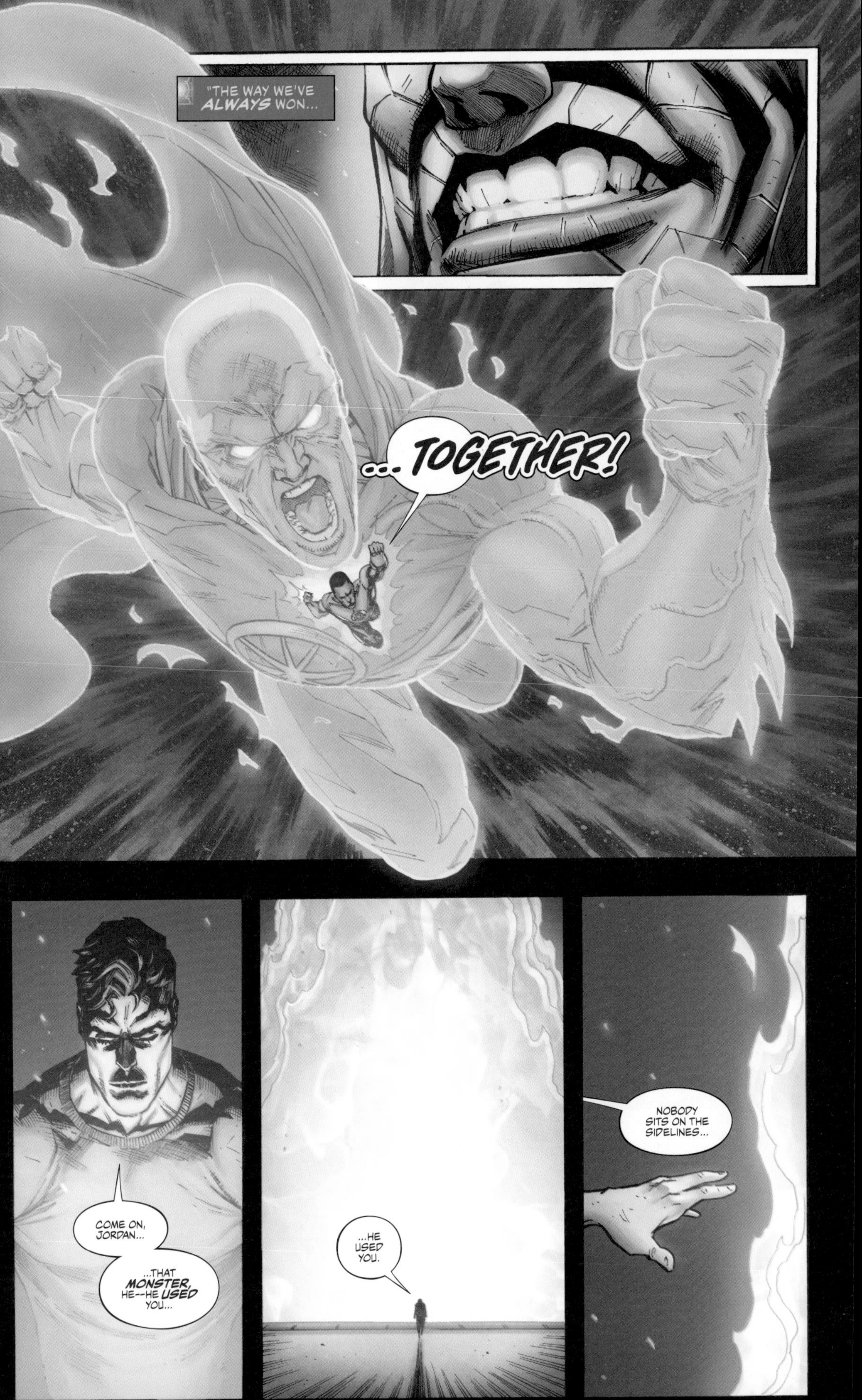
"THE WAY WE'VE ALWAYS WON...
...TOGETHER!
COME ON, JORDAN...
...THAT MONSTER, HE--HE USED YOU...
...HE USED YOU.
NOBODY SITS ON THE SIDELINES...

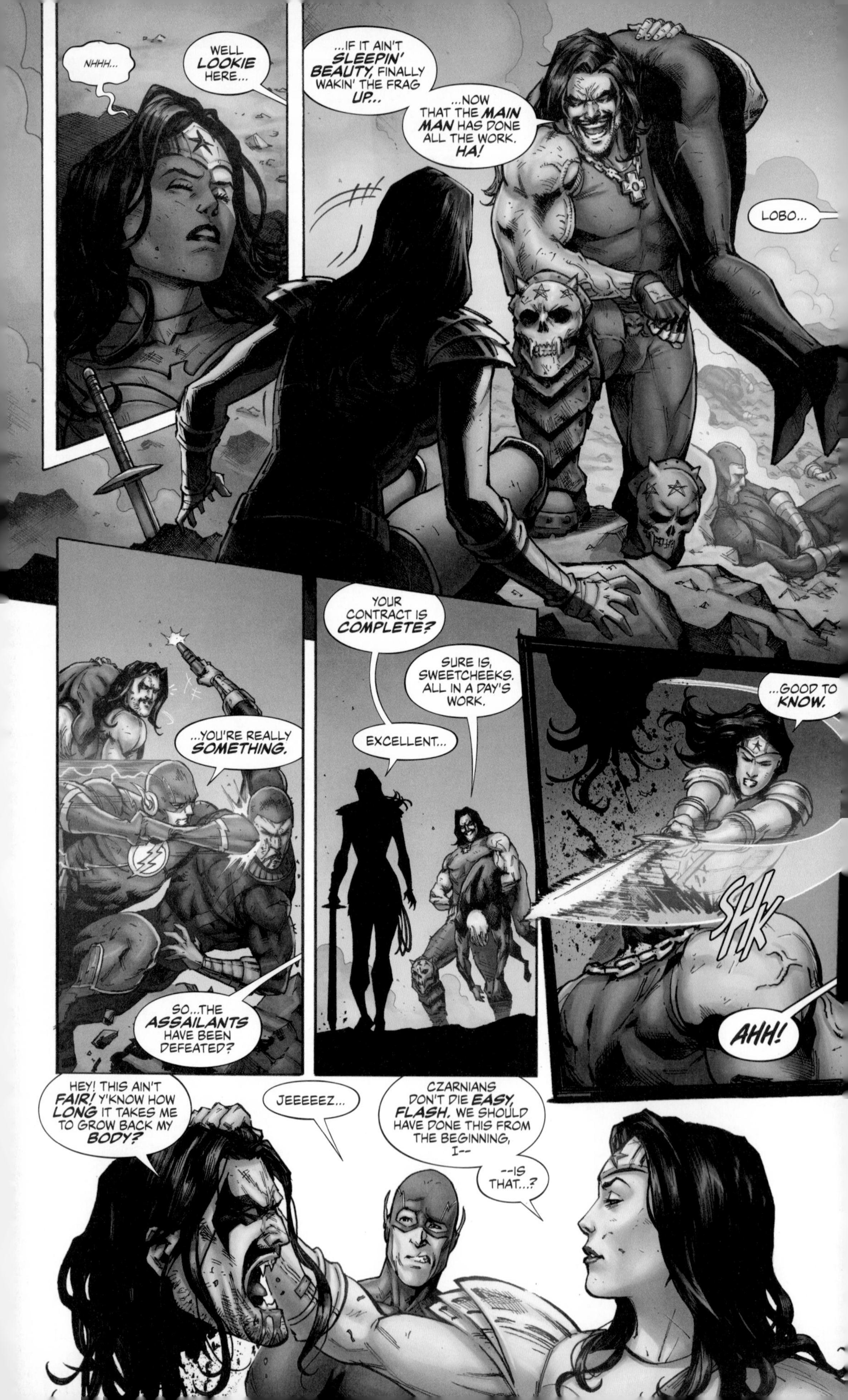
NHHH...
WELL LOOKIE HERE...
...IF IT AIN'T SLEEPIN' BEAUTY, FINALLY WAKIN' THE FRAG UP...
...NOW THAT THE MAIN MAN HAS DONE ALL THE WORK. HA!
LOBO...
...YOU'RE REALLY SOMETHING.
SO...THE ASSAILANTS HAVE BEEN DEFEATED?
YOUR CONTRACT IS COMPLETE?
SURE IS, SWEETCHEEKS. ALL IN A DAY'S WORK.
EXCELLENT...
...GOOD TO KNOW.
SHK
AHH!
HEY! THIS AIN'T FAIR! Y'KNOW HOW LONG IT TAKES ME TO GROW BACK MY BODY?
JEEEEEZ...
CZARNIANS DON'T DIE EASY, FLASH. WE SHOULD HAVE DONE THIS FROM THE BEGINNING, I--
--IS THAT...?

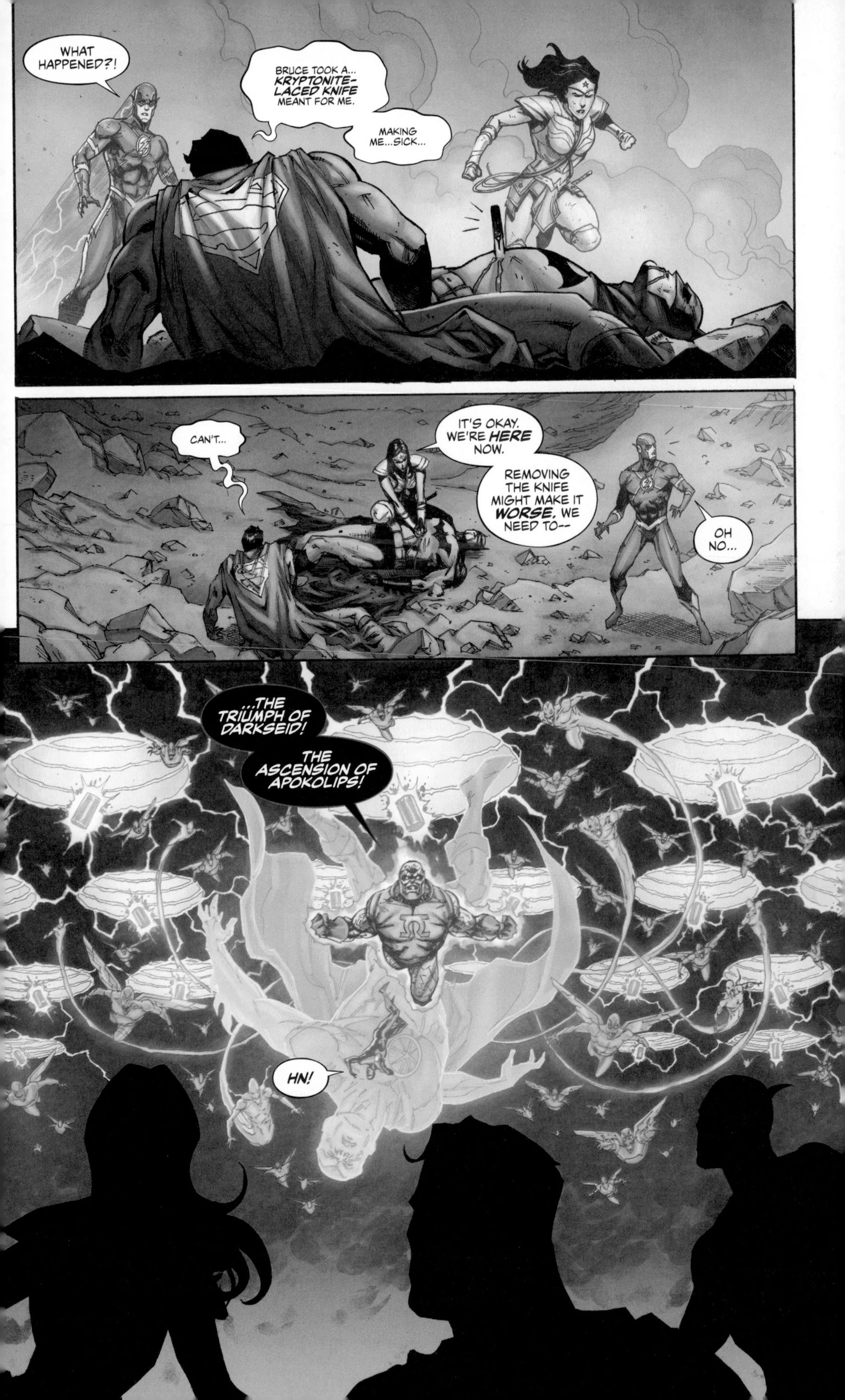
WHAT HAPPENED?!
BRUCE TOOK A... KRYPTONITE-LACED KNIFE MEANT FOR ME.
MAKING ME...SICK...
CAN'T...
IT'S OKAY. WE'RE HERE NOW.
REMOVING THE KNIFE MIGHT MAKE IT WORSE. WE NEED TO--
OH NO...
...THE TRIUMPH OF DARKSEID!
THE ASCENSION OF APOKOLIPS!
HN!

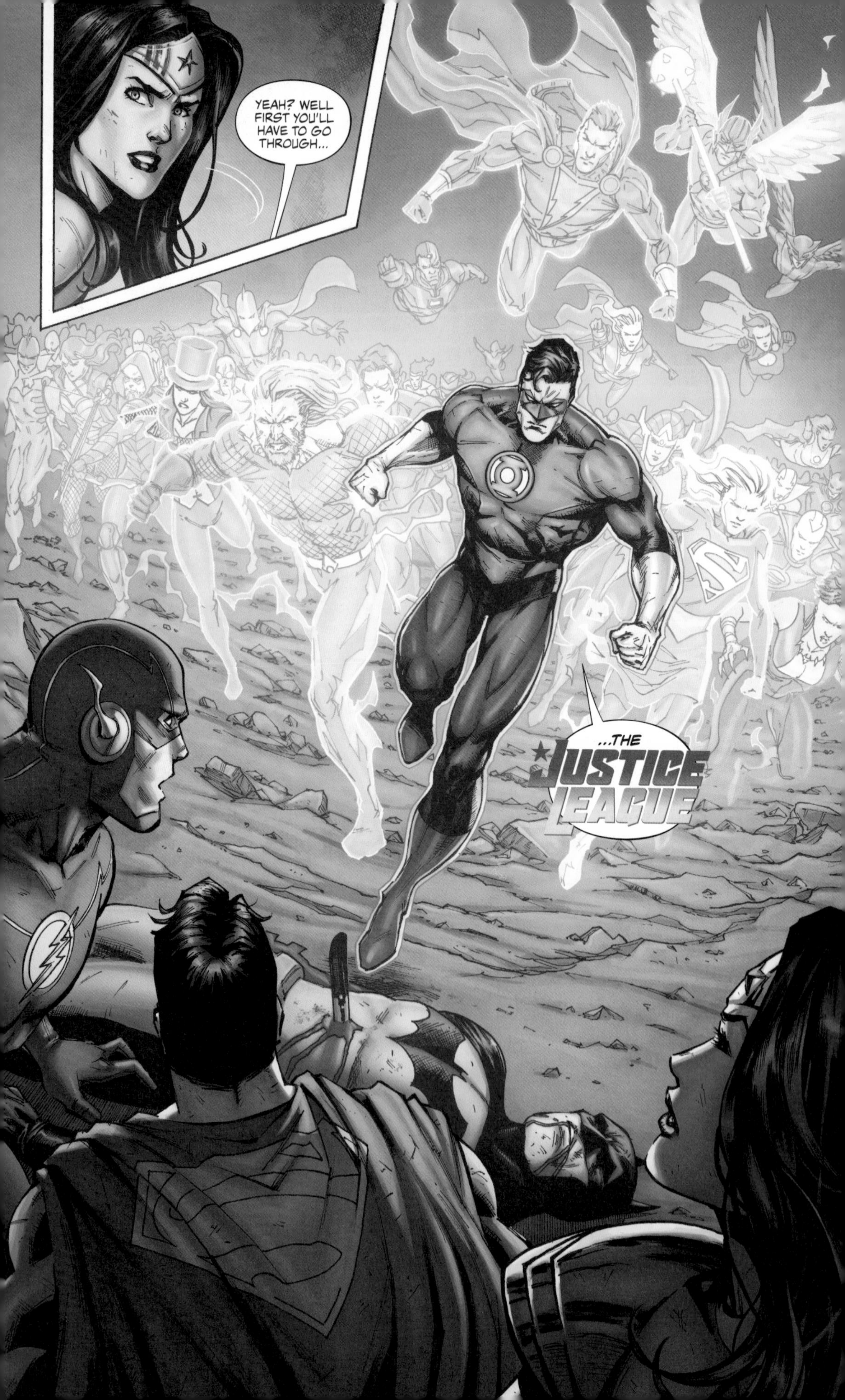
YEAH? WELL FIRST YOU'LL HAVE TO GO THROUGH...
...THE JUSTICE LEAGUE

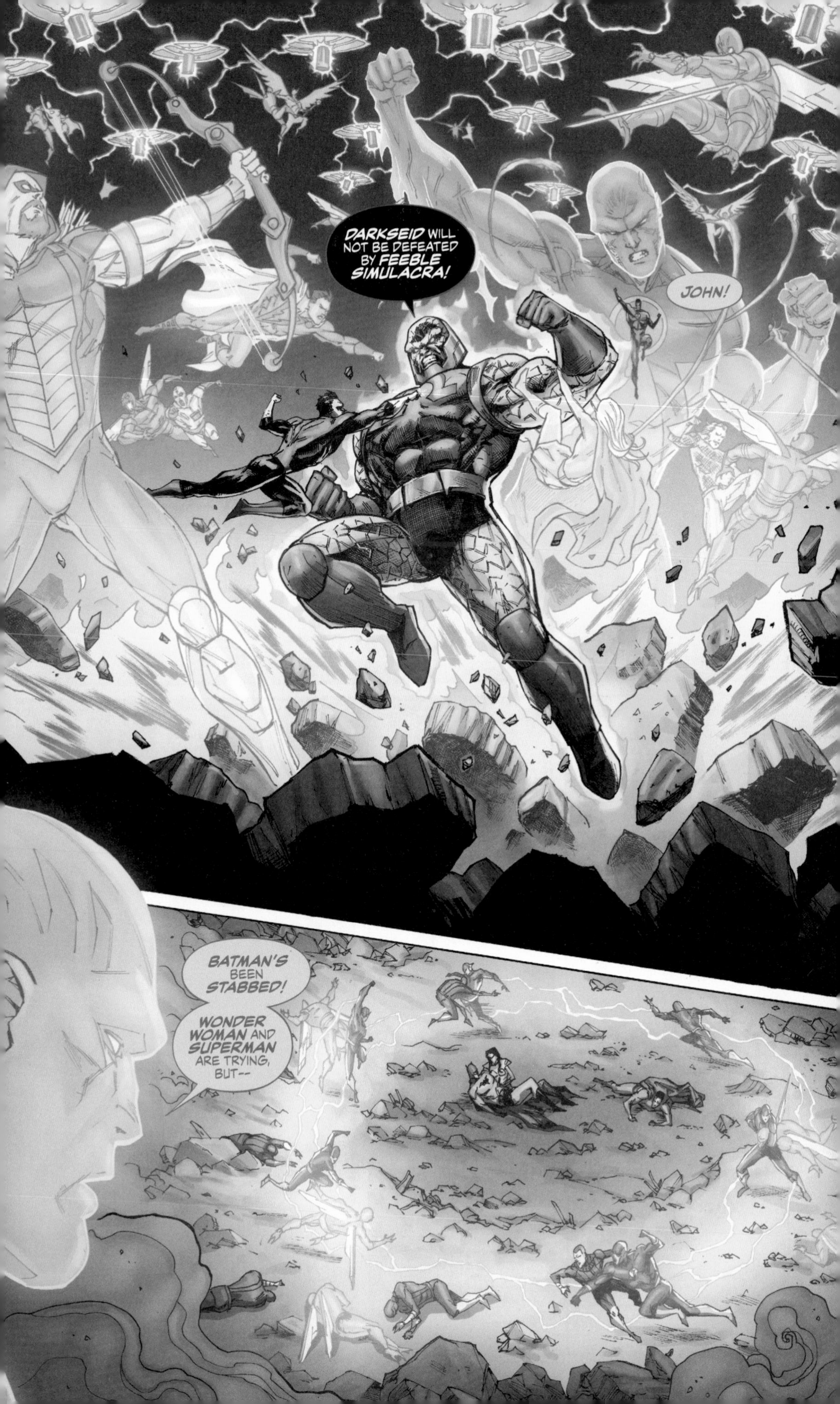
DARKSEID WILL NOT BE DEFEATED BY FEEBLE SIMULACRA!
JOHN!
BATMAN'S BEEN STABBED!
WONDER WOMAN AND SUPERMAN ARE TRYING, BUT--

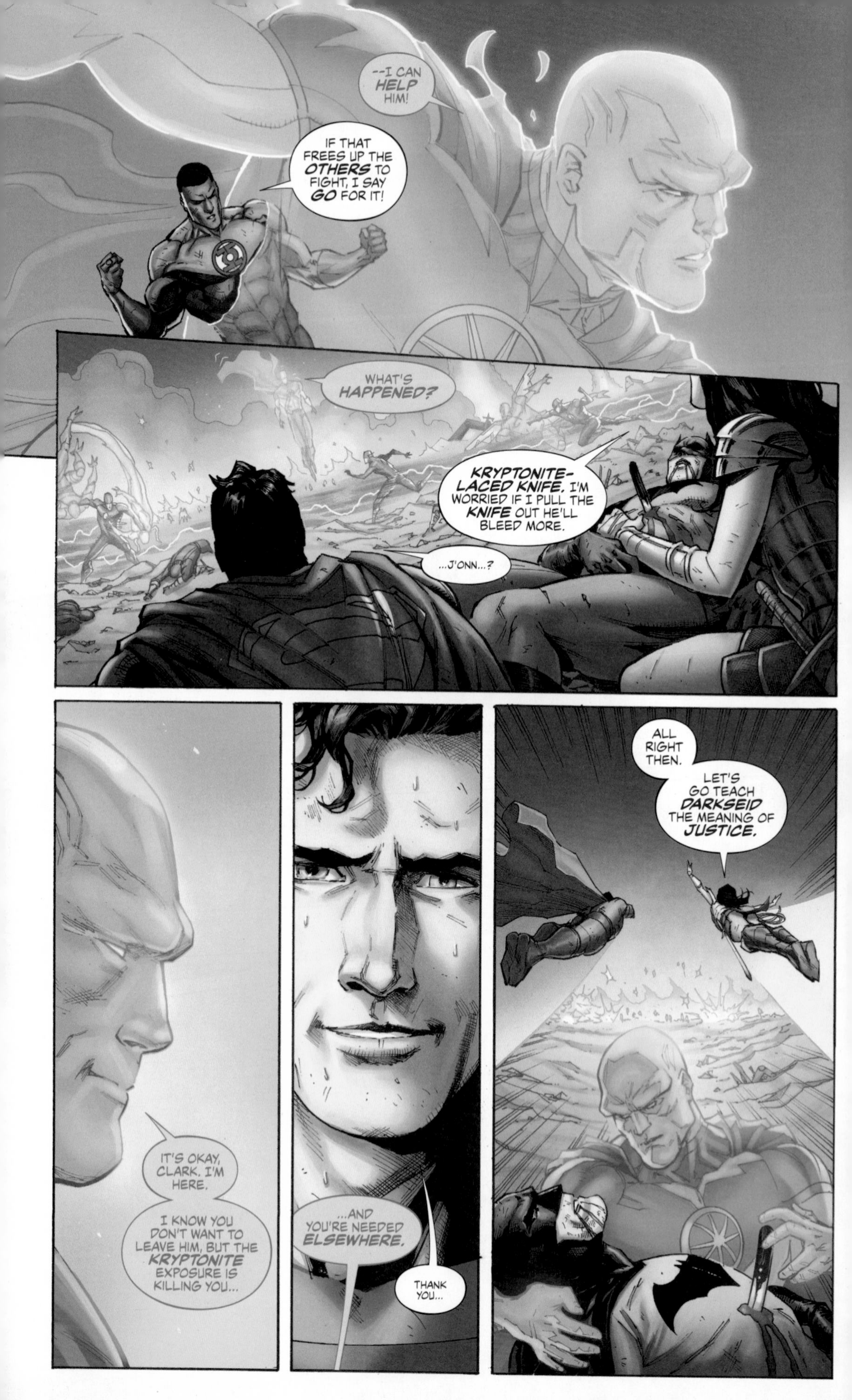
--I CAN HELP HIM!
IF THAT FREES UP THE OTHERS TO FIGHT, I SAY GO FOR IT!
WHAT'S HAPPENED?
KRYPTONITE-LACED KNIFE. I'M WORRIED IF I PULL THE KNIFE OUT HE'LL BLEED MORE.
...J'ONN...?
IT'S OKAY, CLARK. I'M HERE.
I KNOW YOU DON'T WANT TO LEAVE HIM, BUT THE KRYPTONITE EXPOSURE IS KILLING YOU...
...AND YOU'RE NEEDED ELSEWHERE.
THANK YOU...
ALL RIGHT THEN.
LET'S GO TEACH DARKSEID THE MEANING OF JUSTICE.

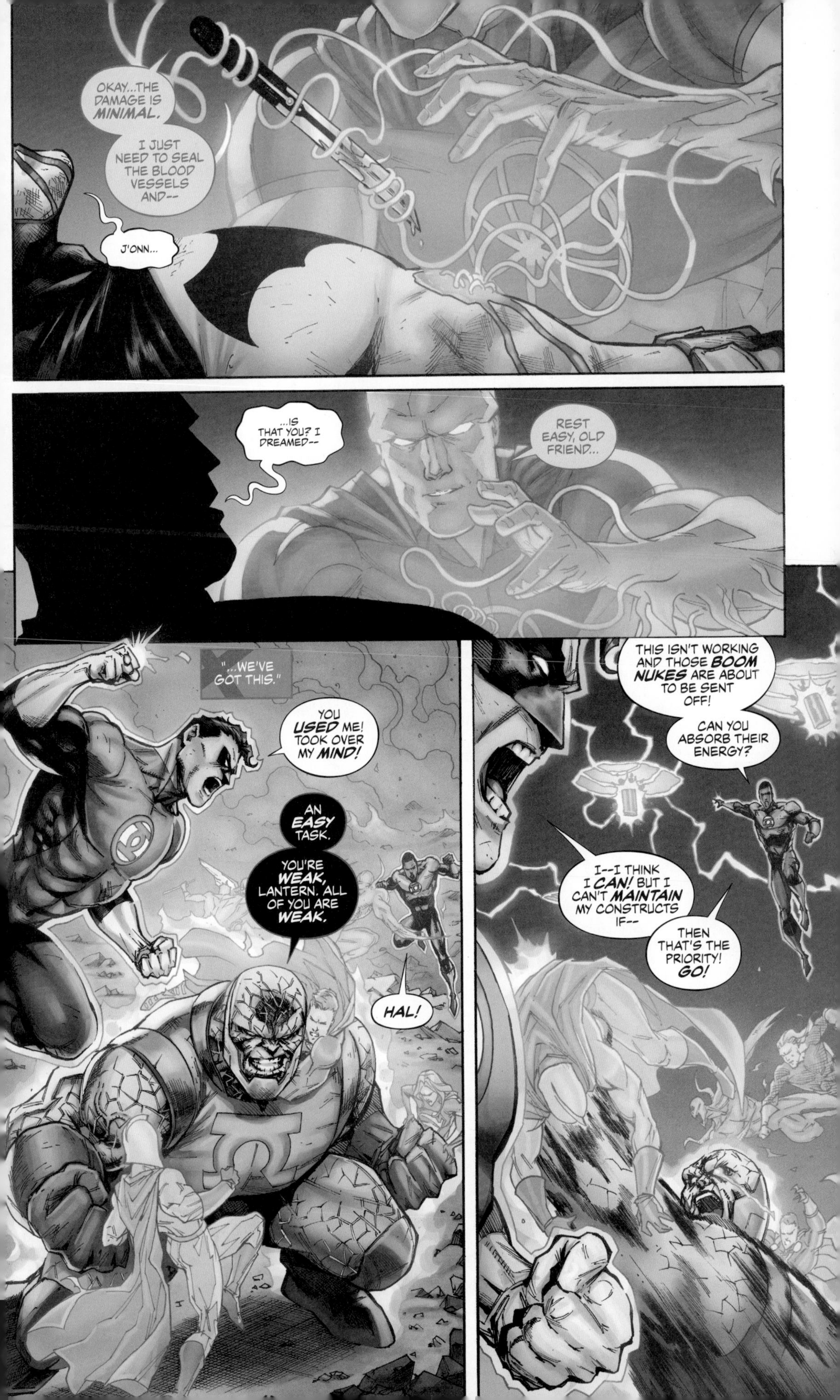
OKAY...THE DAMAGE IS MINIMAL.
I JUST NEED TO SEAL THE BLOOD VESSELS AND--
J'ONN...
...IS THAT YOU? I DREAMED--
REST EASY, OLD FRIEND...
"...WE'VE GOT THIS."
YOU USED ME! TOOK OVER MY MIND!
AN EASY TASK.
YOU'RE WEAK, LANTERN. ALL OF YOU ARE WEAK.
HAL!
THIS ISN'T WORKING AND THOSE BOOM NUKES ARE ABOUT TO BE SENT OFF!
CAN YOU ABSORB THEIR ENERGY?
I--I THINK I CAN! BUT I CAN'T MAINTAIN MY CONSTRUCTS IF--
THEN THAT'S THE PRIORITY! GO!

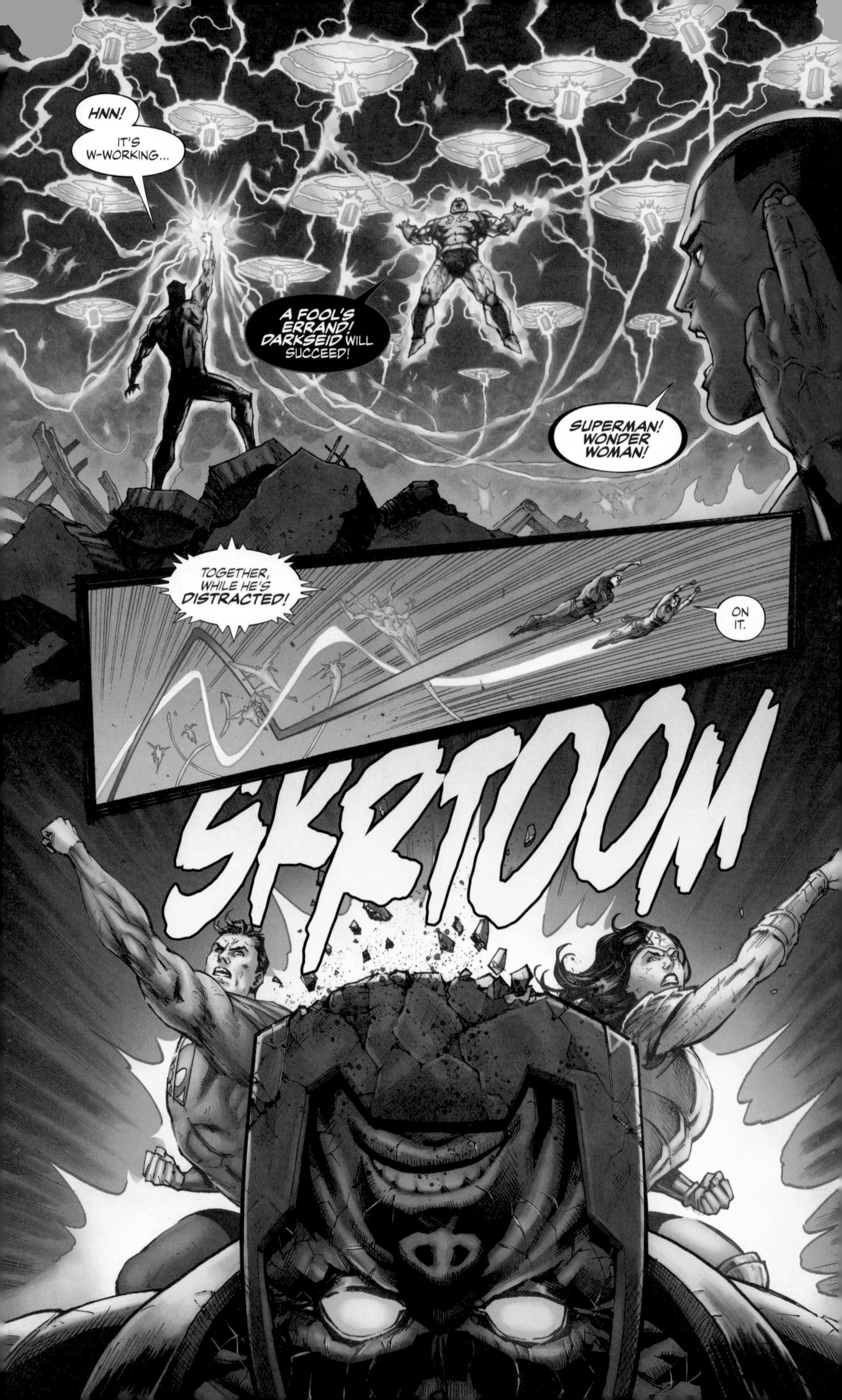
HNN!
IT'S W-WORKING...
A FOOL'S ERRAND! DARKSEID WILL SUCCEED!
SUPERMAN! WONDER WOMAN!
TOGETHER, WHILE HE'S DISTRACTED!
ON IT.
SKRTOOM

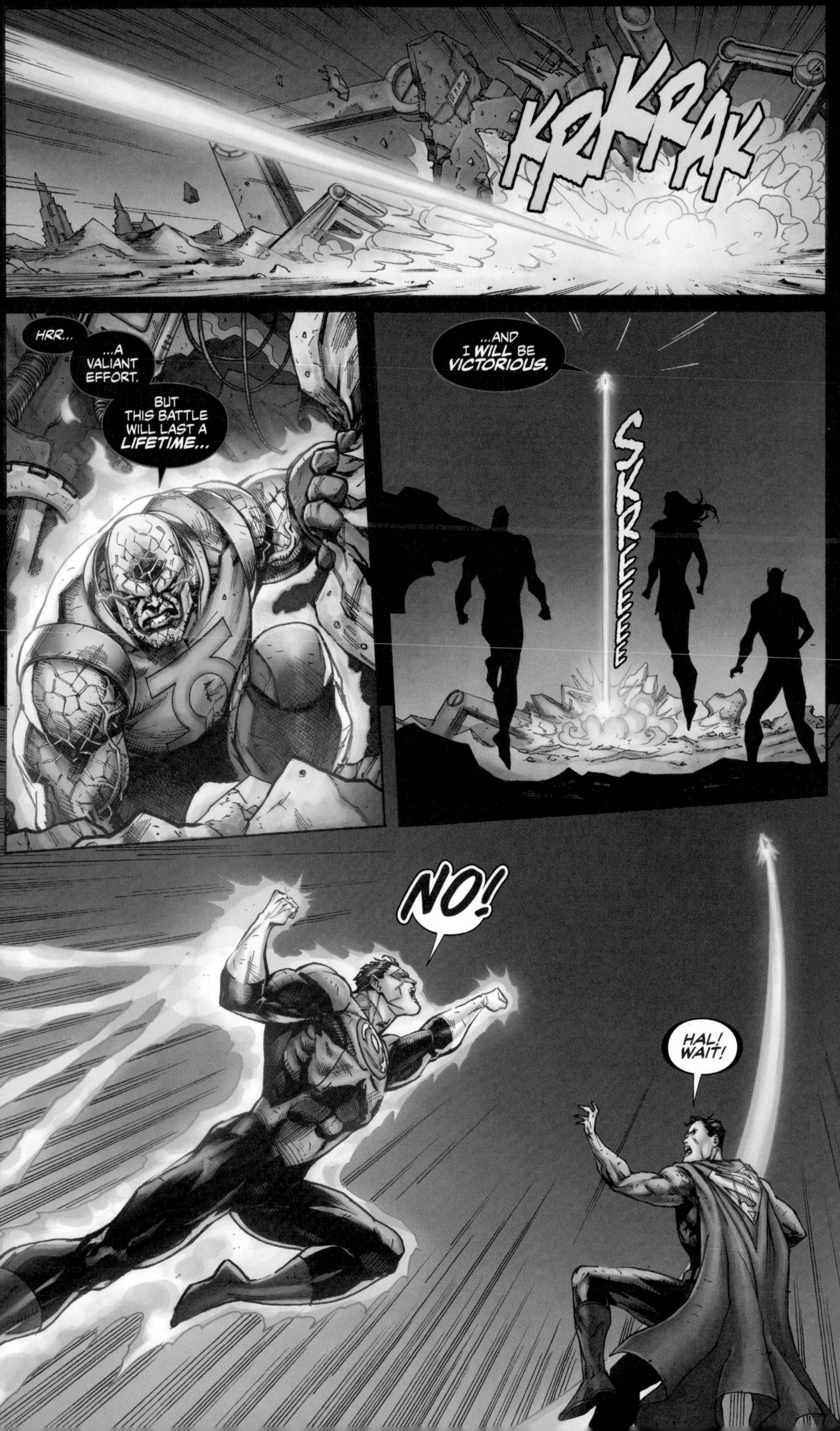
KRAKRAK
HRR...
...A VALIANT EFFORT.
BUT THIS BATTLE WILL LAST A LIFETIME...
...AND I WILL BE VICTORIOUS.
SKREEEEE
NO!
HAL! WAIT!

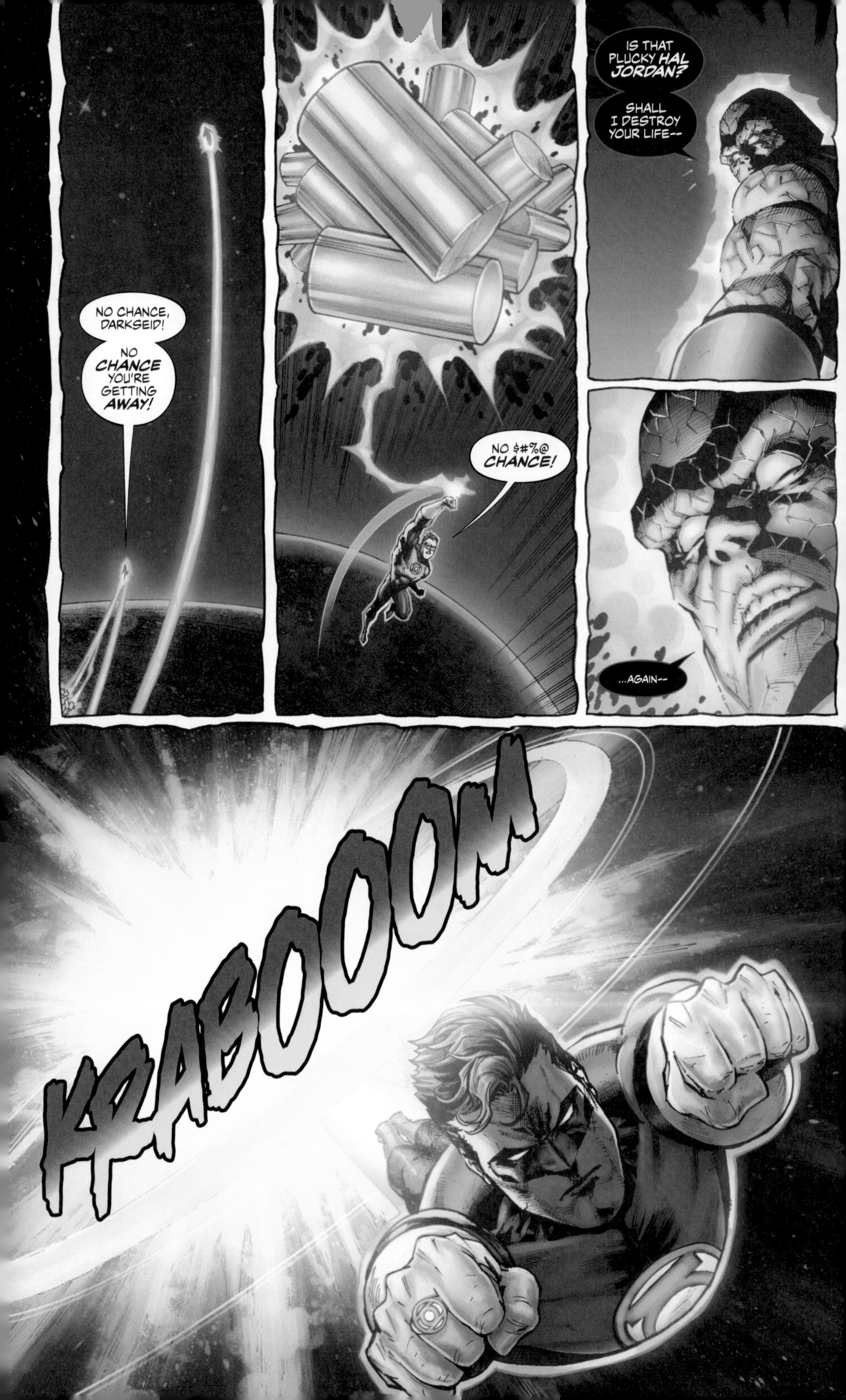
NO CHANCE, DARKSEID!
NO CHANCE YOU'RE GETTING AWAY!
NO $#%@ CHANCE!
IS THAT PLUCKY HAL JORDAN?
SHALL I DESTROY YOUR LIFE--
...AGAIN--
KRABOOOM

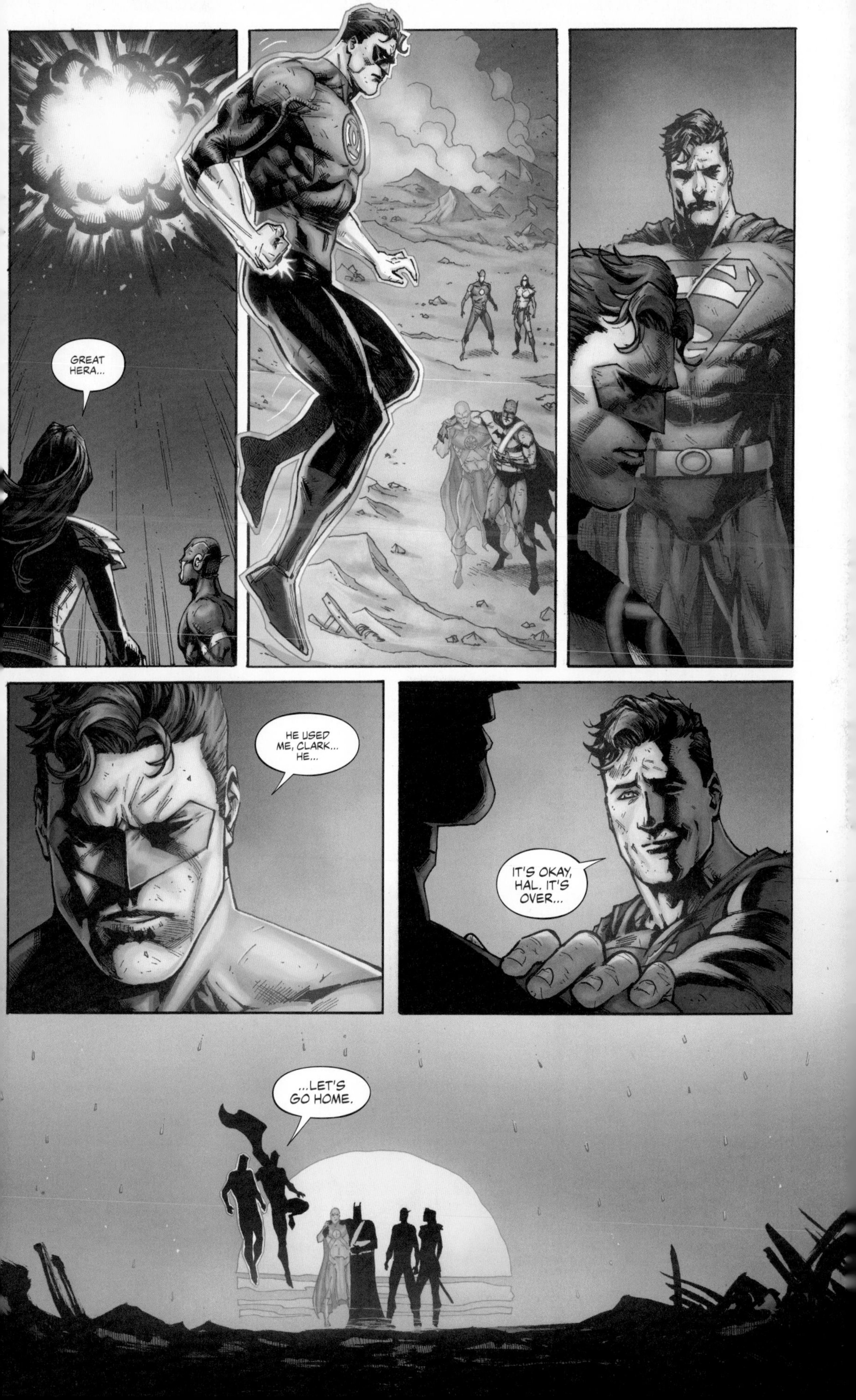
GREAT HERA...
HE USED ME, CLARK... HE...
IT'S OKAY, HAL. IT'S OVER...
...LET'S GO HOME.

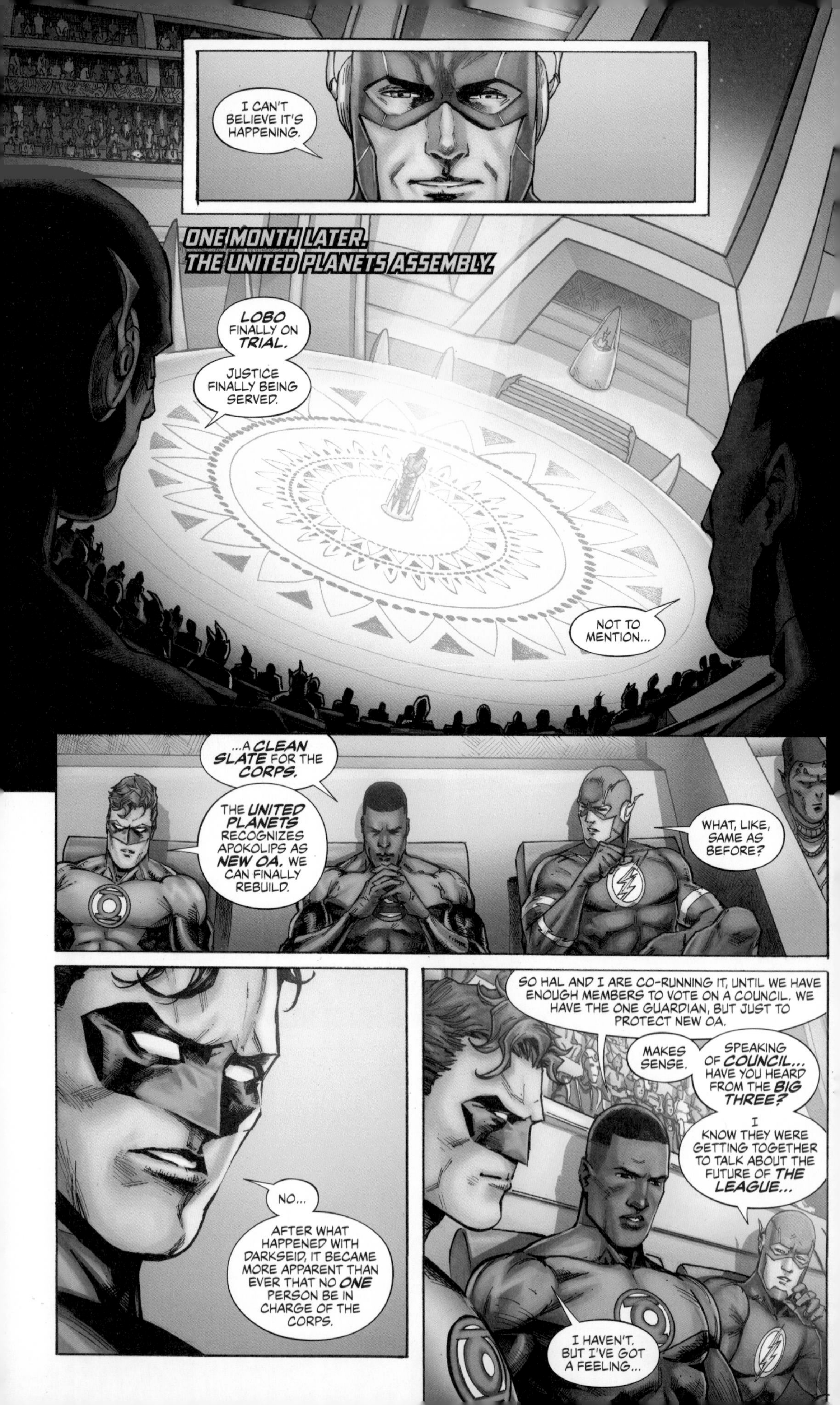
I CAN'T BELIEVE IT'S HAPPENING.
ONE MONTH LATER. THE UNITED PLANETS ASSEMBLY.
LOBO FINALLY ON TRIAL.
JUSTICE FINALLY BEING SERVED.
NOT TO MENTION...
...A CLEAN SLATE FOR THE CORPS.
THE UNITED PLANETS RECOGNIZES APOKOLIPS AS NEW OA. WE CAN FINALLY REBUILD.
WHAT, LIKE, SAME AS BEFORE?
NO...
AFTER WHAT HAPPENED WITH DARKSEID, IT BECAME MORE APPARENT THAN EVER THAT NO ONE PERSON BE IN CHARGE OF THE CORPS.
SO HAL AND I ARE CO-RUNNING IT, UNTIL WE HAVE ENOUGH MEMBERS TO VOTE ON A COUNCIL. WE HAVE THE ONE GUARDIAN, BUT JUST TO PROTECT NEW OA.
MAKES SENSE.
SPEAKING OF COUNCIL... HAVE YOU HEARD FROM THE BIG THREE?
I KNOW THEY WERE GETTING TOGETHER TO TALK ABOUT THE FUTURE OF THE LEAGUE...
I HAVEN'T. BUT I'VE GOT A FEELING...

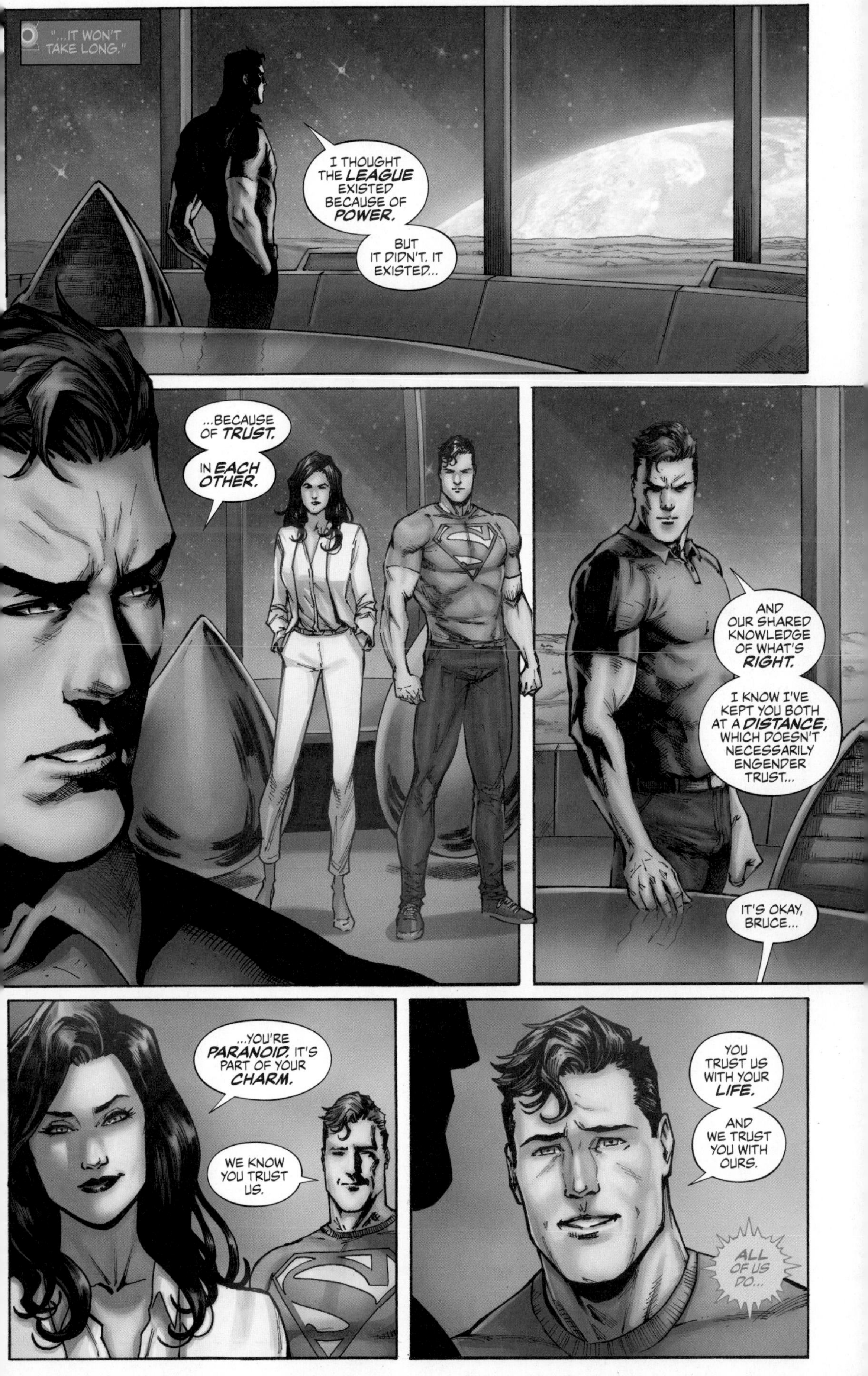
"...IT WON'T TAKE LONG."
I THOUGHT THE LEAGUE EXISTED BECAUSE OF POWER.
BUT IT DIDN'T. IT EXISTED...
...BECAUSE OF TRUST.
IN EACH OTHER.
AND OUR SHARED KNOWLEDGE OF WHAT'S RIGHT.
I KNOW I'VE KEPT YOU BOTH AT A DISTANCE, WHICH DOESN'T NECESSARILY ENGENDER TRUST...
IT'S OKAY, BRUCE...
...YOU'RE PARANOID. IT'S PART OF YOUR CHARM.
WE KNOW YOU TRUST US.
YOU TRUST US WITH YOUR LIFE.
AND WE TRUST YOU WITH OURS.
ALL OF US DO...

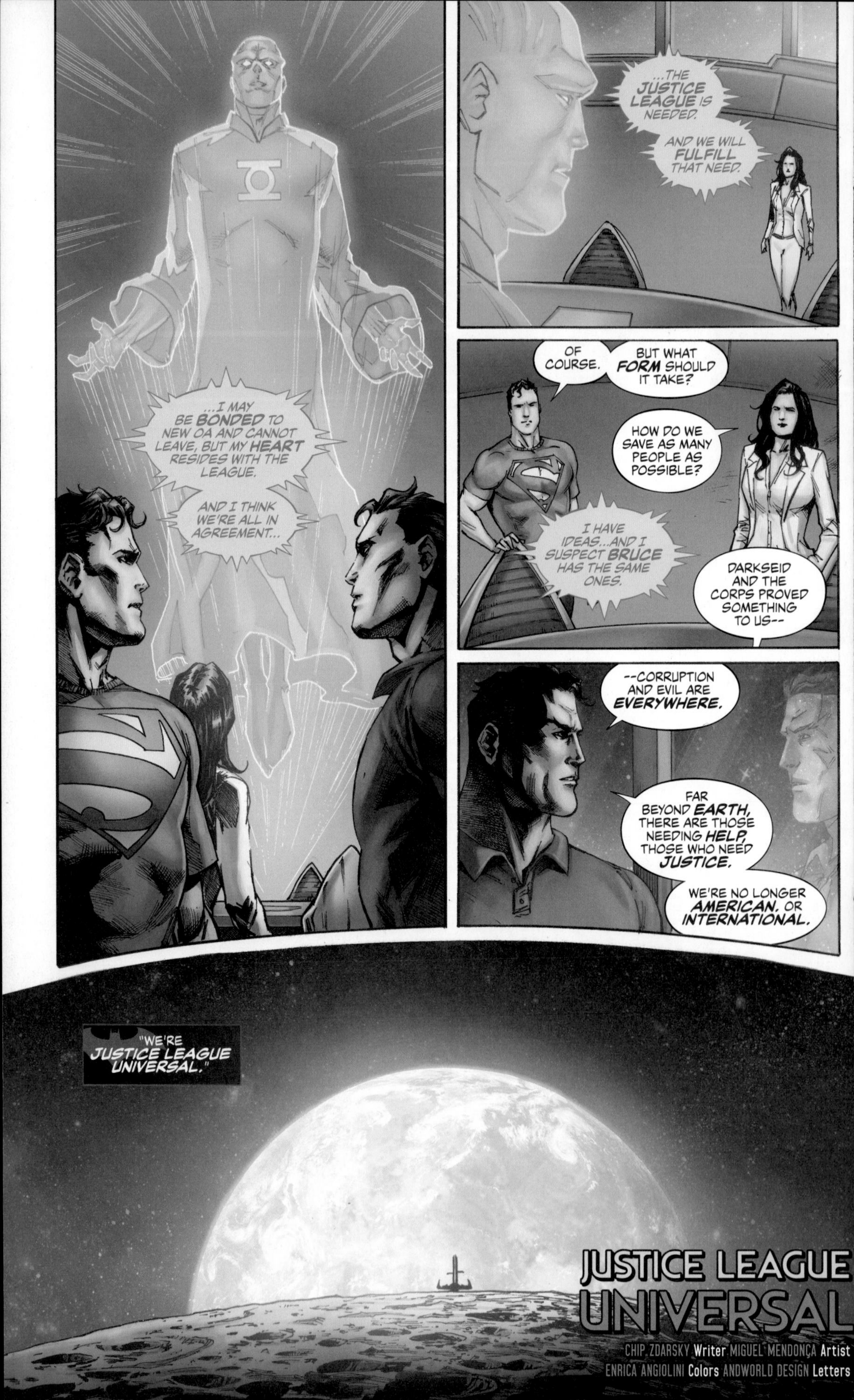
...I MAY BE BONDED TO NEW OA AND CANNOT LEAVE, BUT MY HEART RESIDES WITH THE LEAGUE.
AND I THINK WE'RE ALL IN AGREEMENT...
...THE JUSTICE LEAGUE IS NEEDED.
AND WE WILL FULFILL THAT NEED.
OF COURSE.
BUT WHAT FORM SHOULD IT TAKE?
HOW DO WE SAVE AS MANY PEOPLE AS POSSIBLE?
I HAVE IDEAS...AND I SUSPECT BRUCE HAS THE SAME ONES.
DARKSEID AND THE CORPS PROVED SOMETHING TO US--
--CORRUPTION AND EVIL ARE EVERYWHERE.
FAR BEYOND EARTH, THERE ARE THOSE NEEDING HELP, THOSE WHO NEED JUSTICE.
WE'RE NO LONGER AMERICAN, OR INTERNATIONAL.
"WE'RE JUSTICE LEAGUE UNIVERSAL."
JUSTICE LEAGUE UNIVERSAL
CHIP ZDARSKY Writer MIGUEL MENDONÇA Artist
ENRICA ANGIOLINI Colors ANDWORLD DESIGN Letters

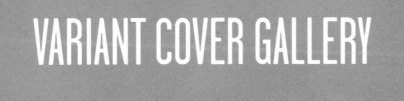

VARIANT COVER GALLERY

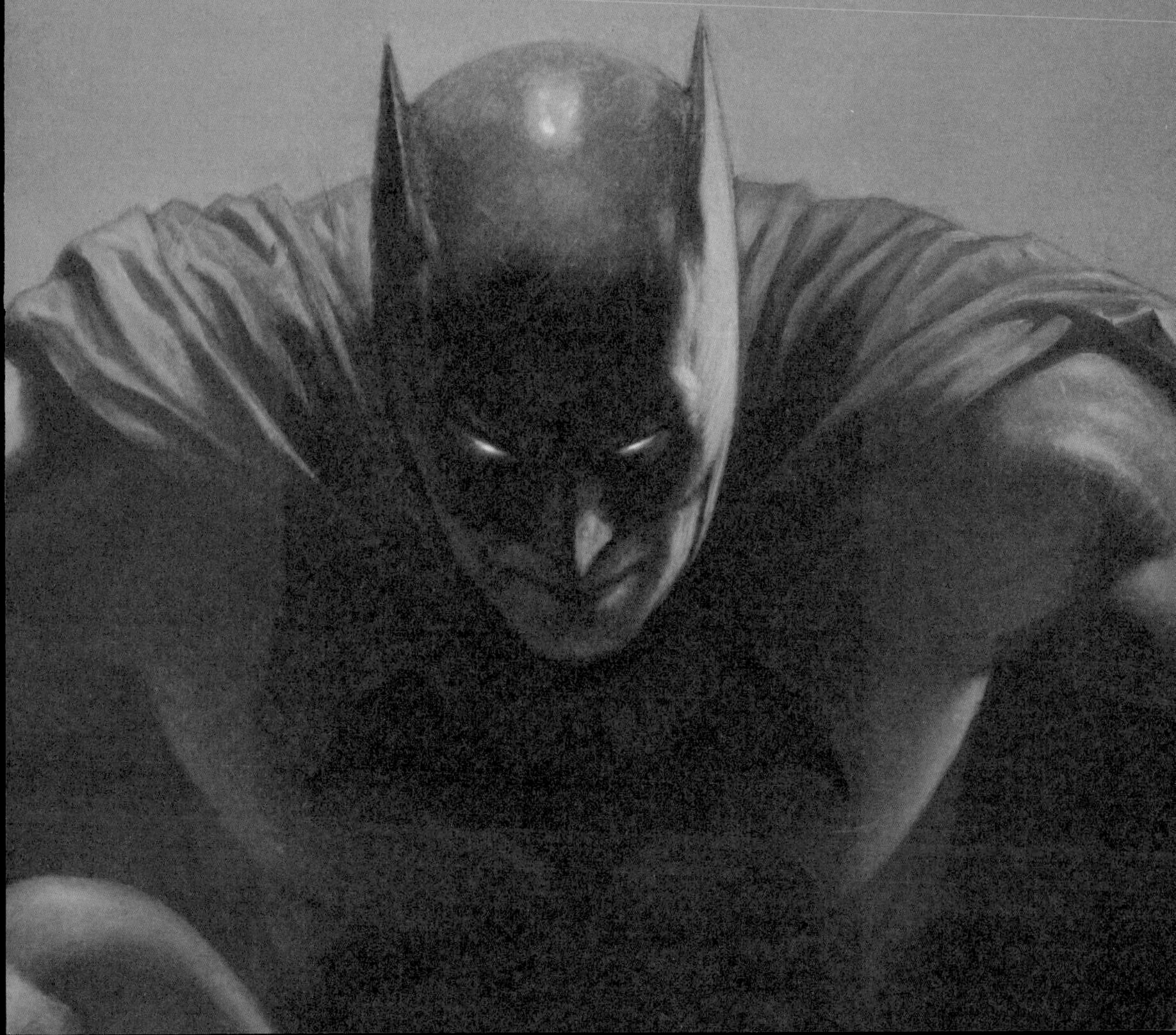

Justice League: Last Ride #2
variant cover art by **INHYUK LEE**

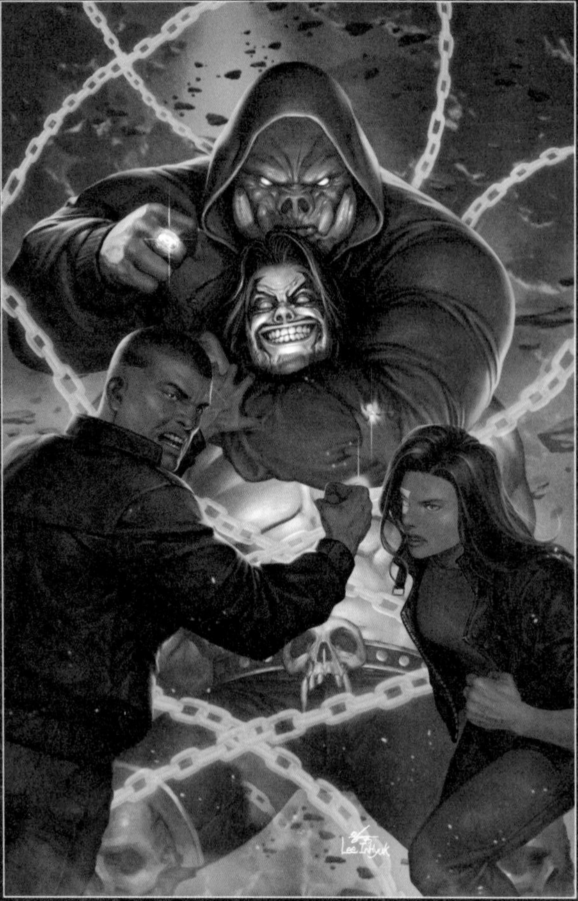

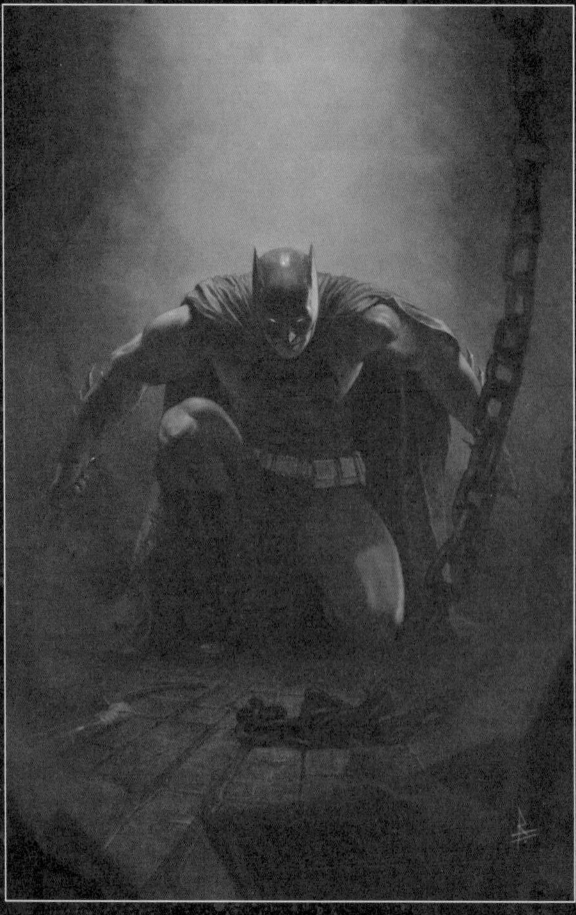

Justice League: Last Ride #3
variant cover art by **RICCARDO FEDERICI**

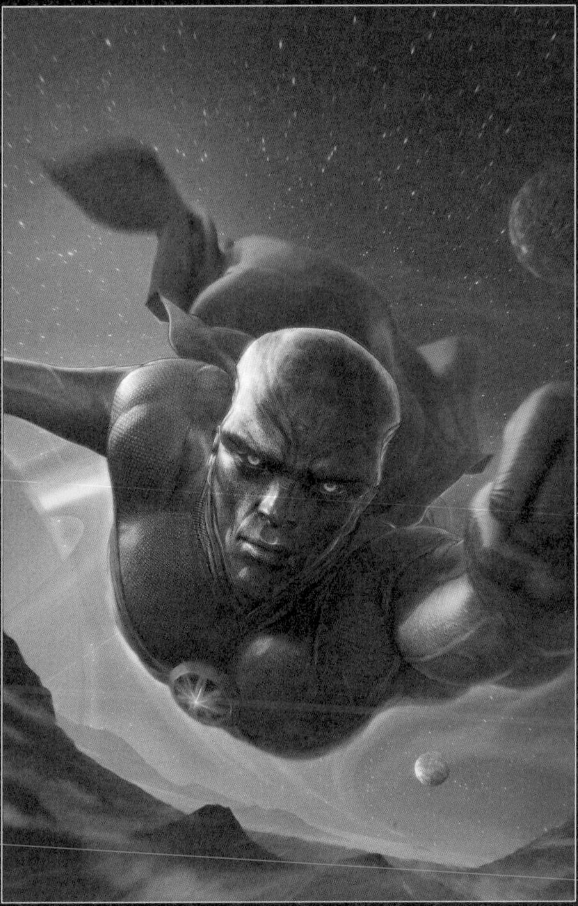

Justice League: Last Ride #4
variant cover art by **TIAGO DA SILVA**

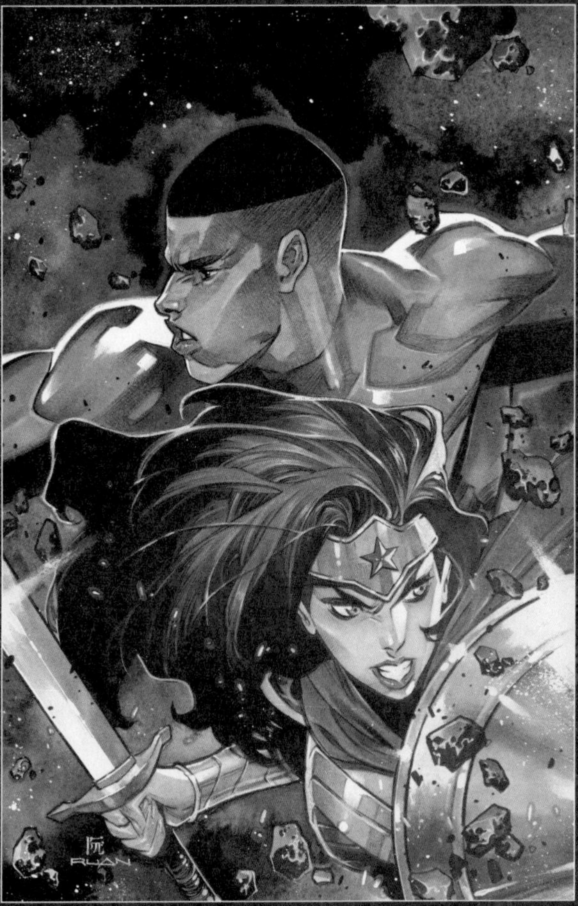
RUAN

Justice League: Last Ride #5
variant cover art by **DIKE RUAN**

Justice League: Last Ride #6
variant cover art by **MICHAEL CHOI**

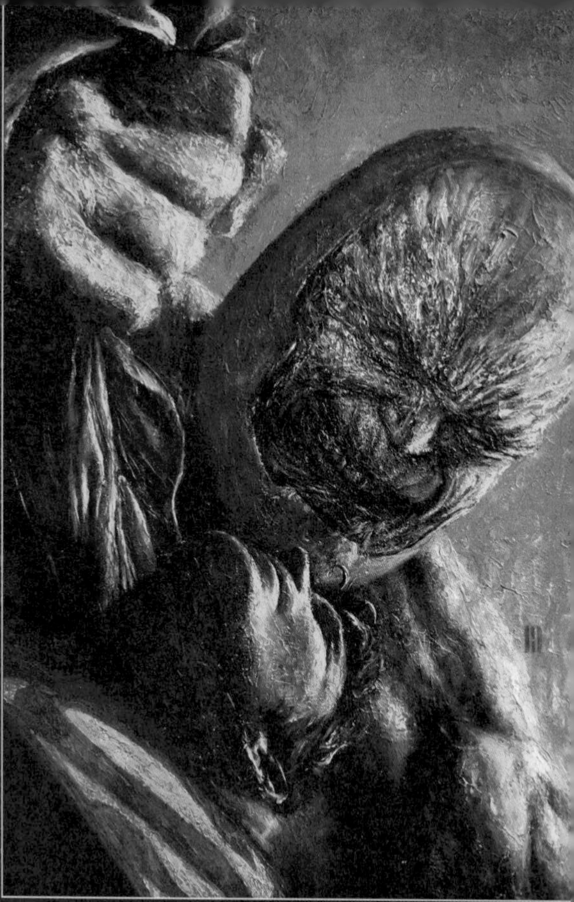

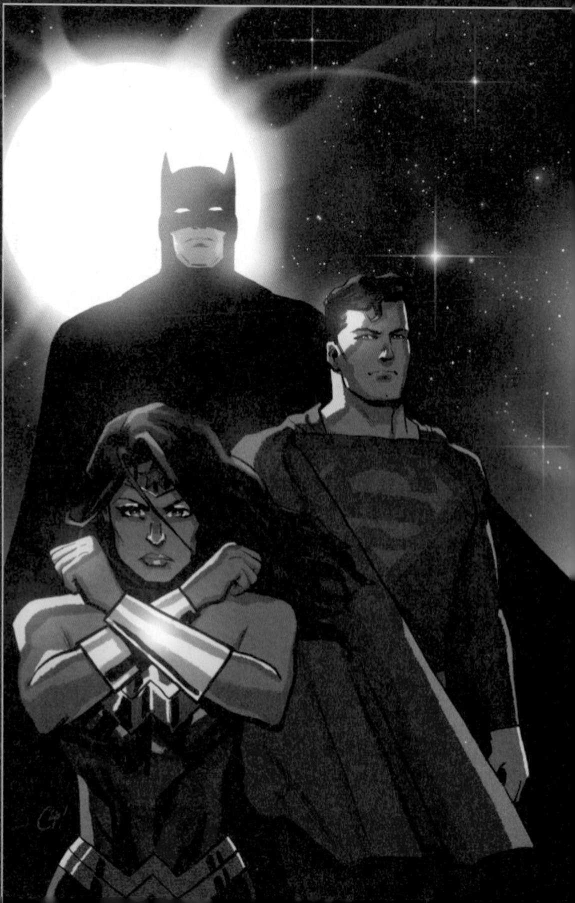

Justice League: Last Ride #7
variant cover art by **CHIP ZDARSKY**